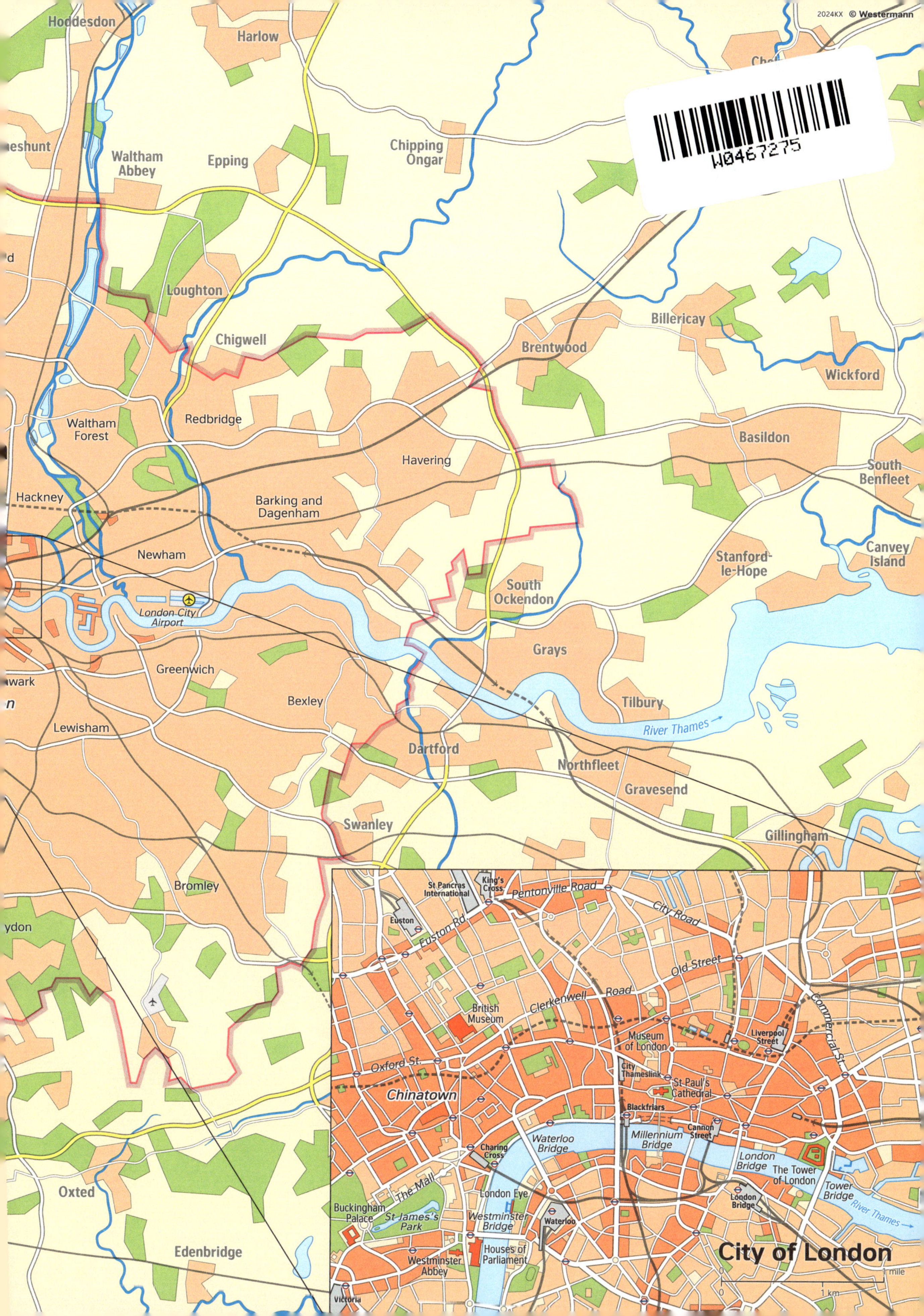
Hoddesdon
Harlow
Waltham Abbey
Epping
Chipping Ongar
Loughton
Chigwell
Brentwood
Billericay
Wickford
Waltham Forest
Redbridge
Havering
Basildon
South Benfleet
Hackney
Barking and Dagenham
Newham
Stanford-le-Hope
Canvey Island
South Ockendon
London City Airport
Grays
Greenwich
Bexley
Tilbury
River Thames
Lewisham
Dartford
Northfleet
Gravesend
Swanley
Gillingham
Bromley
Oxted
Edenbridge
St Pancras International
King's Cross
Pentonville Road
City Road
Euston
Euston Rd
Old Street
British Museum
Clerkenwell Road
Commercial St
Museum of London
Liverpool Street
Oxford St.
City Thameslink
St Paul's Cathedral
Chinatown
Blackfriars
Cannon Street
Waterloo Bridge
Millennium Bridge
Charing Cross
London Bridge
The Tower of London
Tower Bridge
The Mall
London Eye
Buckingham Palace
St James's Park
Westminster Bridge
Waterloo
River Thames
Houses of Parliament
Westminster Abbey
Victoria
City of London
1 mile
1 km

westermann

NOTTING HILL GATE

Textbook 7

Basis-Ausgabe

Erarbeitet von:
Hanna Hoof (Schacht-Audorf), Gabriele Linke (Marburg),
Sascha Mohr (Wiesbaden), Penelope Pedder (Köln),
Maike Pegler (Sarstedt/Gödringen)

sowie Denise Arrandale (Neumünster), Michael Biermann (Hamburg),
Hannelore Debus (Mörfelden-Walldorf), Phil Mothershaw-Rogalla
(Volkmarsen-Külte), Susanne Quandt (Bremen)

Fachliche Beratung:
Martina Pods-Sievers (Ahrensburg), Martin Weber (Wiesbaden)

Story „Jamie and Lucy“ von Lisa Fast

Notting Hill Gate 7
Basis-Ausgabe
Textbook

Zusatzmaterialien zu Notting Hill Gate 7

Für Lehrkräfte:

- Textbook für Lehrkräfte 7 (ISBN 978-3-14-128290-0)
- Materialien für Lehrkräfte 7 (ISBN 978-3-14-128296-2)
- Lernerfolgskontrollen 7 (ISBN 978-3-14-128322-8)
- CD für Lehrkräfte 7 (ISBN 978-3-14-128310-5)
- DVD für Lehrkräfte 7 (ISBN 978-3-14-128316-7)
- Online-Diagnose zu Notting Hill Gate 7
  www.onlinediagnose.de

Für Schülerinnen und Schüler:

- Workbook 7 (inkl. Audios) (ISBN 978-3-14-128216-0)
- Interaktive Übungen 7 (WEB-14-128226)
- Arbeitsbuch Inklusion 7 (inkl. Audios)
  (ISBN 978-3-14-128232-0)
- Klassenarbeitstrainer 7 (ISBN 978-3-14-128248-1)
- Grammatiktrainer 7 (ISBN 978-3-14-128388-4)
- Wortschatztrainer 7 (ISBN 978-3-14-128242-9)

Das digitale Schulbuch und digitale Unterrichtsmaterialien für Schülerinnen und Schüler und für Lehrkräfte finden Sie in der BiBox – dem digitalen Unterrichtssystem passend zum Lehrwerk. Mehr Informationen über aktuelle Lizenzen finden Sie auf www.bibox.schule.

www.westermann.de/nhg

DIGITAL+

Alle digitalen Ergänzungen zum Buch erkennen Sie an dem Symbol **DIGITAL+**. Dazu zählen Audiotracks, Videoclips, Arbeitsblätter zur Medienbildung, zusätzliche Übungen zu den Practise-Seiten und Zusatzmaterialien zum Buch. Gehen Sie auf **www.westermann.de/webcode** und geben Sie den Webcode **WES-128206-001** ein. Sie können auch den QR-Code scannen.

Druck A[1] / Jahr 2024
Alle Drucke der Serie A sind im Unterricht parallel verwendbar.

Redaktion: Doris Bos sowie Lisa Fast und Dr. Katja Nandorf
Vokabelanhang: Doris Bos
Illustrationen: Mario Ellert, Bremen
Umschlaggestaltung: LIO Design GmbH, Braunschweig
Layout: LIO Design GmbH, Braunschweig
Druck und Bindung: Westermann Druck GmbH, Georg-Westermann-Allee 66, 38104 Braunschweig

ISBN 978-3-14-**128206**-1

So arbeitest du mit dem Buch

Im Buch findest du folgende Verweise:

1 audio	Hier gibt es einen Audiotrack, den du auch online abrufen kannst.
2 video	Hier gibt es einen Videoclip, den du auch online abrufen kannst.
3 workbook	Hier siehst du, auf welcher Seite im Workbook es weitere Übungen gibt.
4 wordbank	In den Wordbanks findest du Wörter nach Wortfeldern geordnet.
5 skill	Auf den Skills-Seiten findest du Tipps und Strategien fürs Lernen.
6 grammar	Zu dieser Aufgabe gibt es Erklärungen und Beispiele im Grammatik-Teil.
7 media worksheet	Dieser Hinweis kennzeichnet Aufgaben, in denen du Medienkompetenz aufbaust und trainierst. Zu diesen Aufgaben gibt es Arbeitsblätter, die du über den Webcode oder den QR-Code auf Seite 2 abrufen kannst.
DIGITAL+ practise more	Dieser Hinweis zeigt, dass es zusätzliches Material auf der Webseite gibt.

In den Units gibt es verschiedene Arten von Aufgaben:

8 CHOOSE YOUR LEVEL	Bei diesen Aufgaben gibt es drei unterschiedliche Schwierigkeitsgrade: **I leicht II mittel III schwierig**
9 GET TOGETHER Partner A: I Go to page 128. II Go to page 131. III Go to page 134. Partner B: I Go to page 137. II Go to page 140. III Go to page 143.	Hier arbeitest du mit einem Partner oder einer Partnerin zusammen. Entscheidet, wer Partner A und wer Partner B ist und wählt jeweils einen Schwierigkeitsgrad. Geht dann zur entsprechenden Seite und bearbeitet die Aufgabe.
10 CHOOSE YOUR TASK	Hier gibt es drei Aufgaben, von denen du dir eine aussuchen kannst. Du kannst mit einem Partner oder einer Partnerin oder in einer Gruppe arbeiten.
TARGET TASK	In der Target Task (Zielaufgabe) wendest du an, was du gelernt hast. Du erarbeitest ein kleines Produkt, das du in der Klasse vorstellen und in deinem Portfolio aufbewahren kannst.

Ein ausführliches Inhaltsverzeichnis befindet sich auf den Seiten 248 bis 253.

Lily and Harry Norris

- 13 years old (twins)
- live with their mums, Olivia and Sarah
- used to live in Brighton
- their grandparents live in Bristol
- have got two rabbits, Double and Trouble
- like playing board games
- Lily's hobby is upcycling
- Harry plays the guitar in the school band

Ava Kogan

- 13 years old
- lives with her mum, her dad and her two brothers: Joshua (8) and Noah (14)
- has got a dog, Ollie
- likes skateboarding
- wants to be an engineer when she grows up
- her grandma Edyta lives in Poland

Tarek Adil

- 14 years old
- lives with his dad
- has got an uncle, Sami
- his family is originally from Egypt
- plays hockey in a team
- likes science fiction books and cooking

1 What can you see in the pictures?
2 Which of the foods in the pictures do you like?
3 Have you ever cooked a meal? What was it?

Food

Part A Delicious dishes

- Du unterhältst dich über Essen aus aller Welt.
- Du hörst dir einen Podcast an.
- Deine Klasse stellt ein internationales Kochbuch zusammen.

Part B At a restaurant

- Du liest etwas über einen Restaurantbesuch.
- Du sprichst über Speisekarten.
- Ihr präsentiert in einem Rollenspiel eine Szene in einem Restaurant.

Favourite food

1 workbook p. 4/1-2

What do you like to eat? Collect the names of your favourite dishes in class and talk about them.

You can say:

My favourite dish is …

I really like … It's yummy.

spaghetti · pizza · curry · chips · pasta with tomato sauce · mashed potatoes with sausages · …

Different dishes

2a

Look at the pictures on this double page and talk about them.

You can say:

There is … / There are …

In the first / second / third / fourth picture, I can see …

2b

Read the four texts on this double page. Where are the dishes from?

1

BFF

Emily
Greetings from our family holiday in Greece.
Look what Dad has ordered! Salad with cucumber, olives, tomato and grilled octopus!
He loves it, but I don't like it.
Have you ever tried anything like this? 2:05 pm

Emily

2

Foodlover

Foodlover I've just eaten the best Sunday roast ever at my aunt's house. I'm so full now! There was so much I couldn't finish it. Have you had your roast dinner today?

Isabel3589 This looks absolutely delicious! Are those mashed potatoes?
Foodlover Yes, and a lot of gravy!

AyazLondon I've just moved to London, I have never eaten a Sunday roast! What is it?
Foodlover It's a traditional British dish, you usually have it for lunch on Sundays.
It's roast meat, vegetables, Yorkshire pudding and potatoes. You should try it! You can also get really good vegetarian versions in restaurants here in London!
AyazLondon Yorkshire pudding? Is it sweet?
Foodlover: No, it's not sweet. It's savoury.

3 https://www.katie.co.uk/Berlinstreetfood × –

KATIE'S BLOG

Berlin street food

I spent a week in Berlin in the summer – since then my comfort food has been Lahmacun. I first tried it in Berlin and it was so good! Lahmacun is a thin rolled flatbread filled with minced meat, onions and tomato. It's very spicy. It's a dish from Turkey, but there are similar dishes in many other countries, like Lebanon or Egypt. I've found some places in London where you get good Lahmacun, too!

There's also a German speciality you must try when you are in Berlin: currywurst. You sometimes get currywurst in London, too – but it's not as good as it is in Berlin!

4 https://www.worldfoodfestival/streetfood × –

Fantastic street food at the World Food Festival ** * * by Jason and Laura * * **

Shakshuka

Our number one street food is very popular in Israel and North Africa: Shakshuka. It's a savoury, healthy and vegetarian dish served with flatbread. The tomatoes were really good, the eggs were fresh and there was just a little bit of garlic. All in all: perfect.

2c CHOOSE YOUR LEVEL skill: reading p. 154

I Unscramble the sentences and write them down.

1 in Greece. – You can eat – grilled octopus –
2 British dish. – is a traditional – The Sunday roast
3 is – Yorkshire pudding – savoury.
4 Currywurst – German speciality. – is a

II Match the sentence parts. Write down the sentences.

1 In Greece
2 The Sunday roast
3 Yorkshire pudding
4 Lahmacun

A is not sweet.
B is a dish from Turkey.
C you can eat grilled octopus.
D is a traditional British dish.

III True or false? Correct the false statements and write down all the sentences.

1 In the holiday, Emily's dad had a salad with grilled octopus.
2 You can't get a vegetarian Sunday roast in London.
3 Lahmacun is filled with minced meat, cheese and olives.
4 In Lebanon or Egypt you can find dishes that are similar to Lahmacun.
5 Katie thinks that the currywurst in London is better than the currywurst in Berlin.

2d skill: talking with people p. 152, workbook p. 5/3

Walk around the classroom. Talk to your classmates.

You can ask:	You can answer:
Have you ever tried …?	*Yes, I have. / No, I haven't.*
Have you ever eaten …?	*Yes, I have. / No, I haven't.*
Did you like it?	*Yes, I did. / No, I didn't.*
What was it like?	*It was delicious / yummy / disgusting / …*

GRAMMAR HELP the present perfect (R) p. 172-173

Schau dir die Beispielsätze an. Kannst du erklären, wann man das *present perfect* benutzt? Achte besonders auf die Signalwörter *never*, *just*, *not yet* und *already*.

I have never tried a vegetarian roast.	Ich habe noch nie einen vegetarischen Braten probiert.
Dad has just eaten lots of salad. Now he is full.	Papa hat gerade viel Salat gegessen. Jetzt ist er satt.
Mum hasn't finished her salad yet.	Mama hat ihren Salat noch nicht fertig gegessen.
We have already made lunch. It's ready now.	Wir haben schon Mittagessen gemacht. Es ist jetzt fertig.

Auf den Seiten 172 und 173 findest du ausführliche Erklärungen und weitere Beispiele zum *present perfect*. Eine Liste mit unregelmäßigen Verben gibt es auf den Seiten 245-247.

What have they done?

3
grammar: present perfect (R) p. 172, workbook p. 5/4

Unscramble the sentences and write about Ollie and the children.

1 yet. – Ava – hasn't finished – her breakfast
2 yet. – hasn't tidied – the kitchen – Tarek
3 already – eaten – Ollie has – all his food.
4 Harry and Lily – yet. – haven't done – their homework

You can write:

1. Ava hasn't finished her breakfast yet.

…

Have you tried Lahmacun?

4
grammar: present perfect (R) p. 172, wordbank: eating and eating out p. 160, workbook p. 5/5

Write about three or more dishes that you have tried.

You can write:

I have tried … and I liked it. It was good. / …

I have tried … and I didn't like it. It was …

It's a savoury / sweet …

Food words

5a
wordbank: eating and eating out p. 160, skill: working with words p. 150

Make a list of English food words that are similar to food words in German or in other languages.

You can write:

English	*German*	*???*
tomato	*Tomate*	…
…	…	…

5b

Work with a partner. Compare your lists and add words from your partner's list.

International week

6a

Look at the web page. What is it about?

https://www.worldfoodfestival/streetfood

Holland Park School Cafeteria

International week

Next week it's international week at the school cafeteria. Come and enjoy dishes from around the world!

MONDAY	TUESDAY	WEDNESDAY	THURSDAY	FRIDAY
Currywurst	Fried noodles	Chicken tikka masala	Vegetarian sushi	Spaghetti bolognese

Germany	*China*	*India*	*Japan*	*Italy*

6b audio 1/1

Listen to Lily, Harry, Ava and Tarek. What is Lily and Harry's problem? What do they all decide to do? Take notes.

6c CHOOSE YOUR LEVEL skill: listening p. 151

I Listen again and answer the questions.

1 Is Harry OK? What is his problem?
2 Who do Lily and Harry meet?
3 What are they talking about?

You can write:
1. Harry is …
2. Lily and Harry meet …
3. They are talking about …

II Listen again and answer the questions.

1 What did Harry have for lunch?
2 What did Harry eat for breakfast?
3 What did Lily have for lunch?
4 What is Harry looking forward to?

III Listen again and answer the questions.

1 Why is Harry annoyed?
2 Why didn't Harry eat in the cafeteria?
3 Why is Harry looking forward to next week?
4 What does Tarek miss on the menu?

6d workbook p. 6/6-7

Do you have a cafeteria at your school? What is your favourite dish there?

Home cooking

7a audio 1/4

Listen and read along. What are the children talking about?

The children are in the kitchen at Tarek's house.

Harry: What could we cook? Have you got any ideas?

Ava: We could make one-pot pasta!

Tarek: What's that?

Ava: You cook everything together in one pot – it's quick and easy and you only have to wash one pot! Noah and I sometimes make it for dinner.

Harry: Quick and easy sounds good – I'm still starving!

Tarek: What do we need? I don't think we have any meat.

Ava: We need pasta, veggies, tomatoes, herbs and spices. Let's see what you've got!

Tarek: All the spices are in the drawer over there. Lily, could you check what there is in the fridge? And could you please get the pasta from the cupboard, Ava?

Lily: There aren't many onions. But there are a lot of carrots and peppers and there's some cabbage. And there isn't much cheese.

Tarek: Ava, do we need any cheese?

Ava: We could add some cheese if you like. Oh, here are cans of chickpeas and tomatoes. But there is not much pasta left … Hm, there's a big jar with small yellow crumbs. What is it?

Tarek: It's couscous.

Ava: What is it like?

Tarek: It's really good, and it's super easy to cook. You just bring water to the boil, add the couscous and some salt, cover it and let it stand for five minutes. We often have it.

Harry: Cool! Can't we cook a dish from Egypt then, Tarek? What do you think?

Tarek: Couscous is NOT from Egypt, but we can try to cook a meal with it. But I'm not sure how to put it all together and what spices we need.

Ava: Can't we search for a recipe online?

Lily: Sure, wait a second … Ah, here, I've found something. It's a dish from Morocco. And here is a cook-along video. Look, it says we need couscous, veggies, an onion, garlic, chickpeas and a lot of spices.

7b

What is the children's first idea? What do the children decide to cook in the end?

7c CHOOSE YOUR LEVEL skill: reading p. 154, workbook p. 7/8

I Read the dialogue again. Choose the correct words and phrases from the brackets and write down the sentences.

1 One-pot pasta is (quick and difficult / quick and easy).
2 We need (pasta and couscous / pasta and veggies).
3 All the spices (are in the drawer over there / are in the cupboard).
4 There aren't many (tomatoes / onions) and there isn't much (cheese and pasta / fruit and water).

II Read the dialogue again. Complete the sentences and write them down.

1 One-pot pasta is quick and easy and …
2 All the spices are …
3 There aren't many …
4 There isn't much …
5 There are cans of …

III Read the dialogue again. Correct the sentences and write them down.

1 "Noah and I sometimes make it for lunch."
2 "We need pasta, veggies, tomatoes, ketchup and spices."
3 "There aren't many carrots."
4 "Do we need any meat?"
5 "Can't we cook a dish from China then?"

A cook-along video

8a video 1, skill: watching a video clip p. 156

Watch the video clip. What do you have to do after you have put the couscous in the pot?

8b

Copy the following verbs:
chop, cut, heat, slice, cook, enjoy, cover, stir in
Then watch the video clip again and put the verbs in the correct order.

International food

9 CHOOSE YOUR TASK wordbank: eating and eating out p.160, skill: writing p.153, C: media worksheet 13

A **Draw your favourite dish and label it.**

B **Write and design your dream menu for an international week at your school cafeteria.**

C **Write a text message to a friend and describe a dish that you know and like.**

Vegan Steven

10a audio 1/5

Listen to the limerick. What is it about?

10b

What do you know about vegan and vegetarian food? Collect words.

10c workbook p.8/9

Learn the limerick by heart and present it.

There was a young vegan called Steven,
Who just would not kill for no reason,
This kid would not eat
No cheese or no meat
And he hated the foxhunting season.

Benjamin Zephaniah

LAND & LEUTE 1 video 2

Essen in Großbritannien

Traditionelle britische Gerichte sind *fish and chips* (Fisch mit Pommes frites) und *Sunday roast* (Sonntagsbraten) mit *Yorkshire pudding*. *Yorkshire pudding* wird aus den gleichen Zutaten wie Pfannkuchen gemacht, man backt ihn aber im Ofen und isst ihn als Beilage zu herzhaften Gerichten.
Das englische Wort *pudding* bedeutet sonst allgemein „Nachtisch".
Einige britische Gerichte haben ungewöhnliche Namen, wie zum Beispiel *toad in the hole* (wörtlich: Kröte im Loch) – Würstchen in einem großen *Yorkshire pudding*. *Bangers and mash* (wörtlich: Knaller und Brei) sind Würstchen mit Kartoffelpüree, und *bubble and squeak* (wörtlich: Blase und Quieken) ist gebratenes Kartoffelpüree mit Kohl oder anderem Gemüse.

chicken tikka masala

Neben traditionellem britischen Essen kann man in Großbritannien auch Essen aus aller Welt bekommen. Besonders indisches Essen ist sehr beliebt. Eines der beliebtesten Gerichte ist *chicken tikka masala* – manche Menschen sagen sogar, dass es das Nationalgericht Nummer eins der Briten ist. Es ist ein ursprünglich indisches Gericht, dem eine Soße aus Joghurt, Kokosmilch und einer Mixtur aus verschiedenen Gewürzen *(masala)* hinzugefügt wird.

Hast du schon einmal ein traditionelles britisches Gericht gegessen oder kennst du ähnliche Gerichte?

Dishes with funny names

11a video 3, skill: watching a video clip p. 156

Watch the video clip.
Which name do you like best?

11b

Watch the video clip again.
Make a list of the dishes that really exist.
Which dish would you like to try?

11c workbook p. 9/10-11

Do you know any dishes with funny names in other languages? Try to translate the names into English. Describe the dishes to the class.

You can say:

In Germany, there is "Arme Ritter".
That's "poor knights" in English.
It is white bread fried with milk and egg.

Foods invented by accident

12a audio 1/8, skill: listening p. 151

What do you think "by accident" means? Guess.
Then listen to the first part of the podcast and find out. Were you right?

12b audio 1/9

Listen to the podcast. What foods do the people talk about? Take notes.

12c CHOOSE YOUR LEVEL skill: mediation p. 155, workbook p. 10/12

A German friend has some questions about the podcast. Read the questions first. Then listen again and answer your friend's questions in German.

I
1 Wer hat denn das Sandwich erfunden?
2 Wer hat das Eis am Stiel erfunden?

II
1 Warum wurde das Sandwich erfunden?
2 Wie wurde das Eis am Stiel erfunden?

III
1 Wer hat denn das Sandwich erfunden und warum?
2 Wer hat das Eis am Stiel erfunden und wie kam es dazu?
3 Was war eigentlich auf dem ersten Sandwich?

Much or many?

13 grammar: quantifiers (R) p. 174

Choose the correct word and write down the sentences.

1 I need **much/many** tomatoes for the sauce.
2 Have you got **much/many** favourite dishes?
3 How **much/many** ice cream have you eaten this week?
4 I'd like to go to a restaurant, but I haven't got **much/many** money.

Cookbook language

14a

Complete the sentences with the correct verbs and write them down.

bring · add · cook · wash

1 ??? the water to the boil.
2 ??? the veggies before you cut them.
3 ??? the pasta for ten minutes.
4 ??? some salt.

14b workbook p. 10/13

Read the recipe. Then tell a friend in English how to cook spaghetti.

SPAGHETTI

Nimm pro Person 100–125 g Spaghetti. Koche Wasser mit etwas Salz. Wenn das Wasser kocht, gib die Spaghetti in den Topf. Nach ca. 8 Minuten sind die Spaghetti fertig.

Odd one out

15

Find the odd one out. Make more "odd one outs" with food words for a partner.

1 pot – fork – knife – spoon
2 carrot – potato – banana – onion
3 spices – chickpeas – tomatoes – carrots
4 potatoes – chickpeas – rice – milk

Cooking

16 CHOOSE YOUR LEVEL wordbank: eating and eating out p. 160

Copy the word web.

I Add two or more words to every branch.

II Add three or more words to every branch. You can add another category.

III Add four or more words to every branch. Add other categories.

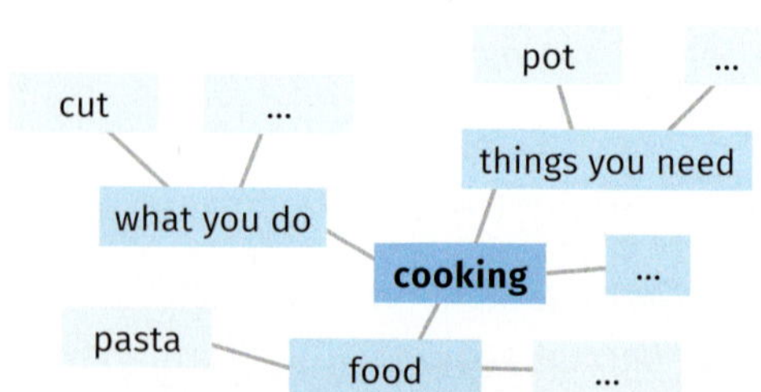

Our international cookbook TARGET TASK

17 workbook p. 11/14, wordbank: eating and eating out p. 160, media worksheet 1

Your task is to make an international cookbook in your class.
Before you start, look at these steps:

STEP 1

In class, decide what kind of cookbook you want to create: a book, a digital cookbook, ...

STEP 2

Work with a partner or in small groups. Think of dishes from different countries.
Then choose a dish, for example:

- a family recipe
- something you have tried in a restaurant
- something you have eaten on holiday
- ...

STEP 3

Find an English name for the dish or write down the original name.
Then find a recipe for the dish.

STEP 4

Make a list of ingredients. Write down how to prepare your dish.
You can add a photo for each step or even make a tutorial.

STEP 5

Put all the recipes together in your cookbook.
If you like, sort the recipes in your cookbook: starters, main courses, desserts.
Try them out! You can organize a class party and serve your dishes!

COUSCOUS *for two people*

Ingredients:

- *olive oil*
- *1 red onion*
- *3 red or yellow peppers*
- *1 carrot*
- *garlic*
- *1 can of chickpeas*
- *½ teaspoon of: paprika, coriander, cumin, cinnamon*
- *cayenne pepper, salt and pepper*
- *1½ cups of vegetable stock*
- *1 cup of couscous*

Wash the vegetables and cut them.
Chop the onion and slice the garlic.
Heat the olive oil and cook the vegetables.
Add the spices and the vegetable stock.
Cook until the vegetables are soft.
Add the couscous.
Take the pot from the cooker, cover it and let it stand for five minutes.
Enjoy!

Restaurants in your area

1 workbook p. 12/1

What kinds of restaurants are there in your area? Talk about them.

You can say:

There is an Italian restaurant in my area.
You can eat … there.
… is the best …

Italian · Greek · Turkish · Vietnamese · Thai · ...

fast food restaurant · takeaway · ...

Restaurant reviews

2a

Look at the pictures. Which restaurant would you like to go to? Which restaurant would you not like to go to? Why?

You can say:

I would like to go to … because I like …
I wouldn't like to go to … because I don't like …

2b skill: reading p. 154

Now skim the reviews. Which restaurant would you like to go to now? Say why.

Sushi Blue
It's not cheap, but the food is very good!
The fish is the freshest that I've ever tasted.
The service is very quick and friendly. It is more expensive than other sushi restaurants in the area, but you get better quality.

I would go again.

Pizza Extra Notting Hill
Stay away from this restaurant!
I had the worst pizza I've ever had in my life.
It was burnt, the vegetables were disgusting and the service was terrible! I waited over an hour for the most disappointing pizza I've ever had.
My friend's pizza was as bad as mine.

We will never go back.

https://www.eatingout/reviewsxxxx × –

The Taj Mahal

This place has the hottest curry you can find in London!
The vindaloo curry was so spicy that I could not finish it.
Even the vegetable korma was a bit too hot for my children. We had to add lots of yoghurt to finish our food. But the rice was perfect and the naan bread was yummy.

Only go there if you like *really* hot food!

https://www.eatingout/reviewsxxxx × –

The Black Horse

Very nice atmosphere, food OK, but not as good as the food we ate at The King's Head in North London the day before.
My fish was a bit overcooked, but the chips were delicious. My wife had a very juicy veggie burger with a side of chips.
The large choice of desserts was great.
The pub is cosy – we stayed for two hours and could have stayed longer!
The pub also has a beautiful garden where children can play.

2c CHOOSE YOUR LEVEL

I Read the first two reviews and take notes. What did people like at Sushi Blue and Pizza Extra? What did they not like?

II Read the first three reviews and take notes. What did people like at Sushi Blue, Pizza Extra and The Taj Mahal? What did they not like?

III Read the four reviews and take notes. What did people like at these restaurants? What did they not like? Which restaurant do you think is the best and which is the worst? Why?

2d skill: talking with people p. 152

What does a good restaurant need? Collect ideas. Talk to a partner.

You can say:

I think a good restaurant must offer …
In my opinion, a good restaurant should …
… is important to me.

GRAMMAR HELP the comparison of adjectives (R) p. 175

Erinnerst du dich noch daran, wie man im Englischen Dinge oder Personen miteinander vergleichen kann? Schau dir die Beispiele an und erkläre, wie die Formen gebildet und verwendet werden.

The food at Sushi Blue is fresher and more expensive than the food at Pizza Extra.	Das Essen bei Sushi Blue ist frischer und teurer als das Essen bei Pizza Extra.
The fish is the freshest that I've ever tasted.	Der Fisch ist der frischeste, den ich je probiert habe.
Sushi Blue is the most expensive sushi restaurant in the area.	Sushi Blue ist das teuerste Sushi-Restaurant in der Gegend.
My friend's pizza was as bad as mine.	Die Pizza meines Freundes war so schlecht wie meine.

Auf Seite 175 findest du weitere Beispiele und Erklärungen zur Steigerung von Adjektiven.

Tasty food

3a grammar: comparison of adjectives (R) p. 175

Compare different kinds of food. Write three or more comparisons with 'than' or 'as … as'. You can look at the box for help.

as tasty as · tastier than · as good as · better than · as fresh as · fresher than · as delicious as · more delicious than · healthier than · spicier than · …

You can write:

Hot dogs are as tasty as …

… are tastier than …

…

hot dog

chicken curry

salad

vegetable soup

?

???

3b grammar: comparison of adjectives (R) p. 175, wordbank: eating and eating out p. 160, workbook p. 12/2-4

Write three or more statements about your favourite food or restaurant. Look at the box for help.

the tastiest · the best · the freshest · the most delicious · the healthiest · the spiciest · the cheapest · …

You can write:

The pizza at … is …

It's … restaurant I know.

The restaurant has … food in our area.

Where is the stress?

4a audio 1/11

Listen to the words and repeat them.

perfect · dessert · vegetable · disgusting · expensive · restaurant · beautiful · delicious

4b

Is the stress on the first or the second syllable? Make two lists.

first syllable	second syllable
perfect	*dessert*
…	…

DIGITAL+ practise more 6-7

Making plans

5a audio 1/12

**Listen to Ava's mum Fiona talking to Grandmother Edyta.
What are they talking about?**

5b CHOOSE YOUR LEVEL skill: listening p. 151

I Listen again. Then match the sentence parts and write the sentences in your exercise book.

1 The family is planning to
2 Grandma Edyta wants to
3 They don't want to go to
4 They decide to go to

A an Indian restaurant.
B a Chinese restaurant.
C go to a restaurant.
D try something different.

II Listen again. Are the statements true or false? Take notes. Then copy the true statements into your exercise book.

1 The family is planning to go to a restaurant on Wednesday evening.
2 Grandma Edyta is allergic to raw fish.
3 Sushi is Grandma Edyta's favourite food.
4 Joshua loves Turkish food.
5 There is a Chinese restaurant on Portobello Road.
6 Edyta likes the Indian restaurant near the station.

III Listen again and take notes. Then correct these statements.

1 The family is planning to go to a restaurant on Tuesday evening.
2 Fiona is allergic to raw fish.
3 Grandma Edyta would like to go to a sushi restaurant.
4 Joshua loves Turkish food.
5 Fiona suggests a Vietnamese restaurant on Portobello Road.
6 The Indian restaurant doesn't have many vegetarian dishes.

5c wordbank: eating and eating out p. 160, workbook p. 14/5

**Is there a restaurant you and your family go to on special occasions?
Or do you prepare something special to eat?
Tell your class about it.**

You can say:
We always go to … on my dad's birthday.
My mum always cooks … when …
…

At The Palace of India – part one

6a
wordbank: talking about pictures p. 166, grammar: present progressive (R) p. 176

Look at the picture. What are the people doing?

You can say:

The waiter / Ava / … is …

The guests / The Kogans are …

arriving · smiling · looking at · eating · drinking · showing · …

6b
audio 1/13

Listen to the dialogue and read along. What food does everybody order?

Waiter: Good evening and welcome to The Palace of India. Have you got a reservation?

Mrs Kogan: Hello, yes, the name is Kogan – a table for six.

Waiter: Certainly. Let me show you to your table. Please come this way. Take a seat.

***

Waiter: Here are your menus. Today I can recommend a tikka masala with salmon and home-made mango ice cream for dessert. Can I bring you some drinks to start with?

Mr Kogan: We'd like to look at the menu first, but can we please have a bottle of water for the table?

Waiter: Of course. I'll be back in a minute with your water and I'll take your order.

***

Waiter: So, have you decided what you would like to eat?

Mrs Kogan: Yes, two vegetable kormas for the boys and a chicken tikka masala for me, please. What are you having, Edyta?

Edyta: I'd like the tikka masala with salmon please, with rice on the side.

Waiter: What about the others?

Ava: I'm starving! I'll have the butter chicken with rice *and* some naan bread, please.

Waiter: Of course. And for you, sir?

Mr Kogan: I'll have the lamb vindaloo, please.

Waiter: Just to warn you, our vindaloo is extremely spicy.

Mr Kogan: I love hot food! I'll be OK.

Waiter: OK, great.

6c
workbook p. 14/6-7

These sentences are not very polite. Rewrite them in a more polite way. Look at the text for help.

1 Your table is over there. Sit down.
2 Do you want a drink?
3 We want a bottle of water.
4 What do you want to eat?

The menu

7a

Read the menu of The Palace of India. What do they serve with all main courses?

DRINKS

Lemonade, cola, mineral water	*£2.20*
Mango lassi *(a cool yoghurt drink)*	*£3.00*

STARTERS

Poppadoms *(fried chickpea crackers) with a selection of dips*	*£1.85*
Onion bhaji *(golden fried onions)*	*£2.30*
Vegetable samosa *(fried pastry filled with potatoes and vegetables)*	*£3.95*

MAIN COURSES **** We serve all main courses with rice or naan bread. ****

Butter chicken *(chicken cooked in a mild sauce with garlic, tomato and coriander)*	*£10.95*
Korma *(a mild curry with coconut cream)* *Choose from vegetable, lamb or chicken.*	*£13.95*
Tikka Masala *(a curry with ginger, tomato, coriander and chilli)* *Choose from vegetable, lamb, chicken or fish.*	*£13.95*
Vindaloo *(our hottest curry with lots of chilli)* *Choose from vegetable, lamb or chicken.*	*£9.95*
Palak paneer *(soft cheese in a spinach curry)*	*£7.95*
Mixed kebab plate *(grilled lamb, chicken and beef with salad)*	*£11.95*

7b CHOOSE YOUR LEVEL skill: mediation p. 155

I You are at The Palace of India with your grandmother. Answer three of her questions in German.

II You are at The Palace of India with your grandmother. Answer five of her questions in German.

III You are at The Palace of India with your grandmother. Answer her questions in German.

1 Was ist ein *mango lassi*?
2 Was gibt es denn alles als Vorspeise? Ist da etwas ohne Zwiebeln dabei?
3 Bekommt man auch was zum Hauptgericht dazu, Kartoffeln oder so?
4 Welche Vorspeise ist vegetarisch?
5 Was genau ist ein *vegetable samosa*?
6 Was ist eigentlich *butter chicken*? Ist da wirklich nur Butter in der Soße?
7 Gibt es ein besonders scharfes Gericht?

7c

You have £20 to spend. What would you order? Make notes and talk to a partner.

At The Palace of India – part two

8a audio 1/14

Listen to the rest of the dialogue and read along. Who has not finished his or her food? Why?

Waiter: Is everything OK with your food? Can I get you any more drinks?
Noah: Really yummy, thank you.
Mrs Kogan: Yes, it's really good.
Mr Kogan: I'll have another mango lassi, please!
Waiter: Of course.
Mrs Kogan: How is the vindaloo?
Mr Kogan: It is really spicy!
Edyta: Are you OK?
Mr Kogan: Yes, yes, very good!

***

Noah: I can't eat anymore. I'm full already! I'll have to leave the rest. Do you think I can take it home?
Edyta: I'm sure that will be OK. Sebastian, you haven't finished either! Was it too spicy for you?
Mr Kogan: Umm, no, err … I just … I'm getting full. But I think I'll have just one more mango lassi …

***

Waiter: Would you like to see the dessert menu? We also have teas and coffee.
Mrs Kogan: No, thank you very much. We've all eaten too much already.
Mr Kogan: Can we get the bill, please?
Waiter: Of course. I'll be back in a minute. Would you like to pay with cash or card?
Mr Kogan: Card, please.
Waiter: OK. Just a minute. I'll bring the card machine over.

***

Edyta: What a great meal, thank you!
Mrs Kogan: I'm happy you enjoyed it!
Mr Kogan: And the mango lassi is really excellent.
Mrs Kogan: We can take some home if you need some more …

8b wordbank: eating and eating out p. 160, skill: writing p. 153, workbook p. 16/8-10

After the trip to the restaurant, Ava texts her friends. Write down three or more sentences.

You can write:

Hi guys, I'm just back from The Palace of India.
The food was …
I had …
Dad had …

Ordering food

9 GET TOGETHER workbook p. 17/11

Get together with a partner.
Decide what you would like to order.

Partner A
- I Go to page 128.
- II Go to page 131.
- III Go to page 134.

Partner B
- I Go to page 137.
- II Go to page 140.
- III Go to page 143.

Eating out

10 CHOOSE YOUR TASK wordbank: eating and eating out p. 160, C: skill: writing p. 153, media worksheet 9, workbook p. 17/12

A Write a menu for your dream restaurant.
B Collect useful phrases that you need when you are at a restaurant.
C Write about a good or a bad restaurant experience. It can be a real experience or you can make one up. You can look at 2b on pages 18 and 19 for help.

A

STARTER
small muffins and chocolate soup

MAIN COURSE
chocolate cake with strawberries

DESSERT
ice cream with chocolate sauce

B

Eating out

Could I have a …, please?

I would like the …, please.

What is …?

Can I have chips with my burger?

A difficult customer

11a video 4, skill: watching a video clip p. 156

Watch the video clip. What is happening?

11b

What do you think the lady is going to eat in the end? Collect ideas.

11c skill: writing p. 153, workbook p. 18/13

Later that evening the waiter and the lady both send text messages to a friend. Choose one of them and write his or her text message.

You can write:

Guess what happened to me today. I …

Can you believe what …? I … Then …

What is going on?

12 CHOOSE YOUR LEVEL

I Look at the pictures and read the texts. Are the people happy or not?

You can say:
I think, the … in picture … is …

II Look at the pictures and read the texts. Then match the captions to the pictures.

You can say:
Picture … matches caption …

A A disgusting experience

B Waiting for my lunch

C Sitting next to a famous person

III Look at the pictures and read the texts. Then choose one picture and think about what could happen next. Make notes.

Sorry, will be late. I'm still sitting here waiting for my lunch.

OMG! I can't believe that I'm having dinner at the same restaurant as Preppy Rappy!

So disgusting! I found a spider in my soup!!! But I'm getting a free dessert now.

At the restaurant

13a skill: mediation p. 155

You are at a restaurant with your family. Two English-speaking tourists at the table next to you ask you for help with the German menu. Can you help them?

Tourist: We would like soup, one vegetarian main course and one with meat. We'd also like a dessert!
You: Then you could order …

13b skill: performing a scene p. 159, workbook p. 18/14

Take notes and act out the conversation with a partner. Remember to be polite.

Ratsstübl

Vorspeisen und Suppen
Kleiner bunter Salat
Kartoffelsuppe
Tomatensuppe

Hauptgerichte
Schnitzel mit Bratkartoffeln
Backfisch mit Salzkartoffeln
Spaghetti Bolognese
Bratwurst und Kartoffelpüree mit Salat
Gemüselasagne
Grillgemüse mit Käse überbacken

Nachtisch
Erdbeerkuchen
Vanilleeis mit heißen Früchten

DIGITAL+ practise more 8

Our restaurant role play TARGET TASK

14 workbook p. 19/15, wordbank: eating and eating out p. 160, skill: performing a scene p. 159, media worksheet 2

Your task is to present a scene at a restaurant. Before you start, look at these steps:

STEP 1

Get together in small groups and plan your role play. Decide:

- What type of restaurant is it?
  (A fast food restaurant, a very expensive restaurant, a takeaway, ...?)
- What can you eat there?
- Who are your characters? What are they like?
- ...

STEP 2

What is going to happen in your scene? Will it be a good or a bad experience?
Think of an unusual event, for example:

- someone finds something disgusting in their food
- someone famous visits the restaurant
- something funny happens
- ...

STEP 3

Decide who will play which part.

STEP 4

Make notes for your role play. Collect words and phrases you will need.
You can write cue cards for each character.

STEP 5

Practise your role play. You can use props or costumes if you like.

STEP 6

Perform your scene. If you like, you can film your scene and show it to the rest of the class.

Check out

Kannst du einen Blogeintrag zum Thema Essen verstehen?	Workbook, p. 20
Kannst du ein Gespräch zum Thema Kochen verstehen?	Workbook, p. 20
Kannst du über Gerichte sprechen, die du schon einmal probiert hast?	Workbook, p. 20
Kennst du wichtige Redewendungen, die man bei einem Restaurantbesuch braucht?	Workbook, p. 21
Kannst du jemandem sprachlich aushelfen, der eine Speisekarte nicht versteht?	Workbook, p. 21
Kannst du einen kurzen Text über ein Restaurant schreiben?	Workbook, p. 21

Delicious disaster

Hi, I'm Jamie and this is my sister Lucy. We live with our mum and dad.

Well, he's not our *real* dad, but he behaves like one and we like him a lot. Our mum met him when I was three and Lucy was one.

Mum's a hairdresser. She works in the city centre and she's really good. Dad sells fridges.

Last week, Dad's sister Sally came to our place for dinner. We like her very much, she's really cool.

That morning Mum said, "Tonight is going to be very busy. I've got a lot to do at work today, and Dad won't be home before seven. You'll have to let Sally in and then we'll order some pizza as soon as I'm home." Both my parents are quite bad at cooking so we order in a lot. Or get takeaways. But we're all really good at making sandwiches.

When I came home from school that day, no one was there and I went to the kitchen to get a snack. While I was looking for some snacks, I found this really fancy cookbook Mum has: *French kitchen: 300 traditional recipes.* I looked through it and there were lots of pictures of really yummy-looking food. The last part of the book was *Suggestions for menus.* There were ideas for three-, four- and even twelve-course menus!!!

Just at that moment Lucy came home and found me staring at the cookbook.
"What are you doing?" she asked and looked at the cookbook. "Oh, that looks yummy. Why do we never have anything like that?"
At that moment I had an idea. "Lucy," I said. "Why don't we cook our dinner for tonight?
"But we can't cook," Lucy said.
"Well, that's what cookbooks are for," I said. "You have to start somewhere – look at that four-course meal with chicken. It doesn't look too difficult. Mum makes chicken nuggets all the time."
"OK, let's try it," Lucy said. "What do we do first?"

disaster = *Katastrophe;* fancy = *nobel;* course = *Gang;* four-course-meal = *Vier-Gänge-Mahlzeit*

I looked at the cookbook. "I think we'll have to go shopping first," I said. "Let's take the pizza money." So we went shopping. To our great surprise, salad for the first course, some cheese and tomatoes for the second course, a chicken, potatoes and vegetables for the main course and fruit and cream for the dessert were cheaper than our usual pizza dinner.

"Right, let's do this," I said when we got home. "You could start peeling the potatoes. I'll prepare the chicken." "Alright," Lucy said and started to peel the potatoes.

About half an hour later the kitchen looked like a battlefield.

There was not much left of the potatoes, but we had lots of peels. I was still trying to cut the chicken, but it didn't look right. On the pictures in the cookbook there was a lot less blood and mess.

"Maybe you could start whipping the cream for the dessert," I told Lucy. "OK," she said and took out the mixer.
Big mistake! Lucy was as bad at whipping cream as she was at peeling potatoes. The cream went everywhere!
When Sally arrived at half past six, we hadn't even started with the first two courses yet … There was food everywhere, and I was still holding the knife. Sally laughed so hard she almost cried.

We explained our plan to her and she said: "Oh, that's a lovely idea. But I don't think we have enough time for that now. Why don't we do that another day? We can quickly make some pancakes for tonight. And maybe we should clean the kitchen first?"
She started laughing again.
So we cleaned the kitchen and Sally showed us how to make pancakes. With her help it was quite easy and we managed not to make any more mess.

When Mum and Dad came home, the kitchen was clean and there were lots of pancakes on the table. Mum and Dad were so surprised!
We all sat down and had a lovely pancake dinner. I ate five, Lucy ate three and Dad ate twelve!!!
"That was sooooo good. Thank you guys," Mum said.
"Maybe you can do the cooking from now on. Then we wouldn't always have to eat takeaways or sandwiches."
"That's a brilliant idea, dear," Dad said and licked his fingers. "They could learn to prepare some more dishes. Something with chicken maybe. Chicken's not too difficult."

surprise = *Überraschung;* peel = *schälen, Schale;* battlefield = *Schlachtfeld;* mess = *Unordnung;* whip cream = *Sahne schlagen;* hadn't even started = *hatten noch nicht einmal angefangen;* manage = *es schaffen;* lick = *ablecken*

Curious about curry?

Curry is a traditional dish in many countries such as India, Pakistan and Bangladesh. The word 'curry' comes from the word 'kari' meaning 'sauce' in Tamil – a language spoken in South India and other parts of Asia.

There are many types of curries. They can be very spicy or mild, but they all use a combination of spices.
In most curries you find chillies, coriander, cumin and turmeric. Many curries also include ginger, cardamom and garlic. A mix of some of these spices also goes into curry powder, a spice mix very popular in the Western world.

curry

curry powder

a spice and tea stall at a market in India

So why is curry – and Indian food in general – so popular in the UK today? In the 17th century, Britain and India started trading goods like spices and tea.
At that time in Britain, Indian spices were very expensive, and only rich people could buy them.

In the 18th and 19th centuries, British influence in India grew, and the British East India Company, which controlled large parts of trade in India, became more and more powerful.

In 1858, India officially became a British colony until it became independent in 1947. Many people from India have moved to Britain and brought their culture and eating habits with them.
Today there are thousands of Indian restaurants all over the country.

Find out more about an Indian dish or spice and report your findings to the class.

2

1 Look at the pictures. What are the people doing?
2 What is important for a healthy lifestyle?
3 What sports do you like?

Healthy living

Part A Keeping fit

- Du unterhältst dich über verschiedene Sportarten.
- Du hörst dir ein Interview an.
- Du sammelst und präsentierst Tipps für einen gesunden Lebensstil.

Part B At the doctor's

- Du sprichst über Gesundheitsthemen.
- Du siehst dir ein Video darüber an, wie man jemanden aufheitert, der krank ist.
- Du stellst ein Rollenspiel vor.

What's the right sport for you?

1a

Answer the questions to find out: what could be a good sport for you?

1 Do you like playing games?
- **A** Yes, I do.
- **B** No, I don't.

2 Do you like ball sports?
- **A** Yes, I do.
- **B** No, I don't.

3 Where do you prefer to be?
- **A** Indoors.
- **B** Outdoors.

4 Do you like water sports?
- **A** Yes, I do.
- **B** No, I don't.

5 Are you a good loser?
- **A** Yes, I am. I don't care if I win or lose.
- **B** No, I'm not. I get really angry.
- **C** I'm not, but I try not to show it.

6 Do you prefer doing sports in a team or do you prefer being on your own?
- **A** I prefer doing sports in a team.
- **B** I prefer being on my own.

Different sports:

Water sports:	swimming · diving · rowing · ...
Team sports:	football · hockey · basketball · American football · ...
Sports you can do on your own:	marathon · darts · yoga · running · weight training · climbing · ...

1b workbook p. 22/1-3

Work with a partner. Talk about what you think could be a good sport for you. Take turns.

You can say:

I like … I think … could be a good sport for me.
I prefer … so I think … is a good idea.
I don't like … but I think …
…

Finding the right sport

2a skill: reading p. 154

Scan the profiles and find out:

1 Who loves being in nature?
2 Who likes maths?
3 Who does not like being alone?

Hi, I'm Kristin. I love being active. I'm not good at sitting still. I like spending time outside with my friends – that makes me really happy. I don't like being alone. Having people around me is very important to me.

Hi, I'm Ben. I like to choose when and where I train. I don't really like team sports because I like being on my own.
I love spending time in nature. It feels great to reach a goal just by using my own skills and strengths. Living a healthy life is important to me so I try to eat healthy food in order to stay fit.

Hi, I'm Amira. I don't like big groups of people. I prefer being indoors – on my own or with my best friend.
I'm not much of an outdoor person.
My favourite subject at school is maths. I'm good at logical thinking and solving puzzles. I'm not a very good loser. It makes me really angry when I'm not the best at something.

2b CHOOSE YOUR LEVEL wordbank: keeping fit p. 162

I Read Kristin's profile. What does she like? What does she not like? Take notes. Look at 1a again. What could be a good sport for her?

You can write:
Kristin likes being …
Kristin doesn't like being …
… could be a good sport for her.

II Read Ben's profile. Take notes on what he likes and what he does not like. Write down what could be a good sport for him.

You can write:
Ben likes being … He doesn't like …
I think … could be a good sport for Ben because he likes …

III Read Amira's profile. Take notes on what she likes and does not like. What is she good at? Think of a good sport for her and write her a short message.

You can write:
Hi Amira, you say that you like …
… could be a good sport for you because …
You don't like … so maybe …
…

GRAMMAR HELP the gerund p. 177

Die *ing*-Form von Verben hast du schon beim *present progressive* kennengelernt, wie etwa in diesem Satz: *The children are playing football.* Schau dir nun folgende Sätze an. Wie werden die *ing*-Formen hier benutzt?

Swimming keeps you fit.	(Das) Schwimmen hält dich fit.
Do you like diving?	Magst du Tauchen? (= Tauchst du gerne?)
I'm good at climbing.	Ich bin gut im Klettern.

In diesen Fällen nennt man die Formen *gerund*. Auf Seite 177 findest du weitere Beispiele und Erklärungen.

A sport for Matilda

3 grammar: gerund p. 177, workbook p. 23/4

Read what Matilda said and copy it. Complete it with the words from the box.

swimming · playing · sitting · going · spending · running

I don't like ??? at home. I want to find a sport that I really like. I've tried ???, but I stopped ??? to the pool after a few weeks.
Maybe a team sport is better for me. I'm really good at ??? fast and I prefer ??? time outside. How about ??? rugby? Do you think it's a cool sport?

Doing sports

4 grammar: gerund p. 177, workbook p. 23/5

What do you think about different sports and activities? Write four or more sentences. You can use words from the boxes.

You can write:
I think swimming is …
Doing karate is not …
I think … can be …
…

swimming · doing karate · running · cycling · playing football · playing basketball · ...

fun · exciting · boring · easy · difficult · exhausting · ...

What are you good at?

5 grammar: gerund p. 177, wordbank: keeping fit p. 162, workbook p. 24/6

What sports and activities are you good at? Write three or more sentences.

You can write:
I'm good at playing …
I'm good at …
…

DIGITAL+ practise more 9

An interview

6a skill: working with words p. 150, media worksheet 3

Match the definitions to the words. Look up the words you do not know.

1 They tell you how to play a game.
2 A ... is what you need in order to do something well.
3 A series of games where the best team or player wins a prize at the end.
4 When you focus on something, you ...
5 Training is a ...

A skill
B physical activity
C rules
D concentrate
E tournament

6b audio 1/20, skill: listening p. 151

You are going to hear the words from 6a in an interview. What do you think the interview is about? Collect ideas in class. Then listen to the interview. Were you right?

6c CHOOSE YOUR LEVEL

I Listen again and choose the right word to complete the statements. Write down the statements.

1 Chess is a ??? (new / very old) game.
2 You need a lot of ??? (training and practice / lessons) to be good.
3 Being fit can help you ??? (win / concentrate) when you play for hours.

II Listen again and take notes. Copy the true statements and correct the false statements.

1 Chess is sometimes called “the game of kings”.
2 You can’t play chess online.
3 Anna likes chess because it is relaxing.
4 There are four elements that make a sport a sport.

III Listen again and take notes. Copy the true statements and correct the false statements.

1 Chess is probably 150 years old.
2 In Anna’s opinion, chess is a game.
3 You have to learn different strategies.
4 Being fit does not help you in a game of chess.
5 Chess is very competitive.

6d wordbank: expressing opinions p. 165, media worksheet 15, workbook p. 24/7-9

What do you think? Is chess a sport?

You can say:

I think chess is a sport because ...
I don’t think chess is a sport because ...

Feeling good

7a skill: reading p. 154

Scan the posts and write down what sports the teenagers do.

× –

ELLIE, 13

I love dancing and I'm in a dance group. It's so much fun moving to the music and practising together as a team. You exercise and have a great workout without even noticing it. After the training I'm really exhausted, but I always feel great. At school I really hate PE lessons. Our teacher thinks it's the most important subject ever, but I am not very good at running, jumping and playing football, so the sports that we usually do are not for me. Why can't we do something like dancing?

RYAN, 15

I love playing wheelchair basketball. Playing in a team with your friends is great fun. I go to practice twice a week, and we play matches against other teams at the weekends.
My dream is to play for the national team some day.
In the summer holidays we always go to a special practice camp for a week. There we also learn about things like looking after ourselves – how to get enough sleep and what to eat and how not to stress too much. This is also important to be good at your sport.

ALEX, 16

I don't like the fact that most sports are about competing against others and winning. But I know that doing something for my body is important.
So I tried running and cycling – but I didn't like that very much.
I wanted to find an indoor activity.
One day I went to yoga class with my mum and I really liked it!
I do yoga regularly now and I love it.
Yoga not only keeps me fit and flexible, it also helps me to learn about myself. I now know how to relax when feeling stressed.
Even my marks at school are better now. So, if you have the chance – try it out!

MIRA, 14

I've always been quite sporty – but last year I broke my leg and was in hospital for some time. I spent a lot of time watching TV or playing computer games. I also ate a lot of sweets.
When my leg got better, the rest of me wasn't feeling too well.
I felt tired and sad most of the time.
My mum had the idea that I should start swimming again and eat less chocolate. It was really hard, but after about three weeks I felt a lot better. The swimming helped my leg, and I can ride my bike to school again. Of course I still eat sweets, but not as many as before, and I eat a lot more fruit and vegetables because I can really feel that that's better for me.

7b CHOOSE YOUR LEVEL

I Read two or more of the posts and answer the questions about them.
II Read three or more of the posts and answer the questions about them.
III Read all of the posts and answer the questions.

Questions on Ellie's post:
1 What does Ellie think about PE at school?
2 What does she like about dancing?

Questions on Ryan's post:
1 What does Ryan like about playing wheelchair basketball?
2 What does Ryan learn in the summer holidays?

Questions on Alex's post:
1 What kinds of sports does Alex not like?
2 Why does yoga make him feel good?

Questions on Mira's post:
1 What happened when Mira had to stop doing sports?
2 What made her feel better?

7c workbook p. 25/10-11

What makes you feel good? Make notes and talk to a partner about it.

You can write:	You can say:
- doing sports	*... makes me feel good.*
- being with my friends	*I love ...*
- listening to music	*... is what I'm good at. It makes me ...*
...	...

LAND & LEUTE 2 video 5

Schulsport im Vereinigten Königreich

Viele Schulen im Vereinigten Königreich haben drinnen und draußen Bereiche für alle möglichen Sportarten. Die Schülerinnen und Schüler üben während des Schuljahres verschiedene Sportarten aus, sowohl Teamsportarten wie Fußball und Hockey als auch Individualsportarten wie Badminton und Geländelauf. Damit jeder sehen kann, für welche Schule sie bei Wettkämpfen antreten, tragen sie auch beim Sport eine Schuluniform, normalerweise ein T-Shirt, Shorts und Strümpfe in den Schulfarben.
Im Sommer gibt es an den meisten Schulen ein Sportfest. Die Schülerinnen und Schüler messen sich in verschiedenen Aktivitäten. Beim Sportfest kann man wie auch bei anderen Aktivitäten im Schuljahr für sein Haus Punkte gewinnen. Die meisten Schulen sind in vier oder fünf verschiedene Häuser unterteilt. Am Ende des Jahres gewinnt das Haus mit den meisten Punkten einen Pokal.

Vergleicht Schulsport im Vereinigten Königreich mit dem an eurer Schule oder an Schulen anderer Länder, über die ihr etwas wisst. Was ist gleich? Was ist anders?

Martin's favourite sport

8a video 6, skill: watching a video clip p. 156, workbook p. 26/12

Watch the video clip.
What is Martin's favourite sport?

8b CHOOSE YOUR LEVEL skill: mediation p. 155

A friend wants to know what Martin is talking about. Read his or her questions. Then watch the video clip again.

I Take notes and answer two or more of the questions in German.
II Take notes and answer three or more of the questions in German.
III Take notes and answer four or more of the questions in German.

1 Wie lange macht Martin seinen Sport schon?
2 Wie oft ist er schon getaucht?
3 Warum braucht er manchmal einen „dry suit"?
4 Wieso hat er eine so große Uhr?
5 Was sind das für Fotos, die er zeigt?
6 Was ist ein „buddy check"?

Sports

9 CHOOSE YOUR TASK wordbank: keeping fit p. 162, C: media worksheet 10, workbook p. 27/13

A Find a picture of your favourite sport or draw one and label it.
B Create a poster, a flyer or an advert for your favourite sport.
C Write a post about a sport you like doing or watching.
You can look at the posts on pages 36 and 37 again.

Sports poems

10a audio 1/23-25

Listen to the poems and read along.

Choose your sports

Let's turn off our video games,
and run outside.
From so many sports,
we may choose and decide.
Baseball, soccer,
and basketball are fun.
Let's grab some friends,
and play in the sun.
(...)
Whatever sports,
you decide to play,
enjoy them with friends,
each and every day.

SKATEBOARDING

Knee pads, elbow pads,
start the show.
Grab your helmet;
Come on, let's go!

Margo L. Dill

What
Can You
Do With a
Football
?

Well...

You can
kick it - you can catch
it - you can bounce it - all
around. **YOU CAN GRAB IT** you can
pat it you can roll it - on the ground.
You can throw it ***you can head it***
you can hit it - with a bat. You can
biff it you can boot it you can spin
it **you can shoot it.** You can
drop it you can stop it. Just
like that!

James Carter

10b

Which of the words in the first two poems are rhyming words? Collect them on the board.

10c

Look at the two boxes and find the rhyming pairs. Write them down. You can add more.

fun · trick · match · dream · ball · throw

go · team · catch · run · all · kick

10d wordbank: keeping fit p. 162, workbook p. 28/14

Be a poet. Write a sports poem. You can use one of the poems in 10a to help you.

10e

Work with a partner or in small groups. Choose a poem and learn it by heart.

Word families

11 skill: working with words p. 150

How many words that belong to each word family can you find? Write them down. You can use a dictionary to help you.

run · play · swim · dance · train

You can write:

run: runner, running, …

play: playground, …

…

A sports idol

12a audio 1/26

Listen to the interview with Jada. What does she say about Tony Hawk and his "Skatepark Project"?

12b CHOOSE YOUR LEVEL skill: listening p. 151, workbook p. 28/15

I Listen again. Choose the right words from the box and write down the sentences.

started · keeping · skating

1 Jada started ??? when she was six.
2 Skateboarding is a great sport for ??? fit.
3 Tony Hawk ??? the Skatepark Project.

II Listen again and match the sentence parts. Write down the sentences.

1 Jada started competing
2 Looking out for each other is
3 Skateboarding is a great sport
4 Jada's idol is

A Tony Hawk.
B for keeping fit.
C when she was ten.
D important for skateboarders.

III Listen again and complete the sentences. Write them down.

1 Jada started ??? when she was six years old.
2 Jada loves being able to do a new trick after hours of ???.
3 Tony Hawk is her ???.
4 Tony Hawk was really good at ??? new tricks.
5 Jada started ??? yoga because it helps her to ???.

12c wordbank: keeping fit p. 162, workbook p. 28/16

Who is your sports idol? Write four or more sentences about him or her. You can make one up if you do not have a sports idol.

You can write:

My idol is … He / She is …

He / She was born in …

He / She is a …

I like him / her because he / she is …

DIGITAL+ practise more 10

Tips for a healthy lifestyle TARGET TASK

13 workbook p. 29/17, wordbank: keeping fit p. 162, presenting something p. 168, skill: presentations p. 158

Your task is to collect and present tips for keeping fit and healthy.
Before you start, look at these steps:

STEP 1

In class: think about how you would like to present the tips.
You could make:

- leaflets
- posters
- slides for a slide show
- a short video clip
- ...

STEP 2

Get together with a partner or in a small group and collect information.
You can look at the unit again and / or search the Internet.
Make notes.
Think about the following:

- How much sleep do you need?
- What should you do before you go to sleep? What should you not do? (switch off your mobile phone, switch off the TV, read a good book, ...)
- What should you eat? What should you not eat?
- What kind of sport do you like?
- What is good for you?
- How often should you do sports?
- What else could you do to keep fit and to relax? (yoga, pilates, ...)
- ...

STEP 3

Create your poster, leaflet, slide show, short video clip, ...
Edit it with a partner or in a small group.

STEP 4

Present your work, for example in a gallery walk.
Which tips do you think are the most important ones?

STEP 5

Give each other feedback. Remember to be polite.

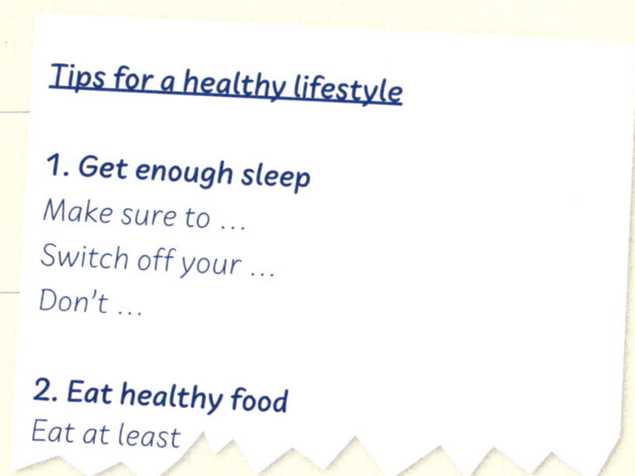

What's the matter?

1a

Look at the pictures on this double page. What is the matter with the people?

You can say:
Matthew / Sarah / Linda / Tom / Demir has …

a toothache · a swollen wrist · a bad cold · a stomach ache · a wound

1b audio 1/27

Listen to the dialogues and read along. What is each patient's problem?

Matthew: Ow, my shoulder and my wrist hurt so much! And look, my wrist is swollen.
John: I know.
Matthew: What if my wrist is broken?
John: Don't worry too much. They'll probably take an X-ray, and if it is broken, you will get a cast.
Matthew: But if I have a cast, I'll miss the match next week! Ow – it really hurts!

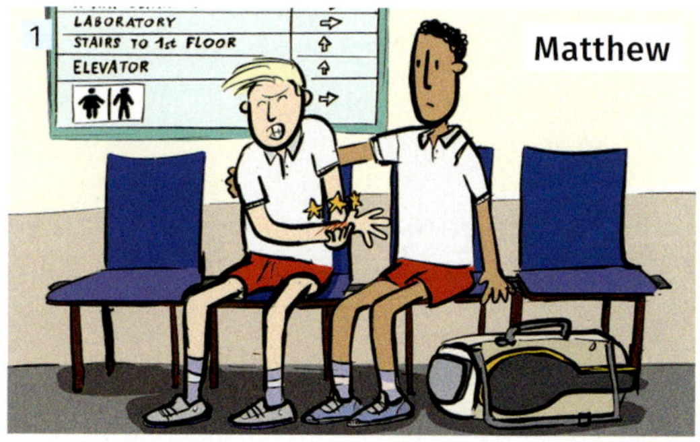

Sarah: My tooth hurts so much!
Mum: Then I'll make an appointment at the dentist's for you.
Sarah: Oh no!
Mum: If it hurts so much, you'll have to go to the dentist. The toothache will only get worse if you don't go.
Sarah: I know. But I really hate going to the dentist.

Receptionist: Good morning, Dr Hill's practice. This is Jemima speaking. How can I help you?
Linda: Hello, this is Linda Miller. I think I've caught a cold. I have a headache and a sore throat, and my nose just won't stop running. I also have a fever and a cough.
Receptionist: Oh yes, you don't sound too good. Let me see … If you come in at twelve o'clock, the doctor can see you just before his lunch break.
Linda: That sounds good. Thanks.

Mum: Oh dear. What's happened?
Tom: I fell on my knee and it really hurts.
Mum: Let me have a look at it. Oh, it's bleeding. We have to clean the wound. If we don't do that, you will get an infection. Then I'll put a plaster on it. If it doesn't get better soon, we'll go and see a doctor.

Nurse: Good morning, Demir. How are you feeling today?
Demir: My stomach still hurts.
Nurse: Well, it's only been two days since your operation, but you can have some toast today.
Demir: Oh, great. I'm so hungry.
Nurse: Yes, I know. But please eat slowly. It'll be quite painful if you eat too fast. And here is your medicine for today.

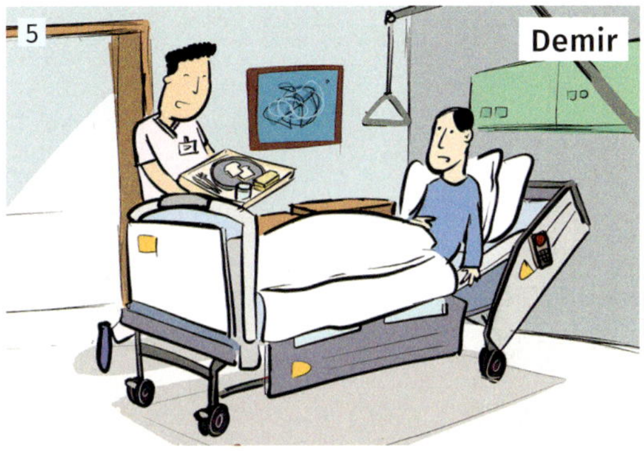

1c CHOOSE YOUR LEVEL skill: reading p. 154

I Read the first three dialogues again. What health problems do the people have?

You can write:
Matthew: shoulder hurts, wrist is swollen
Sarah:
Linda:

II Read the first three dialogues again.
Collect words for body parts and words for health problems.

You can write:

body part:	***problem:***
shoulder, wrist, …	*hurt, …*

III Read all the dialogues again. Collect words for body parts and words for health problems.

1d skill: performing a scene p. 159, media worksheet, 2, 5, workbook p. 30/1-2

Work with a partner. Try to imagine how the people are feeling in each situation and do a dramatic reading of one of the dialogues. You can record it if you like.

GRAMMAR HELP conditional clauses 1 p. 178

Wenn du sagen möchtest, was unter bestimmten Bedingungen geschehen wird, benutzt du Bedingungssätze. Diese Sätze bestehen aus zwei Teilen. Sieh dir die Beispiele an. Was fällt dir auf?

If you have a broken wrist, you will miss the tennis match.
Wenn / Falls du ein gebrochenes Handgelenk hast, wirst du das Tennisspiel verpassen.

The toothache will only get worse if you don't go to the dentist.
Die Zahnschmerzen werden nur schlimmer werden, wenn / falls du nicht zum Zahnarzt / zur Zahnärztin gehst.

If you come in at twelve o'clock, the doctor can see you just before his lunch break.
Wenn / Falls du um 12 Uhr kommst, kann der Arzt dich direkt vor seiner Mittagspause drannehmen.

Auf Seite 178 findest du weitere Erklärungen zur Bildung und Verwendung von Bedingungssätzen.

If you ...

2 grammar: conditional 1 p. 178

Match the sentence parts. Write the sentences in your exercise book.

1 If you don't see a doctor,
2 If you break your leg,
3 If you stay in bed,
4 If you don't eat slowly,
5 You'll feel a lot better soon if
6 You will catch a cold

A if you don't wear a warm jacket.
B it will get worse.
C your stomach will hurt.
D you take your medicine.
E you'll get well soon.
F you will get a cast.

What if ...?

3a grammar: conditional 1 p. 178

Write sentences. There can be more than one solution.

If you have a really bad cold, you ??? (will / must) stay at home.
If you stay at home, you ??? (will / can) play lots of video games.
If you play lots of video games, you ??? (will / can) become really good at playing video games.

3b grammar: conditional 1 p. 178, workbook p. 31 / 3

Choose one of the sentence beginnings below and write about a chain of events like in 3a. Write three or more sentences starting with "If ...".

A If the weather is nice tomorrow, I'll go to the park. If I go to the park, I'll ...
B If it's rainy tomorrow, I will / I won't ...
C If my mum / dad goes to ..., she / he will ... If she / he ....
D If ...

DIGITAL+ practise more 11

Tarek's accident

4a

Look at the picture. What can you see? What do you think is going to happen next?

4b audio 1/28

Listen to the dialogue and read along. Who is Tarek's coach going to call?

Tarek: Ow! I banged my head really hard.
Coach: Tarek, are you alright? Can you get up? Let me help you!
Tarek: Ow, I don't think I can! I can't move my foot, it hurts too much. I'm feeling dizzy, too.
Coach: OK, stay down then. I'll call an ambulance. Could somebody call Tarek's dad, please?
Chris: I can call Mr Adil.
Coach: Thanks, Chris. Tell him that I'll let him know which hospital we're at as soon as I know.

4c audio 1/29, skill: listening p. 151

Listen to Tarek's coach calling the emergency services. What is going to happen next?

4d CHOOSE YOUR LEVEL workbook p. 32/4-5

I Listen again. Choose the right words and write down what Tarek's coach explains to the operator.

There was ??? (a match / an accident) on the playing field. One of my players is hurt. He is able to ??? (talk / see). He can't stand on his ??? (left foot / right foot) and he is feeling ??? (sad / dizzy).

II Listen again. Choose the right words and write down what Tarek's coach explains to the operator.

There was an accident ??? (on the playing field / on the playground). During a hockey match, ??? (three / two) players ran ??? (into a wall / into each other). One of them can't stand on his ??? (right / left) foot and is feeling ??? (dizzy / cold). His head ??? (is bleeding / hurts).

III Listen again. Imagine you are Tarek's coach. Answer the operator's questions.

1 What is your emergency?
2 How many people are hurt?
3 Is the person able to talk?
4 What exactly is wrong with him?
5 How old is he?
6 Where are you exactly?

At the hospital

5a skill: working with words p. 150, media worksheet 3

Look up the words and phrases in a dictionary. Write them down and add the German meanings.

injury · examine · sprained ·
put on a bandage · X-ray

5b audio 1/32

Listen and read along. What do you find out about Tarek's injuries?

In the waiting room

Coach: Ah Tarek, there's your dad. Hello Mr Adil.
Dad: Tarek! Are you OK? Does it hurt? Have you seen a doctor yet?
Tarek: Calm down, Dad. It's not that bad.
Coach: Yes, we've already seen a doctor. She's examined his head, there is nothing wrong with it.
Dad: Phew.
Coach: But the doctor wants to take an X-ray of his foot. We were just waiting for you, there are a few papers to sign.
Dad: Oh yes, of course.
Coach: Is it OK if I go back to the team?
Dad: Yes sure, thanks for taking care of him. Tarek, I'll just go and sign those papers.
Tarek: OK, Dad.

***

In the doctor's practice

Dr Weston: Well, hello Mr Adil. I'm Doctor Weston. I've met your son already.
Dad: Hello.
Dr Weston: So, Tarek. How are you feeling now?
Tarek: My head is a lot better. But my foot still hurts really badly.
Dr Weston: Yes, I can imagine. But the good news is that it's not broken. You've got a

sprained ankle. It's very important that you rest your ankle for the next few days. We'll put a bandage on it and you must keep it up as much as possible.
Dad: What about school?
Dr Weston: He should stay at home for the next two days. And no sports for at least three weeks.
Tarek: No sports? That'll be so boring. And I won't be able to play in our next hockey match.
Dad: I promise that I'll play that hockey video game with you if it gets too boring. And I'm sure your friends will visit you. Thanks a lot, Doctor Weston.
Dr Weston: No problem. Please make an appointment for a check-up in about a week. Bye, Tarek.
Tarek: Bye. And thank you.

5c CHOOSE YOUR LEVEL skill: reading p. 154

I Read the dialogues again. Unscramble the words in brackets and copy the sentences.

1 Tarek's dad arrives at the ??? (s-t-l-p-**h**-o-i-a).
2 He has to sign a few ??? (r-**p**-p-s-a-e).
3 Tarek's ??? (l-k-**a**-n-e) is sprained.
4 He has to ??? (e-t-**r**-s) it for the next few days.

II Read the dialogues again and write down the sentences in the correct order.

1 Tarek's coach goes back to the team.
2 Tarek's coach says that the doctor wants to take an X-ray.
3 Tarek's ankle is only sprained.
4 Tarek's dad arrives at the hospital.

III Read the dialogues again. Are the sentences true or false? Correct the false sentences.

1 Tarek's dad cannot come to the hospital.
2 Tarek's coach has gone back to the team before Tarek's dad arrives.
3 No one has examined Tarek's head yet.
4 Tarek's dad has to sign a few papers.
5 Tarek's ankle is broken.
6 Tarek should stay at home for two days.

5d skill: performing a scene p. 159, workbook p. 33/6-7

Work in groups of three. Practise reading out one or both of the two scenes.

What now?

6 grammar: modal verbs (R) p. 179, workbook p. 34/8-11

Copy the sentences and fill in the gaps with the words from the box.

will be able to · will be able to · will be able to · will have to · won't be able to

1 Tarek's dad has arrived at the hospital. – Now he ??? find out what happened.
2 Tarek has a sprained ankle. – Now he ??? do sports for the next three weeks.
3 Tarek can't walk properly. – Now he ??? stay at home for two days.
4 Tarek can't do sport for three weeks. – But he ??? play video games with his dad.
5 Tarek has to rest his ankle for a few days. – Then he ??? walk properly again soon.

Cheering Tarek up

7a

Read the text message.
What do you think: who is Ava writing to?

poorTarek

Ava Hi guys! I think we should try to cheer Tarek up a little. I was wondering if we should maybe get him some chocolate or bake him a cake. And what do you think about one of those "Get well soon" balloons? Or a card?
Monday 7:17pm

7b

What are Ava's ideas for cheering Tarek up?

You can say:
Ava's ideas are to get him chocolate, …

7c wordbank: health p. 163

Work with a partner and collect more ideas for cheering up someone who is ill.

7d

Talk about your ideas in class.
What are the three best ideas?

You can say:
I think … is the best idea.
In my opinion, … is a very good idea.

Poor Ellie

8a video 7, skill: watching a video clip p. 156

Watch the video clip.
What is wrong with Ellie?

You can say:
Ellie is …
She feels …

8b workbook p. 35/12-13

Watch the video clip again. What do Ellie's family and friends do to cheer her up?
Take notes and talk about it.

What do they miss?

9 GET TOGETHER audio 1/34

Get together with a partner.
Listen to Ben and Jacob in hospital and find out what they are talking about.

Partner A	Partner B
I Go to page 129.	I Go to page 138.
II Go to page 132.	II Go to page 141.
III Go to page 135.	III Go to page 144.

Helping out at the doctor's

10a audio 1/35, skill: listening p. 151

An exchange student called Sophie is staying with you. She does not speak much German. One day she must go to the doctor. Listen to Sophie. What is wrong with her? Take notes.

10b skill: mediation p. 155, workbook p. 36/14

You have to take Sophie to the doctor. Explain what is wrong to the German doctor.

You can say:

Sophie hat … Sie kann …

What's wrong?

11 wordbank: health p. 163

Work in small groups. Mime an injury or an illness. The others have to guess what it is and tell you what to do to get better. Take turns.

toothache · fever · cold · stomach ache · sprained ankle · broken leg · wound · …

You can say:

Have you got a …?

You should …

…

Being ill and getting well

12 CHOOSE YOUR TASK wordbank: health p. 163, C: skill: writing p. 153

A **Design or draw a "Get well soon" card.**

B **Look at the meme. Make your own meme.**

C **Have you ever been ill or to hospital? Write a short text about it.**

A

B

C

Last year I had to go to hospital. I was a bit nervous because it was my first time in a hospital. After the operation I didn't feel well, but the girl in my room was really nice. We talked and played lots of different games.

Who's asking?

13 CHOOSE YOUR LEVEL workbook p.36/15

I Complete the questions from an emergency call with words from the box.

How many · What · Where · What

1 ??? is your emergency?
2 ??? exactly happened?
3 ??? people are hurt?
4 ??? exactly are you?

II Read the questions. Which ones does a doctor ask and which ones a patient? Make two lists.

1 Where does it hurt?
2 How much chocolate have you eaten?
3 Will I have to stay at home for a week?
4 How exactly did it happen?
5 Will I be able to walk again soon?
6 How are you feeling?

III Unscramble the questions. Which ones does a doctor ask and which ones does a patient ask? Make two lists.

1 got – as well – have you – a fever
2 move – like this – can you – your fingers
3 hit you – the ball – did – where exactly
4 how long – in bed for – stay – will I have to
5 how long – a headache for – have you – had
6 will I – when – do sport – again – be able to

Can you hear the *r*?

14a audio 1/36

Listen to the sentences. In which of the marked words can you hear the "r"? Can you guess why?

1 <u>There</u> are some papers to sign.
2 The waiting room is over <u>there</u>.
3 My <u>shoulder</u> and my wrist hurt.
4 Where does your <u>shoulder</u> hurt?
5 The <u>doctor</u> is in the doctor's practice.
6 You can see the <u>doctor</u> now.
7 I'll put a <u>plaster</u> on your knee.
8 Don't remove the <u>plaster</u> too soon.

14b

Listen again and repeat the sentences.

Odd one out

15

Find the odd one out. Why is it the odd one out?

1 doctor – examine – dentist – nurse
2 leg – tooth – stomach ache – ankle
3 hospital – swollen – broken – sprained
4 medicine – chocolate – cake – toast

DIGITAL+ practise more 12-13

A medical problem TARGET TASK

16 workbook p. 37/16, wordbank: health p. 163, skill: performing a scene p. 159, media worksheet 2

Your task is to do a role play about a medical problem.
Before you start, look at these steps:

STEP 1

Get together with a partner or in a small group and plan your role play.
Decide the following:

- What is wrong with the patient? What happened?
  - *I fell off a horse / my bike / my skateboard / … and hurt my shoulder / arm / knee / …*
  - *My shoulder / wrist / arm / leg / stomach / knee / … is swollen / is broken / hurts.*
  - *I have a toothache / stomach ache / headache / sore throat / fever / cough / …*
- Where are you? (At the doctor's? At the hospital? At home? On the phone?)
- Who are the characters in your scene?
- What do the characters say? How do they feel?
  - *Good morning! How can I help you?*
  - *This is … / I have a … I would like to see the doctor.*
  - *The doctor can see you at …*
  - *Thanks. See you later.*

STEP 2

Collect ideas for your scene and make notes. You can also write cue cards.
Make sure each character has something to say.

STEP 3

Decide who will play which part and practise your role play.
You can use props or costumes if you like.

STEP 4

Act out your scene. If you like, you can film your scene and show it to the rest of the class.

Check out

Kannst du verstehen, wenn jemand darüber spricht, welchen Sport er oder sie mag?	Workbook, p. 38
Kannst du deine Meinung zu einer Sportart ausdrücken?	Workbook, p. 38
Kannst du Reimwörter finden und eigene Reime schreiben?	Workbook, p. 38
Kannst du darüber schreiben, was unter bestimmten Bedingungen passieren wird?	Workbook, p. 39
Kennst du wichtige Wörter und Redewendungen zum Thema Krankheit und Arztbesuch?	Workbook, p. 39
Kannst du jemandem beim Arzt sprachlich aushelfen?	Workbook, p. 39

Sports day

We finally had our sports day yesterday. I was so excited that I almost couldn't sleep the night before. This year I was going for the top!

My training programme had been really good, and I had signed up for as many events as I could.

I began the day with a healthy breakfast: a banana milkshake, fried eggs and porridge.

"Don't you think they meant you should have ONE of these for breakfast?" asked Dad, who was reading the newspaper at the kitchen table.

"Well, since I've signed up for ten events, this should be OK," I told him.

"You signed up for ten events? What were you thinking?" my brother Jamie asked. "We only have to take part in one. I only have the football match at eleven, and the rest of the day is free."

"I'm sorry we won't be there to cheer you on, darling," Mum said. "I have to work and Dad has this really important customer to visit."

If you ask me, no one in my family was very interested, as usual.

Our school looked brilliant that day. There were flags and streamers in our school colours everywhere, the sun was shining, and everyone was happy. Well, almost everyone.

"I hate sports day. All that running and sweating," my best friend Makena said.

"I'm off to my chess game. I'm so glad chess is one of the disciplines today. See you later."

Since my day was about to get busy, I hurried to get to my first event – the mini javelin. I could not wait for my javelin to land because I had to be on time for my second event, the 1500-metre race. During the run I didn't look left or right. I just ran, ran, ran. When I crossed the finishing line, I just kept running to get to the long jump on time so I didn't hear who won. But since I didn't see anyone else near me, I was pretty sure I was first.

At the long jump I did my three jumps, and then I ran to the next event, the 300-metre hurdles. I didn't knock over any of the hurdles because of my technique.

had been = *war gewesen;* had signed up = *hatte angemeldet;* flag = *Fahne;* streamer = *Wimpel;* discipline = *Disziplin, Teilgebiet im Sport*

Luckily, the high jump was right next to the track for the 300-metre hurdles so I could walk over immediately after crossing the finishing line.
Once again, I left before they announced the winner. Next was the lunch break, and I wanted to be the first at the cafeteria. Super athletes need lots of carbohydrates and I still had five more events to do.
I felt quite full after lunch so it was good that the next two disciplines were throwing rather than running: discus and softball throw. Once again, I did well – the other students' discuses and softballs landed nowhere near mine.
After the throwing events I was in great form again. I did the triple jump, and then I had to hurry to get to the relay in time. I was the first runner on my team, which was good because I could run over to my last event for the day as soon as I was finished.

The last event was easy – walking. I can walk with my eyes closed, and that is what I did. Once again, there was no one at the finishing line when I crossed it – probably because I was so fast that everyone else was way behind me.

I was really happy with myself. Now, the last thing to take part in was the award ceremony so I walked back to the main playing field, where there was a small stage.

"Well done, Lucy," said Ms Fisher, my PE teacher, and handed me a large trophy. "You're the only student who managed to compete in ten disciplines. That's a new school record, and I'm very pleased to present you with this *School Champion of the Hearts* trophy."
I was so happy! I heard Jamie and Makena and my house cheer really loudly for me. What a success!

"Yes, very well done, Lucy," added Mr Dunkerley, our headteacher. "You came last in every single event, but you showed great spirit! We're really proud of you."

announce = *bekannt geben;* carbohydrate = Kohlenhydrat; award ceremony = *Preisverleihung;* success = *Erfolg;* spirit = *hier: Kampfgeist*

Paralympics

Every four years thousands of athletes from all around the world come together and compete in the Paralympics. The Paralympics always take place in the same year as the Olympics and usually in the same place. There are summer and winter games.
In the Paralympics, athletes with a disability compete against each other. The first official Paralympic Games took place in Rome in 1960 with 400 athletes from 23 countries.

In the Tokyo 2020 Summer Paralympics, more than 4,000 athletes from over 160 countries competed in 22 different sports.
Paralympic sports include athletics, football 5-a-side (blind football), paratriathlon, sitting volleyball and wheelchair rugby.

Sitting volleyball

In sitting volleyball the players sit on the floor – so the net is much lower. The rules are similar to volleyball, for example there are also six players on a team.

Paratriathlon

A triathlon is made up of three sports – swimming, cycling and running. At the Paralympics it consists of 750m swimming, 20km cycling and a 5km wheelchair or running race.

Football 5-a-side

Football 5-a-side – or blind football – is a kind of football for athletes who can't see much or who are blind.
The field is smaller, and there are boards along the field to keep the ball inside. There are five players in a team, including the goalkeeper. Teams are allowed to have sighted goalkeepers and sighted guides. The guide can help the team by directing the players from outside the field. The ball has bells inside so the players can hear where it is.

Find out more about a Paralympic athlete or sport and present your findings to the class.

3

1. Look at the pictures. What do you think: where are the people?
2. What are the people doing?
3. Have you ever been to events like these? What was it like?

What's on?

Part A At the car boot sale

- Du sprichst über Wochenendaktivitäten.
- Du findest etwas über *Kofferraum-Flohmärkte* heraus.
- Du machst ein Rollenspiel über das Kaufen und Verkaufen von gebrauchten Dingen.

Part B Festivals

- Du findest etwas über Festivals im Vereinigten Königreich heraus.
- Du liest einen Artikel darüber, wie Festivals umweltfreundlicher werden können.
- Du machst ein Poster über ein Festival.

Weekend activities

1

Talk to a partner about weekend activities. Think about where you can go, what you can do there, what the activities cost, ...

You can say:

At the weekend, I sometimes go to …
I like to …
… is free. / … is not expensive. / … costs …
…

What's on in London?

2a skill: reading p. 154

Read these tips for events in London at the weekend. What can you do if you do not want to spend much money?

LONDON WEEKEND TIPS

your guide to fun events in London

PORTOBELLO ROAD MARKET | Notting Hill — Saturday and Sunday 9am – 7pm

Find anything from clothes to arts & crafts at hundreds of shops and stalls. There are some stalls which are only open on Saturdays, so come early to find the best things and to avoid the crowds.

CHARITY RUN | Finsbury Park — Saturday 11am

Run 5km for charity – this charity run is perfect for people who like running and doing something good at the same time. All money goes to charity. Registration fee: children £10, adults £14.99.

FAMILY FILM CLUB | The Barbican Cinema — Saturday 11am

Watch a family film at the Barbican Cinema. Adults can only come if they bring a child, and children can only come with an adult. Tickets cost £3.50.

CAR BOOT SALE | Notting Hill — Sunday 10am – 6pm

Visit the biggest car boot sale in Notting Hill and look for second-hand items that you can't find anywhere else. The entrance fee is only £1.50 and goes to charity.

THE LION KING | Lyceum Theatre — Sunday 2:30pm

A great show for people who love musicals. See the famous musical now and remember it forever. Tickets from £23.50.

2b wordbank: what's on? p. 164, workbook p. 40/1-2

Work with a partner and talk about the events. Where would you like to go? What would you like to do?

You can say:

I would like to go to … because I love …
I would love to do … / watch … / … because …

What to do?

3a audio 2/2

Listen and read along. What are the friends talking about? What do they decide in the end?

Ava: Hi guys, finally Friday! What are you up to this weekend? Would you like to do something together?
Tarek: I have no plans so far.
Lily: Me neither. Any ideas?
Ava: We could go to the cinema. We haven't been there for ages.
Harry: That's too expensive, I haven't got enough pocket money left.
Ava: We could go to the Family Film Club at the Barbican. The tickets are just £3.50.
Tarek: But you have to take an adult with you! I don't want that! Can we please find something else?
What about the charity run on Saturday?
Or a game of football?
Ava: Oh, Tarek. You always want to do sports. I'd rather do something else. Actually, I really need a new hoodie. We could go shopping together.
Harry: Shopping would be OK. I'm sure I could get some money from our mums for new clothes. They keep telling me to get a new pair of jeans.
Lily: But you don't have to buy new things. I could help you with upcycling second-hand hoodies and jeans. We could go to a flea market! I need to get some ideas for my next upcycling project anyway.
Ava: Should we go to Portobello Road Market then?
Harry: OK with me. Maybe that guy who sells those really funny T-shirts is still there.
Tarek: I only remember the funny guy that sells old cameras that nobody needs ...
But Portobello Road Market is always so crowded at the weekend.
And there are so many shops which are pretty expensive.
Lily: Hm, there's a car boot sale on Sunday. Shall we go there then?
Harry: Why not? And it's even for charity – I'll definitely get money for that.
Ava: That's a cool idea. Do you want to meet at 10:30 on Sunday?
Tarek: Sounds great.
Harry: Yeah.
Ava: Great! See you on Sunday then!

3b CHOOSE YOUR LEVEL skill: reading p. 154

I **Read again. Which activities do Ava and Harry suggest? Take notes.**
II **Read again. Which events do the children talk about? Take notes.**
III **Read again. Who suggests what? Take notes for each person.**

3c workbook p. 41/3-4

Which of the weekend tips from number 2a is your favourite? Write a short text message in which you suggest the event to a friend.

GRAMMAR HELP relative clauses p. 180

Wenn du Personen oder Dinge genauer beschreiben willst, kannst du Relativsätze benutzen. Meist beginnt ein Relativsatz mit einem der Relativpronomen *who, which* oder *that*. Sieh dir die Beispielsätze an. Wann verwendest du welches Relativpronomen? Auf welches Wort bezieht es sich jeweils?

There are some stalls which are only open on Saturdays.	Es gibt ein paar Stände, die nur samstags offen sind.
Maybe that guy who sells those really funny T-shirts is still there.	Vielleicht ist der Typ noch da, der diese lustigen T-Shirts verkauft.
Look for stalls that you can't find anywhere else.	Suche nach Ständen, die du sonst nirgendwo finden kannst.
There is a funny guy that sells old cameras.	Es gibt einen lustigen Typen, der alte Kameras verkauft.

Auf Seite 180 findest du weitere Erklärungen und Beispiele, auch zur Verwendung des Relativpronomens *that*.

Tips for the weekend

4 grammar: relative clauses p. 180, workbook p. 42/5

Write sentences.

There is a **car boot sale**		takes place in Notting Hill.
At the car boot sale there are **people**		are especially interesting for children.
There is a **cinema**	who	like running.
You can see **films** there	which	has a Family Film Club.
At the theatre you can see a **musical**		sell second-hand clothes.
On Saturday, there is a **charity run** for people		is very famous.

Making plans

5 grammar: relative clauses p. 180

Complete the sentences. Use 'who', 'which' or 'that'.

1 The friends are talking about **activities** ??? they can do at the weekend.
2 Tarek suggests **activities** ??? have to do with sports.
3 Harry would like to see if the **guy** ??? sells funny T-shirts is still at Portobello Road Market.
4 The **car boot sale** ??? takes place on Saturday is the biggest in Notting Hill.

It's a person who …

6 grammar: relative clauses p. 180

Write four or more sentences for a partner. He or she has to find out who or what it is.

actor / actress · camera · book · teacher · ...

You can write:

It's a person who acts in films.
It's a thing which you can use to take pictures.
It's a … that …

LAND & LEUTE 3 video 8

Secondhand-Shopping im Vereinigten Königreich

Secondhand-Shopping wird immer beliebter, nicht nur, weil es billiger ist, gebrauchte Dinge zu kaufen, sondern auch, weil es besser für die Umwelt ist.
Man kann Secondhand-Ware auch zum Upcyceln verwenden und so aus gebrauchten Dingen neue machen.
Im Vereinigten Königreich gibt es viele Flohmärkte, aber auch Wohltätigkeitsläden. Dort kann man Dinge wie Bücher, Kleidung, Schmuck oder sogar Möbel kaufen, die gespendet wurden. In diesen Läden arbeiten hauptsächlich Ehrenamtliche, die kein Geld für ihre Arbeit bekommen.

At a car boot sale

Es lassen sich günstig gute Sachen finden und manchmal sogar interessante Schätze entdecken. Das Geld, das eingenommen wird, wird für einen guten Zweck verwendet.

Gibt es bei euch in der Gegend solche Läden? Habt ihr schon einmal auf einem Flohmarkt Dinge gekauft oder verkauft? Sprecht in der Klasse darüber.

Look at that!

7a audio 2/5

Listen to Ava, Lily, Harry and Tarek. Where are they?

7b CHOOSE YOUR LEVEL skill: listening p. 151, workbook p. 42/6-8

I Listen again. What does Ava want to buy? Write it down.

a hockey stick · a fish · a hoodie

II Listen again. Which of these things do the children talk about? Write them down.

books

telephones

bicycle bells

vegetables

a singing fish

paintings

toys

clothes

III Listen again. Who wants to buy what at the car boot sale? Take notes.

You can write:

Ava: …

Lily: …

Looking for bargains

8a audio 2/6, skill: reading p. 154

Look at the pictures and the heading above. What do you think the dialogues are about? Then listen and read along. Were you right?

Dialogue 1

Harry: Look, there's a jeans stall. This pair looks OK, doesn't it?
Tarek: Yes, it does.
Seller: Hi guys. Good taste – those are original jeans from the 1950s, and I can sell them to you for just £249.
Harry: Oh, I thought second-hand clothes are cheaper than new ones.
Seller: Well, why don't you look at the jeans over there then? They're all good quality. They start from £5.
Harry: Great. Thanks.
Tarek: What do you think about these ones?
Harry: I like them. Excuse me, could I try these on?
Seller: Sure, just go behind that curtain.
Harry: What do you say, Tarek?
Tarek: They look good on you.
Seller: Do they fit?
Harry: Yes, they do. I think I'll take them. How much are they?
Seller: This pair is £7.
Harry: Great. Here you are.
Seller: £10, thanks. And here's £3 change.
Harry: Thank you. Bye.
Seller: Have a nice day! Bye.

Dialogue 2

Seller: Hello, can I help you?
Lily: We're just looking. But thank you.
Seller: OK.
Lily: I really like this old flowerpot. It's only 50p and it would make a great lamp.
Tarek: Why don't you just buy a lamp? There's a nice one.
Lily: But that's not as much fun as making your own lamp. I also like this coffee grinder. Excuse me, how much is this? There's no price tag.
Seller: Oh, I got that from a man who lives in his grandparents' old house and keeps finding interesting things. His grandparents brought that back with them from a holiday in Italy because they liked Italian coffee so much. It's really old. There's also a coffee pot that came with it. See?
Lily: Oh, it's great. How much for both and this flowerpot?
Seller: I can give you the flowerpot for free if you take the other two things for £12, well, let's say £10.
Lily: That's a fair price. Here you are. Thank you! – Hey guys, I think I've just found a bargain!

Dialogue 3

Lily: OK, that was a very successful day. I found lots of good things for my next lamp. Did you find anything, Tarek?

Tarek: Yes, I got five new science fiction books for only £2.50. They're in my rucksack.

Ava: Is there any more room on your shelves for new books?

Tarek: No, I have to get rid of some old ones.

Ava: If you want to get rid of old stuff, you could take it to a charity shop. There is a small one on Portobello Road.

Harry: I've got an idea! Why don't we sell some of our old things at a flea market?

Lily: I like Harry's idea. I think selling things at a flea market would be fun.

Harry: Yes! We have so many old board games that we don't play anymore. And Double and Trouble's old cage and ...

Lily: Oh no, not the old cage. I've got an idea for that ...

8b CHOOSE YOUR LEVEL

I Read dialogue 1 again. Complete the sentences and write them in your exercise book.

1 Harry and Tarek look at a jeans ???.
2 Harry tries on a pair of jeans behind a ???.
3 He thinks he'll ???.
4 The jeans cost ???.

II Read dialogues 1 and 2 again. Complete the sentences and write them in your exercise book.

1 Harry and Tarek are at a ???.
2 Harry buys ???.
3 He spends ???.
4 Lily buys ???.
5 She spends ???.

III Read the dialogues again and answer the questions.

1 How much are the cheapest jeans at the jeans stall?
2 How much are the jeans that Harry buys?
3 What does Lily buy?
4 How much does Lily pay?
5 What kind of books has Tarek bought?
6 How much did he pay for them?

8c wordbank: expressing opinions p. 165, media worksheet 15, workbook p. 43/9

Lily says that buying a lamp is not as much fun as making your own lamp. What do you think?

How much is it?

9a wordbank: buying and selling p. 164

Look at the prices. Ask and answer questions with a partner. Take turns.

You can ask:
How much is the …?
How much are the …?

You can answer:
It's …
They are …

1 £1.50

2 80p

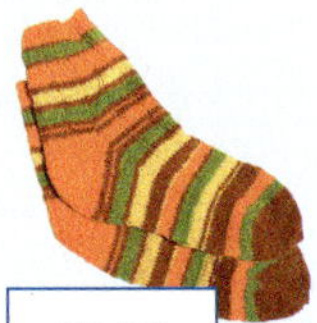

3 £3.90

4 £5.25

5 £7

9b skill: searching the internet p. 157, workbook p. 44/10

How much do the items cost in euros? You can find out on the Internet.

You can say:
One pound fifty is one euro … cents.
…

Tom's day out

10a video 9, skill: watching a video clip p. 156

Watch the video clip. Where is Tom? What is he doing?

10b CHOOSE YOUR LEVEL

Watch the video clip again.

I Answer the questions. You can find help in the box.
1 Which animal does Tom buy?
2 What kind of book does he buy?

a children's book · a giraffe · an elephant · a guitar · a travel guide · …

II Answer the questions.
1 What day is it?
2 What does Tom buy at the first stall?
3 How much does he pay for it?

III Answer the questions.
1 What does Tom buy at the first stall?
2 At the second stall Tom buys several things. Why does he buy them?
3 What does Tom buy at the third stall?
4 How much does the woman want for it and how much does Tom pay for it in the end?

At the market

11 skill: mediation p. 155

You are at a market in England with a friend who does not speak English very well. Help him or her. Write down what you say.

Your friend: Oh, schau mal da an dem Stand, da gibt es Marmelade und – Chutney? Könntest du mal fragen, was das ist?

(1) You: *Gern.*

Excuse me, what is …?

Seller: Chutney is really popular in the UK, especially mango chutney. It's a kind of sauce. It's originally from India. This one contains tomatoes and onions. You can eat it with vegetables, fish or meat.

(2) You: *Das ist … Man kann es …*

Your friend: Das hört sich gut an. Das könnte ich meinen Eltern mitbringen. Wie teuer ist denn ein Glas?

(3) You: …

Seller: £3.50. We've also got other kinds. This one contains pumpkin and carrots for example.

(4) You: …

Your friend: Super, mein Vater liebt Kürbis. Ich nehme beide. Dann habe ich zwei tolle Geschenke für meine Eltern.

(5) You: …

Seller: Great. That's £7 then.

Out and about

12 CHOOSE YOUR TASK B: wordbank: events p. 165, C: buying and selling p. 164

A **Think of an object you could upcycle. Find a photo or draw a design and write a caption.**

B **Create an event calendar for your dream weekend.**

C **Imagine you want to sell something really odd. Advertise it!**

A

Old pair of jeans makes cool new bag

C

Do you like fish?
Do you like music?
Then this is the **perfect item** for you!

This decorative fish sings one of 20 songs for you whenever you walk past it. It looks great in any room! So, what are you waiting for? Come and get your singing fish today for **only £35!**

I'd like the blue one

13 grammar: prop words one and ones p. 181, workbook p. 44/11-12

Complete the sentences with 'one' or 'ones' and write them in your exercise book.

1 Which **T-shirt** do you like better? The red ??? or the green ????
2 I don't like these **socks**. The blue ??? are nicer.
3 This **ring** is too small for me. Have you got a bigger ????
4 Have you got another **book** like this ????
5 Which **shoes** are cheaper? The brown ??? or the black ????
6 This **cup** is broken. Have you got another ????

Buying and selling

14 CHOOSE YOUR LEVEL workbook p. 46/13-16

I Match the English and the German phrases and write them down.

Excuse me, how much is this?	Das kostet £6.
It's £6.	Und hier ist Ihr Wechselgeld.
I'll take it. Here you are.	Entschuldigung, wie viel kostet das?
And here's your change.	Ich nehme es. Hier, bitte.

II Read the phrases. What does the customer say? What does the seller say? Make a table.

Excuse me, how much is this? · It's £6. · You can have it for £4.50. · Have you got another one of these? · I'll take it. · Here's your change. · Can I help you? · That's too much. I only have £4.

You can write:

seller	*customer*
It's …	*Excuse me, …*
…	…

III Match the sentence parts. Then sort the sentences into two lists: one for the seller, one for the customer.

1 Excuse me, can
2 Hi there, are you
3 Do you need
4 This cap is quite expensive,
5 Thank you, we're just

A how much is that one?
B looking.
C looking for anything special?
D anything else?
E I try these on?

DIGITAL+ practise more 15

Second-hand shopping TARGET TASK

15 workbook p. 47/17, wordbank: buying and selling p. 164, skill: performing a scene p. 159, media worksheet 2

**Your task is to do a role play of a second-hand shopping situation.
Before you start, look at the following steps:**

STEP 1

**Get together in small groups and plan your role play.
Think about:**

- Where does your role play take place? At a car boot sale, a flea market, ...?
- How many people do you need? Who are they? What are they like?

STEP 2

What is going to happen in your shopping situation? Collect ideas.

- What can you buy? What can you sell?
- How much are the items?
- Make up an interesting story behind one or more of the objects.

STEP 3

Decide who will play which part.

STEP 4

**Make notes for your role play.
Collect words and phrases you will need.
Write cue cards for each character.**

STEP 5

**Practise your role play.
You can use your cue cards.**

STEP 6

**Present your role play.
Make a video recording or act it out in class.**

Remember to be friendly and polite!

Good morning. / Hello.
Excuse me, could you ...?
..., please.
Thank you.
You're welcome!
Have a nice day.
Thanks. Bye.

A festival

1a

Look at the poster. What festival is it about? Where and when does it take place? What can visitors expect?

1b

What do you know about the Vikings? Collect information in class.

You can say:

I think they lived …

The Vikings were …

…

The Jorvik Viking festival

2a

wordbank: talking about pictures p. 166

Describe the pictures in 2b. What are the people doing?

You can say:

In picture number …, the people are …

2b

Andy is a student in York. He likes travelling around the UK and writes a travel blog as *Adventuring Andy*. Read his post about the Jorvik Viking Festival.

1 March

Hey guys,

It's me, Adventuring Andy. Last weekend the *Jorvik Viking Festival* took place here in York. York has an interesting Viking past. The Vikings conquered York in 866. They lived here in the 9th and 10th centuries and had a big influence on everyday life.

What can I say? The festival was amazing. On my first day I checked out a show fight at the festival combat arena. When I arrived, two Viking warriors in armour were fighting each other while hundreds of people were watching.

After that I was really hungry. When I walked into the dining room, lots of people were already eating delicious Viking food.

The next day, I watched the *Best Beard Competition*. That's a competition where men, women, children and even dogs – really anyone – present their beards. The beards don't have to be real. Although it was raining, everyone there had such a great time!

3

Then I went to the *Birds of Prey Show* at Barley Hall. While I was watching the birds, I listened to the bird trainer. He told us a lot about the role of birds in old Viking stories.

My personal highlight was the *Battle Spectacular* in which two Viking hordes fought against each other. Then there was a breathtaking firework display. Throughout the festival, you could tell that all the visitors were really enjoying this trip to the Viking world.

4

Follow me for more interesting festival content. Coming soon: *Highland Games* and the *Notting Hill Carnival*.

2c CHOOSE YOUR LEVEL skill: reading p. 154

I Read the post in 2b again. Write captions for the pictures in the post.

You can write:

Picture 1: A show … *Picture 2: Delicious …*
Picture 3: … *Picture 4: …*

II Read the post again. Put these pictures in the correct order and write captions for them.

A

B

C

D

III Read the post again. List all the events and activities that Andy mentions. What can you say about the activities?

2d wordbank: events, expressing opinions p. 165

Which part of the Jorvik Viking festival do you find the most interesting? What do you find the least interesting? Say why.

You can say:

I find the … the most interesting because …
I find … the least interesting because …
…

2e workbook p. 48/1

Do you know any events like this? Talk about them in class.

GRAMMAR HELP the past progressive p. 182-183

Du benutzt das *past progressive* um zu beschreiben, was zu einem bestimmten Zeitpunkt in der Vergangenheit gerade passierte.
Sieh dir die Beispiele an. Was fällt dir auf?

At 3 o'clock, two Viking warriors were fighting each other.	Um drei Uhr kämpften gerade zwei Wikingerkrieger gegeneinander.
Although it was raining, everyone there had such a great time!	Obwohl es gerade regnete, hatte jeder solchen Spaß!
Throughout the festival, the visitors were enjoying this trip to the Viking world.	Während des Festivals genossen die Besucher diesen Ausflug in die Welt der Wikinger.

Auf den Seiten 182 und 183 findest du weitere Erklärungen, auch zu verneinten Sätzen und Fragen.

Preparing for the competition

3 grammar: past progressive p. 182

Joe is taking part in the Best Beard Competition. Write about what he was doing in the morning.

1 At 6:30, Joe ??? (have) breakfast.
2 At 7:00, he ??? (wash) his beard.
3 At 7:45, he ??? (style) his beard.
4 At 8:00, he ??? (put on) his costume.

What were they doing?

4a grammar: past progressive p. 182

Look at the pictures. What was happening? Write sentences in your exercise book.

1 5pm, two Vikings / fight

2 7pm, Andy / eat

3 10am, men, women, children and dogs / take part in competition

4 2pm, Andy / watch

5 9pm, visitors / watch

You can write:
At 5pm, two Vikings were …
At 7pm, Andy was …
…

4b grammar: past progressive p. 182-183, workbook p. 49/2

What were you doing yesterday at 6pm, last Saturday at 10am, this morning at 7am, ...? Work with a partner. Ask and answer questions. Take turns.

You can ask:
What were you doing yesterday at 6pm?
What were you doing last Saturday at …?

You can answer:
I was talking to my dad. / I was …

DIGITAL+ practise more 16-17

Opinions

5a audio 2/8

Listen to the three statements. Who is a fan of the Jorvik Viking Festival and who is not?

5b CHOOSE YOUR LEVEL skill: listening p. 151

I Listen to the first two statements again and complete the sentences.

1 The Viking Lodge is a hotel in ...
2 Over the year they have ...
3 Cathy absolutely loves ...
4 She always has ...

all kinds of guests · the Jorvik Viking Festival · the centre of York · the time of her life

II Listen to the three statements again. Complete three or more of the sentences.

Statement 1 (Chris)
1 Chris Cooper runs a ??? in York.
2 ??? is the best month of the year for the hotel.

Statement 2 (Cathy)
3 Cathy made her ??? from an old teddy bear.
4 She made a lot of new ??? from all over the world.

Statement 3 (Edward)
5 Edward has lived in York all his ???.
6 Last year, pickpockets stole Edward's ??? out of his pocket.

III Listen to the three statements again. Answer the questions.

1 What is the "Viking Lodge"?
2 Who stays there?
3 What is the best month of the year for the Viking Lodge?
4 What does Cathy say about her shoes?
5 What kind of competition does Cathy take part in every year?
6 How long has Edward lived in York?
7 Why is February not Edward's favourite month?

5c wordbank: events p. 165, workbook p. 49/3-4

In class, collect positive and negative aspects of having a big festival in your area. Take notes.

You can write:

positive: many tourists, ...
negative: too many people, ...

You can say:

I think ... / In my opinion ...
On the one hand, ... / ... is a positive aspect.
On the other hand, ... / ... is a negative aspect.

More festivals

6a

Andy checked out three more festivals.
Look at the photos. What can you see?

6b skill: reading p. 154

Read Andy's blog posts.
Which festival do you find interesting?

29 June

Hey festival lovers,

Today I'm going to tell you about one of the biggest open-air music festivals in the world: the Glastonbury Festival in south-west England. It started in the 1970s and got bigger every year. At the Glastonbury Festival you sleep in tents, and when it rains everything is muddy at the end of the festival. But this isn't a problem for anyone. Every year, there are thousands of tents but it is not just a huge camping site, of course. At the festival itself there is so much to see. At Glastonbury there are always world-famous musicians, and you can listen to really good live music. A lot of people bring their children with them, and there's even an area with activities just for children.

I definitely recommend going there. The atmosphere is really special – it's like diving into another world.

4 August

Hey guys,

It's me again. This time I checked out the Notting Hill Carnival. It was impressive, loud and colourful! People from all over the world celebrate it in London every year in August. The carnival is a happy and cheerful event, but its beginnings in 1959 were quite serious. The organizers wanted to draw attention to the difficult situation of Caribbean immigrants.

If you like multicultural events, steel drums, colourful costumes and impressive parades, this is the right event for you. You can also taste a lot of different Caribbean dishes and drinks.
I had a really great time. I loved the final parade on Monday the most. Over 60 bands in fantastic costumes – where else can you see such a spectacle?

---

29 August
Hi there, lads and lasses!
Can you guess where I am? That's right, I'm in Scotland, in Braemar! I came here to see the world-famous Highland Games. They take place every summer in lots of different places.
Well, let me tell you this: the Highland Games are really worth a visit. You'll hear a lot of bagpipes and see men in kilts. There are many events to watch, for example Highland dancing, throwing the hammer or the most popular sport of all: tossing the caber. Here, you have to lift a big log and toss it so that it turns over and lands on the other end. Amazing!

6c CHOOSE YOUR LEVEL workbook p. 50/5-6

I Read the post about the Glastonbury Festival again. Copy the sentences and complete them.

1 The Glastonbury Festival started in the 1970s and ??? every year.
2 At the Glastonbury Festival, you sleep in ???.
3 You can listen to ??? musicians and ??? live music.
4 The ??? is really special.

II Write down four or more questions about the Glastonbury Festival. Then work with a partner and ask and answer the questions. Take turns.

You can write:
What is the Glastonbury Festival?
What can you …?
Where do / is …?
When does / is …?
How many …?

III Write down five or more questions about the Glastonbury Festival, the Notting Hill Carnival or the Highland Games. Then work with a partner and ask and answer the questions. Take turns.

Andy's picture show

7a wordbank: talking about pictures p. 166

Andy took a lot of pictures on his trips. Look at these four. What can you see? Where do you think Andy took them?

1

2

3

4

7b video 10, skill: watching a video clip p. 156, workbook p. 51/7

Andy is showing his pictures to a friend. Watch the video clip. What was new to you? What did you find the most surprising?

You can say:

… was new to me.

I found … the most surprising.

Party!

8 CHOOSE YOUR TASK C: wordbank: events, expressing opinions p. 165, media worksheet 5, workbook p. 52/8

A Create your own look! How would you dress if you went to a festival or a carnival? Draw your costume and label it.

B Look at the pictures of the festivals on pages 70-72 again and write slogans for one or more of the festivals.

C What do you think people who live in Glastonbury think about the festival? Write down what someone who lives there might say. Record it.

B

Help the environment!

9a skill: reading p. 154

Read the newspaper article. What problem does it describe?

How to clear up Britain's biggest events

Over three million people attend UK festivals each year and produce 23,500 tons of waste, which means 2.8kg of waste per person, per day. It is the UK's plan to be plastic-free by 2042, and festivals must become greener.

What's the plan?
In 2018, the British government published a plan on how to reduce waste over the next 25 years. Part of that plan was to get rid of plastic bags, food packaging and plastic straws. These and other products made of plastic have been in use a lot at festivals across the country. For example, in the past visitors threw away more than one million plastic bottles at each Glastonbury Festival, and it cost organizers almost £800,000 to get rid of the waste every year. Since 2019, visitors are no longer allowed to bring plastic bottles in order to help protect the environment. Another problem at the festival is the large number of tents that people leave at the festival site.

Do green festivals exist?
At 'No Planet B', the UK's first 'zero waste' festival, there was a list of 'zero waste rules'. For example, festival guests had to bring their own bottles, and the organizers asked them to use digital tickets and not paper.

9b skill: mediation p. 155, workbook p. 53/9

Your sister has some questions. Read the article again and answer them in German.

1. Wieso ist denn da ein Bild von so vielen Zelten?
2. Was steht da über das Jahr 2042?
3. Was steht da mit 800.000?
4. Was steht in dem Artikel darüber, wie man Festivals umweltfreundlicher macht?

Which festival?

10 GET TOGETHER

Get together with a partner.
Read and talk about different festivals.

Partner A	Partner B
I Go to page 129.	I Go to page 138.
II Go to page 132.	II Go to page 141.
III Go to page 135.	III Go to page 144.

Check your spelling

11 grammar: past progressive p. 182

Look at the verbs in the box. What are their -ing forms? Sort them into three lists in your exercise book.

run · have · watch · happen · put · talk · listen · make · sit · dance · drive · swim · play · stop · get

You can write:

run - running	*have - having*	*watch - watching*
...		

When it started to rain

12 CHOOSE YOUR LEVEL grammar: past progressive p. 182, workbook p. 53/10-11

What were the people at the festival doing when it started to rain?

I **Choose three or more of the pictures and write sentences.**

II **Choose four or more of the pictures and write sentences.**

III **Write sentences about the pictures.**

You can write:

Picture A: Jill and Suzy were setting up their tent when it started to rain.
Picture B: Becky was eating ... when ...
...

A Jill and Suzy / set up tent

B Becky / eat

C Levi / listen to

D Sheree / talk on the phone

E Juan / sleep

F the people / dance

Writing about a festival

13 workbook p. 54/12-14

Match the sentence parts.

1 The atmosphere
2 I listened
3 I can definitely
4 I had a

A to a lot of cool music.
B really great time.
C is really special.
D recommend going there.

DIGITAL+ practise more 18

A blog post TARGET TASK

14 workbook p. 55/15, wordbank: events p. 165, skill: writing p. 153, media worksheet 1, 10

Your task is to write a blog post about a festival or an event.
Before you start, look at these steps:

STEP 1
What do you want to write about?
A carnival, a music festival, a street party, …?
It can be a festival or event you have been to.
You can also make something up.

STEP 2
Collect ideas. Think about the following:
- Where did the event or festival take place?
- When did it take place? For how long?
- How much was it? Or was it free?
- What could you see or do there?
- Who was it for?
- What was special about it?
- What did you like about it?
- …

STEP 3
Plan your post.

STEP 4
Write a first version of your post.
You can ask a classmate or your teacher to give you feedback.

STEP 5
Edit your post and write the final version.

× –

3 March

Hi everyone,

It's me, …, again.
Last weekend, I was at …

Look forward to next week's blog – I'll write about …

Your …

Check out

Kannst du einem Flyer mit Veranstaltungstipps Informationen entnehmen?	Workbook, p. 56
Kannst du ein Verkaufsgespräch verstehen?	Workbook, p. 56
Kannst du jemandem in einer Einkaufssituation sprachlich aushelfen?	Workbook, p. 56
Kannst du einen Blogeintrag zu einem Festival verstehen?	Workbook, p. 57
Kannst du Fragen zu einem Blogeintrag formulieren und beantworten?	Workbook, p. 57
Kannst du einen Zeitungsbericht verstehen?	Workbook, p. 57

Medieval mischief

You can't imagine how glad I am to be back home! This weekend Mum forced us all to go to the *Medieval Weekend at Arundel Castle*. We had to sleep in a tent and wear funny costumes and I almost got killed.
But let me start at the beginning.
Two weeks ago, one of Mum's customers told her about this "really great event" which was "so much fun".
Mum said "we never do things together" and "I'm sure it'll be good for us as a family".
My plan had been to spend the weekend at my best friend Joe's house. He's got a really good console and he has loads of games. I was looking forward to finally improving my score.
But no.
On Friday I found myself in the car, stuck between Lucy on one side and a spinning wheel and a sword on the other. Mum had borrowed those from her friend "to make it more authentic".
The boot of the car was completely full of camping gear and costumes and tins of baked beans.

Lucy was really excited because there were going to be horses, and she had always wanted to go horse riding.
When we arrived, a guy dressed like a knight showed us where to park the car and where to put up the tent. There were people dressed in medieval clothing everywhere.

The next morning, Mum woke us up and served porridge in wooden bowls. Except she called it "gruel". More authentic, you know. After breakfast, Lucy wanted to go and see the horses.
"But first, let's get dressed," Mum said and handed me something that looked like a brown curtain.
"What's that?" I asked. "It's a tunic. Just put it on. You'll look just like a medieval teenager," Mum said happily. Then she handed Lucy another curtain (beige) and grabbed the spinning wheel.
"Why are you taking the spinning wheel with you?" Lucy asked.
"It's for the mother-daughter living picture competition I've registered us for," Mum replied.
"You've done WHAT?" Lucy asked. "I thought we were going horse riding and then I could go back to the tent and read my book." "Oh no, dear," Mum said. "And now let's go and make some beautiful memories."

medieval = *mittelalterlich;* mischief = *Unfug;* force = *zwingen;* spinning wheel = *Spinnrad;* sword = *Schwert;* had borrowed = *hatte geliehen;* camping gear = *Campingausrüstung;* gruel = *Grütze;* tunic = *Tunika;* living picture competition = *Wettbewerb der lebendigen Bilder*

"That's a great idea," Dad said and looked like he was trying really hard not to laugh. But Mum didn't notice. She just smiled at him. "It is, isn't it?" she said.
So we all followed Mum to the stage in the middle of the festival ground. She set herself and Lucy and the spinning wheel up, and a jury came by and looked at all the mothers and daughters spinning and baking and doing all that other stuff women did in the Middle Ages. Then the jury went off to decide who had created the best living picture.
"OK," Lucy said, "that's it. I'm off to find the horses now." And she was gone.

Since there were posters all over the place advertising a show fight in the combat arena somewhere near our tent, I thought it might be a good idea to offer to take the spinning wheel back to the tent and check out the arena. Mum was happy with that, too.
I was nearly at our tent when someone behind me suddenly shouted: "Careful! Get out of the way everyone!!!" I turned around and saw the biggest horse I'd ever seen galloping towards me. On its back was my sister, barely hanging on. "Lucy!" I shouted.
"Help!" Lucy shouted.

I jumped out of the way and fell on my left knee. It really hurt, but I saved the spinning wheel!
Meanwhile, the horse with Lucy on its back was galloping away.
But another horse was already on its way. Someone who was a lot better at riding than my little sister was trying to help her.
Behind him came Mum and Dad, running and out of breath and clearly panicking.

Dad panicked even more when the knight's sword almost cut my ear off. That was the moment when I decided I liked the 21st century very much. Not so many swords and less gruel, much safer.

I don't know how, but the knight managed to bring Lucy and the horse back. Lucy was fine and she wanted to get back on her horse and try again, but my knee hurt so much that they had to take me to the emergency tent first.

When we came back, Mum said, "Alright, that was a bit too authentic. Even for me. I'm so glad they invented modern medicine. I think I'm ready to go home, order some pizza and watch TV on the couch in our living room."

Just at that moment, Mum and Lucy were called back to the stage and the jury announced that they had won the mother-daughter living picture competition. They got the first prize: a week at a Middle Ages Camp in the Cotswolds for the whole family.

the Middle Ages = *das Mittelalter*; I'd ever seen = *ich je gesehen hatte*; gallop = *galoppieren*; meanwhile = *inzwischen*

The legend of King Arthur

Glastonbury is not only famous for its music festival, it is also connected with the legend of King Arthur. It is said that King Arthur was buried in Glastonbury at the ruins of Glastonbury Abbey. Another place connected with King Arthur is Glastonbury Tor, a tall hill with a tower. Some people say that it is the mythical island of Avalon.

There are different versions of the legend of King Arthur, and it is not clear if King Arthur really existed. However, there are many stories about King Arthur and also about the wizard Merlin, Arthur's loyal friend and counsellor. A well-known part of the legend is the story about the sword in the stone and how Arthur became king.

Once upon a time, when King Uther Pendragon of Britain had died, there was no new king. For years, many men fought to get to the throne, but no one won and still there was no new king.

In one corner of the kingdom lived a young man, Arthur. He lived in the castle of Sir Ector and his son, Sir Kay. They had taken in Arthur when he was a baby and had raised him. Now Arthur was sixteen years old.

One morning, a great stone with a sword appeared in the middle of the town. On the stone there were these words:

"He who pulls this sword from its stone shall be the rightful King of Britain."

The town was full of talk of this stone. Who had put it there? Where did it come from? Who would be the next king? For days, people tried to pull the sword from the stone, but it did not move. When Sir Ector, Sir Kay and Arthur walked past, Sir Kay also tried to pull the sword from the stone, but Arthur paid little attention.

Later, Kay was preparing for a tournament and couldn't find his sword. He asked Arthur to look for it.
Some time later, Arthur came back with a sword. "That ... that's not Kay's sword! Wh-where did you find this?" stuttered Sir Ector, who already recognized the sword. Arthur explained that he had taken the sword out of the stone because he couldn't find Kay's sword. "You are our new king! My brother is king!" cried Sir Kay.

Later, the great wizard Merlin appeared, and he explained everything to Arthur. "Your real father was the great King Uther, but he could not raise you and I gave you to Ector to raise you like his own child. But now your time has come to rule Britain."
And so Arthur ruled Britain, kindly and bravely, and the people were finally happy.

Do you know any stories, books or films about the legend of King Arthur? Search the Internet for more information and talk about it in class.

4

1 Describe the photos.
2 What do you think? How are the people feeling?
3 Choose one photo. What could be the story behind it? Collect ideas.

You are not alone

Part A Exploring roots

- Du erfährst etwas über die Wurzeln und Lebensgeschichten verschiedener Menschen.
- Du sprichst darüber, was an deinem Wohnort besonders für dich ist.
- Du stellst eine Lebensgeschichte vor.

Part B Giving a helping hand

- Du übst, Gefühle und Situationen zu beschreiben.
- Du lernst, wie man um Rat fragt und Ratschläge gibt.
- Du stellst eine Szene darüber vor, wie man jemandem helfen kann.

The place where you live

1 workbook p. 58/1

What do you like about the city or village where you live? What is special about it? Make notes and share your thoughts in class.

a halfpipe · restaurants · friendly people · kebab stalls · ...

You can say:

There is / are … in …
I like … because …
… is my favourite place in …

Living in London

2a

Read what four people from London posted on this website. Why did they come to London? Where in London do they live now? Take notes.

********************** LIVING IN LONDON **********************

Jenna

My name is Jenna, and I am 16 years old. I was born in Korea, but my parents moved to London when I was four because they found better jobs here.

I have one brother. We live in south-west London, in Merton. There's a Korean church in our neighbourhood and we go there every Sunday. I like going to church because I always meet my friends there.

My first memory of London was when I went on the London Eye. It was lots of fun, and the view was amazing! The riverside near the London Eye is my favourite place in London.

My grandparents still live in Korea. We fly to Korea every two years to visit my grandparents.

We speak Korean and English at home. I like Korea, but I feel at home in London.

Leon

Hi, I'm Leon. I'm from Spain, but we moved to Bayswater last year because my mum got a job here in London. We lived in northern Spain and I loved it there! My hobby is mountain biking, and it's hard to find a good place for that here.

I would like to go back to Spain as soon as possible.

I miss my friends very much.

I also don't like my school here. When I first came here, I didn't understand much of what people said and sometimes people thought I was stupid just because of my accent.

The only thing I like about London is that there are a lot of parks here – Hyde Park is my favourite.

My name is Sam. My family has always lived in London. I grew up in Battersea and now I live in Hammersmith. I went to university in Bristol, but I didn't like it very much because I missed London so much.
There are so many things to do here. You can go shopping, visit museums, go to parks or lots of concerts and shows …
My favourite place in London is the Science Museum. There are always new exhibitions and I often go there. I love London.
I don't want to live anywhere else!

Sam

Hello, I'm Erika. I'm from Sweden, and I came to London in 2006 to go to university here. I met my husband here. He's from Ghana and we both liked the lively atmosphere in London so much that we decided to stay here. We got married in 2014 and moved to Elephant & Castle in 2016. What I like most about this part of London are the people. I often meet someone I know in the street! There is a very strong community here.
My husband and I have a son and a daughter and we talk to them a lot about our family roots – both the West African side and the Swedish side. We all like cooking and we often cook dishes that are a mixture of West African, Swedish and British food.

Erika

2b CHOOSE YOUR LEVEL skill: reading p. 154

I **Read the first two texts again. What do Jenna and Leon like about London? Take notes. In which lines did you find the information?**

You can write:
Jenna likes going to church.
In lines 6 and 7 she says: "I like …"

II **Read the first three texts again. What do the people like about London? Take notes. In which lines did you find the information?**

III **Read the texts again. What do the people like about London? Take notes. In which lines did you find the information?**

2c skill: talking to people p. 152, workbook p. 58/2-3

If you could live anywhere in the world, where would you like to live? Why? Work in small groups and talk about your dream places to live.

in the country | in a big city | in a small village | in London | …

You can say:
I would like to live … because there are …
I would like to live … because I could have …

many shops · many animals · many things to do · not so many cars · a garden · a horse · …

GRAMMAR HELP the simple past (R) p. 184–185

Die Zeitform *simple past* kennst du schon. Du benutzt sie, wenn du über etwas sprechen möchtest, das in der Vergangenheit liegt und abgeschlossen ist. Sieh dir die Beispielsätze an. Erinnerst du dich? Wie bildest du die Formen? Worauf musst du bei der Verneinung und bei Fragen im *simple past* besonders achten?

My parents moved to London when I was four. They found better jobs here.	Meine Eltern zogen nach London, als ich vier war. Sie fanden dort bessere Jobs.
I didn't like Bristol very much. Why did the people come to London?	Ich mochte Bristol nicht sehr. Warum kamen die Leute nach London?

Auf den Seiten 184 und 185 sind die wichtigsten Punkte zum *simple past* noch einmal zusammengefasst.

Writing about the past

3a
grammar: simple past (R) p. 184

Write down the simple past forms of these verbs and use them to write three or more true or false statements about the people from pages 80 and 81.

1 move 2 live 3 be 4 like
5 grow up 6 meet 7 go

You can write:

Jenna's parents moved to Korea from London.
Leon …

3b
grammar: simple past (R) p. 184, workbook p. 59/4

Work with a partner. Your partner has to correct the false statements. Take turns.

Who, what, when, where?

4a
grammar: simple past (R) p. 185

Unscramble the questions and write them down.

1 move to – where – Jenna's parents – did
2 in London – was born – who
3 Sam – did – to university – go – where
4 to study – went – who – to London
5 when – move to Elephant & Castle – did – Erika's family

4b
grammar: simple past (R) p. 184

Look at pages 80 and 81 again and write down the answers to the questions from 4a.

4c
grammar: simple past (R) p. 184, wordbank: family history p. 166, workbook p. 60/5

Write three or more statements about yourself and your family.

You can write:

I was born in …
My great-grandmother came from …
…

DIGITAL+ practise more 19

London neighbourhoods

5a audio 2/14

Listen to the podcast. Match the neighbourhoods with the pictures.

A Golders Green
B Southall
C Chinatown
D Brixton

1

2

3

4

5b CHOOSE YOUR LEVEL skill: listening p. 151, workbook p. 60/6-8

I Listen to the podcast again and take notes. Complete the sentences and write them down.

Brixton · Southall · Chinatown

1 There are more than 80 different Chinese restaurants in ???.
2 ??? is sometimes called "Little India".
3 You will find a lot of Caribbean restaurants and reggae music shops in ???.

II Listen to the podcast again and take notes. Complete the sentences and write them down.

1 Many tourists visit ???.
2 In ??? you can try dishes from many South Asian countries.
3 Many people in ??? have an African or Caribbean background.
4 The largest Jewish community in London lives in ???.

III Listen to the podcast again. Choose the correct information and write it down.

1 A Chinese immigrants have lived in Chinatown for more than 200 years.
  B There is a parade for Chinese New Year in Chinatown in December.
2 A Southall is in South London.
  B Many people who live in Southall have an Indian background.
3 A You can hear more than 130 different languages in Brixton.
  B Over 50% of the population in Brixton has an African or Caribbean background.
4 A Only Jewish people live in Golders Green.
  B Many of the people who live in Golders Green have German or Polish roots.

LAND & LEUTE 4 video 11

Multikulturelles London

Großbritannien ist schon immer multikulturell gewesen. Nach dem Zweiten Weltkrieg sind viele Menschen aus ehemaligen britischen Kolonien nach Großbritannien gekommen, zum Beispiel aus Indien, Pakistan, Hongkong und einigen afrikanischen Ländern. Viele sind vor allem nach London gekommen, weil sie dort auf bessere Jobs hofften.

Die Einwanderer haben ihre Kultur und ihre Sprachen mitgebracht. London ist der Schmelztiegel dieser Kulturen. In London werden mehr als dreihundert verschiedene Sprachen gesprochen.

In einigen Stadtteilen kann man einen starken Einfluss der verschiedenen Gruppen sehen. Beispielsweise leben viele Menschen aus Bangladesch im Osten Londons. Die bekannteste Gegend dort ist die *Brick Lane*, in der man sogar Straßenschilder auf Bengali sehen kann, einer Sprache, die hauptsächlich in Bangladesch und Indien gesprochen wird.

Es gibt auch viele Menschen in London, die Polnisch, Türkisch, Gujarati, Panjabi oder Urdu sprechen.

Welche Sprachen sprechen deine Mitschüler und Mitschülerinnen? Macht eine Umfrage.

The Grandparent Project

6a

What do you think: what is "The Grandparent Project"?

6b

skill: mediation p. 155

Your grandparents have found this website. Tell them in German what it is about.

Connecting children & grandparents all over the world

This programme helps children all over the world to write their grandparents' stories and learn about their family history.

→ Interview your grandparents and listen to their story.
→ Write your grandparents' story. If you like, you can put it into a digital format, make a drawing or create a multimedia series.
→ Learn creative storytelling skills.

6c

What questions would you ask in an interview for the Grandparent Project? Collect ideas in class.

You can ask:

What did you do in your free time?
Where did you meet Grandma / Grandpa?
Tell me about your parents. Were they ...? ...

Edyta's life story – part one

7a audio 2/17

Ava has decided to take part in the Grandparent Project and talks to her grandmother Edyta in Poland on the phone. Listen and read along. Who do they talk about?

Ava: Hi Grandma. Thanks for helping me with this project.
Edyta: Of course. I'm looking forward to talking to you about our family history. Where would you like to start?
Ava: Maybe with your parents? I know that my great-grandfather left Poland and came to England. Can you tell me more about it?
Edyta: Of course. My father, your great-grandfather Radek, was a pilot. When World War II began in 1939, he and many other Polish pilots went to England and joined the Royal Air Force to help fight the Nazis.
Ava: And what happened after the war?
Edyta: He decided to stay in Britain.

Ava: And how did he meet your mother?
Edyta: Oh, he knew her already. She was from the same town in Poland as he was. In 1946 my mother – your great-grandmother Agata – left Poland and emigrated to Great Britain to marry him and start a new life in London.
Ava: How did she feel about it? Was it hard for her to move to a foreign country?
Edyta: It wasn't easy at first. She didn't speak any English and she was homesick. But they lived in a neighbourhood with a lot of Polish people, so it was OK. She learnt to speak English, and after a while she felt at home. And then my oldest brother, Pavel, was born in 1951.
Ava: When was your brother Jan born?
Edyta: Jan was born in 1955 and then I was born in 1958 …

7b CHOOSE YOUR LEVEL skill: reading p. 154, workbook p. 61/9-10

I **Read the dialogue again. What do you learn about Edyta and her brothers? Take notes.**

II **Read the dialogue again. What do you learn about Edyta's mother Agata? Take notes.**

III **Read the dialogue again. What do you learn about Edyta's father Radek? Take notes.**

Edyta's life story – part two

8a wordbank: talking about pictures p. 166

Look at the pictures. What do you think happened in Edyta's life?

8b audio 2/18, skill: reading p. 154

Listen to the dialogue and read along. What does Edyta say about speaking Polish?

Ava: You looked so cute when you were a baby. I remember the old photo of you in your funny baby dress ...

Edyta: Ha, ha. That was the latest fashion for babies then! But I had a wonderful childhood. We lived in a nice house and I loved playing in our garden.

Ava: You speak English and Polish. How did you learn to speak both languages?

Edyta: Well, at school I always spoke English, and at home we mostly spoke Polish. It was very important to my parents that my brothers and I were able to speak Polish with our family in Poland.

Ava: It's a shame that I don't speak Polish that well. Did you have Polish lessons at school?

Edyta: No, I didn't. But I went to a Polish theatre group once a week. That's where I met your grandad Filip.

Ava: He was Polish too, wasn't he?

Edyta: Actually, we were both British. We just came from Polish families.

Ava: Oh. Right. But you still spoke Polish at home. That's why Dad can speak Polish a lot better than Noah, Joshua and me.

Edyta: Yes, we did. And we often spent the summer holidays in Poland when your father was little.

Ava: Yes, he told us about that. He really liked it there. But back to you. What about your job? Did you like it?

Edyta: Yes, I did. I liked working as a nurse and, when your father was old enough, I went back to my job.

Ava: Grandpa Filip died when Dad was still quite young, didn't he?

Edyta: Oh, that was a very sad time for

all of us. Your father was at university in Manchester and I felt a bit lonely at that time, but then I began to visit my family in Poland more often.
Ava: And how did you get the idea to move to Poland?
Edyta: My cousin had the idea and I liked it.
Ava: Do you miss anything about London?
Edyta: Sure. I miss you. That's why I come to visit as often as I can. But Poland feels as much like home as London. I feel like I have two homes.
Ava: "Two homes". That's a good title for my story for the Grandparent Project. I think I have a lot to write about now.
Edyta: I really enjoyed talking to you. Just let me know if you want to know anything else about our family.
Ava: Thanks for answering all my questions.
Edyta: You're welcome, darling.

8c CHOOSE YOUR LEVEL skill: writing p. 153, media worksheet 11

I Choose three or more of the pictures from 8a and write captions for them.

You can write:

Picture 1: Edyta in her funny baby dress
Picture …

II Choose three or more of the pictures from 8a and write speech or thought bubbles for Edyta.

You can write:

Picture 1: "I …"
…

III Choose two or more of the pictures from 8a and write Edyta's diary entries or letters for those days.

You can write:

Dear diary,
Today was a great day. I …
…

London, 24 March 1982
Dear Janina,
Today, I …
Love,
Edyta

8d wordbank: family history p. 166, workbook p. 63/11-13

What does 'home' mean to you? Is it a place? A feeling? People? Collect ideas in class.

You can write:

To me, 'home' means …
Home is …

Tell us more

9 CHOOSE YOUR TASK A+B: wordbank: family history p. 166, C: skill: searching the internet p. 157, media worksheet 6

A **Create a picture or collage about what 'home' means to you and label it.**
B **What were important events in your own life? Make a timeline.**
C **Find a map of London on the Internet. Choose a neighbourhood that looks interesting to you. Find out more about it. Then write a fact file.**

Interviewing grandparents

10 CHOOSE YOUR LEVEL grammar: simple past (R) p. 185, workbook p. 64/14-15

Read the following answers to interview questions. Write questions to the answers.

I
1 I was born in 1959.
2 My grandmother had three children.
3 I went to school in Bristol.

You can write:
When were you …?
How many … did your …?
Where did you …?

II
1 My father was from Italy.
2 My mother had two brothers.
3 My parents got married in 1952.
4 I went to school in Exeter.

You can write:
Where was your …?
How many … did …?
When did …?
Where …?

III
1 My mother was born in Egypt.
2 My father had two brothers and a sister.
3 My parents moved to Liverpool in 1955.
4 Yes, I did. I liked going to school a lot.

Adjectives and nouns

11

Match all the adjectives to the nouns. There can be more than one solution.

better · foreign · happy · good · sad · wonderful

job · place · time · language · roots · family · childhood · life · people

How to pronounce the letter *s*

12a audio 2/20

Listen and repeat.

parks · roots · things · brothers · towns · accents · groups · friends

12b

Make two lists in your exercise book and listen again. Write the words in your lists.

/s/	/z/
parks	*things*
…	…

12c audio 2/21

Listen and check your lists.

DIGITAL+ practise more 20

A life story TARGET TASK

13 workbook p. 65/16, wordbank: family history p. 166, media worksheet 1

Your task is to present someone's life story.
Before you start, look at these steps:

STEP 1

Who do you want to present? You could choose:

- yourself
- someone from your family
- a famous person
- someone from a book or film
- ...

STEP 2

Think of questions you would like to ask the person and decide how you want to present his or her life story. You could:

- create a poster
- create a photo story with speech and thought bubbles
- create a collage with labels
- create a timeline with photos
- write a text about the person's life
- ...

STEP 3

Find out as much as you can about the person's life story. Think about:

- the family (parents, grandparents, ...)
- the places where the person lived
- important people in the person's life
- the person's school, university, job, ...
- ...

STEP 4

Create your work.

STEP 5

Present your work.

How are you today?

1
skill: talking with people p. 152, wordbank: feelings p. 167, workbook p. 66/1

Work in small groups.
How are you feeling today?
Talk to each other.

happy · sad · angry · bored · worried · nervous · ...

You can say:
I'm happy / sad because ...
I feel OK. How about you?

What's up?

2a
wordbank: talking about pictures p. 166

Look at the pictures. Describe the situations. What do you think: how are the people feeling?

You can say:
In picture A, there are ...
They are ...
The boy looks ...
I think the girl on the left is feeling ...
...

2b
audio 3/1, skill: listening p. 151

Listen to the dialogues. Which picture from 2a goes with which dialogue?

You can say:
I think picture ... goes with dialogue ...

2c

Read the three dialogues. What are the problems?

Dialogue 1

Louise: Hi Emily! What's wrong? You look sad.
Emily: Hi Louise. Oh, it's about Chloe. We had an argument.
Louise: Why, what happened?
Emily: She wanted to copy my French homework. But I said no and that she should do her homework herself because our French teacher always notices and is very strict. Now Chloe is so angry with me that she won't talk to me anymore.
Louise: Should I try to talk to her?
Emily: Thanks, Louise – that would be great!

Dialogue 2

Toby: Hi guys. Anyone up for hanging out at my place this afternoon?
Jack: I'm in!
Paul: I have maths tuition on Tuesdays.
Toby: Why don't you ask your mum if you can skip the lesson?
Paul: I don't think that she will let me. She's not happy with my marks. Just because I got a D in my last test …
Jack: And what does your dad say?
Paul: Oh, no chance, he is even stricter! It's really annoying. What if I join you guys later?
Toby: Yeah, good idea. We'll save some snacks for you!
Paul: That would be great. Thanks, guys.

Dialogue 3

Faisal: Guys, have you heard about James and Delia? Delia invited James to her party, but she says that he won't come.
Linda: Why not? What happened?
Faisal: She says that he says that her party will be lame – because she didn't invite his rugby friends.
Matt: But Delia doesn't even know his rugby friends!
Faisal: Exactly. Why should she invite people that she doesn't know? Now James is angry and says that he doesn't even want to go to Delia's party. He's telling everybody that he'll have his own party on that day!
Linda: That's so silly. Delia must be really upset. I'll go and talk to her.

2d CHOOSE YOUR LEVEL skill: reading p. 154

I Complete the sentences with words from the box and write them in your exercise book.

1 Emily looks ???.
2 Chloe is ??? with Emily.
3 Paul's mum is not ??? with his marks.

strict · sad · angry · happy · afraid

II Match the sentence parts. Write the sentences in your exercise book.

1 Emily tells Louise that
2 Louise thinks that
3 Paul explains to his friends that
4 Delia says that

A he has to go to maths tuition before he can join them.
B James won't come to her party.
C Chloe is wrong.
D she is sad because she had an argument with Chloe.

III Are the sentences true or false? Copy the true sentences and correct the false sentences.

1 Emily tells Louise that she is sad because she got a bad mark in maths.
2 Louise thinks that Chloe is right.
3 Paul has to go to maths tuition on Fridays.
4 Paul says that his mum is even stricter than his dad.
5 Delia wants to invite James's rugby friends to her party.

2e workbook p. 66/2

Choose one of the situations from 2c.
What do you think will happen next? Collect ideas.

You can say:
I think … will …

GRAMMAR HELP reported speech 1 p. 186

Wenn du wiedergeben möchtest, was jemand anderes sagt, benutzt du indirekte Rede *(reported speech)*. Schau dir die Sätze an und achte dabei vor allem auf die Pronomen und die Verbformen. Was fällt dir auf?

Direkte Rede:	Indirekte Rede:
Louise: “You look sad.” Louise: „Du siehst traurig aus.“	Louise tells Emily that she looks sad. Louise sagt Emily, dass sie traurig aussehe.
Emily: “We had an argument.” Emily: „Wir hatten einen Streit.“	Emily says that they had an argument. Emily sagt, dass sie einen Streit gehabt hätten.

Auf Seite 186 findest du weitere Beispiele und Erklärungen zur indirekten Rede.

Text messages

3 grammar: reported speech 1 p. 186, workbook p. 66/3-4

What do the people say in their text messages? Write at least one sentence for each text message.

James
Hi everyone, my party will be at my house this Saturday. We start at four! James

Matt
Hi James, I'm really sorry. I can't come. I've already said yes to Delia's party. Matt

Faisal
Hi guys, I can get the present for Delia. You can give me the money on Monday.

Phil
Hi James, I'll be there and I'll bring my friends from the football team. Phil

You can write:

James says that his party …
Matt says that he is …
Faisal says that he can …
Phil says that …

Feelings

4a wordbank: feelings p. 167

How do you think the people are feeling? Make notes.

OK · sad · proud · stressed · lonely · happy · …

Mia

Eric

Michelle

Oliver

4b audio 3/2, skill: listening p. 151, grammar: reported speech 1 p. 186

Listen to the statements and take notes. Compare with your notes in 4a. Then write about the people.

You can write:

Mia says that she is …
Eric says that his …
…

DIGITAL+ practise more 21

Lily's problem

5a

Read the text messages. Why does Lily want to talk to Noah?

Lily Norris

Lily Hi Noah, how r u? R u busy right now? 5:14pm

Noah No, I'm not busy. What's up? 5:15pm

Lily It's about a guy from the chemistry club – I think he's in your class. 5:17pm

Noah Tom Miller is in the chemistry club. What about him? 5:18pm

Lily Yes, that's him. Can I call you? I'd like to talk to you. 5:19pm

Noah Yes, of course. 5:21pm

Lily Gr8. Talk to you in a sec. 5:21pm

5b audio 3/3

Listen to Lily talking to Noah on the phone. What is Lily's problem?

5c CHOOSE YOUR LEVEL skill: listening p. 151

I Listen again. What does Noah say? Take notes.

You can write:
Tom: no right to …

II Listen again. Then write down Noah's ideas.

You can write:
Noah says that he could …
He says that Lily could …

III Listen again and answer the questions.

1 Why did Lily tell Tom to delete the photo?
2 What was Tom's reaction when Lily asked him to delete the photo?
3 What do Lily's mums always say about the Internet?
4 What does Noah say Lily could do now?

5d skill: talking with people p. 152, workbook p. 68/5

What can you do if you have a problem? Who could you talk to? Talk about it with a partner.

You can say:
We could …

Seeking advice

6a

Look at the headline of the website. What kind of content do you expect?

6b

skill: reading p. 154

Read the texts. Who is writing? Who is the website for?

× –

LONDON TEEN HELP – ASK OUR EXPERTS ONLINE

School, parents, friends – there's a lot that teenagers can have problems with. If you need advice, we're here to help. Send your questions to our team of experts. We'll answer every question and post some of them anonymously with our answers on this website.

Q

Dear expert,

I have a problem with a boy. He took a silly photo of me with his phone after school. I told him to delete it, but he said no. He says that the photo is his and that he can keep it and do whatever he wants with it – even put it on the Internet. I really don't want that and I tried to talk to him about it, but he only laughs at me. Now I don't know what I can do to stop him. Can you help me?

Thanks a lot,

Sunnyday

A

Dear Sunnyday,

I'm sorry to hear about your situation, but I'm sure there's a solution to your problem. That boy has no right to keep or publish that photo. You did not agree to anything so he must delete it if you say so. I think that he does not know that he is doing something wrong. I suggest that you talk to him as soon as possible to make that really clear to him. I would also suggest that you ask a parent or a teacher to help you.

All the best and good luck!

Your expert

Q

Dear expert,

I am 13 years old and I have a problem with my parents. They are very strict when it comes to online time. I am not allowed to be online more than one hour per day. That's just enough time to do some work for school, check my messages and answer them. All my friends are online all day. They chat and play online video games. I am completely left out unless I go to a friend's house and go online with them. My parents worry about my marks. They think I won't do my homework if I spend more time online and they don't listen to my arguments. Help! What can I do?

Lonelygirl

A

Hi Lonelygirl,
I know how important it can be to be online. Teenagers today live in a very digital world – you use laptops or tablets at school and at home. Have you explained to your parents that you're not only online for fun but that you also communicate with your classmates about school matters, do research and so on? Maybe you could keep a diary to show your parents how much time you need for your online school work alone? You could also ask them to let you have more time online so that you can prove that your marks won't get worse. There are also official websites that give parents an idea of how much screen time is OK for children and teenagers. I wish you good luck!
Your expert

Q

Dear expert,
I am 14 and I have a problem that I can't solve. There is this girl in the chemistry club at my school and I really like her – but I am too shy to tell her. Last week, after school, we walked home together and we took funny pictures of each other with our phones. She did not like one of the photos that I took of her – but I think she looks cute in it, so I didn't want to delete it when she asked me to. I thought it was really funny and told her that I might put the photo on the Internet. She got so angry with me that she doesn't look at me or talk to me anymore. What can I do now? I really want her to like me again. Can you help me?
Anonymous

A

Dear Anonymous,
Why don't you talk to her again and apologize? You are definitely not allowed to keep that photo or put it on the Internet if she doesn't want you to do so. And don't you think she might be happy if you tell her the real reason for keeping the picture? Teasing her is definitely the wrong way! Just tell her that you like her. Good luck!
Your expert

6c CHOOSE YOUR LEVEL skill: writing p. 153

I **In your own words, describe Sunnyday's problem. Write two or more sentences. Can you guess who Sunnyday is?**

You can write:
Sunnyday has problems with …
She doesn't want that …

II **In your own words, describe Sunnyday and Lonelygirl's problems. Write three or more sentences for each person. Can you guess who Sunnyday is?**

III **In your own words, describe the people's problems. Write three or more sentences for each person. Can you guess who Sunnyday and Anonymous are?**

6d wordbank: expressing opinions p. 165, skill: talking with people p. 152, workbook p. 68/6-9

Work in small groups. What do you think about the answers on the website? Are they helpful? Have you got any other ideas?

Solving the problem

7 skill: writing p. 153, workbook p. 70/10-11

Work with a partner. Write a dialogue between Tom and Lily in which they try to solve the problem.

You can write:

Tom: *I wanted to talk to you about …*
Please listen to me and …
I'm sorry that …
I didn't mean to …
…

Lily: *But you …*
It's important to me that …
…

Tom / Lily: *Why don't we …?*
Let's …
…

A person to talk to

8a video 12, skill: watching a video clip p. 156

Watch the video clip.
Where does the woman work?

8b workbook p. 71/12

Watch the video clip again.
What does the woman talk about?

You can say:

The woman talks about …
She says that …

8c wordbank: expressing opinions p. 165

Would you talk to a school counsellor about your problems? Why or why not? Work with a partner. You can talk in German.

Sheree's problems

9 GET TOGETHER audio 3/5

Get together with a partner.
Listen to Sheree's call to the teen helpline.

Partner A	Partner B
I Go to page 130.	I Go to page 139.
II Go to page 133.	II Go to page 142.
III Go to page 136.	III Go to page 145.

Dealing with feelings

10 CHOOSE YOUR TASK A, C: wordbank: feelings p. 167, B: skill: performing a scene p. 159, media worksheet 2, 5

A **Draw at least eight emojis and label them.**

B **Work in groups or pairs and read out one of the dialogues from pages 90/91. You can record your reading.**

C **Make a word search for a partner with words for feelings.**

Helping out

11 skill: mediation p. 155, workbook p. 71/13

Bob is an exchange student at your school. He does not speak much German. He is upset because he has lost his rucksack. Help him to get it back.

Bob: I can't find my rucksack! I think I left it on the bus yesterday when we were on the school trip. Could we call the bus company and ask if they have found my rucksack?

(1) You: *Yes, sure. I'll call their office. (…) Guten Tag, …*

Office manager: Wie spät war das? Und wo hat er denn gesessen? Welche Farbe hat der Rucksack?

(2) You: *What time …? And …? What …?*

Bob: It was about three in the afternoon and I was sitting in the middle of the bus on the left. It's a red rucksack.

(3) You: …

Office manager: Alles klar. Da muss ich mal eben mit einem Kollegen sprechen, einen Moment bitte. (...) Ich habe eine gute Nachricht! Sie haben einen Rucksack gefunden. Das muss seiner sein. Ihr könntet ihn heute Nachmittag abholen.

(4) You: *She says …*

Bob: Oh great, thank you very much. Where can we pick it up?

(5) You: …

Office manager: In der Husarenstraße 10. Direkt beim Busbahnhof.

(6) You: …

Your problem or mine?

12 workbook p. 72/14-15

Copy the sentences and fill in the correct words from the brackets.

1 Your brother is wrong: it's not your problem, it's ???. (he / his)
2 The photo belongs to me, it's ??? and I can do whatever I want with it. (mine / my)
3 She took my cap and now she says that it's ???. (her / hers)
4 Who left the dirty T-shirt in the living room? Is it ???? (your / yours)
5 The TV belongs to all of us, it's ???. (ours / our)
6 Do you think the ball in our garden belongs to our neighbours? - Yes, I think it's ???. (theirs / their)

Linking parts

13 CHOOSE YOUR LEVEL

I Choose the correct word and write down the sentences.

1 I feel worried **because / but** my dog is sick.
2 **So / When** I have too much to do, I feel stressed.
3 I wanted to go the party **when / but** now I can't.

II Match the sentence parts and write down the sentences.

1 I feel stressed
2 My parents are really strict
3 I'm angry with my brother
4 I'm really sad

A and don't allow me to stay up late.
B when I have too much homework.
C because I can't go to my friend's party.
D but he only laughs at me.

III Choose the correct linking word and write down the sentences.

1 I always feel sad when/but my parents have an argument.
2 My friend is angry because / and I forgot her birthday.
3 I got a very rude message from a classmate when/and I definitely won't answer it.
4 My sister can stay up late because / but I have to be in bed by nine.

How to pronounce the letters *th*

14 audio 3/10

Listen to the words and repeat them. Then sort them into two lists: words with /ð/ as in "this" and words with /θ/ as in "thanks".

this · thanks · that · think · thought · then · through · there · they

DIGITAL+ practise more 21

Giving a helping hand TARGET TASK

15 workbook p. 73/16, wordbank: seeking and giving advice p. 167, skill: performing a scene p. 159, media worksheet 2

Your task is to prepare a scene about helping somebody.
Before you start, look at these steps:

STEP 1

Work in small groups. Choose a situation in which you can give advice or help, for example:

- A friend always panics before tests.
- A classmate tells you that his or her best friend says bad things behind his or her back.
- The new pupil in your class looks very sad and lonely.
- ...

STEP 2

Make notes for your scene. You can look at the box for help. You do not have to write the complete script but you can write cue cards for each character.

Think about what you can do.	You can sit next to him or her. · You can spend time with him or her. · You can try to talk to ... · ...
Think about what you can say.	You are not alone. · It's not your fault. · Maybe you could ... · Maybe it would help to ... · ...
Ask questions to find out more.	What exactly is the problem? · Why ...? · Do you think ...? · Are you afraid of ...? · ...
Talk about your experience.	When I had this problem, I ... · I've tried ... · I know someone who ... · He / She ... · ...
Think about who else could help.	Could you talk to your parents? · Could you ask a teacher for advice? · ...

STEP 3

Decide who will play which part and practise your scene.

STEP 4

Perform your scene. If you like, you can film your scene and show it to the rest of the class.

Check out

Kannst du einem Blogeintrag Informationen entnehmen?	Workbook, p. 74
Kannst du über vergangene Ereignisse schreiben?	Workbook, p. 74
Kannst du einen Podcast über Stadtteile in London verstehen?	Workbook, p. 74
Kannst du verstehen, worum es geht, wenn jemand über ein Problem spricht?	Workbook, p. 75
Kannst du wiedergeben, was jemand sagt?	Workbook, p. 75
Kannst du deine Meinung zu einem Problem äußern?	Workbook, p. 75

Wrong impressions

A couple of months ago, my English teacher, Mr Rogers, asked me after class if I could help a student from another class with her work for English Literature because she didn't like to read and wasn't doing well in her exams. I wasn't happy about that, especially when he said, "It's Marianne Hamilton from your year." Until that day I had talked to Marianne exactly three times.

The first time was in the queue at lunch break. She said, "Oh, could you pass me a fork, please? I forgot to take one," and I said, "Yeah sure. Here you are." The second time was during the music project all the students in our year did together. She said, "Could you move your chair, please?" and I said, "Yeah sure. Sorry."

The third time was in our school library. I was there with my friends having fun when she said, "Could you please be quiet? I am trying to work here," and I said, "Yeah sure."

Well, anyway, I had always been a bit shy around Marianne. I thought that she was probably quite boring and one of those students who are good at everything and always on time and always do their homework and always study before exams.

I don't like studying too much. I'm good at English by accident. I just like reading and writing about what I've read. That helps a lot.
"If you help Marianne for about one hour every week, I can let that count as your group project for this year," Mr Rogers went on. At my school we have to do one group project in English every year. I hate doing group projects. I wasn't sure what was worse, but then I thought I may as well give it a try so I said, "Yeah, OK, I'll help her."

"Brilliant!" Mr Rogers said and seemed very happy. He told me to come back to his room at the end of the school day. Marianne was there, too, and we worked out a plan together. She didn't seem to be too excited about Mr Rogers' idea, either. All she said was, "Yes. OK. Yes, Saturday is fine. We can meet at my house. Just give me your phone number and I'll text you my address." Which she did. On Saturday, Marianne's mum let me in. The house was really nice. Marianne's mum seemed nice, too. She gave us a plate of biscuits and some lemonade and told us to have fun. I wasn't sure I'd have much fun in the next hour but at least there were biscuits. Really good chocolate biscuits. We went upstairs and Marianne opened the door to her room. It was full of books!

impression = *Eindruck*; exam = *Prüfung*; queue = *Schlange*; by accident = *zufällig, aus Versehen*; count = *zählen*; give a try = *ausprobieren*

Really, there were books EVERYWHERE. "Whoa," I said, "I thought you didn't like reading?"

"I LOVE reading" she said, "It's just that I didn't like the first book we had to read in Year 7. I hated it. I don't like books with animals as the main characters. I think they're silly. I think we should read books about real people. So I wrote what I thought was bad about the book. But it is Mr Rogers' favourite book and now he thinks that I'm not good with books. I can say and write and do whatever I want – he has this image of me and I can't change it."

"That's not fair of him," I said, "I liked the book but maybe only because my dad read it to my sister and me when we were younger. I'm not sure I would like it as much otherwise. But now Mr Rogers seems to like me and I get good marks."

"See?" Marianne said, "He's got this opinion and it's really hard to change it. I really like the book we're reading now, but I'm sure he won't give me anything better than a C. So, why bother? – What are you reading at the moment?" "*Noah can't even*," I said, "It's about a boy who's …" "Oh, I've read it," Marianne interrupted me, "I loved it. Have you ever read this one?" and she pulled a book from the pile next to her bed.

We spent the next three hours discussing books, and Marianne let me borrow five of her books that I hadn't read yet. I didn't help her with her homework at all, but we had a good time and set a date for Marianne to come to my place so that she could borrow some of my books. From then on, we spent all our "lessons" talking about books and reading. When Mr Rogers asked how it was going, we always smiled and told him that we were working hard and that Marianne was doing very well. The day before her next exam, we studied a little but not too much. Then we went out for ice cream.

Three days later Marianne got her very first A in an English exam. She told me that Mr Rogers had smiled at her when he returned her exam paper and said: "That was very well done. I'm happy that my plan worked out so well."

bother = *sich Mühe geben;* interrupt = *unterbrechen;* pull = *ziehen;* pile = *Stapel, Haufen;* set a date = *sich verabreden;* A = *etwa: 1, sehr gut;* paper = *hier: Klassenarbeit, Klausur;* work out = *hier: aufgehen*

On the Move Again

You know
You gotta go.
No time to grieve
You just gotta leave.

Get away from the pain
On the move again.

Take the train.
Catch a plane.

Make the trip
In a ship.

Take a hike
Ride a bike.

Go by car.
Going far.

Use your feet
On the street.

Get stuck
In a truck.

Then you arrive
And you're alive.

What you leave behind
Won't leave your mind.

But home is where you find it.
Home is where you find it.
Home is where you find it.
Home is where you find it.

Michael Rosen

5

1 Look at the pictures. What can you see?
2 What can you do with the objects?
3 Which of the objects do you use? Which of them would you like to use?

Everyday science

Part A Inventions

- Du liest etwas über verschiedene Erfindungen.
- Du lernst, wie man über Erfindungen, Erfinder und Erfinderinnen schreibt.
- Du stellst deine Ideen für eine neue Erfindung vor.

Part B Communication

- Du liest über eine Projektwoche an der Holland Park School.
- Du siehst dir eine Präsentation an.
- Du hältst einen dreiminütigen Vortrag über einen Aspekt der Geschichte der Kommunikation.

Everyday objects

1a

What objects from your everyday life could you not live without? Talk about them in class.

mobile phone · fridge · tablet · book · TV · toothbrush · pen · ...

You can say:
I couldn't live without a ...
I really need my ...

1b

Look at these pictures.
Match them to the definitions.

You can say:
Picture number ... goes with definition ...

1

2
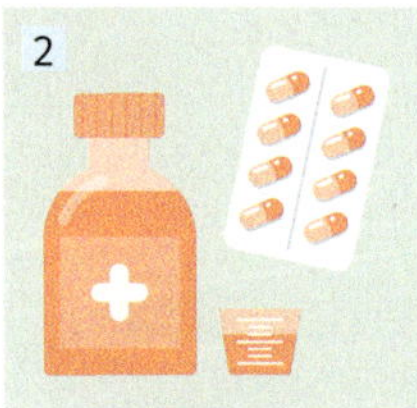

3
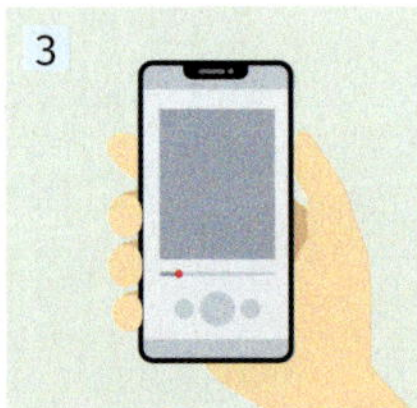

4

5

6
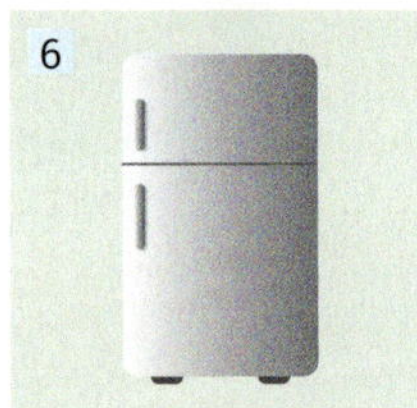

A A telephone that has lots of apps.
B A type of transport which has two wheels and needs muscle power to move.
C Lots of pages with text that was written by an author.
D A small computer that you can take with you.
E An electric cupboard which you use to keep your food cool.
F Something that helps you to get better when you are ill.

1c

skill: talking with people p. 152, workbook p. 76/1

Which of the objects from 1b do you find most important? Why?
Share your thoughts with a partner.

You can say:
I think the ... is most important because ...
What do you think?

British inventions

2a

Look at the pictures. Which invention came first? Which one came last? Work with a partner.

You can say:
I think the ... came first, then the ...

telephone

toothbrush

TV

steam locomotive

2b

Read the article. Did you put the inventions in the correct order?

British inventions

British inventors are very creative. Let's have a look at some of their inventions.

The toothbrush

People have always cleaned their teeth, but toothbrushes as we know them today were invented in 1780 by a man named William Addis. His toothbrush was made of horsehair and cow bone. The basic design of the toothbrush has not changed much, but today other materials are used.

The steam locomotive

In 1802, the first high-pressure steam engine for locomotives was invented by Richard Trevithick. Some years later, Robert and George Stephenson built a steam locomotive that could pull passenger trains. Soon this invention was used all over the world. Today, most trains are pulled by locomotives with electric or diesel engines.

The telephone

The telephone was invented in 1875. It was patented by Alexander Graham Bell from Scotland, but the American Thomas Watson helped him with his invention. The first phone call was made between Bell and Watson in the same building. Soon long-distance phone calls were possible as well, but they were extremely expensive. In 1927, the first three minutes of the first transatlantic telephone call cost $75 – half the price of a car at that time.

The television

The first working television was presented in London in 1927 by John Logie Baird.

2c CHOOSE YOUR LEVEL skill: reading p. 154, workbook p. 76/2

I Choose the correct words to complete the sentences and write them down.

1 Toothbrushes were made of **wood / horsehair and cow bone** in 1780.
2 Today, most **trains / ships** are pulled by locomotives with electric or diesel engines.

II Match the sentence parts and write down the sentences.

1 William Addis invented a toothbrush that
2 Steam locomotives
3 The first telephone calls

A could pull passenger trains.
B were extremely expensive.
C was made of horsehair and cow bone.

III Copy the sentences and complete them.

1 The basic design of the ??? has not changed much.
2 Steam locomotives were used all over the ???.
3 The first ??? was made between Bell and Watson in the same building.
4 The first working ??? was presented in London in 1927.

GRAMMAR HELP the passive p. 187

Aktivsätze stellen den oder die Handelnden in den Vordergrund. Bei Passivsätzen dagegen ist es nebensächlich oder nicht bekannt, wer oder was handelt. Die Handlung selbst steht im Vordergrund. Sieh dir die Beispielsätze an. Was fällt dir auf?

An author wrote lots of pages. Ein/e Autor/in schrieb viele Seiten.	Lots of pages were written by an author. Viele Seiten wurden von einem Autor/einer Autorin geschrieben.
Many people used this invention. Viele Menschen verwendeten diese Erfindung.	This invention was used by many people. Diese Erfindung wurde von vielen Menschen verwendet.
Today, electric engines pull many trains. Heutzutage ziehen Elektromotoren viele Züge.	Today, many trains are pulled by electric engines. Heutzutage werden viele Züge von Elektromotoren gezogen.

Weitere Erklärungen findest du auf Seite 187.
Die Liste mit den unregelmäßigen Verbformen findest du auf den Seiten 245 bis 247.

Inventions

3a grammar: passive p. 187

Unscramble the sentences and write them down.

1 were invented – a lot of things – by British inventors
2 by William Addis – the first toothbrush – was invented
3 the first steam locomotive – in Britain – was built
4 in Scotland – of the telephone – was born – the inventor

3b grammar: passive p. 187, workbook p. 76/3

Copy the sentences and complete them with words from the box.

1 The fridge ??? to keep your food cool.
2 A laptop is a small computer that ??? anywhere.
3 The telephone ??? in 1875.
4 Steam locomotives ??? by railway companies.

was invented · were used · can be taken · is used

Important inventions

4 grammar: passive p. 187, workbook p. 77/4-5

Rewrite the sentences in the passive.

1 Doctors give medicine to sick people.
2 A British inventor invented the telescope.
3 William Addis made the modern toothbrush.
4 In the 1820s, steam locomotives pulled trains.
5 Thomas Watson helped Alexander Graham Bell.

You can write:

Medicine is given to sick people by …
The telescope was …
The toothbrush was …
Trains were …
Alexander …

A day out

5a

Look at Ava's computer screen.
What is on at the London Science Museum?

You can say:

There is a section on …

There is an exhibition about …

5b audio 3/12

Listen to Ava, Lily and Harry. What are they talking about?

5c CHOOSE YOUR LEVEL skill: listening p. 151

I Listen again and choose the correct sentence ending.

1 Ava is looking at the website of **the London Science Museum / the Museum of London**.
2 They have a section on **animals / science and medicine**.
3 Ava wants **Harry and Lily / Tarek, Harry and Lily** to come, too.

II Listen again and choose the correct answer.

1 Which section of the London Science Museum ist Ava excited about?
A science and medicine
B everyday technology
C clock design

2 Who was Stephen Hawking?
A Ava's neighbour
B an inventor
C a scientist

3 What is the everyday technology section about?
A inventions that have changed our lives
B the history of computers
C space travel

III Listen again. Match the sentence parts and write down the sentences.

1 Ava's mum is going to take Ava and her brothers
2 Ava is really excited
3 There are always special exhibitions
4 The everyday technology section is about

A on different topics or people.
B inventions that have changed our lives.
C to the London Science Museum.
D about the everyday technology section.

5d skill: searching the Internet p. 157, media worksheet 6, workbook p. 78/6

What would you like to see at the London Science Museum?
Find out more on the Internet and tell your class.

You can say:

I would like to see …

Visiting the London Science Museum

6 skill: mediation p. 155

You are at the London Science Museum. A German family does not understand the visitor information. Help them and answer their questions in German.

TICKETS
The museum is free to visit.
We recommend you book a free ticket online in advance.

OPENING TIMES
The museum is open from Wednesday to Sunday from 10am to 6pm.
Exhibition areas start to close 30 minutes before the museum closes.

FOOD AND DRINK
1. There are several cafés in the museum.
2. You can bring your own food and drink, which can be eaten in the picnic area outside.
3. Eating in the exhibition rooms is not allowed.

GETTING HERE
The museum is located on Exhibition Road in South Kensington. The nearest tube station is South Kensington.

PLEASE NOTE
We are renovating some of our exhibitions. To find out which exhibitions are closed, please see our home page.

1 Was muss man zum Thema Tickets wissen?
2 Wie sieht es mit den Öffnungszeiten aus?
3 Wo im Museum kann man etwas essen?
4 Wie kommt man zum Museum?
5 Was muss man sonst noch beachten?

Everyday technology

7a

Read the info texts that Ava and her friends saw at the London Science Museum. What objects did they look at?

1 Everyday technology that ... ***saves time***

Zip

When you look around you – how many zips can you count? They are everywhere! On trousers, jackets, bags, rucksacks, ... Just imagine how long it would take to button all these things. But that's what people did until zips were first used for clothes. Although early versions of the zip appeared from the 1870s onwards, the clothes industry only discovered in the 1930s how useful zips can be.

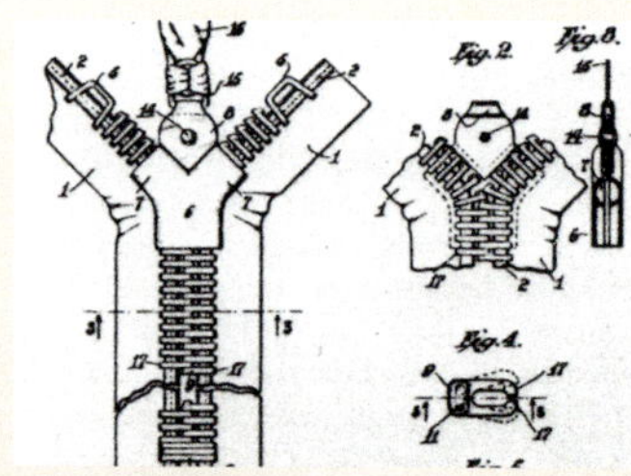

construction drawing for one of the first zips

2 Everyday technology that … ***saves lives***

Seat belts

Early seat belts were simple straps of leather that you fastened in front of you like a belt. They kept you in your seat but did not really prevent injuries.
But in the 1950s, Swedish engineer Nils Bohlin invented the kind of seat belt that looks like the letter Y. It is a lot more comfortable and safer and it is still used in cars today.

Nils Bohlin with his invention in 1958

3 Everyday technology that … ***keeps food fresh***

Tins and tin openers

For centuries, people looked for ways to keep food fresh, especially meat and fish. Peter Durand had an idea in 1810. If you put food inside tins, close them and then heat them, the food inside the tins can be stored for a long time and the food inside can still be eaten years later.
The tin opener was only invented in 1870. Until then, people had to use other tools to open their tins.

an early tin

4 Everyday technology that … ***was invented by accident***

Penicillin

Until 1942, a small wound could actually kill you if it became infected with bacteria. But in 1928, Alexander Fleming accidentally discovered penicillin, the first antibiotic. He was tidying up some Petri dishes with different bacteria in his lab when he noticed something unusual on one dish – there were bacteria all over the dish except for one area where some mould was growing. It looked like the mould was killing the bacteria. This discovery was the beginning of modern antibiotics. It is estimated that penicillin has saved at least 200 million lives since its first use as a medicine in 1942.

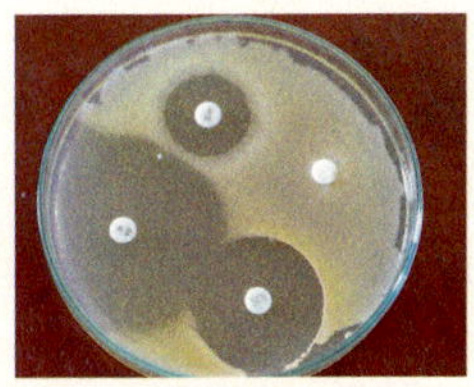

antibiotic mould killing bacteria

7b CHOOSE YOUR LEVEL skill: reading p. 154, workbook p. 78/7

I Read the info texts 1 and 2 again and complete the sentences with the words from the box.

1 The clothes industry discovered in the 1930s how useful ??? can be.
2 Early ??? were simple straps of leather.
3 A Swedish engineer invented the ??? seat belt that looks like the letter Y.

kind of · zips · seat belts

II Read the info texts 1 to 3 again and match the sentence parts.

1 First versions of a zip
2 Until the 1930s,
3 The first seat belts
4 The tin opener

A did not prevent injuries.
B was only invented in 1870.
C zips were not used on clothes.
D appeared from the 1870s onwards.

III Read the info texts 1 to 4 again and complete the sentences.

1 The clothes industry discovered very late how ???.
2 Early ??? were simple straps of ???.
3 For centuries, people looked ???.
4 The beginning of modern antibiotics was when Fleming discovered ???.

LAND & LEUTE 5 video 13

Die Industrielle Revolution

Die sogenannte „Industrielle Revolution" nahm vor ungefähr 300 Jahren im Vereinigten Königreich ihren Anfang. Seit den 1730er Jahren veränderten viele Erfindungen auf Gebieten wie der Landwirtschaft, dem Verkehr und der Industrie das Alltagsleben dramatisch. Diese Erfindungen wurden bald überall auf der Welt übernommen. Eine der wichtigsten Erfindungen war vermutlich die Dampfmaschine, die 1765 von James Watt verbessert wurde. Sie machte Produktionsprozesse schneller und billiger. Diese Erfindungen hatten sowohl positive als auch negative Auswirkungen auf das Leben der Menschen, aber ohne sie wäre unser Alltag heute nicht vorstellbar.

Welche positiven und negativen Aspekte der Industriellen Revolution fallen dir ein? Tauscht euch in der Klasse aus.

Useful inventions?

8a video 14, skill: watching a video clip p. 156

Watch the video clip. What is George watching on TV and why? What inventions are presented? You can take notes in German.

8b wordbank: inventions p. 168, workbook p. 79/8-9

How useful are the inventions to you? Rate each one from 1 (not useful) to 10 (very useful). Compare your ratings with a partner.

You can say:

I think the … is very useful. I would give it a 9.

I think the … is not so useful. I would …

Writing about inventions

9 CHOOSE YOUR TASK A + B: wordbank: inventions p. 168, C: skill: writing p. 153, workbook p. 80/10

A **Look at 2b on page 105 again. Draw one of the inventions and write about it.**

B **Write quiz cards for a partner. Describe an invention. Your partner has to guess what it is. Take turns.**

You can write:

You use it to see when it is dark.

You can use it when there is no electricity.

C **Imagine there was no electricity last Tuesday. Write about your day.**

In the morning, I got up really late because my mobile didn't work. I couldn't listen to music while I had breakfast and … Then …

Visiting a German museum

10
skill: mediation p. 155, media worksheet 2, 5

You want to take a British friend to the Technik Museum in Speyer. Look at the brochure and work with a partner. He or she plays the role of your friend and asks you two or more questions in English about the museum. Take turns. You can record your dialogues.

TECHNIK MUSEUM SPEYER

Im Technik Museum in Speyer erwarten Sie mehr als 3000 Ausstellungsstücke: Flugzeuge, klassische Automobile, Lokomotiven, U-Boote, Schiffe und viele andere technische Meisterleistungen. Zu den größten Attraktionen zählen eine Boeing 747, die russische Raumfähre BURAN und das voll zugängliche U-Boot U9.

Wir haben **365 Tage im Jahr geöffnet**.
Montag bis Freitag: 9–18 Uhr
Samstag, Sonntag, Feiertage: 9–19 Uhr

Unser **Restaurant** bietet jeweils von 9 bis 18 Uhr eine Auswahl an kalten und warmen Speisen.

Die **Buslinien 564 und 565** bringen Sie direkt vom Bahnhof zum Museum.

Eintrittspreise

Kinder 5–14 J.	15,00 €
Erwachsene	19,00 €

Funny inventions

11a

Look at the pictures and guess what you can do with the inventions.

11b

Match the descriptions to the pictures. Were you right in 11a?

Emma: "My invention is a good idea for birthday parties. All I do is watch my biscuit baker."

Leona: "My invention is practical. With my cleaning skates I can clean the floor and have fun at the same time."

Chris and Claire: "With our invention we always know the answers to the homework. We can read the teacher's book with our X-ray glasses."

11c
skill: writing p. 153, media worksheet 13, workbook p. 81/11-13

I **Choose one of the inventions from the box and write about it.**
II **Choose two of the inventions from the box and write about them.**
III **Write about the inventions from the box.**

close-your-eyes lamp · singing toilet roll · homework butler

More inventions

12 CHOOSE YOUR LEVEL grammar: passive p. 187

I Unscramble the sentences and write them down.

1 in 1860. – invented – Dog biscuits – were
2 by Levi Strauss. – Blue jeans – designed – were
3 made – The first – cornflakes – in 1894. – were
4 teddy bear – The first – made – in 1902. – was

II Unscramble the two texts about dog biscuits and cornflakes. Copy one of them into your exercise book.

III Unscramble the two texts and copy them into your exercise book. Find headings for them.

For a long time, dogs were given almost exactly the same food as their owners ate: meat, vegetables and bread. Cornflakes were first made in 1894 by John Harvey Kellogg. They were originally created as a healthy food for the patients at the hospital where he worked. In 1860, James Spratt had the idea to produce special biscuits for dogs. Although there was no sugar in the first recipe, they soon became very popular as a breakfast food. They were made of flour, vegetables and a little meat and became very popular with rich dog owners.

Nouns and verbs

13a

Copy the verbs from the box. Add the nouns. You can find help in a dictionary.

begin · collect · invent · spell · build · meet · celebrate · end

You can write:
begin – beginning
collect – …

13b workbook p. 82/14–15

Look at the endings of the nouns. What do you notice? Sort them into two lists. Add more nouns.

Where is the stress?

14a audio 3/18

Listen to the words and repeat them.

vegetarian · invention · television · toothbrush · information · smartphone · communicate · inventor · understand

14b

Where is the stress? On the first, second or third syllable? Make three lists.

first syllable	second syllable	third syllable
television	*invention*	*vegetarian*
…	…	…

DIGITAL+ practise more 22

ACTIVATE PRACTISE DEVELOP **PRACTISE** APPLY

Ideas for a new invention TARGET TASK

15 workbook p. 83/16, skill: giving a presentation p. 158, wordbank: inventions, presenting something p. 168, media worksheet 13

Your task is to present your ideas for a new invention.
Before you start, look at these steps:

STEP 1
Work with a partner or in a small group.

STEP 2
Think of objects that should be invented or objects that you would like to improve.
You can think of something from the following categories:
- food
- school
- tasks at home
- free time and holidays
- medicine
- travel
- …

STEP 3
Agree on one object and be creative: what should the object be able to do?
How could it help people? Which problem should it solve?
Make notes and make a draft.

STEP 4
Decide how you would like to present your idea. You can:
- make a collage and label it
- draw a picture and label it
- write a text
- …

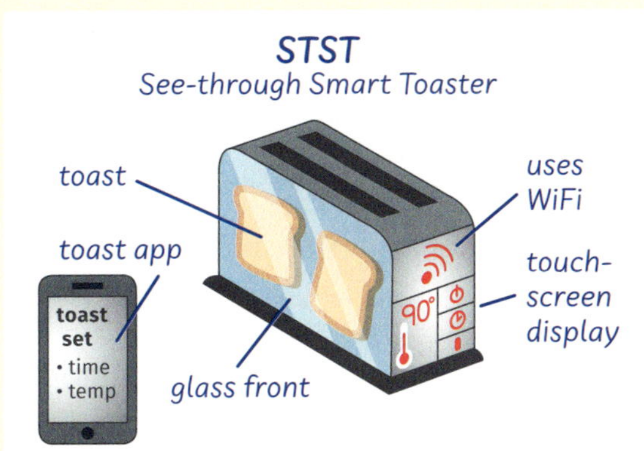

STEP 5
Create your collage, picture, text, …
Check it.

STEP 6
Present your ideas in class.

Communication

1 workbook p. 84/1

How do people communicate with each other? Collect ideas in class.

You can say:

Many people use … to communicate.

Some people use …

Project week at Holland Park School

2a skill: reading p. 154

Scan the noticeboard. What is the topic of the project week? What workshops are there?

PROJECT WEEK – COMMUNICATION IN THE PAST AND PRESENT

Workshop 1: Written communication – from hieroglyphs to emojis
From hieroglyphs in ancient Egypt to then writing postcards and letters on paper to sending texts with your smartphone – in this workshop we are going to look at the development of writing and the history of written communication. For the presentation we are going to learn different ways to do a digital presentation.

Workshop 2: The history of the telephone
From the beginnings to your smartphone – in this workshop we are going to focus on the development of the telephone. We are going to build models of low-tech telephones that work without electricity. At the end of the workshop we are going to present our results on different posters.

Workshop 3: Radio and TV
No streaming, no video on demand, no podcasts – can you imagine life in the early days of radio and TV? In this workshop we are going to look at the history of radio and TV and record our own radio or TV show to present our findings.

GENERAL INFORMATION

All groups have to do research at the library.

At the end of the week all students are going to show their results and give short presentations on their topic.

All groups have to write handouts for the other students.

2b CHOOSE YOUR LEVEL workbook p. 84/2

I Read the texts on the noticeboard and correct the statements.

1 In workshop 1, students are going to learn how to do a poster presentation.
2 The students in workshop 2 are going to focus on the development of radios.
3 In workshop 3, students are going to look at the history of writing.

II Are the statements true or false?
Read the texts on the noticeboard and correct the false statements.

1 Students can explore the future of written communication in workshop 1.
2 In workshop 1, students are going to make paper.
3 In workshop 2, students are going to look at the beginnings of the telephone.
4 They are going to build models of high-tech telephones in workshop 2.
5 In workshop 3, students are going to create posters about their findings.

III Read the texts on the noticeboard and answer the questions.

1 What kind of presentation are the students in workshop 1 going to do?
2 How are the students going to present the results of workshop 2?
3 What are the newer developments in the area of radio and TV?
4 Where do all students have to do research?
5 What do all groups have to prepare for the other students?

Talking about the workshops

3a audio 3/19, skill: listening p. 151

Listen to Ava, Lily, Harry and Tarek. Who is going to take part in which workshop?

You can write:

Ava is going to take part in workshop …
Lily is going to …
…

3b skill: talking with people p. 152, workbook p. 84/3

Which workshop would you be interested in? Talk to a partner.

You can say:

I would be interested in the workshop on …
I would choose … because …

GRAMMAR HELP the going to-future (R) p. 188–189

Wenn du sagen möchtest, was jemand für die Zukunft plant oder beabsichtigt, benutzt du das *going to-future*. Du benutzt es auch, wenn du ausdrücken möchtest, dass etwas mit großer Wahrscheinlichkeit passieren wird. Schau dir die Beispiele an. Was fällt dir auf?

Harry thinks the workshop is going to be a bit boring.	Harry denkt, dass der Workshop ein bisschen langweilig sein wird.
We are going to produce our own show.	Wir werden unsere eigene Show produzieren.
I am not going to choose the workshop on the history of the telephone.	Ich werde den Workshop über die Geschichte des Telefons nicht auswählen.

Auf den Seiten 188 und 189 findest du weitere Erklärungen und Beispiele zum *going to-future*.

They are going to …

4 grammar: going to-future p. 188, workbook p. 85/4

Write down what is going to happen.

Anna: get dirty

Tim and Bob: miss bus

Suzy: fall off horse

Dan: wake up soon

You can write:

Anna is going to get dirty.

Tim and Bob are …

Plans

5a grammar: going to-future p. 188

Read Lily's planner.
What is she going to do next week?
What is she not going to do? Write it down.

Monday afternoon: meet Ava
Tuesday: ~~do yoga with Olivia~~
Wednesday: hand in English homework
Thursday: do research
Friday afternoon: ~~do some upcycling~~, go skateboarding (park)

You can write:

Next Monday afternoon, Lily is going to …

Next Tuesday, Lily is not going to …

5b grammar: going to-future p. 188–189, workbook p. 85/5

Work with a partner. Ask and answer questions about his or her plans for next week.

You can ask:

Are you going to … next Monday afternoon?

Are you going to …?

You can answer:

Yes, I am.

No, I'm not. I'm going to …

DIGITAL+ practise more 23

At the library

6a audio 3/20

Listen to the dialogue and read along. Why are the friends at the library?

Tarek: Lily, why did you bring your tablet? I thought we came here for the books.
Lily: Yes, we did. But I'm going to take notes on my tablet.
Harry: Cool. You're connected to the school network and the Internet, aren't you? Can I use your tablet when you're done with it, Lily?
Lily: Sure. I'm going to have a look at the books first, so you can use the tablet now. I hope they have some useful books on ancient Egypt.
Ava: Hey guys, look. I've found all these books on the history of TV and radio. Harry, come on! You're in my workshop, too.
Harry: No, thanks, Ava. I'm going to use modern methods and research online.
Tarek: But Mr Patel told us to use books.
Harry: No, he didn't. He told us to go to the library to do research. And where are we now? Right. I'm going to find all the information I need on the Internet.

6b audio 3/21

Listen to the rest of the dialogue. What are the friends talking about?

6c CHOOSE YOUR LEVEL skill: listening p. 151

I Listen again. Choose the correct word or phrase and write down the sentences.

1 Harry used a **search engine / dictionary** and has 59 pages of information now.
2 Mr Patel said it was **not important / important** that the students really understand the texts.
3 Harry **has named / has not named** his sources.

II Listen again. Complete the sentences.

1 Harry copied all the ??? into his document.
2 He has no idea what is ??? and what is not.
3 Lily says that he has to ??? his sources and save the ??? to the pages where he found his information.
4 Ava gives Harry a ??? and Tarek suggests that he should make a poster about his findings.

III Listen again. Copy the true sentences and correct the false sentences.

1 Harry used a search engine and has 59 pages of information now.
2 Harry understands all the texts and knows exactly what is important.
3 Lily says that they have to name their sources.
4 Harry has saved the links of the pages where he found his information.

6d workbook p. 86/6-7

Listen to the rest of the dialogue again and take notes on what is important when doing research online. Use your notes and write down tips in German.

The history of communication

7a skill: reading p. 154

Lily found some information for her project. Skim the texts. Match the headings to the texts.

The invention of paper | Modern communication | Rock art | First letters

You can say:

Text number … matches the heading …

1. The beginning of writing can be seen in rock art – pictures that people painted on stone.
Some of these pictures are more than 28,000 years old. There are different theories on why people created them. Maybe they wanted to remember special events or tell a story or maybe the pictures had a religious function.

2. Already in 9,000 BC, people used pictures and signs on stone tablets to make notes. The first letters, the hieroglyphs, were invented by people in ancient Egypt about 3,000 BC. With hieroglyphs, people could tell longer stories in writing. People in ancient Egypt also invented papyrus, which made writing a lot easier.

3. Before papyrus and paper were invented, people used stone or clay tablets to write on. Paper was first used by the Chinese around 105 AD. From then on paper was used in communication for letters and – perhaps even more important – books.

With the invention of the modern printing press in the 15th century, information could travel faster and wider than ever before.

4. The invention of the computer changed the way we communicate once more. 🙂
The first email was sent in 1971 by computer engineer Raymond Tomlinson. The rise of the Internet began in the 1990s and smartphones appeared in the 2000s. 😉
Texting, messaging and emojis 🙂 have made it even easier and quicker to keep in touch with each other, and many people like a simple and uncomplicated 'thumbs up'. 👍

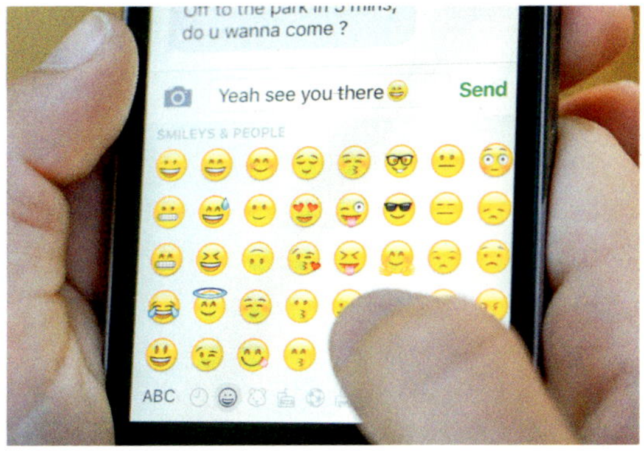

7b CHOOSE YOUR LEVEL

I Choose one of the texts and read it. Take notes on the most important facts.

II Choose two of the texts and read them. Take notes on the most important facts.

III Choose three of the texts and read them. Take notes on the most important facts.

7c workbook p. 87/8-9

Share your findings in class. Organize them in a table.

What?	*When?*	*Where?*	*Who?*	*Other information*
pictures on stone	…	…	…	…
…	…	…	…	…

An interview

8 skill: talking with people p. 152, wordbank: communication p. 169, workbook p. 87/10

Work with a partner. Interview each other about your communication habits.

You can ask:

How often do you text someone?
Do you write letters or postcards?
How do you contact your grandparents?
Have you ever made a video call?
What's your favourite way to communicate?
…

You can answer:

I often / sometimes / never text …
Yes, I do. / No, I don't. I …
I write / text / phone …
Yes, I have. / No, I haven't. I …
My favourite way to communicate is …
…

A challenge

9a video 15

Watch the video clip. What is Zara's challenge?

You can say:

Zara's challenge is to …

…

9b skill: watching a video clip p. 156, workbook p. 88/11

Watch the video clip again and take notes. What are difficult situations for Zara? How does she solve her problems?

You can say:

Difficult situations for Zara are …

She solves her problems by …

…

Modern technology

10 CHOOSE YOUR TASK C: wordbank: inventions p. 168, media worksheet 13

A **Design at least one new emoji and explain what it stands for.**

B **Imagine a day without your phone, your tablet and your console. Describe the situations in which you would miss them. How do you help yourself?**

On a day without my phone,

I wouldn't be able to …

I could …

My friends would …

C **Design an app that solves one of your everyday problems. Write down what problem you want to solve and how the app can help.**

Two inventions

11 GET TOGETHER workbook p. 88/12-14

Get together with a partner.
Read and talk about two different inventions.

Partner A	Partner B
I Go to page 130.	I Go to page 139.
II Go to page 133.	II Go to page 142.
III Go to page 136.	III Go to page 145.

Being online

12a

What are "dos and don'ts"? Share your ideas in class.

12b
skill: mediation p. 155

Read this list from a British magazine. Tell a partner in German what the rules say.

SIX DOS AND DON'TS FOR USING THE INTERNET

1. Only give your password to your parents, not to anyone else!
2. Don't post personal information like your name, address, phone number etc.
3. Be careful what you download. Check links before clicking on them and don't trust just anybody.
4. Don't befriend people online that you don't know in real life.
5. If someone bullies you on the Internet, don't react! Show their messages to your parents or a teacher.
6. Always treat other people on the Internet in the way you would like to be treated. Use respectful language.

12c
wordbank: going online p. 169, media worksheet 7, workbook p. 89/15

Work with a partner. Can you think of any more dos and don'ts for using the Internet? Collect as many as you can and share your ideas in class. You can collect your ideas in German.

A presentation

13a
video 16

Watch Jason's presentation. What is it about?

13b
skill: watching a video clip p. 156

Go to www.westermann.de/webcode and enter the webcode WES-128206-001 to find the feedback sheet. Watch the presentation again and fill it in.

13c
wordbank: presenting something p. 168, workbook p. 90/16

Give some written feedback. Do not forget to mention the positive aspects.

You can write:

At the beginning, you spoke loudly and clearly. That was good.
The pictures were very helpful.
Your summary was …
was …

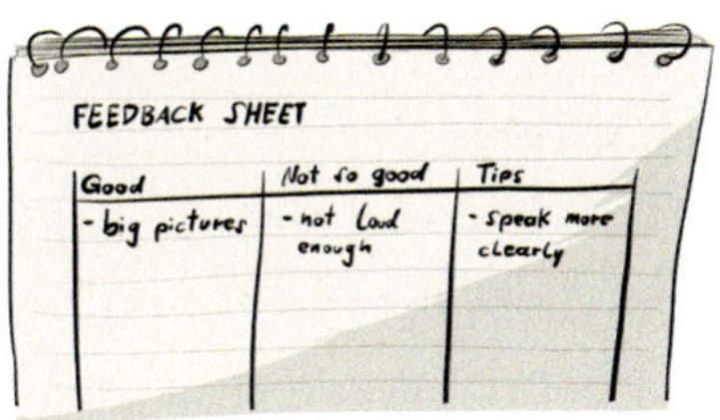

Mr Patel's feedback

14 audio 3/25, skill: listening p. 151, workbook p. 90/17

Listen to Mr Patel. He is giving feedback on another presentation. Is he happy with the student? Say why or why not.

You can say:

I think Mr Patel is happy / not happy with the student because he says …

Giving feedback

15 CHOOSE YOUR LEVEL

I Match the German and the English sentences. Write them down.

1 Das hast du gut gemacht!
2 Deine Informationen waren richtig.
3 Du hast alle Quellen genannt.
4 Die Bilder hatten die richtige Größe.

A You named all your sources.
B You did a great job!
C The pictures were the right size.
D Your information was correct.

II Match the German and the English sentences. Write them down.

1 Deine Präsentation war sehr interessant.
2 Du hast etwas zu schnell gesprochen.
3 Ich konnte einige der Bilder nicht richtig sehen, weil sie zu klein waren.
4 Du hast frei vorgetragen.

A You spoke a bit too fast.
B You spoke freely.
C Your presentation was very interesting.
D I couldn't see some of the pictures because they were too small.

III Match the sentence parts. Write down the sentences.

1 It was good that you spoke
2 I liked your
3 Why don't you use
4 You could
5 You were very well

A add some more pictures.
B prepared. You could answer all the questions.
C loudly and clearly.
D introduction. It gave me an idea about what to expect.
E words like "because" the next time?

DIGITAL+ practise more 24

A three-minute talk TARGET TASK

16 workbook p. 91/18, skill: searching the Internet p. 157, presentations p. 158, media worksheet 4, 6

Your task is to give a three-minute talk.
Before you start, look at these steps:

STEP 1

Decide what you would like to talk about. Think about:

- an invention you find interesting or useful
- one aspect of the history of communication
- ...

STEP 2

Do your research.

- Do some research on your topic. Use books or the Internet.
- Find some good pictures. Do not forget to list your sources.
- Choose texts which are easy to understand.
- Write down the most important facts in your own words.

STEP 3

Prepare your presentation.

- Read through your findings.
- Organize the information. What is important? What is not?
- In which order do you want to present the facts?
- You can make a digital presentation or a poster.
- Write the most important facts of your presentation on cue cards.

STEP 4

Practise your presentation with a partner.

- Use your cue cards.
- Give each other feedback.

STEP 5

Give your presentation.

In my presentation, I'm going to talk about …
This is a picture of …
Now I'd like to talk about …
If you look at this …, you'll see …
My next point is …
Finally, …

Check out

1. Kannst du über Erfindungen sprechen? Workbook, p. 92
2. Kannst du einem Gespräch Informationen entnehmen? Workbook, p. 92
3. Kannst du Informationen aus einem deutschen Museumsflyer auf Englisch wiedergeben? Workbook, p. 92
4. Kannst du einem Aushang die wichtigsten Inhalte entnehmen? Workbook, p. 93
5. Kannst du über Zukünftiges schreiben? Workbook, p. 93
6. Kannst du Feedback formulieren? Workbook, p. 93

A field trip

Last Tuesday, all the students at my school in years 8 to 10 went to the Science and Industry Museum in Manchester. I love science, so I was quite excited to go. Jamie wasn't that excited, but he said it would be better than a day at school.

We went to Manchester by train, but I didn't see Jamie at all because there were so many of us. My group almost lost Daniel Thomas from my class twice before we even got to the museum.

The first time was at the station in Manchester. Ms Barlow, one of the teachers who was with us, counted us to make sure no one was missing. "40, 41, 42," Ms Barlow went. "42, 42, wait, where's 43? There should be 43 of us. MS KERSHAAAAAAW!"
Ms Kershaw is the other teacher who went with us because 43 students were about 42 too many for Ms Barlow, who is always a bit nervous. Also, Ms Barlow doesn't teach our class so she didn't know Daniel Thomas. She didn't know that he always gets lost. Sometimes he gets lost at school on his way to class …
But anyway, Ms Barlow was getting really nervous: "Ms Kershaw! There's one student missing. WHO IS MISSING? WHO IS …?"
Suddenly, Daniel Thomas said, "I'm here. Everything is OK."
"Oh," Ms Barlow said. "Yeah, alright. Let's go then."

The museum was not too far from the station so we walked there because Ms Barlow and Ms Kershaw thought it would be good for us to get some exercise. But maybe that wasn't such a good idea because we lost Daniel Thomas for the second time. On the way he met this very nice little old lady who asked him where Manchester Cathedral was. Daniel Thomas told her that he didn't know because he was from London, and then the lady told him that she liked London a lot, and then they talked about London for a bit. Ms Kershaw, who counted us at the entrance of the museum, didn't get as nervous as Ms Barlow at the station, but when Daniel Thomas appeared, she wasn't very friendly to him.

When we were finally ready and could go inside, there were sooooo many cool things. We started with a guided tour of the exhibition.
"Hi, I'm Ben," the guide said. "I'll show you around our Science of the Future exhibition today.
This way please, we'll begin with the section on drones."

field trip = *Exkursion;* be missing = *fehlen;* get lost = *verloren gehen;* guided tour = *Führung;* section = *Abteilung;* drone = *Drohne*

Ben was really nice, and he told us about how science and technology and inventions might develop in the future. We were allowed to try things out, and he asked me to control a robot just by moving my eyeballs. The robot followed my eyeballs, and I could give it simple orders by opening and closing my eyes. That was brilliant.

Daniel Thomas almost got lost again at the station with the VR glasses. He put on a pair and then just walked around. We found him when he crashed into one of the tables at the back of the exhibition hall.

Ben continued to be friendly, but he seemed to become a bit nervous, too. He did the rest of the tour a lot faster than the first bit. But that was good, because after the tour we were allowed to walk around the museum by ourselves. "But remember to be back at the meeting point near the main entrance at two o'clock for our lunch break. Don't break anything and stay inside the exhibition area. Don't leave the museum and don't go anywhere you're not allowed to go. Is that clear?" Ms Kershaw asked.
"Yes, Ms Kershaw," we all said.

I wandered around and met Jamie at the Textiles Gallery. Jamie is always reading books about the past so this part of the museum was exactly right for him.
There was a lot about Manchester's past as the centre of the cotton industry. There was a real Spinning Jenny, and one of the people working at the museum showed us how it worked. She even let us try it. I wasn't very good at spinning, but Jamie was really talented. The next time Mum takes us to anything medieval, HE gets the spinning wheel!

Just when we wanted to leave the Textiles Gallery, I saw Daniel Thomas walking through a door with a sign on it that said "NO ENTRY!"
"Oh no," I thought. "Not again."
I knew exactly what was going to happen: Ms Kershaw would count at the meeting point, Daniel Thomas would be missing, Ms Barlow would be first nervous and then hysterical, we might even have to miss lunch and maybe our train, then someone would call the police ... but I would not let that happen!
"Come on, Jamie," I said and pulled him with me through the door. "Hey! What ...?" Jamie said, "Lucy, we can't just go there. We're not allowed here. There might be ... Wow!"

develop = *sich entwickeln;* eyeball = *Augapfel;* order = *Befehl;* meeting point = *Treffpunkt;* spinning wheel = *Spinnrad;* entry = *Zutritt*

"Wow!" was about right. We were standing in a huge hall with shelves everywhere. On the shelves were collections of everything you can imagine. There were old machines, furniture, books and paintings.

Then I saw Daniel Thomas. He was looking at a huge machine which had a wheel and something that looked like a hammer.

"That's an early steam engine," Jamie said.

"And over there is a time travelling machine. Unfortunately it's broken so we now have visitors from the future in Manchester. But they don't show themselves.", Daniel Thomas replied.

"But that's a …" Jamie began.

"Oh, and there's a telescope that lets you see the people who live on Mars," Daniel Thomas went on.

"No, that's a …" Jamie tried to say again. But then he seemed to get it – that this was the best part of the museum because there was no one there to tell us what everything was. We could make up our own stories!

"Oh yes," he said and pointed at something that looked like a collage of newspapers, umbrellas and shoes, "that's a piece of art from a group of people who live on the underground in London. They travel on the Tube all the time and collect the things that people forget.

They take everything to a secret tunnel, which they call "the place where it happens", and they create art." Daniel Thomas was looking at Jamie as if he thought Jamie was the cleverest person he had ever met. "Whoa, you're really good at this. Let's go on," he said.

We had so much fun! We found a calculator for numbers that haven't been invented yet, the last egg of the last British dragon, and a lot of other interesting things. Sometimes you find the best places when you are lost!

Luckily, at quarter to two, we found a clock that was still working and showed the correct time.

We were on time for the lunch break so Ms Barlow didn't have to get nervous again.

On the way back to the station, I made sure that I could always see Daniel Thomas.

But when we were finally safely on the train, I relaxed a little.

At the station in Stoke-on-Trent Ms Barlow counted us again.

"40, 41, 42," she went. "42, 42, WHERE IS 43?"

steam engine = *Dampfmaschine;* time travelling = *Zeitreisen;* secret = *geheim;* had met = *hatte getroffen;* be lost = *sich verirrt haben*

Inventions inspired by nature

burdock plant

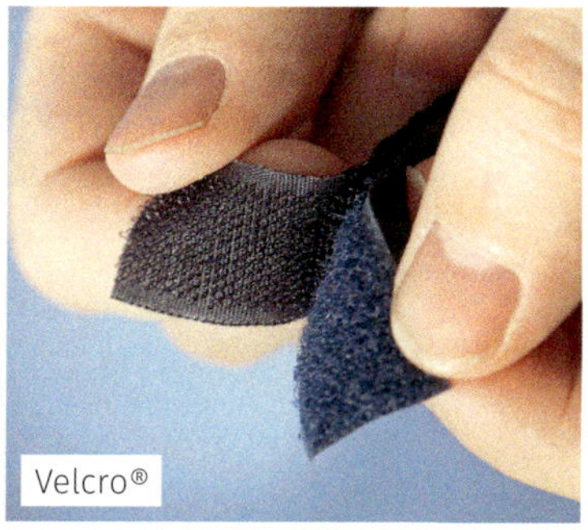
Velcro®

Did you know that the hook-and-loop fastener, or Velcro®, was inspired by the burdock plant?
The seeds of the plant stick to clothes because they have lots of little hooks.

bat

walking stick for the blind

Bats can fly in complete darkness because they give off sounds that echo back.
Scientists invented a walking stick for the blind that was inspired by bats. Like a bat, the walking stick can send and receive sound waves. The stick 'sees' objects on the ground and warns the user.

kingfisher

The first Japanese high-speed train could travel over 200 km/h. But going that fast caused a loud noise when the train left a tunnel. Engineers turned to nature to solve the problem. The high-speed train was inspired by the kingfisher.
Their beaks hardly make a ripple when they hit the water to catch fish. Today, Japan's high-speed trains have long, beak-like noses and leave tunnels quietly.

high-speed train

Find out more about one of the inventions or find out about another invention that was inspired by nature. Report your findings to the class.

Ordering food

9a UNIT 1, p. 25 PARTNER A

You and your partner would like to order some food. You are looking at two different menus. Tell your partner about your restaurant and agree on one menu.

Paolo's Pizza Palace – Italian restaurant

SPECIAL OFFER FOR 2
- 2 Pizzas
- 2 Drinks
- 2 Desserts

for just £29.99

DRINKS

Water, lemonade, cola	£2.20
Orange or apple juice	£2.50

STARTERS

Mixed salad	£6.30
Tomato soup *with bread*	£5.95

PIZZAS

Margherita *tomatoes, cheese*	£10.95
Fresh from the sea *tomato sauce, octopus*	£13.95
Farmhouse *tomato sauce, bacon, mushrooms, onions*	£13.95
Spinach *mozzarella, spinach, garlic*	£11.95

DESSERTS

Tiramisu	£3.95
Ice cream	£2.95

You can say:

I've got a menu from an Italian restaurant.
They have …
I really like …
I don't like …
Let's order …
…

You can ask:

What menu have you got?
Have they got … ?
Do you like …?
How much is …?
What about …?
…

9b UNIT 1 p. 25 PARTNER A

Look at the menu you agreed on. Write down what you would like to order.

9c UNIT 1 p. 25 PARTNER A

Do a role play – you call the restaurant and order your food.
Your partner answers the phone.
You can record your dialogue if you like.

You can say:

I would like to order …
How much is it?
How long will it take?
Thank you very much.

What do they miss?

9a UNIT 2, p. 48 PARTNER A, audio 1/34, skill: listening p. 151

Copy the table. Then listen to Jacob and Ben in hospital. What does Ben miss? Complete the table for Ben.

Ben			meeting friends at school	ice hockey practice	sleeping in
Jacob			inline skating	going swimming	playing the guitar with his band

9b UNIT 2, p. 48 PARTNER A

Work with your partner. Find out what Jacob is missing. Ask and answer questions and complete the table for Jacob. What activity do both of the boys miss?

Which festival?

10a UNIT 3, p. 73 PARTNER A

Read the table. Then ask and answer questions with your partner and write down the information for the gaps.

You can ask:

Which festival is …?

Where is the …?

You can answer:

The … is in …

It's in / on …

It costs … pounds (and … pence).

Which festival?	Where?	When?	How much?	Other information
1	2	usually in February	different fees for different events	three days with Viking events all around York
The Garlic Festival	Isle of Wight	third weekend in August	one day for adults: £12.50, for children: £7.50	garlic lovers from around the world come to the Isle of Wight
The Children's Festival	Edinburgh	27 May to 4 June	adult or child as part of family: £9.00	12 events at different places, lots of activities
The Big Feastival	the Cotswolds	August	weekend for adults: £187.95, weekend for children: £41.80	a family-friendly festival with great music, great food and lots of activities for children

10b UNIT 3, p. 73 PARTNER A, wordbank: what's on? p. 164

Which festival would you like to go to? Why? Tell your partner.

You can say:

I would like to go to the … because I like …

…

Sheree's problems

9a UNIT 4, p. 96 PARTNER A, audio 3/5, skill: listening p. 151

Listen to Sheree's call to the teen helpline. Which of these problems does Sheree have? Write down the correct sentences.

1 Her parents are very strict.
2 She is not allowed to play video games.
3 She is really bad at school.
4 She has to do too many chores.
5 Her sister never has to help.

9b UNIT 4, p. 96 PARTNER A

Tell your partner about Sheree's problems. Then listen to your partner. What advice does Gemma from the teen helpline offer? Take notes.

9c UNIT 4, p. 96 PARTNER A

Work with your partner and match Gemma's tips to Sheree's problems.

You can say:

When Sheree says …, Gemma suggests …

…

Two inventions

11a UNIT 5, p. 120 PARTNER A, skill: reading p. 154

Read the text about the hippo roller. Take notes about the most important facts.

The hippo roller

The problem: many people have to walk very far to get clean water. Then they must carry the water on their head. That means that they cannot transport a lot of water.
The idea: the hippo roller. You fill it with water and roll it, so you do not have to carry the water. Getting water is a lot easier when you use the hippo roller because you can transport more water in one go.

11b UNIT 5, p. 120 PARTNER A

Use your notes and tell your partner about the hippo roller.

You can say:

Many people have to …

That means that…

When you use the hippo roller you can …

…

Ordering food

9a UNIT 1, p. 25 PARTNER A

You and your partner would like to order some food. You are looking at menus from two different restaurants. Tell your partner about your restaurant and agree on one menu.

Paolo's Pizza Palace - Italian restaurant

SPECIAL OFFER FOR 2
- 2 Pizzas
- 2 Drinks
- 2 Desserts

for just £29.99

DRINKS

Water, lemonade, cola	£2.20
Juice (orange, apple)	£2.50

STARTERS

Garlic bread Fresh bread with garlic	£1.85
Mixed salad Salad with our special dressing	£6.30
Tomato soup Home-made tomato soup with freshly-baked bread	£5.95

PIZZAS

Margherita tomatoes, cheese, basil	£10.95
Fresh from the sea tomato sauce, octopus	£13.95
Farmhouse tomato sauce, bacon, mushrooms, onions	£13.95
Spinach mozzarella, spinach, garlic	£11.95
Ham-ster tomato sauce, ham, onions	£11.95

DESSERTS

Tiramisu	£3.95
Ice cream	£2.95
Sorbet	£2.95

You can say:

I've got a menu from an Italian restaurant.
They have …
I really like …
I don't like …
Let's order …
…

You can ask:

What menu have you got?
Have they got … at your place?
Do you like …?
How much is …?
What about …?
…

9b UNIT 1 p. 25 PARTNER A

Look at the menu you agreed on. Write down what you would like to order.

9c UNIT 1 p. 25 PARTNER A

Do a role play – you call the restaurant and order your food.
Your partner answers the phone.
You can record your dialogue if you like.

You can say:

I would like to order …
How much is it? How long will it take?
Thank you very much.

What do they miss?

9a UNIT 2, p. 48 PARTNER A, audio 1/34, skill: listening p. 151

Copy the table. Then listen to Jacob and Ben in hospital. What does Ben miss? Complete the table for Ben.

Ben				*ice hockey practice*	*sleeping in*
Jacob			*going swimming*	*playing the guitar with his band*	

9b UNIT 2, p. 48 PARTNER A

Work with your partner. Find out what Jacob is missing. Ask and answer questions and complete the table for Jacob. What activity do both of the boys miss?

Which festival?

10a UNIT 3, p. 73 PARTNER A

Read the table. Then ask and answer questions with your partner and write down the information for the gaps.

You can ask:

Which festival is …?
Where is the …?
When is the …?

You can answer:

The … is in …
It's in / on …
It costs … pounds (and … pence).

Which festival?	Where?	When?	How much?	Other information
1	2	*usually in February*	*different fees for different events*	*three days packed with Viking events all around York*
The Garlic Festival	*Isle of Wight*	*third weekend in August*	*one day for adults: £12.50 for children: £7.50*	*garlic lovers from around the world come to the Isle of Wight to get a taste*
The Children's Festival	*Edinburgh*	*27 May to 4 June*	*adult or child as part of family: £9.00*	*12 performances at different places, lots of additional activities*
The Big Feastival	*the Cotswolds*	3	*weekend for adults: £187.95, weekend for children: £41.80*	*a family-friendly festival with great music, great food and lots of activities for children*

10b UNIT 3, p. 73 PARTNER A, wordbank: what's on? p. 164

Which festival would you like to go to? Why? Tell your partner.

You can say:

I would like to go to the … because I like …

Sheree's problems

9a UNIT 4, p. 96 PARTNER A, audio 3/5, skill: listening p. 151

Listen to Sheree's call to the teen helpline. What are her problems? Take notes.

You can write:

Her parents …

She is not allowed to …

She has to …

9b UNIT 4, p. 96 PARTNER A

Tell your partner about Sheree's problems. Then listen to your partner. What advice does Gemma from the teen helpline offer? Take notes.

9c UNIT 4, p. 96 PARTNER A

Work with your partner and match Gemma's tips to Sheree's problems.

You can say:

When Sheree says …, Gemma suggests …

…

Two inventions

11a UNIT 5, p. 120 PARTNER A, skill: reading p. 154

Read the text about the hippo roller. Take notes about the most important facts.

The hippo roller

The problem: many people have to walk very far to get clean water. The traditional way is to carry the water on your head. That means that one person cannot transport a lot of water.

The idea: the hippo roller. You fill it with water and pull or push it, so you do not have to carry all the weight. Getting water is a lot easier because you can transport more water in one go, which saves a lot of time and energy.

11b UNIT 5, p. 120 PARTNER A

Use your notes and tell your partner about the hippo roller.

You can say:

Many people have to …

The traditional way is to …

That means that…

When you use the hippo roller you can …

…

Ordering food

9a UNIT 1, p. 25 PARTNER A

You and your partner would like to order some food. You are looking at menus from two different restaurants. Tell your partner about your restaurant and agree on where to order.

Paolo's Pizza Palace – Italian restaurant

SPECIAL OFFER FOR 2
- 2 Pizzas
- 2 Drinks
- 2 Desserts

for just £29.99

DRINKS

Water, lemonade, cola	£2.20
Juice (orange, apple)	£2.50

STARTERS

Garlic bread *Fresh bread with olive oil and garlic*	£1.85
Mixed salad *Salad with fresh tomatos and our special dressing*	£6.30
Tomato soup *Home-made tomato soup with freshly-baked bread*	£5.95

PIZZAS

Margherita *tomatoes, cheese, basil*	£10.95
Fresh from the sea *tomato sauce, octopus*	£13.95
Farmhouse *tomato sauce, bacon, mushrooms, onions*	£13.95
Cheer for cheese *tomato sauce, four different kinds of cheese*	£12.95
Spinach *mozzarella, spinach, garlic*	£11.95
Ham-ster *tomato sauce, ham, onions*	£11.95

DESSERTS

Tiramisu	£3.95
Ice cream	£2.95
Sorbet	£2.95

9b UNIT 1 p. 25 PARTNER A

Look at the menu you agreed on. Write down what you would like to order.

You can say:

I've got a menu from an Italian restaurant.
They have …
I really like …
I don't like …
Let's order …
…

You can ask:

What menu have you got?
Have they got … at your place?
Do you like …?
How much is …?
What about …?
…

9c UNIT 1 p. 25 PARTNER A

Do a role play – you call the restaurant and order your food. Your partner answers the phone. You can record your dialogue if you like.

You can say:

I would like to order …
How much is it?
Thank you very much.
…

What do they miss?

9a UNIT 2, p. 48 PARTNER A, audio 1/34, skill: listening p. 151

Copy the table. Then listen to Jacob and Ben in hospital. What does Ben miss? Complete the table for Ben.

Ben					*sleeping in*
Jacob					*playing the guitar with his band*

9b UNIT 2, p. 48 PARTNER A

Work with your partner. Find out what Jacob is missing. Ask and answer questions and complete the table for Jacob. What activity do both of the boys miss?

Which festival?

10a UNIT 3, p. 73 PARTNER A

Read the table. Then ask and answer questions with your partner and write down the information for the gaps.

You can ask:

Which festival is in / on …?
Have you got any other information on …?
…

You can answer:

It's …
Yes, there is / are …
…

Which festival?	Where?	When?	How much?	Other information
1	2	*usually in February*	3	*three days packed with Viking events all around York*
The Garlic Festival	*Isle of Wight*	*third weekend in August*	*one day for adults: £12.50, for children: £7.50*	*garlic lovers from around the world come to the Isle of Wight to get a taste*
The Children's Festival	*Edinburgh*	*27 May to 4 June*	4	*12 performances at different places, lots of additional activities*
The Big Feastival	*the Cotswolds*	5	*weekend for adults: £187.95, weekend for children: £41.80*	*a family-friendly festival with great music, great food and lots of activities for children*

10b UNIT 3, p. 73 PARTNER A, wordbank: what's on? p. 164

Which festival would you like to go to? Why? Tell your partner.

Sheree's problems

9a UNIT 4, p. 96 PARTNER A, audio 3/5, skill: listening p. 151

Listen to Sheree's call to the teen helpline. What are her problems? Take notes.

9b UNIT 4, p. 96 PARTNER A

Tell your partner about Sheree's problems. Then listen to your partner. What advice does Gemma from the teen helpline offer? Take notes.

9c UNIT 4, p. 96 PARTNER A

Work with your partner and match Gemma's tips to Sheree's problems.

Two inventions

11a UNIT 5, p. 120 PARTNER A, skill: reading p. 154

Read the text about the hippo roller. Take notes about the most important facts.

The hippo roller

The problem: in a lot of African countries, people have to walk long distances to get clean water. The traditional way is to carry the water on your head. But that means that one person cannot transport a lot of water. Often children have to do this chore. This chore takes up a lot of their time, so they cannot go to school.

The idea: the hippo roller. You fill it with water and push or pull it, so you do not have to carry all the weight. Getting water is a lot easier when you use it because you can transport more water in one go, which saves a lot of time and energy. Unfortunately, it does not solve the problem that there is not enough clean water for everyone.

11b UNIT 5, p. 120 PARTNER A

Use your notes and tell your partner about the hippo roller.

Ordering food

9a UNIT 1, p. 25 PARTNER B

You and your partner would like to order some food. You are looking at two different menus. Tell your partner about your restaurant and agree on one menu.

The Wonton Wok – the best Chinese restaurant in town

Special offer for just £25.50
- 2 soups
- 2 main courses
- 2 desserts

DRINKS

Water, lemonade, cola	£2.20
Green tea	£1.95

SOUPS

Chicken soup Delicious hot soup	£5.40
Spring soup Vegetable soup	£2.30

MAIN COURSES

Spring rolls Five large spring rolls with meat	£9.95
Vegetarian spring rolls Five large spring rolls with vegetables	£7.95
Mango chilli chicken Chicken cooked with mango and chilli	£11.95
Dim Sum A selection of traditional Chinese food	£11.95

DESSERTS

Baked banana with honey	£3.95
Ice cream	£2.95

You can say:

I've got a menu from a Chinese restaurant.
They have …
I really like …
I don't like …
Let's order …
…

You can ask:

What menu have you got?
Have they got …?
Do you like …?
How much is …?
What about …?
…

9b UNIT 1 p. 25 PARTNER B

Look at the menu you agreed on. Write down what you would like to order.

9c UNIT 1 p. 25 PARTNER B

Do a role play – your partner calls the restaurant and orders your food.
You answer the phone.
You can record your dialogue if you like.

You can say:

Hello, this is the Wonton Wok.
What can I do for you?
It's … pounds …
It will take … minutes.
…

What do they miss?

9a UNIT 2, p. 48 PARTNER B audio 1/34, skill: listening p. 151

Copy the table. Then listen to Jacob and Ben in hospital. What does Jacob miss? Complete the table for Jacob.

Jacob			*inline skating*	*going swimming*	*playing the guitar with his band*
Ben			*meeting friends at school*	*ice hockey practice*	*sleeping in*

9b UNIT 2, p. 48 PARTNER B

Work with your partner. Find out what Ben is missing. Ask and answer questions and complete the table for Ben. What activity do both of the boys miss?

Which festival?

10a UNIT 3, p. 73 PARTNER B

Read the table. Then ask and answer questions with your partner and write down the information for the gaps.

You can ask:

Which festival is …?

Where is the …?

You can answer:

The … is in …

It's in / on …

It costs … pounds (and … pence).

Which festival?	Where?	When?	How much?	Other information
The Viking Festival	*York*	*usually in February*	*different fees for different events*	*three days with Viking events all around York*
The Garlic Festival	*Isle of Wight*	*third weekend in August*	*one day for adults: £12.50, for children: £7.50*	*garlic lovers from around the world come to the Isle of Wight*
1	*Edinburgh*	*27 May to 4 June*	*adult or child as part of family: £9.00*	*12 performances at different places, lots of activities*
The Big Feastival	2	*August*	*weekend for adults: £187.95, weekend for children: £41.80*	*a family-friendly festival with great music, great food and lots of activities for children*

10b UNIT 3, p. 73 PARTNER B, wordbank: what's on? p. 164

Which festival would you like to go to? Why? Tell your partner.

You can say:

I would like to go to the … because I like …

…

Sheree's problems

9a UNIT 4, p. 96 PARTNER B, audio 3/5, skill: listening p. 151

Listen to Sheree's call to the teen helpline. Which of these solutions does Gemma from the teen helpline suggest? Write down the correct sentences.

1 Talk to her parents.
2 Ask her parents to look at an official website about screen time for teenagers.
3 Do everything her parents say.
4 Have a family meeting.
5 Move out.

9b UNIT 4, p. 96 PARTNER B

Tell your partner about Sheree's problems. Then listen to your partner. What advice does Gemma from the teen helpline offer? Take notes.

9c UNIT 4, p. 96 PARTNER B

Work with your partner and match Gemma's tips to Sheree's problems.

You can say:

When Sheree says …, Gemma suggests …

…

Two inventions

11a UNIT 5, p. 120 PARTNER B, skill: reading p. 154

Read the text about the pot-in-pot fridge. Take notes about the most important facts.

The pot-in-pot fridge

The problem: in many countries, some people have no electricity. That means they have no fridges to keep their food fresh.
The idea: you take two pots, sand and water to build a simple fridge. You put the smaller pot inside the bigger pot and fill the gap between the pots with wet sand. You put your food inside the smaller pot. When the water in the sand evaporates[1], the smaller pot becomes cooler, and fresh vegetables stay fresh for three to four weeks.

1 (to) evaporate = verdunsten

11b UNIT 5, p. 120 PARTNER B

Use your notes and tell your partner about the pot-in-pot fridge.

You can say:

Many people don't have …

So they cannot …

But you only need … to build …

…

Ordering food

9a UNIT 1, p. 25 PARTNER B

You and your partner would like to order some food. You are looking at menus from two different restaurants. Tell your partner about your restaurant and agree on one menu.

The Wonton Wok – the best Chinese restaurant in town

Special offer for just £25.50
- 2 soups
- 2 main courses
- 2 desserts

DRINKS

Water, lemonade, cola	£2.20
Juice (lychee, apple)	£2.50
Green tea	£1.95

SOUPS

Chicken soup Delicious hot soup	£5.40
Spring soup Vegetable soup	£2.30
Fish and tofu soup Fresh fish, tofu and vegetables	£3.95

MAIN COURSES

Sweet and sour pork Pork in a sweet and sour sauce	£13.95
Spring rolls Five large spring rolls with meat	£9.95
Vegetarian spring rolls Five large spring rolls with vegetables	£7.95
Mango chilli chicken Chicken cooked with mango and chilli	£11.95
Dim Sum A selection of traditional Chinese food	£11.95

DESSERTS

Baked banana with honey	£3.95
Lychees	£4.95
Ice cream	£2.95

You can say:

I've got a menu from a Chinese restaurant.
They have …
I really like …
I don't like …
Let's order …
…

You can ask:

What menu have you got?
Have they got … at your place?
Do you like …?
How much is …?
What about …?
…

9b UNIT 1 p. 25 PARTNER B

Look at the menu you agreed on. Write down what you would like to order.

9c UNIT 1 p. 25 PARTNER B

Do a role play – your partner calls the restaurant and orders your food.
You answer the phone.
You can record your dialogue if you like.

You can say:

Hello, this is the Wonton Wok.
What can I do for you?
It's … pounds …
It will take … minutes.
…

What do they miss?

9a UNIT 2, p. 48 PARTNER B, audio 1/34, skill: listening p. 151

Copy the table. Then listen to Jacob and Ben in hospital. What does Jacob miss? Complete the table for Jacob.

Jacob				*going swimming*	*playing the guitar with his band*
Ben				*ice hockey practice*	*sleeping in*

9b UNIT 2, p. 48 PARTNER B

Work with your partner. Find out what Ben is missing. Ask and answer questions and complete the table for Ben. What activity do both of the boys miss?

Which festival?

10a UNIT 3, p. 73 PARTNER B

Read the table. Then ask and answer questions with your partner and write down the information for the gaps.

You can ask:

When is the …?
Which festival is …?
Where is the …?

You can answer:

The … is in …
It's in / on …
It costs … pounds (and … pence).

Which festival?	Where?	When?	How much?	Other information
The Viking Festival	*York*	*usually in February*	*different fees for different events*	*three days packed with Viking events all around York*
The Garlic Festival	*Isle of Wight*	1	*one day for adults: £12.50, for children: £7.50*	*garlic lovers from around the world come to the Isle of Wight to get a taste*
2	*Edinburgh*	*27 May to 4 June*	*adult or child as part of family: £9.00*	*12 performances at different places, lots of additional activities*
The Big Feastival	3	*August*	*weekend for adults: £187.95, weekend for children: £41.80*	*a family-friendly festival with great music, great food and lots of activities for children*

10b UNIT 3, p. 73 PARTNER B, wordbank: what's on? p. 164

Which festival would you like to go to? Why? Tell your partner.

You can say:

I would like to go to the … because I like …
…

Sheree's problems

9a UNIT 4, p. 96 PARTNER B, audio 3/5, skill: listening p. 151

Listen to Sheree's call to the teen helpline. What solutions does Gemma from the teen helpline suggest? Take notes.

You can write:

Gemma suggests that Sheree should …

She says that Sheree could try …

…

9b UNIT 4, p. 96 PARTNER B

Listen to your partner. What are Sheree's problems? Take notes. Then tell your partner what Gemma suggests.

9c UNIT 4, p. 96 PARTNER B

Work with your partner and match Gemma's tips to Sheree's problems.

You can say:

When Sheree says …, Gemma suggests …

…

Two inventions

11a UNIT 5, p. 120 PARTNER B, skill: reading p. 154

Read the text about the pot-in-pot fridge. Take notes about the most important facts.

The pot-in-pot fridge

The problem: in many places people in the country have no electricity. That means they cannot use electrical fridges to keep their food fresh.
The idea: you only need two pots, sand and a little water to build a fridge that works without electricity. You put the smaller pot inside the bigger pot and fill the gap between the pots with wet sand. You put your food inside the smaller pot. When the water in the sand evaporates[1], the smaller pot becomes cooler, and fresh vegetables stay fresh for three to four weeks.

1 *(to) evaporate = verdunsten*

11b UNIT 5, p. 120 PARTNER B

Use your notes and tell your partner about the pot-in-pot fridge.

You can say:

Many people don't have …

So they cannot …

But you only need … to build …

…

Ordering food

9a UNIT 1, p. 25 PARTNER B

You and your partner would like to order some food. You are looking at menus from two different restaurants. Tell your partner about your restaurant and agree on where to order.

The Wonton Wok – the best Chinese restaurant in town

Special offer for just £25.50
- 2 soups
- 2 main courses
- 2 desserts

DRINKS

Water, lemonade, cola	£2.20
Juice (lychee, apple)	£2.50
Green tea	£1.95

SOUPS

Chicken soup *Delicious hot soup with chicken and noodles*	£5.40
Spring soup *Vegetable soup*	£2.30
Fish and tofu soup *Fresh fish, tofu and different vegetables*	£3.95

MAIN COURSES

Sweet and sour pork *Pork in a sweet and sour sauce*	£13.95
Spring rolls *Five large spring rolls with different vegetables and meat*	£9.95
Vegetarian spring rolls *Five large spring rolls with different vegetables*	£7.95
Garlic soy beef *Tender beef cooked in a soy sauce with garlic*	£11.95
Mango chilli chicken *Chicken cooked with mango and just enough chilli*	£11.95
Dim Sum *A selection of traditional Chinese food*	£11.95

DESSERTS

Baked banana with honey	£3.95
Lychees	£4.95
Ice cream	£2.95

You can say:

I've got a menu from a Chinese restaurant.
They have …
I really like …
I don't like …
Let's order …
…

You can ask:

What menu have you got?
Have they got … at your place?
Do you like …?
How much is …?
What about …?
…

9b UNIT 1 p. 25 PARTNER B

Look at the menu you agreed on. Write down what you would like to order.

9c UNIT 1 p. 25 PARTNER B

Do a role play – your partner calls the restaurant and orders your food. You answer the phone. You can record your dialogue if you like.

You can say:

Hello, this is the Wonton Wok.
What can I do for you?
Would you like anything else?
It's … pounds …
It will take forty minutes.
…

What do they miss?

9a UNIT 2, p. 48 PARTNER B, audio 1/34, skill: listening p. 151

Copy the table. Then listen to Jacob and Ben in hospital. What does Jacob miss? Complete the table for Jacob.

Jacob					*playing the guitar with his band*
Ben					*sleeping in*

9b UNIT 2, p. 48 PARTNER B

Work with your partner. Find out what Ben is missing. Ask and answer questions and complete the table for Ben. What activity do both of the boys miss?

Which festival?

10a UNIT 3, p. 73 PARTNER B

Read the table. Then ask and answer questions with your partner and write down the information for the gaps.

You can ask:

Which festival is in … / on …?
How much is the …?
…

You can answer:

It's …
There is … / are …
…

Which festival?	Where?	When?	How much?	Other information
The Viking Festival	*York*	*usually in February*	*different fees for different events*	*three days packed with Viking events all around York*
1	*Isle of Wight*	2	3	*garlic lovers from around the world come to the Isle of Wight to get a taste*
4	*Edinburgh*	*27 May to 4 June*	*adult or child as part of family: £9.00*	*12 performances at different places, lots of additional activities*
The Big Feastival	5	*August*	6	*a family-friendly festival with great music, great food and lots of activities for children*

10b UNIT 3, p. 73 PARTNER B, wordbank: what's on? p. 164

Which festival would you like to go to? Why? Tell your partner.

Sheree's problems

9a UNIT 4, p. 96 PARTNER B, audio 3/5, skill: listening p. 151

Listen to Sheree's call to the teen helpline. What solutions does Gemma from the teen helpline suggest? Take notes.

9b UNIT 4, p. 96 PARTNER B

Listen to your partner. What are Sheree's problems? Take notes. Then tell your partner what Gemma suggests.

9c UNIT 4, p. 96 PARTNER B

Work with your partner and match Gemma's tips to Sheree's problems.

Two inventions

11a UNIT 5, p. 120 PARTNER B, skill: reading p. 154

Read the text about the pot-in-pot fridge. Take notes about the most important facts.

The pot-in-pot fridge

The problem: in many countries people in rural areas have no electricity. That means they cannot use electrical fridges to keep their food fresh.
The idea: you only need two clay pots, sand and a little water to build a fridge that works without electricity. You put the smaller pot inside the bigger pot and fill the gap between the pots with wet sand. You put your food inside the smaller pot. When the water in the sand evaporates[1], the smaller pot becomes cooler. Fresh vegetables stay fresh for three to four weeks in the smaller pot – and people do not have to spend money on electricity!

1 (to) evaporate = verdunsten

11b UNIT 5, p. 120 PARTNER B

Use your notes and tell your partner about the pot-in-pot fridge.

A country profile: India DIGITAL+

Introduction

India is one of the biggest countries in the world.
What do you already know about India and what else would you like to know?
These are some questions you may find interesting:

- What famous sights and places are there?
- What sports are popular in India?
- What animals live in India?
- What languages are spoken in India?
- What is the historical connection with the UK?

Find answers to these and other interesting questions in a project about India!

Plan it

1 In class, collect ideas for topics you could work on. You can make notes in a word web. Here is an example:

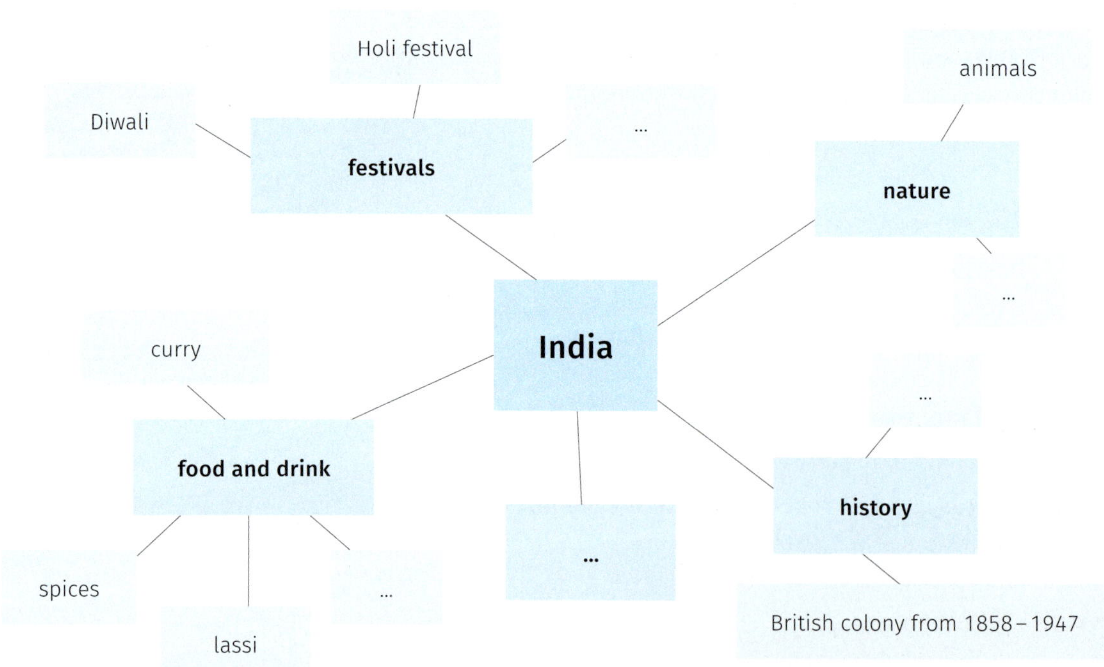

2 **Now collect ideas about what you could create. For example:**

- fact files
- posters
- pages for a computer presentation
- podcasts
- ...

Tip

You can make a class product, for example a brochure: every group creates one page and you put everything together in the end.

India
- capital: New Delhi
- population: about 1.4 billion
- languages: English, Hindi, ...
- ...

3 **Now get together in small groups and make a plan. Write down:**

- what information you need
- how you can find information
- how you want to present your work
- what material you need for your project work (for example: computer, paper, glue, ...)
- who does what and when

Tip

When you as a group have a plan about what to do and how to present your work, you can ask your classmates from other groups for feedback on your plan.

Do it

skill: searching the Internet p. 157, media worksheet 4, 6

And ... action! Do research, collect pictures, write texts, ... and create an interesting fact file, poster, computer presentation, ...

Check it

Check everything. Are there any spelling or grammar mistakes? Are the pictures big enough? Is everything easy to understand? If you want to give a presentation, practise it before you give it.

Present it

skill: presentations p. 158

Present your work. You can ask your classmates for feedback after the presentation.

Music DIGITAL+

Introduction

Music plays an important role in many people's lives. What about you? What does music mean to you? What bands or singers do you like? Do you play an instrument?

Think about the role of music in your life and explore the world of music in a project.

Plan it

1 In class, think about what you would like to do in your project. You can collect ideas in a list, for example:

- Prepare a presentation or a podcast on a band or singer.
- Present a song you like and give some background information on it.
- Write about a concert you have been to.
- Create a poster for a concert or music festival.
- Interview classmates about what music they like or what instruments they play.
- Collect quotations about music and present them in a creative way.
- ...

2 **Now collect ideas about what you could create. For example:**

- fact files
- posters
- pages for a computer presentation
- podcasts
- ...

Tip

You can make a class product, for example a music magazine: every group creates one page and you put everything together in the end.

Billie Eilish
- Birthday: 18 December 2001
- Birthplace: Los Angeles, USA
- Famous songs: Bad guy, ...
- ...

3 **Now get together in small groups and make a plan. Write down:**

- what information you need
- how you can get the information
- how you want to present your work
- what material you need for your project work (for example: computer, paper, glue, ...)
- who does what and when

Tip

When you as a group have a plan about what to do and how to present your work, you can ask your classmates from other groups for feedback on your plan.

Do it

skill: searching the Internet p. 157, media worksheet 4, 6

And ... action! Do research, collect pictures, write texts, ... and create an interesting fact file, poster, computer presentation, ...

Check it

Check everything. Are there any spelling or grammar mistakes? Are the pictures big enough? Is everything easy to understand? If you want to give a presentation, practise it before you give it.

Present it

skill: presentations p. 158

Present your work. You can ask your classmates for feedback after the presentation.

1 WORKING WITH WORDS
Wortschatzarbeit

Im *Dictionary* ab Seite 213 kannst du die Wörter aus diesem Buch und die Lernwörter aus den vorigen Bänden nachschlagen. Wenn du ein Wort suchst, das dort nicht steht, kannst du ein Wörterbuch benutzen.

1. Wörterbücher

- Die Wörter sind alphabetisch geordnet. Du darfst nicht nur auf den ersten Buchstaben achten, sondern musst auch die folgenden Buchstaben angucken: *face* steht beispielsweise vor *false*.

- Hinter den Einträgen stehen Lautschrift und Wortart. Dann folgen in einsprachigen Wörterbüchern eine Definition oder Erklärung des Wortes, in zweisprachigen Wörterbüchern die Übersetzung und Beispiele zur Verwendung des Wortes.

2. Die richtige Übersetzung finden

- Wenn du zum Beispiel ein Rezept liest und dort das Wort *season* findest, schlag im Wörterbuch unter „s", dann „se" / „sea" usw. nach, bis du das Wort findest.

Method:
1. Cut the chicken into slices. Then season the chicken with salt, pepper and curry powder.

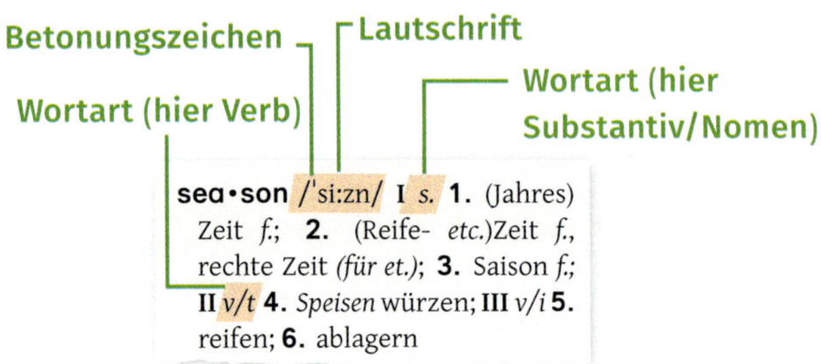

- *season* als Nomen mit der Bedeutung „Jahreszeit" oder „Saison" ergibt hier keinen Sinn. Weiter unten findest du das Verb *season*. Dort steht unter anderem der Eintrag „würzen" – das passt hier gut als Übersetzung.

- Du musst immer alle Einträge durchlesen. Dann entscheidest du, welche Übersetzung am besten passt.

Tipp: Nutze elektronische Hilfsmittel! (media worksheet 3)

- Im Internet gibt es viele Seiten, auf denen du Wörter nachschlagen und dir die richtige Aussprache anhören kannst. Oft gibt es Erklärungen zu den unterschiedlichen Bedeutungen in verschiedenen Zusammenhängen.

2 LISTENING Hören

Folgende Strategien für Hörübungen können dir helfen, Hörtexte besser zu verstehen:

1. Vor dem Hören

- Gibt es eine Höraufgabe im Buch? Lies sie dir genau durch. Was sollst du herausfinden?
- Wie lautet die Überschrift des Hörtextes? Welche Hinweise gibt sie dir?
- Gibt es Bilder? Was ist darauf zu sehen?
- Überlege: Worum könnte es gehen? Was weißt du schon über das Thema?

2. Während des Hörens

- Höre dir den Hörtext einmal ganz an. Wer spricht? Was passiert? Du musst nicht jedes einzelne Wort verstehen. Versuche erst einmal herauszufinden, worum es ganz allgemein geht *(listening for gist)*.
- Achte auch auf die Stimmen der Sprechenden und auf Hintergrundgeräusche. Sie können dir helfen zu verstehen, worum es geht.
- Sieh dir noch einmal die Aufgabe an. Dann höre wieder zu. Achte diesmal auf Details *(listening for detail)* und mache dir Notizen.

Who?	**Where?**	**When?**	**What?**
Wer spricht? Um wen geht es?	Wo findet das Gespräch / die Geschichte statt?	Wann findet das Gespräch / die Geschichte statt?	Was wird besprochen? Was passiert?

3. Nach dem Hören

- Vergleicht eure Ergebnisse. Was habt ihr herausgefunden?

Tipp: Nutze jede Gelegenheit, um Englisch zu hören!

- Alle Hörtexte zum Buch findest du, wenn du auf www.westermann.de/webcode den Webcode WES-128206-001 eingibst oder den QR-Code scannst, den du auf Seite 2 findest.
- Es gibt verschiedene Möglichkeiten, sich Texte in verschiedenen Geschwindigkeiten vorlesen zu lassen. Du kannst probieren, das Tempo nach und nach zu erhöhen.

3 TALKING WITH PEOPLE
Mit anderen sprechen

Sprich so viel Englisch wie möglich mit deinen Mitschülerinnen und Mitschülern.

1. Versuche, so viel wie möglich auf Englisch auszudrücken

- Lerne Ausdrücke auswendig, die du im Gespräch verwenden kannst, z. B. „*There is … / There are … / What about …? / Thank you. / You're welcome.*"
  Auch in den *wordbanks* ab Seite 160 findest du nützliche Ausdrücke.
- Wenn dir ein Wort, z. B. „*spoon*", nicht einfällt, kannst du es umschreiben:
  „*Excuse me, could you pass me the … erm … it's not a fork or a knife. You can eat soup with it.*"

2. Merke dir Redewendungen und Sätze

- Es gibt eine Reihe von Redewendungen und Sätzen, die du im Englischunterricht häufig verwenden kannst. Viele davon findest du bei den *classroom phrases* auf den Seiten 170-171.

3. Wenn du Interviews durchführst

- Schreibe deine Fragen auf.
- Stelle Fragen, auf die man nicht nur mit „ja" oder „nein" antworten kann: Verwende Fragewörter wie *what, when, where, who, how* oder *why*.
- Wenn du etwas nicht richtig verstanden hast, bitte um Wiederholung:
  „*Can you say that again, please?*" oder: „*Can you repeat that, please?*"

4. Sprich so oft Englisch, wie du kannst

- Höre dir die Hörtexte aus deinem Englischbuch an und lies die Texte laut mit. Versuche, die Aussprache der Sprecherinnen und Sprecher nachzuahmen.
- Singe englischsprachige Lieder mit.
- Unterhalte dich auf Englisch mit jemandem, der ebenfalls Englisch sprechen kann.

Tipp: Nimm dich auf! (media worksheet 5)

- Lies einen Text aus dem Buch laut vor oder sprich Englisch und nimm dich auf. Dann kannst du dich selbst anhören und überprüfen, wie dein Englisch klingt.
- Wenn ihr zu zweit zusammenarbeitet, könnt ihr Dialoge und Interviews aufnehmen und gemeinsam prüfen, ob es noch etwas zu verbessern gibt.

4 WRITING
Schreiben

Es ist wichtig, dass du deinen Text planst und nach dem Schreiben überarbeitest.

1. Planen

- Auf www.westermann.de/webcode kannst du den Webcode WES-128206-001 eingeben und dort Anleitungen zu verschiedenen Textsorten, z. B. Brief, E-Mail oder Blogeintrag, finden.
- Wenn du eine Geschichte schreiben willst, kannst du mithilfe von *who, what, where, when* und *why* Ideen sammeln und die Geschichte planen.
- Du kannst in einem *word web* oder in einer Liste passende Wörter sammeln. Sieh in den *wordbanks* ab Seite 160 nach, wenn du Hilfe brauchst.
- Überlege: Was sollte am Anfang stehen? Was folgt darauf? Wie könnte das Ende sein? Wie kannst du den Text interessant machen? Wenn du einen Artikel oder Bericht schreibst, solltest du dir vorher überlegen, wie du ihn gliedern möchtest.

2. Schreiben und überarbeiten

- Schreibe zuerst einen Entwurf *(draft)*.
- Überlege dir eine passende Überschrift.
- Wenn du Bilder einfügen möchtest, vergiss nicht, anzugeben, wo du sie gefunden hast.
- Überarbeite und verbessere *(edit)* dann deinen Text. Du kannst auch andere um Hilfe bitten.
- Schreibe dann deinen Text ins Reine. Das kannst du handschriftlich oder mithilfe eines Textverarbeitungsprogramms am Computer machen.

3. Veröffentlichen

- Zeige deinen fertigen Text deiner Lehrkraft, einem Mitschüler, einer Mitschülerin oder der Klasse.
- Du kannst deinen Text in deinem (digitalen) Portfolio aufbewahren.

Tipp: Texte digital erstellen und veröffentlichen (media worksheet 1, 9-15)

- Wenn du einen Text am Computer schreibst, kannst du zunächst Ideen und nützliche Wörter in einem Dokument sammeln und speichern. Du kannst deine Ideen und deinen Text jederzeit ändern und ergänzen.
- Ihr könnt eure Texte auch zu einem Klassenprodukt zusammenfügen. Vielleicht gibt es die Möglichkeit, dieses Produkt auf der Schul- oder Klassenwebseite zu veröffentlichen.

5 READING Lesen

Folgende Strategien können dir helfen, einen englischen Text zu verstehen:

1. Skimming

Beim *skimming* überfliegst du den Text erst einmal. Du verschaffst dir schnell einen Überblick: Worum geht es? Was passiert? Wer ist dabei? Du musst nicht jedes Wort verstehen.

2. Reading for detail

Du liest den Text gründlich, um möglichst viele Details herauszufinden. Mache dir Notizen. Auf Kopien oder in deinen eigenen Büchern kannst du auch wichtige Textstellen markieren. Die *wh*-Fragen können dir helfen: Who? Where? When? What?

SWIMMING IS HIS LIFE

This young man is going to make it to the top. Leroy Haffner will soon be one of Britain's best swimmers! Leroy was born in Bristol, UK. Swimming has always been his greatest love. He started swimming at the age of four. Three years later he had already won medals for his local club. He took part in one national competition after another. Then last year, Leroy had an injury and couldn't swim for nearly two months. But Leroy didn't give up. He started swimming again – and with great success. Next week, Leroy will participate in the National Championships. His coach, Ted Henley, knows that "Leroy will do really, really well".

3. Scanning

Beim *scanning* suchst du einen Text gezielt nach ganz bestimmten Informationen ab.
Wenn es wichtige Wörter gibt, die du nicht kennst, probiere Folgendes aus:

- Kennst du einzelne Teile eines langen Wortes oder ähnliche Wörter aus dem Deutschen oder aus einer anderen Sprache? Versuche, dir den Sinn des Wortes herzuleiten.
- Kannst du dir die Bedeutung eines unbekannten Wortes aus dem Textzusammenhang herleiten?

Erst, wenn das nicht funktioniert, solltest du das Wort in einem Wörterbuch nachschlagen.

Tipp: Suche dir englische Texte zu Themen, die dich interessieren!

- Du kannst im Internet und in Büchereien nach interessanten Texten auf Englisch suchen.
- Lies so viel du kannst. Am Ende jeder Unit in diesem Buch findest du eine Kurzgeschichte und einen Sachtext oder ein Gedicht.

6 MEDIATION
Sprachmittlung

Manchmal gibt es Situationen, in denen du jemandem helfen musst, der deine Muttersprache oder eine Fremdsprache nicht so gut kann wie du.

1. Gib den Sinn wieder
Übersetze nicht alles Wort für Wort. Wichtiger ist es, den Sinn wiederzugeben.

2. Fasse dich kurz
Bilde einfache, kurze Sätze. Unwichtige Einzelheiten kannst du weglassen.

Was steht denn da?

Science Museum –
New section open now
Don't miss our brand new exhibition section on the history of the computer. From a model of Konrad Zuse's Z3, the first working computer in the world, to the latest tablets, there's a lot to see, learn and try out.

Sie haben eine neue Abteilung zur Geschichte des Computers eröffnet.

Tipp: Keine Angst vor Fehlern!

- Wenn dir ein wichtiges Wort nicht einfällt, kannst du es umschreiben.
- Versuche, dich an Redewendungen zu erinnern. Zum Beispiel kannst du mit „*What about …?*" Vorschläge machen oder mit „*There is … / There are …*" etwas beschreiben.

7 WATCHING A VIDEO CLIP
Videoclips verstehen

Englischsprachige Videoclips anzuschauen macht Spaß und ist auch eine tolle Möglichkeit, die Sprache besser zu lernen. Dabei solltest du einige Dinge beachten:

1. Bevor es losgeht

- Gibt es Bilder aus dem Videoclip? Was ist zu sehen?
- Lies den Titel des Videoclips. Welche Hinweise gibt er auf den Inhalt?
- Worum könnte es gehen? Stelle Vermutungen an.

2. Währenddessen

- Schaue dir den Videoclip in Ruhe an. Was ist dein erster Eindruck? Mache dir Notizen.
  Who? Wer ist zu sehen? Um wen geht es?
  Where? Wo findet das Geschehen statt?
  When? Wann findet das Geschehen statt?
  What? Worum geht es? Was passiert?

- Es ist nicht schlimm, wenn du nicht alles verstehst. Achte auf die Stimmen, Körpersprache und Gesichtsausdrücke der Personen im Videoclip.

- Gibt es eine Aufgabe zu dem Videoclip? Behalte sie im Kopf, während du ein zweites Mal zuschaust. Konzentriere dich stärker auf das, was du hörst. Gibt es Wörter, die immer wieder vorkommen? Notiere sie dir.

- Versuche, gleich danach die Frage zu beantworten. Wenn nötig, schaue dir dann den Clip ein weiteres Mal an. Überprüfe dabei deine Antworten.

3. Hinterher

- Tausche dich mit deinen Mitschülerinnen und Mitschülern aus.

Tipp: Schaue dir Videoclips und Filme auf Englisch an (media worksheet 8)

- Alle Videoclips zum Buch findest du, wenn du auf www.westermann.de/webcode den Webcode WES-128206-001 eingibst oder den QR-Code scannst, den du auf Seite 2 findest.
- Sieh dir Filme, Serien oder Berichte zu Themen, die dich interessieren, auf Englisch an.
- Auf DVDs oder bei Streaming-Diensten kannst du fast immer den englischen Ton und englische Untertitel einschalten. Nach und nach lernst du besser zu verstehen, was gesagt wird.

8 SEARCHING THE INTERNET
Im Internet recherchieren

Hier erfährst du, wie du im Internet zu einem Thema recherchieren kannst.

1. Benutze eine Suchmaschine

- Gute Suchbegriffe erleichtern dir die Suche im Internet. Versuche, auf Englisch möglichst genau zu formulieren, wonach du suchst.
- Gib die Suchbegriffe in eine Suchmaschine ein. Bei vielen Suchmaschinen kannst du Englisch als Sprache wählen. Dann steht dir der nötige Wortschatz gleich zur Verfügung.
- Es kann sein, dass die Suchmaschine sehr viele Treffer anzeigt. Oft genügt es, sich die ersten 10 bis 20 Suchergebnisse anzuschauen.
- Es gibt Webseiten, auf denen du Informationen in einfacherem Englisch finden kannst. Deine Lehrkraft kann dir helfen, sie zu finden.

2. Halte nützliche Informationen fest

- Überfliege erst einmal die Seiten, die dir interessant erscheinen. Du brauchst nicht jedes Wort zu verstehen.
- Dann kannst du dir Notizen zu den Inhalten machen.
- Denke daran, dir das Datum deiner Recherche aufzuschreiben und die Quelle abzuspeichern.
- Wenn du Textausschnitte unverändert aus dem Internet übernimmst, musst du zeigen, dass es Zitate sind. Setze sie in deinem Text in Anführungszeichen und gib die Quelle und das Datum an, an dem du sie gefunden hast.

3. Sei kritisch

- Informationen, die du im Internet findest, sind nicht immer richtig.
- Sei deshalb kritisch und überprüfe die Informationen noch einmal auf anderen Seiten oder in einem Lexikon.

Tipp: Nutze digitale Tools (media worksheet 6, 7)

- Es gibt viele sinnvolle Tools im Internet. Du kannst zum Beispiel Währungen und Maßeinheiten umrechnen oder dir Entfernungen anzeigen lassen.
- Viele englischsprachige Einrichtungen, vor allem Museen, bieten virtuelle Rundgänge an. Du kannst auch virtuell durch britische Städte spazieren.

9 PRESENTATIONS Präsentationen halten

Hier findest du einige Tipps und Tricks für gelungene Präsentationen.

1. Bevor du etwas präsentierst

- Überlege: Was möchtest du zu deinem Thema sagen? Wie viel Zeit hast du?
- Gliedere deinen Vortrag: Überlege, in welcher Reihenfolge du was sagen und wie du anfangen möchtest.
- Fertige ein Poster oder eine Computerpräsentation an, um deinen Vortrag anschaulich zu machen. Wenn du Bilder oder Texte aus dem Internet oder aus einem Buch kopiert hast, dann schreibe immer dazu, wo und wann du sie gefunden hast.
- Notiere Stichpunkte zu dem, was du sagen möchtest, auf Karteikarten.
- Nützliche Redewendungen findest du in der *wordbank* auf Seite 168.
- Übe deinen Vortrag vor dem Spiegel, vor Freunden oder vor deiner Familie.

So sieht ein gelungenes Vortragsposter aus

- *ansprechende Überschrift*
- *interessante Informationen*
- *verständliche Sätze, aber nicht zu viel Text*
- *große Bilder und Schrift: Jeder im Raum muss sie sehen und lesen können.*
- *saubere Schrift*
- *Bilder mit Bildunterschriften*

2. Während du präsentierst

- Sprich langsam und deutlich.
- Sieh deine Zuhörerinnen und Zuhörer an, wenn du sprichst. Achte zum Beispiel bei einer Computerpräsentation darauf, nicht ständig auf den Bildschirm zu schauen.
- Versuche, frei zu sprechen. Du kannst die wichtigsten Punkte von deinen Karteikarten oder deinem Poster ablesen.

3. So wird dein Vortrag spannend und lebendig

- Musik, Videoclips, interessante Bilder oder Zitate machen deinen Vortrag abwechslungsreich.
- Achte darauf, dass dein Vortrag nicht klingt, als würdest du einen Text ablesen.
- Zeige deinen Zuhörerinnen und Zuhörern auf deinem Poster oder auf den Seiten deiner Computerpräsentation, worüber du gerade sprichst.

Tipp: Schau dir Tutorials an (media worksheet 4)

- Zum Präsentieren gibt es viele Tutorials im Internet. Schau dir einige an und überlege, was bei dir schon gut klappt und was du noch verbessern könntest.
- Zum Thema Computerpräsentationen kannst du dir ein passendes Arbeitsblatt herunterladen und dir Tutorials anschauen. Gehe dazu auf www.westermann.de/webcode und gib den Webcode WES-128206-001 ein.

10 PERFORMING A SCENE
Eine Szene vorspielen

Szenische Lesungen, Rollenspiele und Theaterstücke sind eine gute Methode, um Englisch zu trainieren. Denke immer daran, laut und deutlich und nicht zu schnell zu sprechen, damit man dich gut verstehen kann.

1. Szenische Lesung

- Für ein *dramatic reading* musst du deinen Text nicht auswendig lernen. Du solltest ihn aber so gut kennen, dass du auf deine Aussprache, Lautstärke, Betonung und Mimik achten kannst, ohne den Faden zu verlieren.
- Achte darauf, dass Aussprache, Lautstärke, Betonung und Mimik zu dem passen, was du liest.

2. Rollenspiele

- Halte beim Sprechen Augenkontakt zu deinem Gegenüber.
- Versetze dich in die Person hinein, die du darstellst. Denke beim Sprechen an die passende Mimik und Gestik.
- Wechselt auch mal die Rollen und übt mit anderen Partnern. So lernt ihr, spontan zu reagieren.
- Wenn ihr *cue cards* verwendet, denkt daran, nur Stichworte zu notieren, keine ganzen Sätze!

3. Theaterstücke

- Bei Theaterstücken geht es noch mehr als bei Rollenspielen um das Schauspielern. Du solltest deinen Text gut auswendig lernen, damit du dich besser auf das Spielen konzentrieren kannst. Mit der Methode *read – look up – speak* kannst du deine Rolle auswendig lernen: Du liest deinen Satz still, siehst dann auf und sprichst ihn.
- Versetze dich in die Person hinein, die du darstellst. Denke beim Sprechen an die passende Mimik und Gestik.
- Mit Requisiten *(props)* und Kostümen fällt es leichter, in eine Rolle hineinzuschlüpfen.

4. Präsentieren

- Mit Rollenspielen, kleinen Szenen, Sketchen und Theaterstücken könnt ihr zeigen, wie viel Englisch ihr schon könnt. Bei einem Schulfest oder an einem Tag der offenen Tür könnt ihr Eltern oder andere Klassen zu einer Vorführung einladen.

Tipp: Schaut euch selbst zu (media worksheet 2)

- Rollenspiele könnt ihr aufnehmen und so gemeinsam überprüfen, ob es noch etwas zu verbessern gibt.

Eating and eating out

I have never eaten octopus. But I would like to try it.

My family's traditional dish is Sunday roast.

I tried sushi but I didn't like it.

On special occasions we go out for a meal. We often go to a traditional British restaurant.

My favourite food is mashed potatoes with bacon and chips.

Food can be ...

savoury · sweet · tasty · yummy · perfect · delicious · vegetarian · nice · spicy · good · bad · special · disgusting · fried · healthy · fresh · traditional · vegan · hot · grilled · overcooked

Preparing a meal

* *Heat the oil / butter / ...*
* *Chop the tomatoes / vegetables / ...*
* *Slice the onion / cucumber / ...*
* *Cut the potatoes / carrots / ... in half.*
* *Put the vegetables in the pot / ...*
* *Add a teaspoon of salt / sugar / ...*
* *Boil for 10 minutes / half an hour / ...*
* *Stir in the flour / the milk / ...*
* *Add a cup of yoghurt / ...*
* *Cover the pot / ...*
* *Bake for 20 minutes / one hour / ...*

Ingredients

a bag of potatoes · some tomatoes · many carrots · a lot of peppers · a few onions · some cabbage · one cup of chickpeas · some garlic

a little water · some couscous · a bit of bread · a cup of rice

a bottle of milk · a little yoghurt · a piece of cheese

some cumin · a little coriander · pepper · a teaspoon of paprika · cayenne pepper · cinnamon · not too much salt

At a restaurant

On a menu you can find ...

starters · main courses · desserts · drinks · sides · soups · salads

Restaurants can be ...

expensive · good · bad · nice · cosy · cheap · delicious · vegetarian · traditional · perfect · vegan

A restaurant review

My favourite restaurant is ...
The service was quick / good / bad / ...
I had the ...
The food was tasty / healthy / cheap / disgusting / spicy / overcooked / burnt / ...
I had the best / worst ... I have ever eaten.
The atmosphere was friendly / cosy / relaxed / busy / ...
It is not as ... as other restaurants.
It is ... / more ... than other restaurants.

Keeping fit

My favourite sport is swimming. I'm really strong and I like being on my own. I like being indoors and outdoors, so I go swimming at the swimming pool but also in the sea.

I love dancing! I don't like being outdoors, so climbing, cycling and going hiking are not my favourite sports. I prefer indoor sports. Dancing is perfect for me because I like music, too.

I enjoy diving because I like being in the water and watching fish. I love outdoor sports. I just can't be indoors all the time. Being outside makes me happy and I feel less stressed.

Sports

rowing · climbing · swimming · weight training · running · riding · dancing · diving · marathon · triathlon

play: cricket · football · ball sports · rugby · games · golf · chess · tennis · baseball

do: yoga · karate

Sports can be ...

fun · exciting · exhausting · difficult · easy · good for you · dangerous · fast

My sports idol

My favourite sports idol is ... because he / she is fast / good at ... / ...
He / She respects other players and is friendly / funny / ...
He / She trains hard and gives a lot of money to charity.

I don't really know what sport I would like.

You should play / go / do ...

I'm always stressed.

I think doing yoga would be a good idea because it is so relaxing.

I have never tried playing football.

I think you would be good at it because you can run very fast.

Health

To stay healthy, it is important to ...

do sport regularly · get enough sleep · eat healthily · spend time outdoors · drink enough water · don't eat too many sweets · make sure you are not too stressed · do things that make you happy · relax · eat enough fruit and vegetables

At the doctor's

What's the matter?

Where does it hurt?

When did you fall?

Does your toe hurt?

Have you got a headache?

How long have you had a headache for?

You should rest until you feel better.

You will have to stay at home for a week.

There is something wrong with my leg.

It is swollen and it hurts.

My knee is bleeding.

I hurt my ankle.

What do I have to do?

How soon will I feel better?

When will I be able to do sports again?

You can have ...

a sore throat · a fever · a cough · a cold · a headache · an infection · a toothache · a broken arm · an injury · a sprained ankle · a stomach ache

You can feel ...

ill · sick · dizzy · tired · well again

You need ...

a plaster · a cast · some medicine · an ambulance · to go to the dentist's · to rest · to see a doctor · an X-ray · to make an appointment for a check-up · to keep your leg up

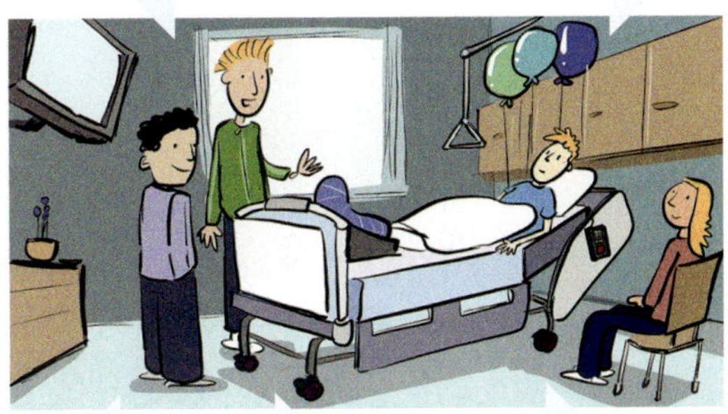

What's on?

What shall we do in London this weekend? Where could we go?

Why don't we go to Portobello Market? You can buy lots of different things there, try food from all over the world and meet interesting people.

My favourite event is the Notting Hill Carnival. I would like to see the costumes and listen to the music. Do you want to go there?

That's always so loud and there are so many people. I really don't want to go there. I would prefer something more quiet.

Portobello Market is not really quiet. What about going to the cinema?

It's so warm and sunny, why don't we do something outside?

There is a summer festival in St James's Park. What about that?

That sounds good. Let's do that! I've never been to an outdoor festival before.

When is it?

this weekend · next month · on 3 July · Sunday morning · Monday afternoon · in the evening · at twelve o'clock

Buying and selling

Can I help you?

Excuse me, I'm looking for a pair of jeans.

Why don't you try it on?

I can give it to you for £25.50.

Anything else?

That'll be £30.80.

Here's your change.

Do you have any dark blue ones?

How much does this pair cost?

How much are these?

Für die Schreibung von Geldbeträgen wird im Englischen zuerst das Währungssymbol geschrieben, dann – ohne Leerzeichen – der Betrag in Ziffern. Es wird ein Punkt und kein Komma verwendet! Zum Beispiel: £4.50 / €3.45

Advertising things

For just £2.50 you can get a …

It's ideal for …

This is the perfect … for you!

Are you looking for a …?

Events

When you go to a music festival, you can listen to lots of different bands.

You can watch many different actors perform at a theatre festival.

When you take part in a charity run, you can do something good while you're having fun.

At a flea market you can sell things you don't need anymore and buy things that other people don't need anymore.

If you like going to the cinema, a film festival is the event for you!

At the Notting Hill Carnival you can watch a brilliant parade.

Events can be ...

loud · crowded · free · exciting · fun · for children · world-famous · interesting

For or against big events?

I think big events are great. You can meet new people and have new experiences. Sometimes you can learn something new.

I don't like big events because there are so many people. It gets very crowded and loud.

It is good that there are more customers in the shops.

Events are good for the people who work at them – for example musicians and actors who perform there.

Many visitors come by car and they leave their rubbish everywhere. That's bad for the environment.

Sometimes they are even free.

Those events are only about making money. The entrance fee can be really expensive.

Expressing opinions

In my opinion, ...

I think that ...

If you ask me, ...

I agree that ...

On the one hand, ...

On the other hand, ...

I would say that ...

Family history

I am originally from Brighton. I moved when I was 19 and went to university in Leeds.

My parents met in London when they were studying there.

My mother spent her childhood in Edinburgh. When she was a teenager, her family moved to Wales.

My brother was born in London. My family moved to Brighton when he was three.

Two years later my parents got married.

My great-grandfather grew up in Trinidad. He started working when he was 16 years old and he met my great-grandmother when he was 18.

They had four children and emigrated to Great Britain in the 1950s.

When did it happen?

in the 1990s · in 2005 · around 2010 · on 22nd October 1999 · in the early 1930s · in the late 1960s · in March 1981

Family

mother · father · son · daughter · child · brother · sister · uncle · aunt · cousin · wife · husband · partner · grandmother · grandfather

Home

For me, home is where my family is.
I don't feel at home without friends and family.
I feel at home when I know everyone in my neighbourhood.
My home is in London / ...
I used to live in a small village in the countryside but I like big cities more, so now I live in London.

Talking about pictures

In the picture there is ... / are ...

The picture shows two children. The girl is sitting on a couch on the left and the boy is sitting on a chair on the right.

There is a table between them. On the table I can see a vase with flowers.

I think it's a very old picture. It's black and white.

The girl could be older than the boy. She looks a bit afraid. The boy doesn't look very happy.

They might be listening to the radio.

Maybe the children are brother and sister.

Feelings

I am feeling ...

angry

afraid

worried

... **excited** because I'm going to a music festival at the weekend.

... **lonely** because all my friends are on holiday.

... **upset** about an argument with my mum.

happy

... **stressed** because I have a problem at school.

bored

... **proud** because I was very good at my maths test.

... **shy** because I have to start a new school.

sad

... **scared** because there's a big black spider in my room.

... **nervous** about my next English test.

Seeking and giving advice

I have a problem with my parents.
They are so strict. Do you have any tips?
What do you think I should do? Can you help?
How shall I deal with them?
I don't know what to do.
I need some advice.
Can you help me / give me some advice, please?

What's the problem?

What happened?
Why are you feeling so sad?

I'm sorry to hear that. Why don't you try to talk to them again?

How about you ask your brothers for help?

I think you should wait for a while and then try again.

Why do you think you can't talk to them?

Have you tried asking your grandma for advice?
Maybe you could speak to her.

Inventions

I proudly present my latest invention. It will solve a lot of problems.

You can save a lot of time and money with this machine.

It can improve people's lives because it helps them with different tasks.

It can work for hours without electricity.

It can be used anywhere.

My invention is very useful if you haven't got enough time.

You only have to switch it on.

It was invented in 1982. · It was invented by James Watt. · It can be used to pull heavy objects. · It can be seen all over the world. · It is used by many people every day. · It was built in 1895. · First versions of this invention appeared in 1723. · It was invented to help people.

Presenting something

Hello and welcome to my presentation about ...
First I would like to introduce the topic of ...
In the second part of my presentation, I will ...
After that I will talk about ...
Finally, I will look at ...
I will first give some information on ...
Here is an example of ...
On this slide you can see ...
This is a photo of ...
This picture shows that ...
It is also important to mention that ...
The last aspect is ...
Thanks for listening. Are there any questions?

Giving feedback

I enjoyed your presentation because you talked about all aspects of the topic.

There was a good summary at the end.

My favourite part of your presentation was when you talked about ...

The best part were the pictures on the third slide.

I think it was a good / fantastic / well-researched / ... presentation.

Well done for giving a good presentation!

You could improve by speaking more loudly / more clearly / more slowly / ...

You need to research more facts / ...

Next time you should have more pictures / less ... / a handout / ...

The presentation was a little hard to understand.

Communication

How do you communicate with your friends and family?

How often do you text your best friend?

What is the best way to communicate with your grandparents?

Have you ever been on a video chat?

I write text messages to my friends.

I send letters or emails to my grandparents.

I send postcards when I am on holiday.

I often call my best friend.

I react with a heart or a smiley to comment on my friend's post.

Dear Mr Kogan,
Dear Mrs Norris,
Dear Grandma,
Hi Ava,

How are you? I'm …

Yours sincerely, …
Lots of love, … / Love, …
I look forward to hearing from you.
Please write to me soon!

Olivia Norris
Lexham Gardens 2A
London W8 5JL
UK

Going online

I'm online for about two hours every day. I chat with my friends, watch videos or play games.

I don't post anything that I don't want to go on the Internet.

My password is strong. Nobody knows it but me and my parents.

I don't share things with people I don't know.

I always ask people for their permission before I take pictures of them.

I delete photos when the person in them asks me to.

Classroom phrases

Wenn man ankommt oder geht

Good morning.	Guten Morgen.
What's for homework?	Was haben wir als Hausaufgabe auf?
See you tomorrow.	Bis morgen.
Bye.	Tschüs.

Wenn es ein Problem gibt

Sorry I'm late.	Tut mir leid, dass ich zu spät bin.
Sorry, I haven't got my exercise book with me.	Tut mir leid, ich habe mein Heft nicht dabei.
Sorry, I haven't got my homework with me.	Tut mir leid, ich habe meine Hausaufgaben nicht dabei.
What's the matter?	Was ist los?
I'm fine.	Mir geht's gut.
I feel sick.	Mir ist schlecht.
I've got a headache.	Ich habe Kopfschmerzen.
Can I open the window, please?	Kann ich bitte das Fenster öffnen?
Can I go to the toilet, please?	Kann ich bitte zur Toilette gehen?

Wenn man Hilfe braucht

Can you help me, please?	Können Sie / Kannst du mir bitte helfen?
I've got a question.	Ich habe eine Frage.
I don't understand this.	Ich verstehe das hier nicht.
How can I do this exercise?	Wie kann ich diese Aufgabe machen?
What's ... in English / German?	Was heißt ... auf Englisch / Deutsch?
What does ... mean?	Was bedeutet ... ?
Is that correct?	Ist das richtig?
Can you write that on the board, please?	Können Sie das bitte an die Tafel schreiben?
Can you spell that, please?	Können Sie das bitte buchstabieren?
Can you say that again, please?	Können Sie / Kannst du das bitte noch einmal sagen?
Can we listen to the audio track again, please?	Können wir den Audiotrack bitte noch einmal hören?
Sorry, I don't know.	Tut mir leid, das weiß ich nicht.
What page, please?	Auf welcher Seite bitte?

Wenn man zusammen arbeitet oder spielt

Whose turn is it?	Wer ist dran?
Do you want to work with me?	Möchtest du mit mir arbeiten?
Let's check ...	Lass uns ... überprüfen.
Let's compare ...	Lass uns ... vergleichen.
Let's talk about ...	Lass uns über ... sprechen.

Wenn man mit dem Computer arbeitet

What's your email address?	Wie ist deine E-Mail-Adresse?
You can click on this link.	Du kannst auf diesen Link klicken.
Can I print that out?	Kann ich das ausdrucken?
Can I download it?	Kann ich es herunterladen?
I saved the links to name the sources.	Ich habe die Links gespeichert, um die Quellen anzugeben.
I did research online. I used a search engine.	Ich habe online recherchiert. Ich habe eine Suchmaschine benutzt.

Was die Lehrerin oder der Lehrer sagt

Open your books at page ...	Öffnet eure Bücher auf Seite ...
Turn to page ...	Blättert zu Seite ...
Look at line ...	Seht euch Zeile ... an.
Look at the next paragraph.	Seht euch den nächsten Absatz an.
Read the text on page ...	Lies / Lest den Text auf Seite ...
Work in pairs / in groups of four.	Arbeitet zu zweit / zu viert.
Listen to the audio track.	Hör dir / Hört euch den Audiotrack an.
Listen to audio track number ...	Hör dir / Hört euch Audiotrack Nummer ... an.
Write about ...	Schreibe / Schreibt über ...
Talk about ...	Sprich / Sprecht über ...
Ask questions about ...	Stelle / Stellt Fragen zu ...
Answer the question, please.	Beantworte / Beantwortet bitte die Frage.
Match the sentences.	Ordne / Ordnet die Sätze zu.
Who wants to read out the text?	Wer möchte den Text vorlesen?
Write down the answers.	Schreibt die Antworten auf.
Act out the dialogue.	Spielt den Dialog vor.
Change roles.	Tauscht die Rollen.
Make your own dialogue / conversation.	Entwirf / Entwerft selbst einen Dialog / ein Gespräch.
Take a card.	Nimm / Nehmt eine Karte.
Come to the board, please.	Komm / Kommt bitte zur Tafel.
Do this exercise at home, please.	Mache / Macht diese Aufgabe bitte zu Hause.
Be quiet, please.	Sei / Seid bitte ruhig.
Sit down, please.	Setz dich bitte. / Setzt euch bitte.
Please speak up.	Sprich / Sprecht bitte lauter.
You can do better.	Das kannst du / könnt ihr besser.
Try again.	Versuch / Versucht es noch einmal.
Well done.	Gut gemacht.

1 THE PRESENT PERFECT: STATEMENTS (REVISION)
Das Perfekt: Aussagen *(revision)*

Das *present perfect* verwendest du, wenn etwas irgendwann in einem Zeitraum von der Vergangenheit bis zur Gegenwart passiert ist.

Du verwendest es auch, wenn ein Vorgang in der Vergangenheit noch Auswirkungen auf die Gegenwart hat.

a) Bejahte Aussagesätze im *present perfect*

DIGITAL+ video 17

Das *present perfect* bildest du mit *have / has* + Partizip Perfekt *(past participle)*.
Statt *have* bzw. *has* kannst du auch die entsprechende Kurzform benutzen.

*I **have cleaned** the kitchen.*
*I**'ve cleaned** the kitchen.* — *Ich **habe** die Küche **sauber gemacht**.*

*He **has finished** his dinner.*
*He**'s finished** his dinner.* — *Er **hat** sein Essen **beendet**.*

Bei regelmäßigen Verben bildest du das Partizip Perfekt, indem du an die Grundform des Verbs die Endung *-ed* anhängst.
Beachte auch die Besonderheiten bei der Schreibung, die auf Seite 184 im Grammatik-Kapitel 13 erläutert werden.

Grundform	*simple past*	*past participle*
clean	cleaned	clean**ed**
help	helped	help**ed**
play	played	play**ed**
tidy	tidied	tidi**ed**
visit	visited	visit**ed**

Die Formen der unregelmäßigen Verben musst du wie Vokabeln auswendig lernen.
Auf den Seiten 245–247 findest du eine Liste dieser Verben. Auf Seite 247 gibt es einen Tipp, wie du die unregelmäßigen Formen gruppieren kannst, um sie dir leichter einzuprägen.

Grundform	*simple past*	*past participle*
be	was / were	**been**
do	did	**done**
have	had	**had**
buy	bought	**bought**

b) Verneinte Aussagesätze im *present perfect*

Die Verneinung bildest du mit *have not / has not* + Partizip Perfekt bzw. mit den Kurzformen *haven't / hasn't* + Partizip Perfekt.

*I **have not cleaned** the kitchen yet.*
*I **haven't cleaned** the kitchen yet.* — *Ich **habe** die Küche noch **nicht sauber gemacht**.*

*He **has not finished** his dinner.*
*He **hasn't finished** his dinner.* — *Er **hat** sein Essen **nicht beendet**.*

2 THE PRESENT PERFECT: QUESTIONS (REVISION)
Das Perfekt: Fragen *(revision)*

Mit einer Entscheidungsfrage im *present perfect* kannst du z. B. fragen, ob jemand etwas irgendwann in der Vergangenheit schon einmal gemacht hat. Der genaue Zeitpunkt ist dabei nicht so wichtig.

a) Fragen und Kurzantworten im *present perfect*

DIGITAL+ video 17

Entscheidungsfragen im *present perfect* bildest du, indem du *have* bzw. *has* an den Satzanfang stellst.

Entscheidungsfrage	Kurzantwort	Kurzantwort
Have you ever been to a Chinese restaurant?	Yes, I have.	No, I haven't.
Has Ava ever eaten a Sunday roast?	Yes, she has.	No, she hasn't.
Have the children finished their dinner?	Yes, they have.	No, they haven't.

b) Fragen mit Fragewort im *present perfect*

Bei Fragen mit Fragewort steht das Fragewort am Satzanfang.

What *have you done?*
Where *have you been?*
Why *hasn't she called yet?*

c) Adverbien der unbestimmten Zeit

Beim *present perfect* ist es nicht wichtig, wann genau in der Vergangenheit etwas passiert ist. Daher werden bei Fragen und Aussagen im *present perfect* häufig Adverbien der unbestimmten Zeit verwendet, z. B. *ever* (= jemals), *never* (= nie), *already* (= schon), *just* (= gerade) und *not yet* (= noch nicht).

Die meisten Adverbien stehen dann direkt vor dem Partizip Perfekt.

Have you ***ever*** *been to London? – No, I've* ***never*** *been there.*
Bist du ***jemals*** *in London gewesen? – Nein, ich bin* ***(noch) nie*** *dort gewesen.*

Has Ava ***already*** *taken Ollie for a walk? – Yes, she has* ***just*** *come back.*
Hat Ava Ollie ***schon*** *Gassi geführt? – Ja, sie ist* ***gerade*** *zurückgekommen.*

Beachte die Ausnahme: *yet* steht am Satzende.

*Have you been to the new restaurant? – No, I have****n't*** *been there* ***yet****.*
Bist du im neuen Restaurant gewesen? – Nein, ich bin ***noch nicht*** *dort gewesen.*

3 QUANTIFIERS (REVISION)
Mengengaben *(revision)*

Some und *any* sind Mengenangaben. Sie bedeuten „einige“, „ein paar“ oder „etwas“. Auch *much*, *many* und *a lot of* („viel, viele“) sind Mengenangaben.

a) Die Mengenangaben *some* und *any*

DIGITAL+ video 18

In bejahten Aussagesätzen benutzt du *some*.

There are ***some*** *apples in the kitchen.*	*In der Küche sind* ***ein paar*** *Äpfel.*
I need ***some*** *milk for my cornflakes.*	*Ich brauche* ***etwas*** *Milch für meine Cornflakes.*

In verneinten Aussagesätzen und in den meisten Fragen verwendest du *any*.
Das Wort wird oft nicht übersetzt. Die Mengenangabe *not ... any* bedeutet „kein“ oder „keine“.

Are there ***any*** *apples? Sind da Äpfel?*	*We have****n't*** *got* ***any*** *apples. Wir haben* ***keine*** *Äpfel.*
Have you got ***any*** *milk? Hast du Milch?*	*There is****n't any*** *milk. Es gibt* ***keine*** *Milch.*

Achtung: Wenn du höflich um etwas bittest oder etwas anbietest, benutzt du auch in Fragen *some*:

Can I have ***some*** *milk, please?*	*Kann ich bitte* ***etwas*** *Milch haben?*
Would you like ***some*** *tea?*	*Möchtest du Tee?*

b) Die Mengenangaben *much, many* und *a lot of*

Much (auf Deutsch „viel“) wird mit Nomen verwendet, die nicht zählbar sind, zum Beispiel *water, milk, juice, time, money*. Die Nomen stehen daher in der Einzahl.

We haven't got ***much*** *milk.*	*Wir haben nicht* ***viel*** *Milch.*
How ***much*** *cheese have we got?*	*Wie* ***viel*** *Käse haben wir?*

Many (auf Deutsch „viele“) wird dagegen mit Nomen verwendet, die zählbar sind, zum Beispiel *apples, eggs, tomatoes*. Die Nomen stehen in der Mehrzahl.

We haven't got ***many*** *apples.*	*Wir haben nicht* ***viele*** *Äpfel.*
How ***many*** *tomatoes have we got?*	*Wie* ***viele*** *Tomaten haben wir?*

Much und *many* werden vor allem in Fragen und verneinten Aussagesätzen verwendet.
In bejahten Aussagesätzen verwendet man eher *a lot of* oder *lots of*. Hier unterscheidet man nicht zwischen zählbaren und nicht zählbaren Nomen.

We need ***lots of*** *juice and* ***lots of*** *snacks for the party.*
Wir brauchen ***viel*** *Saft und* ***viele*** *Snacks für die Party.*

THE COMPARISON OF ADJECTIVES (REVISION)

4 Die Steigerung von Adjektiven *(revision)*

Wenn du Personen oder Dinge näher beschreiben möchtest, verwendest du Adjektive. Wenn du Personen oder Dinge miteinander vergleichen möchtest, kannst du diese Adjektive steigern. Die erste Steigerungsform heißt Komparativ, die zweite Steigerungsform heißt Superlativ.

a) Steigerung von Adjektiven mit *-er* und *-est*

DIGITAL+ video 19

Einsilbige Adjektive (z. B. *cheap* und *old*) werden durch das Anhängen von *-er* und *-est* gesteigert.

Bei manchen Adjektiven ändert sich die Schreibweise, *bigger* z. B. schreibt man mit zwei *g*, ein stummes *e* wie bei *nice* fällt weg.

Auch einige zweisilbige Adjektive können mit *-er* und *-est* gesteigert werden, z. B. Adjektive, die auf *-er*, *-le*, *-ow* und *-y* enden. Bei Adjektiven auf *-y* wird aus dem *-y* ein *-i*.

Einige Adjektive haben unregelmäßige Steigerungsformen. Diese Formen musst du wie Vokabeln lernen.

	Komparativ	Superlativ
cheap	cheap**er**	(the) cheap**est**
old	old**er**	(the) old**est**
big	big**ger**	(the) big**gest**
nice	nic**er**	(the) nic**est**
clever	clever**er**	(the) clever**est**
easy	eas**ier**	(the) eas**iest**
good	**better**	(the) **best**
bad	**worse**	(the) **worst**

b) Steigerung von Adjektiven mit *more* und *most*

Mehrsilbige Adjektive werden mit *more* und *most* gesteigert.
Das Adjektiv bleibt unverändert.

	Komparativ	Superlativ
useful	**more** useful	(the) **most** useful
beautiful	**more** beautiful	(the) **most** beautiful
interesting	**more** interesting	(the) **most** interesting

c) Vergleichssätze

Willst du Personen oder Dinge miteinander vergleichen, dann benutzt du den Komparativ mit *than*.

Noah is older ***than*** *Ava. Noah ist älter* ***als*** *Ava.*
The jacket is more expensive ***than*** *the T-shirt. Die Jacke ist teurer* ***als*** *das T-Shirt.*

Sind die Eigenschaften gleich, benutzt du *as … as*.

Lily is ***as*** *old* ***as*** *Harry. Lily ist* ***so*** *alt* ***wie*** *Harry.*
The jeans are ***as*** *expensive* ***as*** *the jacket. Die Jeans sind* ***so*** *teuer* ***wie*** *die Jacke.*

5 THE PRESENT PROGRESSIVE (REVISION)
Die Verlaufsform der Gegenwart *(revision)*

Mit dem *present progressive* kannst du beschreiben, was gerade passiert oder was auf einem Bild zu sehen ist. Du kannst es auch verwenden, um über Pläne für die (nähere) Zukunft zu sprechen.

The man **is waiting** for his food.

a) Bejahte Aussagesätze im *present progressive*

DIGITAL+ video 20

So bildest du das *present progressive*:

Form von *be (am, is, are)* + Grundform des Verbs + Endung ***-ing***.

*The waiter **is** show**ing** the Kogans to their table.*	*Der Kellner **führt** die Kogans zu ihrem Tisch.*
*The Kogans **are** order**ing** their food.*	*Die Kogans **bestellen** ihr Essen.*

Beachte: Endet das Verb auf einem stummen *-e*, dann fällt das *-e* in der *ing*-Form weg.

*writ**e** → writ**ing***   *danc**e** → danc**ing***   *tak**e** → tak**ing***

Endet das Verb auf einem kurzen betonten Vokal + Konsonant, wird der Konsonant verdoppelt.

*put → pu**tt**ing*   *run → ru**nn**ing*   *get → ge**tt**ing*

b) Verneinte Aussagesätze im *present progressive*

Für die Verneinung fügst du *not* hinter der Form von *be* ein. Oft wird die Kurzform verwendet:

*Harry **is not** danc**ing**.*	*Harry **isn't** danc**ing**.*	*Harry **tanzt (gerade)** nicht.*
*They **are not** watch**ing** TV.*	*They **aren't** watch**ing** TV.*	*Sie **gucken (gerade)** nicht Fernsehen.*

c) Fragen im *present progressive*

Bei Entscheidungsfragen stellst du die Form von *be* (also *am, is* oder *are*) an den Satzanfang. In den Kurzantworten wird die Form von *be* aufgegriffen.

***Is** Ava enjoy**ing** her food?* *Yes, she **is**. / No, she **isn't**.*	***Genießt** Ava **(gerade)** ihr Essen?*
***Are** the Kogans eat**ing** at home?* *Yes, they **are**. / No, they **aren't**.*	***Essen** die Kogans **(gerade)** zu Hause?*

Bei Fragen mit Fragewort steht das Fragewort am Satzanfang:

***What** are you hav**ing** for dinner?*	*Was **isst** du **(gerade)** zum Abendessen?*

6 THE GERUND
Das Gerundium

Wird ein Verb wie ein Nomen verwendet, nennt man die Form Gerundium *(gerund)*. Im Englischen benutzt man dafür die *ing*-Form des Verbs.

a) Das Gerundium als Subjekt

DIGITAL+ video 21

Wie die *ing*-Form eines Verbs gebildet wird, hast du schon auf Seite 176 gesehen. Eine solche Form kann Subjekt eines Satzes sein.

Swimming *keeps you fit.*	*(Das)* ***Schwimmen*** *hält einen fit.*
Cycling *is fun.*	***Radfahren*** *macht Spaß.*
Playing *the guitar is my favourite hobby.*	*Gitarre****spielen*** *ist mein Lieblingshobby.*

b) Das Gerundium nach bestimmten Verben

Das Gerundium folgt oft nach bestimmten Verben, z.B. *like, love, hate, enjoy, suggest, try* und *prefer*.

I ***like being*** *outdoors.*	*Ich* ***bin gerne*** *draußen.*
I don't ***like being*** *alone.*	*Ich* ***bin nicht gerne*** *allein.*
We ***enjoy playing*** *games.*	*Wir* ***genießen*** *es, Spiele zu* ***spielen***.
Do you ***prefer running*** *or* ***swimming***?	***Bevorzugst*** *du* ***Laufen*** *oder* ***Schwimmen***?

c) Das Gerundium nach bestimmten Präpositionen

Auch bei verschiedenen Ausdrücken mit Präpositionen wird das Gerundium verwendet, z.B. *be good at, be interested in, care about* und *look forward to*.

Are you ***good at playing*** *basketball?*
Bist du ***gut darin***, *Basketball* ***zu spielen***?

I'm ***interested in playing*** *hockey.*
Ich ***habe Interesse daran***, *Hockey* ***zu spielen***.

I don't really ***care about winning*** *or* ***losing***.
Es ist mir wirklich egal, *ob ich* ***gewinne*** *oder* ***verliere***.

We're ***looking forward to going*** *to the football match.*
Wir ***freuen uns darauf***, *zum Fußballspiel zu* ***gehen***.

7 CONDITIONAL CLAUSES 1
Bedingungssätze 1

Mit Bedingungssätzen kannst du sagen, was unter bestimmten Bedingungen passieren wird bzw. passieren kann.

Ein Bedingungssatz besteht aus einem *if*-Satz und einem Hauptsatz. Der *if*-Satz nennt eine Bedingung. Der Hauptsatz drückt aus, was passiert, wenn die Bedingung erfüllt ist.
Im *if*-Satz steht das *simple present*, im Hauptsatz meist das *will-future*.

DIGITAL+ video 22

***if*-Satz** (Bedingung: **Wenn** ...)	**Hauptsatz** (Folge: ... **dann** ...)
If you **miss** the bus, **Wenn** du den Bus **verpasst**,	you **will be** late. **wirst** du zu spät **kommen**.
If it **rains**, **Wenn** es **regnet**,	the children **won't go** outside. **werden** die Kinder **nicht** nach draußen **gehen**.

Bedingungssätze können entweder mit dem *if*-Satz oder mit dem Hauptsatz beginnen. Wenn sie mit dem *if*-Satz beginnen, werden sie mit einem Komma getrennt. Wenn sie mit dem Hauptsatz beginnen, verwendest du im Englischen kein Komma.

If *you go to the cinema**,** I'**ll** come with you.*
*I'**ll** come with you **if** you go to the cinema.*

Wenn *du ins Kino gehst, komme ich mit dir.*
*Ich komme mit dir, **wenn** du ins Kino gehst.*

Im Hauptsatz kannst du auch Modalverben (z. B. *can, must*) oder den Imperativ verwenden.

*If you feel sick, you **can stay** at home.*
*Wenn du dich krank fühlst, **kannst** du zu Hause **bleiben**.*

*If you have broken your leg, you **must get** an X-ray.*
*Wenn du dir das Bein gebrochen hast, **musst** du dich röntgen **lassen**.*

*If you need help, **ask** your mum or dad.*
*Wenn du Hilfe brauchst, **frag** deine Mama oder deinen Papa.*

8 MODAL VERBS (REVISION)
Modalverben *(revision)*

Mit *must* kannst du sagen, was jemand tun muss. Mit *mustn't* kannst du sagen, was jemand nicht tun darf. Mit *can* kannst du sagen, was jemand tun kann oder darf.

a) *Must / have to*

Must bedeutet „müssen“. Die Form ist bei allen Personen gleich. Hinter *must* steht die Grundform des Hauptverbs.Du kannst *must* auch durch *have to* bzw. *has to* ersetzen.

*Demir **must** take his medicine. = Demir **has to** take his medicine.*
*Demir **muss** seine Medizin nehmen.*

Die Form *must* gibt es nur im *simple present*. Um z. B. auszudrücken, was jemand in der Vergangenheit tun musste oder in Zukunft wird tun müssen, brauchst du eine Form von *have to*.

*Last week, Demir **had to** go to hospital.* — *Letzte Woche **musste** Demir ins Krankenhaus gehen.*
*Tarek **will have to** stay at home for two days.* — *Tarek **wird** zwei Tage zu Hause bleiben **müssen**.*

b) *Mustn't / not be allowed to*

Mustn't bedeutet „nicht dürfen“. Die Form ist bei allen Personen gleich. Hinter *mustn't* steht die Grundform des Hauptverbs. Du kannst *mustn't* auch durch *not be allowed to* ersetzen.

*Tarek **mustn't** do sports at the moment. = Tarek **isn't allowed to** do sports at the moment.*

Mustn't gibt es nur im *simple present*. In den anderen Zeitformen benutzt du *not be allowed to*.

*Tarek **wasn't allowed to** play video games yesterday.*
*Tarek **won't be allowed to** do sports for three weeks.*

c) *Can / be able to / be allowed to*

Can bedeutet „können“ oder „dürfen“. Die Form ist bei allen Personen gleich. Hinter *can* steht die Grundform des Hauptverbs.

Die Ersatzform für *can* mit der Bedeutung „können“ ist *could* im *simple past* oder *be able to*.

*John **could** play tennis yesterday. = John **was able to** play tennis yesterday. Then he broke his arm.*
*John **will be able to** play tennis again in a few months, but he **won't be able to** play next week.*

Die Ersatzform für *can* mit der Bedeutung „dürfen“ ist *be allowed to*.

*Tarek **couldn't** play video games yesterday. = Tarek **wasn't allowed to** play video games yesterday.*
*Tarek **will be allowed to** play video games while he is ill.*

9 RELATIVE CLAUSES
Relativsätze

Mit Relativsätzen kannst du Personen oder Dinge näher beschreiben.

Relativsätze sind Nebensätze, die Personen oder Dinge näher beschreiben. Ein Relativsatz beginnt meist mit einem Relativpronomen, also z. B. mit *who, which* oder *that.*

DIGITAL+ video 23

Dabei verwendest du *who* für Personen und *which* für Dinge.
That kannst du sowohl für Dinge als auch für Personen benutzen.

	Relativsatz
There is a man Dort ist ein Mann,	**who** sells old cameras. **der** alte Kameras verkauft.
There is a car boot sale Dort ist ein Flohmarkt,	**which** takes place on Sunday. **der** am Sonntag stattfindet.

	Relativsatz
Tarek bought some books Tarek kaufte einige Bücher,	**that** were really cheap. **die** wirklich billig waren.
There are many people Es gibt viele Menschen,	**that** sell things at the car boot sale. **die** auf Flohmärkten Dinge verkaufen.

Relativsätze können auch in der Mitte eines Satzes stehen:
*The man **who is selling old cameras** is funny.*
*Der Mann, **der alte Kameras verkauft**, ist lustig.*

10 THE PROP WORDS ONE AND ONES
Die Stützwörter *one* und *ones*

Wenn du ein Nomen ersetzen willst, das direkt vorher schon genannt wurde, benutzt du stattdessen *one* bzw. *ones*.

Wenn du ein Nomen ersetzen willst, das direkt vorher genannt wurde, benutzt du stattdessen *one* bzw. *ones*. Du musst das Nomen nicht mehr wiederholen. Im Deutschen kannst du es sogar einfach weglassen. Im Englischen ist das nicht möglich.

Du benutzt *one*, um ein Nomen im Singular zu ersetzen.

Englisch	Deutsch
Which T-shirt do you like? The red **one** or the blue **one**?	Welches T-Shirt magst du? Das rote oder das blaue?

Du benutzt *ones*, um ein Nomen im Plural zu ersetzen.

Englisch	Deutsch
Tarek bought some new books and now he has to get rid of some old **ones**.	Tarek hat ein paar neue Bücher gekauft und nun muss er ein paar alte loswerden.

11 THE PAST PROGRESSIVE: STATEMENTS
Die Verlaufsform der Vergangenheit: Aussagen

Mit dem *past progressive* kannst du ausdrücken, was zu einem bestimmten Zeitpunkt in der Vergangenheit gerade passierte.

a) Bejahte Aussagesätze im *past progressive*

DIGITAL+ video 24

Auch für die Vergangenheit gibt es eine *progressive form*, das *past progressive*. Es drückt aus,

- was jemand zu einem bestimmten Zeitpunkt in der Vergangenheit gerade tat oder was gerade passierte.
- was gerade vor sich ging, als plötzlich etwas anderes geschah.

Das *past progressive* wird ganz ähnlich gebildet wie das *present progressive*, nur dass die Form von *be* im *simple past* steht.

Simple past-Form von *be (was / were)* + Grundform des Verbs + Endung *-ing*.

*Andy **was watching** a show.* — *Andy **schaute (gerade)** eine Show an.*
*The people **were eating**.* — *Die Leute **aßen (gerade)**.*

Wenn du beschreiben möchtest, was gerade vor sich ging, als etwas anderes geschah, kannst du das so tun:

past progressive	simple past
The people **were** already **eating** Die Leute **aßen gerade**,	when Andy **came** in. als Andy **hereinkam.**
While Andy **was looking** at a stall, Während **sich** Andy **gerade** einen Stand **anschaute**,	it **started** to rain. **fing** es zu regnen **an**.

was gerade passierte:
past progressive

neues Ereignis:
simple past

b) Verneinte Aussagesätze im *past progressive*

Für die Verneinung fügst du einfach ***not*** hinter die Form von *be* (***was*** bzw. ***were***) ein:

*Andy **wasn't** danc**ing**.* — *Andy tanzte (gerade) **nicht**.*
*Some people **weren't** listen**ing** to the stories.* — *Einige Leute hörten sich **nicht** die Geschichten an.*

12 THE PAST PROGRESSIVE: QUESTIONS
Die Verlaufsform der Vergangenheit: Fragen

Bei einer Entscheidungsfrage im *past progressive* steht *was* bzw. *were* am Satzanfang. Bei einer Frage mit Fragewort steht das Fragewort am Satzanfang.

a) Entscheidungsfragen und Kurzantworten im *past progressive*

DIGITAL+ video 24

Entscheidungsfragen im past progressive bildest du, indem du *was* bzw. *were* an den Satzanfang stellst. In der Kurzantwort wird *was bzw. were* aufgegriffen:

Was *Andy* ***having*** *dinner at 7pm? – Yes, he* ***was****. / No, he* ***wasn't****.*
Aß *Andy um 7 Uhr abends* ***gerade*** *Abendessen? – Ja. / Nein.*

Were *the people* ***dancing****? – Yes, they* ***were****. / No, they* ***weren't****.*
Tanzten *die Menschen* ***(gerade)****? – Ja. / Nein.*

b) Fragen mit Fragewort im *past progressive*

Bei Fragen mit Fragewörtern stellst du das Fragewort an den Satzanfang:

What were *you* ***doing*** *yesterday at 7pm?*
What was *Andy* ***doing****?*
Why were *the people* ***laughing****?*
Who was taking *pictures?*

13 THE SIMPLE PAST: STATEMENTS (REVISION)
Die einfache Vergangenheit: Aussagen *(revision)*

Das *simple past* verwendet man, wenn man über etwas spricht, das in der Vergangenheit liegt und abgeschlossen ist.

a) Formen und bejahte Aussagesätze im *simple past*

DIGITAL+ video 25, 26

Bei den regelmäßigen Verben hängst du *-ed* an die Grundform an:

stay + ***ed*** → *stay**ed***   *look* + ***ed*** → *look**ed***   *visit* + ***ed*** → *visit**ed***

Achte auf die Rechtschreibung: Endet die Grundform des Verbs auf *-e*, dann wird nur *-d* angehängt.

*arriv**e*** → *arriv**ed***

Endet das Verb auf einem kurzen betonten **Vokal + Konsonant**, dann wird der Konsonant verdoppelt.

*sto**p*** → *sto**pped***

Endet das Verb auf **Konsonant + y**, dann wird aus dem *-y* ein *-i* und die Endung lautet *-ied*.

*tid**y*** → *tid**ied***

Unregelmäßige Verben haben im *simple past* eine eigene Form (siehe Seite 245–247).

have → ***had***	*Tarek **had** a great holiday. Tarek **hatte** einen tollen Urlaub.*
go → ***went***	*He **went** to Wales with his father. Er **fuhr** mit seinem Vater nach Wales.*
do → ***did***	*They **did** lots of things together. Sie **machten** viele Sachen zusammen.*

Das Verb *be* hat zwei Formen im *simple past:*
*I / he / she / it **was*** – *you / we / they **were***
*I **was** in London last week, but my friends **were** in Paris.*

b) Verneinte Aussagesätze im *simple past*

Sätze im *simple past* verneinst du im Allgemeinen mit *didn't (= did not).*
Didn't ist bei allen Personen gleich. Danach kommt dann das Verb in der Grundform.

*I **didn't go** to Paris last week.*   *Letzte Woche **fuhr** ich **nicht** nach Paris.*

Bei *was* und *were* hängst du nur *not* oder die Kurzform *n't* an.

*I **wasn't** in Paris last week, and my friends **weren't** in London.*
*Ich **war** letzte Woche **nicht** in Paris, und meine Freunde **waren nicht** in London.*

14 THE SIMPLE PAST: QUESTIONS (REVISION)
Die einfache Vergangenheit: Fragen *(revision)*

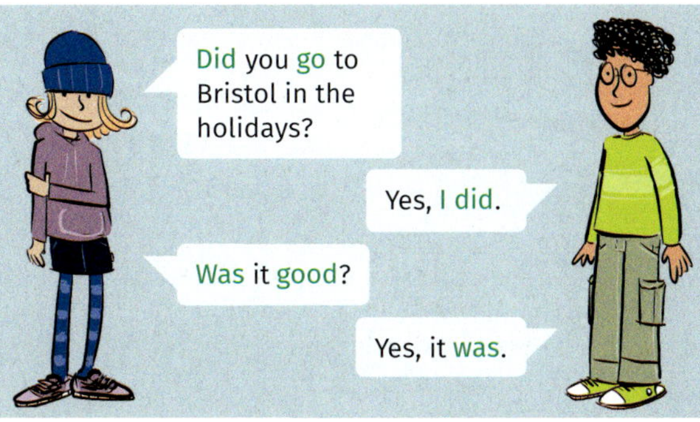

Fragen im *simple past* bildest du in den meisten Fällen mit *did*. Eine Ausnahme sind Sätze mit *was* oder *were*.

a) Entscheidungsfragen und Kurzantworten im *simple past*

DIGITAL+ video 25, 26

Bei Entscheidungsfragen im *simple past* stellst du *did* an den Satzanfang. *Did* ist bei allen Personen gleich.
Achte auch hier darauf, das Verb danach in der Grundform zu verwenden.
In der Kurzantwort wird *did* wieder aufgegriffen.

Entscheidungsfrage	Kurzantwort	Kurzantwort
Did you go on holiday?	Yes, I did.	No, I didn't.
Did Harry visit his grandparents?	Yes, he did.	No, he didn't.

Bei Fragen mit *was* und *were* benutzt du kein *did*.
Hier steht *was* oder *were* am Satzanfang.
In der Kurzantwort wird *was* bzw. *were* wieder aufgegriffen.

Entscheidungsfrage	Kurzantwort	Kurzantwort
Were your parents in Paris last year?	Yes, they were.	No, they weren't.
Was the weather good?	Yes, it was.	No, it wasn't.

b) Fragen mit Fragewort im *simple past*

Bei Sätzen mit Fragewort steht das Fragewort am Satzanfang. Es steht vor *did*.

What *did you do in the holidays?*
Where *did you go?*

Wenn *who* nach dem Subjekt fragt, benutzt du bei Fragen kein *did*:

Who *went to Poland? –* ***Ava*** *went to Poland.* ***Wer*** *fuhr nach Polen? –* ***Ava*** *fuhr nach Polen.*

Bei Fragen mit *was* oder *were* benutzt du kein *did*.

How *was your holiday?*
What *were your favourite places?*

15 REPORTED SPEECH 1
Indirekte Rede 1

Wenn du berichten willst, was jemand anderes sagt, benutzt du indirekte Rede.

Indirekte Rede besteht aus einem Begleitsatz und der wiedergegebenen Aussage. Beide Satzteile können durch *that* verbunden werden.

DIGITAL+ video 27

Wenn der Begleitsatz in der Gegenwart steht, verändern sich die Zeiten in der wiedergegebenen Aussage nicht.

Wenn die Originalaussage Wörter enthält, die nur aus dem Zusammenhang richtig zu verstehen sind, musst du sie in der wiedergegebenen Aussage anpassen.

	Begleitsatz	**wiedergegebene Aussage**
James: "**I** will have **my** own party." James: „**Ich** werde **meine** eigene Party geben."	James says (that) James sagt, dass	**he** will have **his** own party. **er seine** eigene Party geben werde.
Emily: "**We** had an argument." Emily: „**Wir** hatten einen Streit."	Emily says (that) Emily sagt, dass	**they** had an argument. **sie** einen Streit gehabt hätten.
Emily: "Chloe is angry with **me**." Emily: „Chloe ist sauer auf **mich**."	Emily says (that) Emily sagt, dass	Chloe is angry with **her**. Chloe sauer auf **sie** sei.
Tom: "The dog is **here**." Tom: „Der Hund ist **hier**."	Tom says (that) Tom sagt, dass	the dog is **there**. der Hund **dort** sei.

16 THE PASSIVE
Das Passiv

Bei Passivsätzen ist es nebensächlich oder nicht bekannt, wer oder was etwas tut bzw. getan hat.

DIGITAL+ video 28

Aktivsätze sagen uns, wer oder was handelt, hier z. B. *an author*:

An author ***wrote*** *the story in 2010.*
Ein Schriftsteller/Eine Schriftstellerin ***schrieb*** *2010 die Geschichte.*

Wenn es aber nicht wichtig oder nicht bekannt ist, wer etwas tut oder getan hat, kannst du einen Passivsatz verwenden.

The story ***was written*** *in 2010. Die Geschichte* ***wurde*** *2010* ***geschrieben****.*

Das Objekt aus dem Aktivsatz, hier *the story*, wird zum Subjekt des Passivsatzes.

	Subjekt	Verb	Objekt	
Aktivsatz:	An author	wrote	the story	in 2010.
Passivsatz:	The story	**was written**		in 2010.

Das Passiv bildest du so:
Form von ***be*** + **Partizip Perfekt *(past participle)***

Englisch	Deutsch
English **is spoken** all over the world. Matches **are used** to make fire. My computer **was made** in China. These books **were written** in Germany.	Englisch **wird** überall auf der Welt **gesprochen**. Streichhölzer **werden** zum Feuermachen **benutzt**. Mein Computer **wurde** in China **hergestellt**. Diese Bücher **wurden** in Deutschland **geschrieben**.

Wenn du in einem Passivsatz doch einmal die handelnde Person oder die Ursache für etwas nennen willst, hängst du sie mit ***by*** („von", „durch") an den Satz an:

The story was written ***by*** *an author in 2010.*
The first car was invented ***by*** *Karl Benz.*
The house was destroyed ***by*** *a fire.*

17 THE GOING TO-FUTURE: STATEMENTS (REVISION)
Das Futur mit *going to*: Aussagen *(revision)*

I'm going to take part in a cool upcycling workshop next weekend. It's going to be fun!

Das Futur mit *going to* kannst du verwenden, um über Pläne für die Zukunft zu sprechen.
Man verwendet es auch bei Ereignissen, die wahrscheinlich passieren werden.

a) Bejahte Aussagesätze im *going to-future*

DIGITAL+ video 29

Im Deutschen gibt es keine Zeitform, die dem *going to-future* entspricht.
Du hast aber verschiedene Möglichkeiten, es im Deutschen wiederzugeben.

Englisch	Deutsch
I'**m going to do** a drama workshop.	Ich **werde** einen Theaterworkshop **machen**. Ich **möchte / will** einen Theaterworkshop **machen**. Ich **plane / habe vor**, einen Theaterworkshop **zu machen**.

Du bildest das Futur mit *going to* mit einer Form von *be* + *going to* + Grundform des Verbs.

	Langform	Kurzform			
Singular	I am	I'm	going to	do	a drama workshop.
	You are	You're			
	He/She is	He's/She's			
Plural	We are	We're			
	You are	You're			
	They are	They're			

b) Verneinte Aussagesätze im *going to-future*

Für die Verneinung stellst du *not* hinter die Form von *be*. Oft benutzt man Kurzformen.

	Langform	Kurzform			
Singular	I am not	I'm not	going to	do	a cooking workshop.
	You are not	You aren't			
	He/She is not	He/She isn't			
Plural	We are not	We aren't			
	You are not	You aren't			
	They are not	They aren't			

18 THE GOING TO-FUTURE: QUESTIONS (REVISION)
Das Futur mit *going to*: Fragen *(revision)*

Mit einer Frage im *going to-future* kannst du z. B. danach fragen, was jemand für die Zukunft plant.

a) Entscheidungsfragen und Kurzantworten im *going to-future*

DIGITAL+ video 29

Bei Entscheidungsfragen rückt im *going to-future* die Form von *be (am, is, are)* an den Satzanfang.
In der Kurzantwort steht dann die entsprechende Form von *be*.

Entscheidungsfrage	Kurzantwort	Kurzantwort
Are you **going to do** a cooking workshop? **Wirst** du einen Koch-Workshop **machen**?	Yes, I am. Ja.	No, I'm not. Nein.
Is Ava **going to visit** her grandmother? **Wird** Ava ihre Großmutter **besuchen**?	Yes, she is. Ja.	No, she isn't. Nein.
Are the children **going to take part in** a workshop? **Werden** die Kinder an einem Workshop **teilnehmen**?	Yes, they are. Ja.	No, they aren't. Nein.

b) Fragen mit Fragewort im *going to-future*

Bei Fragen mit Fragewort steht das Fragewort an erster Stelle.

What *are you going to do in the holidays?*
When *is the workshop going to start?*
Where *is the workshop going to take place?*

Nach Vokabeln suchen

Alphabetische Wortliste (*Dictionary*): Du suchst nach der Bedeutung eines einzelnen englischen Wortes, das im Textbook vorgekommen ist? Dann nutze die alphabetische Wortliste ab Seite 213. Hier findest du auch die Wörter aus der *Story*, aus den Projekten, aus den *Wordbanks* und von den *Get together*- und *Challenge*-Seiten. Einige englische Wörter, die im Englischen und im Deutschen gleich sind, findest du auf Seite 192.

Wortlisten nach Kapiteln (*Vocabulary*): Du möchtest die Vokabeln zu einem ganzen Abschnitt im Buch lernen? Dann nutze die chronologische Wortliste ab Seite 193. Nach Kapiteln und Seitenzahlen sortiert findest du hier alle Wörter, die neu im Buch vorkommen.

Vokabeln finden
Hier siehst du, zu welcher Aufgabe eines Kapitels die Vokabeln gehören. Die Seitenzahl hilft dabei.

Wichtige Vokabeln erkennen
Wichtige Vokabeln sind fett schwarz gedruckt und farbig markiert. Die solltest du dir merken.

Vokabeln richtig aussprechen
Die Lautschrift zeigt dir, wie die Wörter richtig ausgesprochen werden.

Unit

p. 36, 1	**englische Vokabel** /Lautschrift/	deutsche Übersetzung
	englische Vokabel /Lautschrift/	deutsche Übersetzung
	englische Vokabel /Lautschrift/	deutsche Übersetzung
	englische Vokabel /Lautschrift/	deutsche Übersetzung
	englische Vokabel /Lautschrift/	deutsche Übersetzung
	englische Vokabel /Lautschrift/	deutsche Übersetzung
	englische Vokabel /Lautschrift/	deutsche Übersetzung
	englische Vokabel *(Hinweis)* /Lautschrift/	deutsche Übersetzung

Beispielsätze und Bilder helfen dir dabei, dir Vokabeln einzuprägen.

In farbigen Kästen findest du nützliche Informationen.

Passiver Wortschatz
Vokabeln, die nicht zum Lernwortschatz gehören, sind grau gedruckt. Die brauchst du dir nicht zu merken.

Besondere Hinweise
Zu einigen Vokabeln findest du Angaben, die dir wichtige Hinweise zu ihrem Gebrauch geben:

(pl)	Das Wort kommt hier in seiner Pluralform vor bzw. hat eine unregelmäßige Pluralform.
(no pl)	Dieses Wort hat keine Pluralform.
(informal)	Dieses Wort oder dieser Ausdruck ist umgangssprachlich.
(AE)	Dieses Wort oder dieser Ausdruck kommt aus dem amerikanischen Englisch.
(irr)	Dieses Verb ist unregelmäßig. Du findest eine Liste mit unregelmäßigen Verben auf Seite 245-247.

Die richtige Aussprache

Im Englischen spricht man Wörter oft anders aus als man sie schreibt.
Die Aussprache der Wörter wird mithilfe der Lautschrift in jedem Wörterbuch angegeben.
Man kann so auch neue Wörter richtig aussprechen, ohne sie vorher gehört zu haben.
Die Lautschrift ist eine Schrift, deren Symbole jeden Laut genau bezeichnen.
Hier ist eine Liste mit den Symbolen dieser Lautschrift zusammen mit Beispielwörtern.

The English alphabet

a	/eɪ/
b	/biː/
c	/siː/
d	/diː/
e	/iː/
f	/ef/
g	/dʒiː/
h	/eɪtʃ/
i	/aɪ/
j	/dʒeɪ/
k	/keɪ/
l	/el/
m	/em/
n	/en/
o	/əʊ/
p	/piː/
q	/kjuː/
r	/ɑː/
s	/es/
t	/tiː/
u	/juː/
v	/viː/
w	/ˈdʌbljuː/
x	/eks/
y	/waɪ/
z	/zed/

English sounds

Vokale

/ɑː/	**arm**
/ʌ/	**but**
/e/	**desk**
/ə/	**a, an**
/ɜː/	**girl, bird**
/æ/	**apple**
/ɪ/	**in, it**
/i/	**happy**
/iː/	**easy, eat**
/ɒ/	**orange, sorry**
/ɔː/	**all, call**
/ʊ/	**look**
/u/	**January**
/uː/	**boot**

Doppellaute

/aɪ/	**eye, by, buy**
/aʊ/	**our**
/eə/	**air, there**
/eɪ/	**take, they**
/ɪə/	**here**
/ɔɪ/	**boy**
/əʊ/	**go, old**
/ʊə/	**tour**

Konsonanten

/b/	**bag, club**
/d/	**duck, card**
/f/	**fish, laugh**
/g/	**get, dog**
/h/	**hot**
/j/	**you**
/k/	**can, duck**
/l/	**lot, small**
/m/	**more, mum**
/n/	**now, sun**
/ŋ/	**song, long**
/p/	**present, top**
/r/	**red, around**
/s/	**sister, class** *(stimmlos)*
/z/	**nose, dogs** *(stimmhaft)*
/t/	**time, cat**
/ʒ/	**television**
/dʒ/	**sausage**
/ʃ/	**fresh**
/tʃ/	**child, cheese**
/ð/	**these, mother** *(stimmhaft)*
/θ/	**bathroom, think** *(stimmlos)*
/v/	**very, have**
/w/	**what, word**

Betonungszeichen für die folgende Silbe

/ˈ/	**Hauptbetonung**
/ˌ/	**Nebenbetonung**

Bekannte Wörter

Viele Wörter sind im Englischen und im Deutschen so gut wie gleich. Manche unterscheiden sich nur durch die Groß- bzw. Kleinschreibung – im Englischen werden die meisten Nomen kleingeschrieben. Viele dieser Wörter, die in deinem Buch vorkommen, findest du hier. Bei denen, die anders ausgesprochen werden als im Deutschen, ist die Lautschrift farbig hervorgehoben.

app /æp/
arm /ɑːm/
audio /ˈɔːdiəʊ/
baby /ˈbeɪbi/
ball /bɔːl/
band /bænd/
baseball /ˈbeɪsˌbɔːl/
basketball /ˈbɑːskɪtˌbɔːl/
beige /beɪʒ/
blind /blaɪnd/
blog /blɒg/
burger /ˈbɜːgə/
bus /bʌs/
butler /ˈbʌtə/
butter /ˈbʌtə/
café /ˈkæfeɪ/
cafeteria /ˌkæfəˈtɪəriə/
cent /sent/
champion /ˈtʃæmpjən/
chance /tʃɑːns/
chat /tʃæt/
chicken nugget /ˌtʃɪkɪn‿ˈnʌgɪt/
clip /klɪp/
cola /ˈkəʊlə/
collage /ˈkɒlɑːʒ/
computer /kəmˈpjuːtə/
cool /kuːl/
cornflakes /ˈkɔːnfleɪks/
couch /kaʊtʃ/
couscous /ˈkuːskuːs/
currywurst /ˈkʌriwɜːst/
darts /dɑːts/
definition /ˌdefəˈnɪʃn/
diesel /ˈdiːzl/
digital /ˈdɪdʒɪtl/
dip /dɪp/
display /dɪˈspleɪ/
dressing /ˈdresɪŋ/
element /ˈelɪmənt/
email /ˈiːmeɪl/
emoji /ɪˈməʊdʒi/
etc. (= etcetera) /et ˈsetrə/
euro /ˈjʊərəʊ/
fair /feə/
fan /fæn/
fast food /ˌfɑːst ˈfuːd/
film /fɪlm/
finger /ˈfɪŋgə/
fit /fɪt/
flyer /ˈflaɪə/
form /fɔːm/
format /ˈfɔːmæt/
front /frʌnt/
giraffe /dʒəˈrɑːf/
golden /ˈgəʊldn/
golf /gɒlf/
halfpipe /ˈhɑːfpaɪp/
hammer /ˈhæmə/
handout /ˈhændaʊt/
hieroglyph /ˈhaɪrəglɪf/
high-tech /ˌhaɪ ˈtek/
hobby /ˈhɒbi/
hockey /ˈhɒki/
home page /ˈhəʊm peɪdʒ/
hoodie /ˈhʊdi/
horde /hɔːd/
hot dog /ˌhɒt ˈdɒg/
hotel /həʊˈtel/
ideal /aɪˈdɪəl/
idol /ˈaɪdl/
info /ˈɪnfəʊ/
instrument /ˈɪnstrʊmənt/
international /ˌɪntəˈnæʃnəl/
Internet /ˈɪntəˌnet/
interview /ˈɪntəˌvjuː/
jeans /dʒiːnz/
jury /ˈdʒʊəri/
karate /kəˈrɑːti/
ketchup /ˈketʃəp/
kilt /kɪlt/
laptop /ˈlæpˌtɒp/
limerick /ˈlɪmərɪk/
link /lɪŋk/
live /laɪv/
mango /ˈmæŋgəʊ/
marathon /ˈmærəθn/
material /məˈtɪəriəl/
meme /miːm/
mild /maɪld/
million /ˈmɪljən/
mini /ˈmɪni/
minute /ˈmɪnɪt/
mixer /ˈmɪksə/
modern /ˈmɒdən/
moment /ˈməʊmənt/
mozzarella /ˌmɒtsəˈrelə/
muffin /ˈmʌfɪn/
multimedia /ˌmʌltiˈmiːdiə/
museum /mjuːˈziːəm/
musical /ˈmjuːzɪkl/
name /neɪm/
national /ˈnæʃnəl/
OK (= okay) /ˌəʊˈkeɪ/
olive /ˈɒlɪv/
online /ˈɒnlaɪn/
operation /ˌɒpəˈreɪʃn/
original /əˈrɪdʒnəl/
papyrus /pəˈpaɪrəs/
parade /pəˈreɪd/
paratriathlon /ˌpærətraɪˈæθlən/
park /pɑːk/
partner /ˈpɑːtnə/
party /ˈpɑːti/
patient /ˈpeɪʃnt/
penicillin /ˌpenəˈsɪlɪn/
person /ˈpɜːsn/
pilates /pɪˈlɑːtiːz/
pilot /ˈpaɪlət/
pizza /ˈpiːtsə/
plan /plæn/
planet /ˈplænɪt/
podcast /ˈpɒdˌkɑːst/
pool /puːl/
post /pəʊst/
poster /ˈpəʊstə/
problem /ˈprɒbləm/
quiz /kwɪz/
radio /ˈreɪdiəʊ/
rest /rest/
restaurant /ˈrestrɒnt/
ring /rɪŋ/
rucksack /ˈrʌkˌsæk/
rugby /ˈrʌgbi/
sand /sænd/
sandwich /ˈsænwɪdʒ/
science fiction /ˌsaɪəns ˈfɪkʃn/
service /ˈsɜːvɪs/
show /ʃəʊ/
situation /ˌsɪtʃuˈeɪʃn/
skateboard /ˈskeɪtbɔːd/
skateboarder /ˈskeɪtbɔːdə/
slogan /ˈsləʊgən/
smartphone /ˈsmɑːtˌfəʊn/
smiley /ˈsmaɪli/
snack /snæk/
so /səʊ/
softball /ˈsɒftˌbɔːl/
sorbet /ˈsɔːbeɪ/
spaghetti /spəˈgeti/
streaming /ˈstriːmɪŋ/
super /ˈsuːpə/
sushi /ˈsuːʃi/
T-shirt /ˈtiː ʃɜːt/
tablet /ˈtæblət/
team /tiːm/
teenager /ˈtiːnˌeɪdʒə/
tennis /ˈtenɪs/
test /test/
text /tekst/
ticket /ˈtɪkɪt/
toast /təʊst/
toaster /ˈtəʊstə/
tofu /ˈtəʊfuː/
touch-screen /ˈtʌtʃskriːn/
tour /tʊə/
tourist /ˈtʊərɪst/
training /ˈtreɪnɪŋ/
triathlon /traɪˈæθlən/
tunnel /ˈtʌnl/
tutorial /tjuːˈtɔːriəl/
upcycling /ˈʌpˌsaɪklɪŋ/
vase /vɑːz/
verb /vɜːb/
video /ˈvɪdiəʊ/
video clip /ˈvɪdiəʊ klɪp/
volleyball /ˈvɒlibɔːl/
warm /wɔːm/
webcode /ˈwebˌkəʊd/
website /ˈwebˌsaɪt/
winter /ˈwɪntə/
wok /wɒk/
workshop /ˈwɜːkˌʃɒp/
yoga /ˈjəʊgə/
yoghurt /ˈjɒgət/

p. 6	**grandma** *(informal)* /ˈɡrænˌmɑː/	(die) Oma	
	originally /əˈrɪdʒnəli/	ursprünglich	**originally** = at first
	Egypt /ˈiːdʒɪpt/	Ägypten	

Unit 1 | Part A Delicious dishes

p. 7	**dish** (*pl* **dishes**) /dɪʃ, ˈdɪʃɪz/	(das) Gericht, (die) Speise	**Curry** is a traditional Indian **dish**.
p. 8, 1	**curry** /ˈkʌri/	(das) Curry(gericht)	
	pasta /ˈpæstə/	(die) Nudeln	
	sauce /sɔːs/	(die) Soße	
	yummy *(informal)* /ˈjʌmi/	lecker	
	mashed potatoes *(pl)* /ˌmæʃt pəˈteɪtəʊz/	(der) Kartoffelbrei	
	sausage /ˈsɒsɪdʒ/	(die) Wurst, (das) Würstchen	
p. 8, 2	(to) **order (in)** /ˈɔːdə, ˌɔːdər‿ˈɪn/	bestellen	
	salad /ˈsæləd/	(der) Salat	When you are **full**, you don't want to eat or drink anything.
	full /fʊl/	satt	
	(to) **finish** /ˈfɪnɪʃ/	aufessen	
	absolutely /ˈæbsəluːtli/	absolut	
	potato (*pl* **potatoes**) /pəˈteɪtəʊ, pəˈteɪtəʊz/	(die) Kartoffel	
	vegetarian /ˌvedʒəˈteəriən/	(der/die) Vegetarier/in; vegetarisch	A **vegetarian** doesn't eat fish or meat.
	savoury /ˈseɪvəri/	pikant, salzig	
	BFF (= best friends forever) *(informal)* /ˌbiː‿ef‿ˈef, ˌbest ˌfrendz fərˈevə/	*allerbeste Freunde/Freundinnen*	
	greetings *(pl)* /ˈɡriːtɪŋz/	(die) Grüße	
	Greece /ɡriːs/	Griechenland	
	cucumber /ˈkjuːˌkʌmbə/	(die) Salatgurke	
	grilled /ɡrɪld/	gegrillt	
	octopus /ˈɒktəpəs/	(der) Tintenfisch	
	roast /rəʊst/	(der) Braten; gebraten, geröstet	
	gravy /ˈɡreɪvi/	(die) (Braten)soße	
	Yorkshire pudding /ˌjɔːkʃə ˈpʊdɪŋ/	*britische gebackene Beilage*	
p. 9, 2	**thin** /θɪn/	dünn	There is a **thin** slice of cheese in the burger.
	onion /ˈʌnjən/	(die) Zwiebel	
	spicy /ˈspaɪsi/	würzig, scharf	
	speciality /ˌspeʃiˈæləti/	(die) Spezialität	
	(to) **serve** /sɜːv/	servieren; reichen für	
	disgusting /dɪsˈɡʌstɪŋ/	widerlich	**disgusting** = not nice or yummy
	comfort food /ˈkʌmfət fuːd/	(das) Wohlfühlessen	
	Lahmacun /ˌlɑməˈdʒuːn/	*traditionelles türkisches Gericht*	
	rolled /rəʊld/	gerollt	
	flatbread /ˈflætbred/	(der) Fladen	
	filled /fɪld/	gefüllt	
	minced meat /ˌmɪnst ˈmiːt/	(das) Hackfleisch	

	Turkey /ˈtɜːki/	die Türkei	
	Lebanon /ˈlebənən/	der Libanon	
	Shakshuka /ʃəkˈʃuːkə/	*traditionelles israelisches und nordafrikanisches Gericht*	
	North Africa /ˌnɔːθ‿ˈæfrɪkə/	Nordafrika	
	garlic /ˈɡɑːlɪk/	(der) Knoblauch	
	(to) unscramble /ʌnˈskræmbl/	ordnen, in die richtige Reihenfolge bringen	
p. 11, 6	web page /ˈweb‿peɪdʒ/	(die) Webseite, (die) Internetseite	
	from (all) around the world /frəm‿ˌɔːl‿əˌraʊnd ðə ˈwɜːld/	aus der (ganzen) Welt	
	fried /fraɪd/	gebraten	
	noodle /ˈnuːdl/	(die) Nudel	
	(chicken) tikka masala, (chicken) tikka /ˌtʃɪkɪn ˌtiːkə məˈsɑːlə, ˌtʃɪkɪn ˈtiːkə/	*britisch-indisches (Hühnchen-)Gericht*	
	India /ˈɪndiə/	Indien	
p. 12, 7	**pot** /pɒt/	(der) Topf	 The man is cooking food in a **pot**.
	quick /kwɪk/	schnell, kurz	
	meat /miːt/	(das) Fleisch	
	veggie *(informal)* /ˈvedʒi/	(das) Gemüse	
	herb /hɜːb/	(das) (Gewürz)kraut	
	spice /spaɪs/	(das) Gewürz	There are lots of **spices** in a curry.
	fridge /frɪdʒ/	(der) Kühlschrank	
	cupboard /ˈkʌbəd/	(der) Schrank	
	pepper /ˈpepə/	(die) Paprika; (der) Pfeffer	
	can /kæn/	(die) Dose, (die) Büchse	
	left /left/	übrig	
	recipe /ˈresəpi/	(das) Rezept	Everybody can learn to cook with the help of a **recipe**.
	(to) starve /stɑːv/	verhungern	I'**m starving**! Ich habe einen Bärenhunger!, Ich habe riesigen Hunger!
	drawer /ˈdrɔːə/	(die) Schublade	
	cabbage /ˈkæbɪdʒ/	(der) Kohl	
	chickpea /ˈtʃɪkˌpiː/	(die) Kichererbse	
	jar /dʒɑː/	(das) (Glas)gefäß	
	crumb /krʌm/	(der) Krümel	
	(to) bring to the boil *(irr)* /ˌbrɪŋ tə ðə ˈbɔɪl/	zum Kochen bringen	
	Morocco /məˈrɒkəʊ/	Marokko	
	cook-along video /ˈkʊk‿əˌlɒŋ ˌvɪdiəʊ/	*(das) Mitmach-Koch-Video*	
p. 13, 7	bracket /ˈbrækɪt/	(die) Klammer	
p. 13, 8	(to) **put in** *(irr)* /ˌpʊt‿ˈɪn/	hineintun, hinzufügen	
	(to) **chop** /tʃɒp/	hacken	
	(to) **heat** /hiːt/	erhitzen	
	(to) **slice** /slaɪs/	in Scheiben schneiden	 to **slice** a cucumber
	(to) **stir in** /ˌstɜːr‿ˈɪn/	einrühren, unterrühren	

p. 14, 10	**vegan** /ˈviːgən/	(der/die) Veganer/in; vegan	
	by heart /ˌbaɪ ˈhɑːt/	auswendig	
	(to) **kill** /kɪl/	töten	
	season /ˈsiːzn/	(die) Saison	
	for no reason /fə ˌnəʊ ˈriːzn/	ohne Grund, grundlos	
	foxhunting *(no pl)* /ˈfɒks ˌhʌntɪŋ/	(die) Fuchsjagd	Germany is famous for good **bread**.
p. 15, 11	**bread** /bred/	(das) Brot	
	knight /naɪt/	(der) Ritter	
p. 15, 12	**invented** /ɪnˈventɪd/	erfunden	
	by accident /ˌbaɪ‿ˈæksɪdnt/	zufällig, aus Versehen	**by accident** = not planned
p. 16, 14	cookbook /ˈkʊkˌbʊk/	(das) Kochbuch	
p. 16, 15	odd one out /ˌɒd wʌn‿ˈaʊt/	*(das) Wort, das nicht zu den anderen passt*	
p. 16, 16	branch /brɑːntʃ/	(der) Zweig, (der) Ast	They **are preparing** different meals in their restaurant.
p. 17, 17	**original** /əˈrɪdʒnəl/	ursprünglich	
	(to) **prepare** /prɪˈpeə/	zubereiten	
	starter /ˈstɑːtə/	(die) Vorspeise	
	main (course) /ˈmeɪn kɔːs/	(das) Hauptgericht	
	dessert /dɪˈzɜːt/	(der) Nachtisch	
	(to) **try out** /ˌtraɪ‿ˈaʊt/	ausprobieren	
	oil /ɔɪl/	(das) Öl	
	teaspoon /ˈtiːˌspuːn/	(der) Teelöffel	**teaspoon**
	vegetable /ˈvedʒtəbl/	(das) Gemüse	
	soft /sɒft/	weich	**soft** ≠ hard
	ingredient /ɪnˈgriːdiənt/	(die) Zutat	
	paprika /ˈpæprɪkə/	(das) Paprikapulver	
	coriander /ˌkɒriˈændə/	(der) Koriander	
	cumin /ˈkjuːmɪn/	(der) Kreuzkümmel	
	cinnamon /ˈsɪnəmən/	(der) Zimt	**Paprika**, **coriander**, **cumin**, **cinnamon** and **cayenne pepper** are spices.
	cayenne pepper /ˌkeɪen ˈpepə/	(der) Cayennepfeffer	
	vegetable stock /ˈvedʒtəbl stɒk/	(die) Gemüsebrühe	
	cooker /ˈkʊkə/	(der) Herd	
	Enjoy! /ɪnˈdʒɔɪ/	Guten Appetit!	

Unit 1 | Part B At a restaurant

p. 18, 1	**takeaway** /ˈteɪkəˌweɪ/	(das) Essen zum Mitnehmen, (die) Imbissbude	A **takeaway** is a meal that you buy and take home to eat.
	Italian /ɪˈtæljən/	(der/die) Italiener/in; italienisch	
	Turkish /ˈtɜːkɪʃ/	türkisch	
	Vietnamese /viˌetnəˈmiːz/	(der/die) Vietnamese/Vietnamesin; vietnamesisch	
	Thai /taɪ/	(der/die) Thailänder/in; thailändisch	
p. 18, 2	**review** /rɪˈvjuː/	(die) Kritik, (die) Rezension	
	(to) **skim** /skɪm/	überfliegen	

	cheap /tʃiːp/	billig	**cheap** ≠ expensive
	quality /ˈkwɒləti/	(die) Qualität	
	(to) **stay away from** /ˌsteɪ‿əˈweɪ frɒm/	meiden; sich fernhalten von	
	disappointing /ˌdɪsəˈpɔɪntɪŋ/	enttäuschend	
	mine /maɪn/	meine(r, s)	
	burnt /bɜːnt/	verbrannt, angebrannt	
p. 19, 2	**hot** /hɒt/	scharf	**hot** ≠ mild
	atmosphere /ˈætməsˌfɪə/	(die) Atmosphäre	
	north /nɔːθ/	(der) Norden; Nord-	
	side (dish) /ˈsaɪd‿dɪʃ/	(die) Beilage	A **side dish** is food that you get at the same time as the main course.
	pub /pʌb/	(die) Kneipe	
	vindaloo /ˌvɪndəˈluː/	*indisches Gericht*	
	korma /ˈkɔːmə/	*indisches Gericht*	
	naan bread /ˈnɑːn bred/	*indisches Fladenbrot*	
	overcooked /ˌəʊvəˈkʊkt/	verkocht	
	juicy /ˈdʒuːsi/	saftig	
	cosy /ˈkəʊzi/	gemütlich	
p. 20, 3	**tasty** /ˈteɪsti/	lecker	
	soup /suːp/	(die) Suppe	There is a tablespoon in the **soup**.
p. 20, 4	**syllable** /ˈsɪləbl/	(die) Silbe	
p. 21, 5	(to) **be allergic to** *(irr)* /ˌbi‿əˈlɜːdʒɪk tʊ/	allergisch sein auf	
	occasion /əˈkeɪʒn/	(die) Gelegenheit, (der) Anlass	
	Indian /ˈɪndiən/	(der/die) Inder/in; indisch	
	raw /rɔː/	roh	
p. 22, 6	**waiter/waitress** /ˈweɪtə, ˈweɪtrəs/	(der/die) Kellner/in	
	reservation /ˌrezəˈveɪʃn/	(die) Reservierung	
	certainly /ˈsɜːtnli/	sicher, gerne	
	this way /ˈðɪs weɪ/	hier entlang	
	(to) **take a seat** *(irr)* /ˌteɪk‿ə ˈsiːt/	sich setzen	They **have taken a seat** in a restaurant.
	home-made /ˌhəʊmˈmeɪd/	hausgemacht	
	(to) **take an order** *(irr)* /ˌteɪk‿ən‿ˈɔːdə/	eine Bestellung aufnehmen	
	on the side /ˌɒn ðə ˈsaɪd/	als Beilage	**on the side** = as a side dish
	sir/Sir /sɜː/	Sir; Herr (*Anrede vor Vornamen*)	
	(to) **warn** /wɔːn/	warnen	
	extremely /ɪkˈstriːmli/	äußerst, höchst, außerordentlich	**extremely** = very
	palace /ˈpæləs/	(der) Palast	
	(to) show to the table *(irr)* /ˌʃəʊ tə ðə ˈteɪbl/	zum Tisch führen	
	salmon /ˈsæmən/	(der) Lachs	
	lamb /læm/	(das) Lamm	
	(to) rewrite *(irr)* /ˌriːˈraɪt/	überarbeiten, umschreiben	**to rewrite** = to make changes to a piece of writing
p. 23, 7	**lemonade** /ˌleməˈneɪd/	(die) Limonade	
	mineral water /ˈmɪnrəl ˌwɔːtə/	(das) Mineralwasser	

	lassi /'læsi/	*Joghurtgetränk*	
	poppadom /'pɒpədəm/	*dünnes indisches Brot*	
	cracker /'krækə/	(der) Kräcker	
	selection /sɪ'lekʃn/	(die) Auswahl	cooked /kʊkt/ gekocht mixed /mɪkst/ gemischt
	bhaji /'bɑːdʒi/	*indisches Gericht*	
	samosa /sə'məʊsə/	*indische gefüllte Teigtasche*	
	pastry /'peɪstri/	(der) Brandteig, (der) Blätterteig	
	coconut cream /'kəʊkəˌnʌt kriːm/	(die) Kokosmilch	
	ginger /'dʒɪndʒə/	(der) Ingwer	
	chilli (*pl* chillies) /'tʃɪli/	(der) Chili, (die) Peperoni	
	palak paneer /ˌpɑːlək pə'nɪə/	*indisches Gericht*	
	spinach /'spɪnɪdʒ/	(der) Spinat	
	beef /biːf/	(das) Rindfleisch	
p. 24, 8	(to) **get** *(irr)* /get/	bringen	
	any more /ˌeni 'mɔː/	noch mehr	The mother is not happy. The father is **not** happy **either**.
	not ... either /ˌnɒt‿'aɪðə/	auch nicht	
	bill /bɪl/	(die) Rechnung	You can pay in **cash** or by credit card at a restaurant.
	cash /kæʃ/	(das) Geld, (das) Bargeld	
	(to) **bring over** *(irr)* /ˌbrɪŋ‿'əʊvə/	herbeibringen	to **eat out** = to not eat at home
p. 25, 10	(to) **eat out** *(irr)* /ˌiːt‿'aʊt/	auswärts essen; im Restaurant essen	
	strawberry /'strɔːbri/	(die) Erdbeere	
p. 25, 11	**lady** /'leɪdi/	(die) Frau, (die) Dame	
	both /bəʊθ/	beide	
p. 26, 12	(to) **go on** *(irr)* /ˌgəʊ‿'ɒn/	passieren; weitergehen, weiterreden	
	caption /'kæpʃn/	(die) Bildunterschrift	
	OMG! (= Oh my God!) /ˌəʊ‿em 'dʒiː/	Oh mein Gott!	
	spider /'spaɪdə/	(die) Spinne	
p. 26, 13	**conversation** /ˌkɒnvə'seɪʃn/	(das) Gespräch, (die) Unterhaltung	
	English-speaking /'ɪŋglɪʃ‿ˌspiːkɪŋ/	englischsprachig	There are usually lots of **props** on a theatre stage.
p. 27, 14	**prop** /prɒp/	(die) Requisite	

Unit 2 | Part A Keeping fit

p. 31	**living** /'lɪvɪŋ/	(der) Lebensstil	Wenn man den Ort und nicht die Person meint, sagt man „at the doctor**'s**" – beim Arzt / bei der Ärztin.
	lifestyle /'laɪfˌstaɪl/	(der) Lebensstil	
	(to) **keep fit** *(irr)* /ˌkiːp 'fɪt/	fit bleiben, (sich) fit halten	
	doctor /'dɒktə/	(der/die) Arzt/Ärztin	
p. 32, 1	(to) **prefer** /prɪ'fɜː/	vorziehen, bevorzugen	
	indoors /ˌɪn'dɔːz/	drinnen, im Haus	
	outdoors /ˌaʊt'dɔːz/	draußen, im Freien	**indoors** ≠ **outdoors**
	(to) **win** *(irr)* /wɪn/	gewinnen	
	(to) **lose** *(irr)* /luːz/	verlieren	to **win** ≠ to **lose**
	diving /'daɪvɪŋ/	(das) Tauchen	
	loser /'luːzə/	(der/die) Verlierer/in	

	(to) care about /ˈkeər‿əˌbaʊt/	sich etwas machen aus
	rowing /ˈrəʊɪŋ/	(das) Rudern
	weight training /ˈweɪt‿ˌtreɪnɪŋ/	(das) Krafttraining
	climbing /ˈklaɪmɪŋ/	(das) Klettern
p. 33, 2	(to) **scan** /skæn/	absuchen, überfliegen
	profile /ˈprəʊfaɪl/	(das) Profil, (das) Porträt
	active /ˈæktɪv/	aktiv
	(to) **sit** *(irr)* /sɪt/	sitzen
	(to) **train** /treɪn/	trainieren
	(to) **reach** /riːtʃ/	erreichen
	skill /skɪl/	(die) Fähigkeit, (das) Geschick
	strength /streŋθ/	(die) Kraft, (die) Stärke
	in order to /ˌɪn‿ˈɔːdə tʊ/	um zu
	outdoor /ˌaʊtˈdɔː/	Outdoor-, im Freien
	still /stɪl/	still, bewegungslos
	logical thinking /ˌlɒdʒɪkl ˈθɪŋkɪŋ/	(das) logische Denken
	puzzle /ˈpʌzl/	(das) Rätsel
p. 34, 4	**exhausting** /ɪɡˈzɔːstɪŋ/	anstrengend
p. 35, 6	(to) **look up** /ˌlʊk‿ˈʌp/	hochschauen; nachschlagen
	series /ˈsɪəriːz/	(die) Folge, (die) Serie
	prize /praɪz/	(der) Preis, (der) Gewinn
	physical /ˈfɪzɪkl/	körperlich
	(to) **concentrate** /ˈkɒnsnˌtreɪt/	sich konzentrieren
	chess /tʃes/	(das) Schach
	relaxing /rɪˈlæksɪŋ/	entspannend
	strategy /ˈstrætədʒi/	(die) Strategie
	tournament /ˈtʊənəmənt/	(das) Turnier
	competitive /kəmˈpetətɪv/	*von Konkurrenzdenken geprägt*
p. 36, 7	**dance** /dɑːns/	(der) Tanz
	(to) **move** /muːv/	(sich) bewegen
	wheelchair /ˈwiːltʃeə/	(der) Rollstuhl
	twice /twaɪs/	zweimal
	some day /ˈsʌmˌdeɪ/	eines Tages
	ourselves /aʊəˈselvz/	uns; wir selbst
	sleep /sliːp/	(der) Schlaf
	(to) **stress** /stres/	stressen
	(to) **compete** /kəmˈpiːt/	an einem Wettkampf teilnehmen; kämpfen
	indoor /ˌɪnˈdɔː/	Hallen-
	regularly /ˈregjʊləli/	regelmäßig
	flexible /ˈfleksəbl/	biegsam, gelenkig
	myself /maɪˈself/	mir/mich/ich (selbst)
	stressed /strest/	gestresst

They **are sitting** on the sofa.

Camping is an **outdoor** activity.

Training hard is very **exhausting**.

chess

dance

The girl has a good **sleep**.

The boy is very **flexible**.

	chance /tʃɑ:ns/	(die) Möglichkeit, (die) Gelegenheit	
	(to) exercise /ˈeksəsaɪz/	trainieren	
	workout /ˈwɜ:kaʊt/	(das) Training	
	exhausted /ɪɡˈzɔ:stɪd/	erschöpft	
p. 37, 7	(to) **get better** *(irr)* /ˌɡet ˈbetə/	besser werden; gesund werden	When you are ill, you hope to **get better** very soon.
	most of the time /ˈməʊst‿əv ðə ˌtaɪm/	meistens	
	(to) **make somebody do something** *(irr)* /ˌmeɪk ˌsʌmbədi ˈdu: ˌsʌmθɪŋ/	jemanden dazu bringen, etwas zu tun	My mum **made** me **do** my homework.
	sporty /ˈspɔ:ti/	sportlich	
	for some time /fə ˌsʌm ˈtaɪm/	eine Zeitlang	
p. 38, 8	**check** /tʃek/	(die) Überprüfung, (die) Kontrolle	
	dry suit /ˈdraɪsu:t/	(der) Taucheranzug	
	buddy *(informal)* /ˈbʌdi/	(der) Kumpel	
p. 39, 9	**advert (= ad)** /ˈædvɜ:t, æd/	(die) Werbung, (die) Anzeige	
p. 39, 10	(to) **turn off** /ˌtɜ:n‿ˈɒf/	ausschalten	
	helmet /ˈhelmɪt/	(der) Helm	 **helmet**
	(to) **roll** /rəʊl/	rollen	
	(to) **shoot** *(irr)* /ʃu:t/	schießen	
	like that /ˌlaɪk ˈðæt/	so	
	rhyming word /ˈraɪmɪŋ wɜ:d/	(das) Reimwort	Poems often have **rhyming words.**
	poet /ˈpəʊɪt/	(der/die) Dichter/in	
	soccer *(AE)* /ˈsɒkə/	(der) Fußball	**soccer** *(AE)* = football
	(to) grab /ɡræb/	sich schnappen, greifen	
	each and every /ˈi:tʃ‿ən‿ˌevri/	jede(r, s) einzelne	
	knee pad /ˈni: ˌpæd/	(der) Knieschützer	
	elbow pad /ˈelbəʊ ˌpæd/	(der) Ellenbogenschützer	
	Come on! /ˌkʌm‿ˈɒn/	Komm(t) schon!	
	(to) bounce /baʊns/	(auf)springen	
	all around /ˌɔ:l‿əˈraʊnd/	überall (in)	
	(to) pat /pæt/	einen Klaps geben	
	(to) head /hed/	köpfen	
	bat /bæt/	(der) Schläger	 **bat**
	(to) biff *(informal)* /bɪf/	hauen, schlagen	
	(to) boot /bu:t/	einen Tritt geben	
	(to) spin *(irr)* /spɪn/	drehen, einen Drall geben	
	(to) drop /drɒp/	fallen lassen	
p. 40, 11	(to) **belong** (to) /bɪˈlɒŋ/	gehören (zu)	When something **belongs to** you, it is yours.
p. 40, 12	(to) **be born** *(irr)* /ˌbi: ˈbɔ:n/	geboren werden	
	skating /ˈskeɪtɪŋ/	*hier:* (das) Skateboardfahren	
	(to) look out for /ˌlʊk‿ˈaʊt fə/	*hier:* sich kümmern um	
p. 41, 13	**slide** /slaɪd/	(die) Folie	
	unit /ˈju:nɪt/	(das) Kapitel	
	(to) **switch off** /ˌswɪtʃ‿ˈɒf/	ausschalten	It is dark when you **switch off** the light at night.
	leaflet /ˈli:flət/	(der) Prospekt, (die) Broschüre	

	slide show /ˈslaɪd ʃəʊ/	(die) Bildschirmpräsentation	
	gallery walk /ˈɡæləri wɔːk/	*(die) Gruppendiskussion in Stationsarbeit*	
	the most important ones /ðə ˌməʊst‿ɪmˈpɔːtnt wʌnz/	die wichtigsten	

Unit 2 | Part B At the doctor's

p. 42, 1	**What's the matter?** /ˌwɒts‿ðə ˈmætə/	Was ist los?	
	toothache *(no pl)* /ˈtuːθeɪk/	(die) Zahnschmerzen	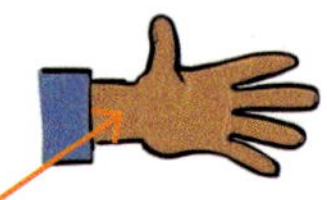
	swollen /ˈswəʊlən/	geschwollen	
	wrist /rɪst/	(das) Handgelenk	**wrist**
	cold /kəʊld/	(die) Erkältung	
	stomach ache *(no pl)* /ˈstʌmək‿ˌeɪk/	(die) Bauchschmerzen	
	wound /wuːnd/	(die) Wunde	
	shoulder /ˈʃəʊldə/	(die) Schulter	When you have a **stomach ache**, your stomach **hurts**.
	(to) **hurt** *(irr)* /hɜːt/	wehtun, schmerzen; verletzen	
	broken /ˈbrəʊkən/	gebrochen	
	(to) **take an X-ray** *(irr)* /ˌteɪk‿ən ˈeksreɪ/	eine Röntgenaufnahme machen	
	cast /kɑːst/	(der) Gips	
	tooth (*pl* **teeth**) /tuːθ, tiːθ/	(der) Zahn	
	appointment /əˈpɔɪntmənt/	(der) Termin	Wenn man den Ort und nicht die Person meint, sagt man „at the dentist**'s**“ – „beim Zahnarzt / bei der Zahnärztin / in der Zahnarztpraxis“ oder „to the dentist**'s**“ – „zum Zahnarzt / zur Zahnärztin“.
	dentist /ˈdentɪst/	(der/die) Zahnarzt/Zahnärztin	
	practice /ˈpræktɪs/	(die) Praxis	
	This is ... speaking. /ðɪs‿ɪz ... ˈspiːkɪŋ/	Hier spricht ...	
	(to) **catch a cold** *(irr)* /ˌkætʃ‿ə ˈkəʊld/	sich erkälten	
	headache /ˈhedeɪk/	(die) Kopfschmerzen	
	sore throat /ˌsɔː ˈθrəʊt/	(die) Halsschmerzen	
	fever /ˈfiːvə/	(das) Fieber	
	cough /kɒf/	(der) Husten	
	(to) **come in** *(irr)* /ˌkʌm‿ˈɪn/	hereinkommen	
	(to) **see** *(irr)* /siː/	empfangen, drannehmen	
	bad /bæd/	*hier:* stark	
	ow (= ouch) *(informal)* /aʊ, aʊtʃ/	aua, autsch	
	receptionist /rɪˈsepʃnɪst/	(die/der) Empfangsdame/Empfangschef	
p. 43, 1	(to) **fall** *(irr)* /fɔːl/	fallen	The **wound** on his knee **is bleeding**.
	(to) **bleed** *(irr)* /bliːd/	bluten	
	infection /ɪnˈfekʃn/	(die) Infektion	
	plaster /ˈplɑːstə/	(der) Gips, (das) Pflaster	
	soon /suːn/	bald	**soon** = in the near future
	(to) **see a doctor** *(irr)* /ˌsiː‿ə ˈdɒktə/	einen Arzt/eine Ärztin aufsuchen	
	stomach /ˈstʌmək/	(der) Magen, (der) Bauch	
	medicine /ˈmedsn/	(die) Medizin, (die) Medikamente	
	health /helθ/	(die) Gesundheit	

	dramatic /drəˈmætɪk/	dramatisch	
	reading /ˈriːdɪŋ/	(die) Lesung	
	oh dear *(informal)* /əʊ ˈdɪə/	oje	
	painful /ˈpeɪnfl/	schmerzhaft	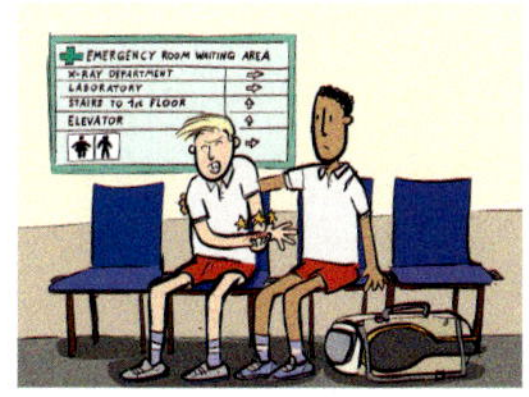
p. 44, 2	(to) **get well** *(irr)* /ˌget ˈwel/	gesund werden	
p. 45, 4	**accident** /ˈæksɪdnt/	(der) Unfall	
	coach /kəʊtʃ/	(der/die) Trainer/in	
	hard /hɑːd/	fest, kräftig	
	(to) **call an ambulance** /ˌkɔːl‿ən‿ˈæmbjʊləns/	einen Krankenwagen rufen	In case of an **emergency**, you have to go to the hospital.
	emergency /ɪˈmɜːdʒnsi/	(der) Notfall	
	(to) bang one's head /ˌbæŋ wʌnz ˈhed/	sich den Kopf anschlagen	
	alright /ɔːlˈraɪt/	in Ordnung	
	dizzy /ˈdɪzi/	schwindlig	
	emergency services *(pl)* /ɪˈmɜːdʒnsi ˌsɜːvɪsɪz/	(der) Notdienst, (der) Rettungsdienst	
	operator /ˈɒpəˌreɪtə/	(der/die) Telefonist/in	
	playing field /ˈpleɪɪŋ ˌfiːld/	(der) Sportplatz	
p. 46, 5	**meaning** /ˈmiːnɪŋ/	(die) Bedeutung	
	injury /ˈɪndʒəri/	(die) Verletzung	
	(to) **examine** /ɪgˈzæmɪn/	untersuchen	
	sprained /spreɪnd/	verstaucht	
	(to) **put on** *(irr)* /ˌpʊt‿ˈɒn/	anlegen, auftragen	
	bandage /ˈbændɪdʒ/	(der) Verband	They are sitting in the **waiting room**.
	waiting room /ˈweɪtɪŋ ˌruːm/	(das) Wartezimmer	
	yet /jet/	schon; noch	
	(to) **calm down** /ˌkɑːm ˈdaʊn/	(sich) beruhigen	
	(to) **sign** /saɪn/	unterschreiben	
	news *(no pl)* /njuːz/	(die) Neuigkeit, (die) Nachrichten	
	ankle /ˈæŋkl/	(der) (Fuß)knöchel	
	(to) **rest** /rest/	ausruhen	When you **promise** something, you tell someone that you will definitely do something.
	possible /ˈpɒsəbl/	möglich	
	(to) **promise** /ˈprɒmɪs/	versprechen	
	X-ray /ˈeksreɪ/	(das) Röntgenbild	
	phew *(informal)* /fjuː/	puh	at the **doctor's practice** = at the doctor's
	doctor's practice /ˈdɒktəz ˌpræktɪs/	(die) Arztpraxis	
	(to) keep up *(irr)* /ˌkiːp‿ˈʌp/	*hier:* hochlegen	
	No problem. /ˌnəʊ ˈprɒbləm/	*hier:* Keine Ursache.	
	check-up /ˈtʃek‿ʌp/	(die) Untersuchung	
p. 47, 5	(to) read out *(irr)* /ˌriːd‿ˈaʊt/	(laut) vorlesen	
p. 47, 6	**properly** /ˈprɒpəli/	richtig	**properly** = correctly
p. 48, 7	**Get well soon!** /ˌget ˌwel ˈsuːn/	Gute Besserung!	
	(to) cheer up /ˌtʃɪər‿ˈʌp/	aufmuntern, aufheitern	
p. 48, 8	(to) **be wrong (with)** *(irr)* /ˌbiː ˈrɒŋ wɪθ/	nicht in Ordnung sein (mit)	

p. 49, 10	(to) **help out** /ˌhelp‿ˈaʊt/	aushelfen	
	exchange student /ɪksˈtʃeɪndʒ ˌstjuːdnt/	(der/die) Austauschschüler/in	An **exchange student** goes to school in another country for some time.
p. 49, 11	**illness** /ˈɪlnəs/	(die) Krankheit	
	(to) mime /maɪm/	mimen, pantomimisch darstellen	
p. 50, 13	emergency call /ɪˈmɜːdʒnsi kɔːl/	(der) Notruf	
p. 50, 14	(to) **mark** /mɑːk/	markieren, kennzeichnen	
p. 51, 16	(to) **fall off** *(informal)* /ˌfɔːl‿ˈɒf/	(herunter)fallen	 She is afraid of **falling off**.
	medical /ˈmedɪkl/	medizinisch	

Unit 3 | Part A At the car boot sale

p. 55	**car boot sale** /ˌkɑː ˈbuːt seɪl/	*(der) Kofferraum-Flohmarkt*	
p. 56, 2	**stall** /stɔːl/	(der) Stand	
	(to) **avoid** /əˈvɔɪd/	meiden, vermeiden	
	crowd /kraʊd/	(die) Menschenmenge	Many people together are a **crowd**.
	charity /ˈtʃærəti/	(die) Wohltätigkeitsorganisation	
	run /rʌn/	(der) Lauf	
	km (= kilometre) /ˈkɪləˌmiːtə/	(der) Kilometer	
	at the same time /ˌæt‿ðə ˌseɪm ˈtaɪm/	gleichzeitig, zur gleichen Zeit	
	second-hand /ˌsekənd ˈhænd/	gebraucht	 People sell **second-hand items** at a **car boot sale**.
	item /ˈaɪtəm/	(der) Gegenstand	
	anywhere /ˈeniˌweə/	irgendwo	
	fee /fiː/	(die) Gebühr, (das) Geld	
	guide /ɡaɪd/	(der) Führer *(Buch)*	
	arts and crafts /ˌɑːrts‿ən ˈkrɑːfts/	(das) Basteln, (die) Bastelarbeit	
	charity run /ˈtʃærəti rʌn/	(der) Wohltätigkeitslauf	
	registration fee /ˌredʒɪˈstreɪʃn fiː/	(die) Anmeldegebühr	
	forever /fərˈevə/	ewig, für immer	
p. 57, 3	**finally** /ˈfaɪnli/	schließlich, endlich	**Pocket money** is money that children get from their parents every week or every month.
	neither /ˈnaɪðə, ˈniːðə/	auch nicht	
	pocket money /ˈpɒkɪt ˌmʌni/	(das) Taschengeld	
	(to) **keep doing something** *(irr)* /ˌkiːp ˈduːɪŋ sʌmθɪŋ/	etwas weiter tun	
	flea market /ˈfliː ˌmɑːkɪt/	(der) Flohmarkt	
	(to) **sell** *(irr)* /sel/	verkaufen	
	nobody /ˈnəʊbədi/	niemand, keiner	
	crowded /ˈkraʊdɪd/	überfüllt	 The concert was **crowded**.
	shall /ʃæl/	sollen; werden	
	(to) be up to something *(irr)* /ˌbi‿ˌʌp tə ˈsʌmθɪŋ/	etwas vorhaben	
	for ages *(informal)* /fər‿ˈeɪdʒɪz/	seit einer Ewigkeit	
	(to) have something left *(irr)* /ˌhæv sʌmθɪŋ ˈleft/	etwas übrig haben	
p. 58	relative clause /ˌrelətɪv ˈklɔːz/	(der) Relativsatz	

p. 59, 7	hockey stick /ˈhɒki stɪk/	(der) Hockeyschläger
	bicycle bell /ˈbaɪsɪkl bel/	(die) Fahrradklingel
	singing /ˈsɪŋɪŋ/	singend
p. 60, 8	**bargain** /ˈbɑːɡɪn/	(das) Schnäppchen
	above /əˈbʌv/	oben, oberhalb
	seller /ˈselə/	(der/die) Verkäufer/in
	taste /teɪst/	(der) Geschmack
	(to) **try on** /ˌtraɪ‿ˈɒn/	anprobieren
	much /mʌtʃ/	sehr
	price /praɪs/	(der) Preis *(Kosten)*
	..., doesn't it? /ˈdʌznt‿ɪt/	..., nicht wahr?
	curtain /ˈkɜːtn/	(der) Vorhang
	flowerpot /ˈflaʊəˌpɒt/	(der) Blumentopf
	lamp /læmp/	(die) Lampe
	coffee grinder /ˈkɒfi ˌɡraɪndə/	(die) Kaffeemühle
	price tag /ˈpraɪs tæɡ/	(das) Preisschild
p. 61, 8	**successful** /səkˈsesfl/	erfolgreich
	(to) **get rid of** *(irr)* /ˌɡet ˈrɪd‿əv/	loswerden
	charity shop /ˈtʃærəti ʃɒp/	*(der) Laden, in dem gebrauchte Dinge zu Wohltätigkeitszwecken verkauft werden*
p. 62, 10	**several** /ˈsevrəl/	einige, verschiedene
	elephant /ˈelɪfənt/	(der) Elefant
	travel guide /ˈtrævl ɡaɪd/	(der) Reiseführer *(Buch)*
p. 63, 11	(to) **contain** /kənˈteɪn/	enthalten
	chutney /ˈtʃʌtni/	*indische Beilage*
p. 63, 12	out and about /ˌaʊt‿ən‿əˈbaʊt/	unterwegs
	(to) upcycle /ˈʌpsaɪkl/	upcyceln
	odd /ɒd/	merkwürdig, seltsam
	(to) advertise /ˈædvətaɪz/	für etwas Werbung machen
p. 64, 13	**one** /wʌn/	eine(r, s)
	sock /sɒk/	(die) Socke
	broken /ˈbrəʊkən/	zerbrochen; kaputt
p. 65, 15	**part** /pɑːt/	(die) Rolle
	You're welcome. /ˌjɔː ˈwelkəm/	Gern geschehen., Keine Ursache.

A **bargain** is something you can buy that costs much less than normal.

new ones /ˈnjuː wʌnz/ neue
these ones /ˈðiːz wʌnz/ diese
a nice one /ə ˈnaɪs wʌn/ ein schöner/eine schöne/ein schönes
some old ones /səm‿ˈəʊld wʌnz/ ein paar alte
a small one /ə ˈsmɔːl wʌn/ ein kleiner/eine kleine/ ein kleines

several = some, different

this one /ˈðɪs wʌn/ diese(r, s) hier
the blue / red / green one /ðə ˈbluː / ˈred / ˈɡriːn wʌn/ der/die/das blaue / rote / grüne
the blue / brown / black ones /ðə ˈbluː / ˈbraʊn / ˈblæk wʌnz/ die blauen / braunen / schwarzen
a bigger one /ə ˈbɪɡə wʌn/ ein größerer/eine größere/ein größeres
another one /əˈnʌðə wʌn/ noch ein/e; ein anderer/ein anderes/ eine andere

Unit 3 | Part B Festivals

p. 66, 1	Viking /ˈvaɪkɪŋ/	(der/die) Wikinger/in; Wikinger-
p. 66, 2	**student** /ˈstjuːdnt/	(der/die) Student/in
	influence /ˈɪnfluəns/	(der) Einfluss
	(to) **check out** *(informal)* /ˌtʃek‿ˈaʊt/	sich ansehen; ausprobieren
	fight /faɪt/	(der) Kampf, (der) Streit

	after that /ˌɑːftə ˈðæt/	danach	first → **after that**
	(to) conquer /ˈkɒŋkə/	erobern	
	combat arena /ˈkɒmbæt‿əˌriːnə/	(die) Wettkampfarena	
	warrior /ˈwɒriə/	(der/die) Krieger/in	
	armour /ˈɑːmə/	(die) Rüstung	
	dining room /ˈdaɪnɪŋ ruːm/	*hier:* (der) Speisesaal	
p. 67, 2	**beard** /bɪəd/	(der) Bart	The man has a **beard**.
	anyone /ˈeniˌwʌn/	jede(r, s); (irgend)jemand	**highlight** = the best part of an event
	highlight /ˈhaɪˌlaɪt/	(der) Höhepunkt	
	battle /ˈbætl/	(der) Kampf	
	spectacular /spekˈtækjʊlə/	atemberaubend, spektakulär	
	content /ˈkɒntent/	(der) Inhalt	
	(to) **mention** /ˈmenʃn/	erwähnen	
	least /liːst/	am wenigsten	
	bird of prey /ˌbɜːd‿əv ˈpreɪ/	(der) Raubvogel	**bird of prey**
	breathtaking /ˈbreθˌteɪkɪŋ/	atemberaubend	
	firework display /ˈfaɪəˌwɜːk dɪˌspleɪ/	(das) Feuerwerk	
	throughout /θruːˈaʊt/	während	
	coming soon /ˌkʌmɪŋ ˈsuːn/	in Kürze erscheinend	
p. 68, 3	(to) **prepare for** /prɪˈpeə fɔː/	sich vorbereiten auf	When you **have put on** clothes, you are wearing them.
	(to) **put on** *(irr)* /ˌpʊt‿ˈɒn/	anziehen (*Kleidung*)	
	(to) style /staɪl/	frisieren	
p. 69, 5	(to) **run** *(irr)* /rʌn/	leiten, betreiben	
	(to) **steal** *(irr)* /rʌn/	stehlen	
	pocket /ˈpɒkɪt/	(die) Hosentasche	
	aspect /ˈæspekt/	(der) Aspekt, (der) Gesichtspunkt	
	on the one hand ... /ˌɒn ðə ˈwʌn hænd/	einerseits ...	
	on the other hand ... /ˌɒn ði‿ˈʌðə hænd/	andererseits ...	
	teddy bear /ˈtedi beə/	(der) Teddybär	**teddy bear**
	pickpocket /ˈpɪkˌpɒkɪt/	(der/die) Taschendieb/in	
p. 70, 6	**not anyone** /ˌnɒt‿ˈeniwʌn/	niemand	
	itself /ɪtˈself/	selbst, sich selbst	
	world-famous /ˌwɜːld ˈfeɪməs/	weltberühmt	
	(to) **dive** /daɪv/	tauchen	
	impressive /ɪmˈpresɪv/	beeindruckend	
	colourful /ˈkʌləfl/	farbenfroh, bunt	The chair is **colourful**.
	cheerful /ˈtʃɪəfl/	fröhlich, vergnügt	
	serious /ˈsɪəriəs/	ernst	
	(to) **draw attention to** *(irr)* /ˌdrɔ‿əˈtenʃn tə/	Aufmerksamkeit lenken auf	An **immigrant** is someone who comes to live in a country from another country.
	immigrant /ˈɪmɪɡrənt/	(der/die) Einwanderer/in, (der/die) Immigrant/in	
	lover /ˈlʌvə/	(der/die) Liebhaber/in	

	open-air /ˌəʊpən‿ˈeə/	im Freien	
	south-west /ˌsaʊθˈwest/	Südwest-	
	tent /tent/	(das) Zelt	**tent**
	muddy /ˈmʌdi/	matschig, schlammig	
	camping site /ˈkæmpɪŋ ˌsaɪt/	(der) Campingplatz	
	organizer /ˈɔːgəˌnaɪzə/	(der/die) Organisator/in	
	Caribbean /ˌkærɪˈbiən/	karibisch	
p. 71, 6	**multicultural** /ˌmʌltiˈkʌltʃərəl/	multikulturell	A **multicultural** class is a class with pupils from many different cultures.
	such /sʌtʃ/	so, solch	
	(to) **be worth** *(irr)* /ˌbiː ˈwɜːθ/	(sich) lohnen, wert sein	When you carry something, you often have to **lift** it first.
	(to) **lift** /lɪft/	(hoch)heben	
	(to) **turn over** /ˌtɜːn‿ˈəʊvə/	(sich) umdrehen	
	(to) **land** /lænd/	landen	
	steel drum /ˌstiːl ˈdrʌm/	*Steeldrum*	
	spectacle /ˈspektəkl/	(das) Spektakel	
	lad *(informal, Scottish)* /læd/	(der) Junge	
	lass *(informal, Scottish)* /læs/	(das) Mädchen	
	bagpipes *(pl)* /ˈbægˌpaɪps/	(der) Dudelsack	**Tossing the caber** is one of the events at the Highland Games.
	tossing the caber /ˌtɒsɪŋ ðə ˈkeɪbə/	(das) Baumstammwerfen	
	log /lɒg/	(der) Baumstamm	
	(to) toss /tɒs/	werfen	
p. 72, 8	**look** /lʊk/	(das) Aussehen, (der) Look	
	(to) **dress** /dres/	sich anziehen, sich kleiden	
	carnival /ˈkɑːnɪvl/	(das) Volksfest, (der) Karneval	
p. 73, 9	(to) **attend** /əˈtend/	besuchen	
	(to) **produce** /prəˈdjuːs/	produzieren	
	waste /weɪst/	(der) Abfall	
	green /griːn/	umweltfreundlich, ökologisch	We should **reduce** the amount of **waste** that we **produce**.
	government /ˈgʌvənmənt/	(die) Regierung	
	(to) **reduce** /rɪˈdjuːs/	reduzieren	
	packaging /ˈpækɪdʒɪŋ/	(die) Verpackung	
	made /meɪd/	hergestellt, gemacht	
	use /juːs/	(die) Verwendung; (der) Einsatz	
	no longer /ˌnəʊ ˈlɒŋgə/	nicht mehr	**no longer** = not anymore
	site /saɪt/	(die) Stelle, (der) Platz	
	(to) clear up /ˌklɪər‿ˈʌp/	aufräumen	
	ton /tʌn/	(die) Tonne	
	straw /strɔː/	(der) Strohhalm	
	across the country /əˌkrɒs ðə ˈkʌntri/	im ganzen Land	
	zero waste /ˌzɪərəʊ ˈweɪst/	verpackungsfrei	
p. 74, 12	(to) **set up** *(irr)* /ˌset‿ˈʌp/	aufbauen	The man **has set up** a stall.

Unit 4 | Part A Exploring roots

p. 79	**root** /ruːt/	(die) Wurzel	
	(to) give a helping hand *(irr)* /ˌɡɪv‿ə ˌhelpɪŋ ˈhænd/	helfen	
p. 80, 1	**village** /ˈvɪlɪdʒ/	(das) Dorf	A **village** is much smaller than a town.
	thought /θɔːt/	(der) Gedanke	
p. 80, 2	**memory** /ˈmemri/	(die) Erinnerung	**memory** = something that you remember
	because of /bɪˈkɒz‿əv/	wegen	
	accent /ˈæksnt/	(der) Akzent	
	Korean /kəˈriːən/	(der/die) Koreaner/in; koreanisch	
	riverside /ˈrɪvəˌsaɪd/	(das) Flussufer	
	Spain /speɪn/	Spanien	
	mountain biking /ˈmaʊntɪn ˌbaɪkɪŋ/	(das) Mountainbikefahren	
p. 81, 2	(to) **grow up** *(irr)* /ˌɡrəʊ‿ˈʌp/	aufwachsen	
	university /ˌjuːnɪˈvɜːsəti/	(die) Universität	
	(to) **get married** *(irr)* /ˌɡet ˈmærid/	heiraten	When two people **get married**, there is usually a big party.
	strong /strɒŋ/	stark	
	community /kəˈmjuːnəti/	(die) Gemeinschaft, (die) Gemeinde	
	mixture /ˈmɪkstʃə/	(die) Mischung	
	the Science Museum /ðə ˈsaɪəns mjuːˌziːəm/	(das) Naturwissenschaftsmuseum	
	Sweden /ˈswiːdn/	Schweden	
	lively /ˈlaɪvli/	lebendig	
	West African /ˌwest‿ˈæfrɪkən/	(der/die) Westafrikaner/in; westafrikanisch	
	Swedish /ˈswiːdɪʃ/	schwedisch	
p. 82, 4	(to) **study** /ˈstʌdi/	studieren; lernen	to **study** = to learn
	great-grandmother /ˌɡreɪt ˈɡrænˌmʌðə/	(die) Urgroßmutter	
p. 83, 5	**south** /saʊθ/	(der) Süden; Süd-	
	population /ˌpɒpjʊˈleɪʃn/	(die) Bevölkerung	**population** = all the people who live in an area
	South Asian /ˌsaʊθ‿ˈeɪʒn/	südasiatisch	
	African /ˈæfrɪkən/	(der/die) Afrikaner/in; afrikanisch	
	Polish /ˈpəʊlɪʃ/	(das) Polnisch; polnisch	
p. 84, 6	(to) **connect** /kəˈnekt/	verbinden	to **connect** = to put things together
	grandpa *(informal)* /ˈɡrænˌpɑː/	(der) Opa	
	storytelling /ˈstɔːriˌtelɪŋ/	(das) Geschichtenerzählen	
p. 85, 7	**war** /wɔː/	(der) Krieg	
	(to) **emigrate** /ˈemɪɡreɪt/	auswandern	When people **emigrate**, they leave their country to live in another country.
	Great Britain /ˌɡreɪt ˈbrɪtn/	Großbritannien	
	(to) **marry** /ˈmæri/	heiraten	
	foreign /ˈfɒrɪn/	ausländisch, fremd	
	(to) **be homesick** *(irr)* /ˌbiː ˈhəʊmˌsɪk/	Heimweh haben	
	while /waɪl/	(die) Weile	

	great-grandfather /ˌɡreɪt ˈɡrænˌfɑːðə/	(der) Urgroßvater
	World War II /ˌwɜːld ˌwɔː ˈtuː/	der Zweite Weltkrieg
	The Royal Air Force /ðə ˌrɔɪəl_ˈeə fɔːs/	(die) Königliche Luftwaffe
	air force /ˈeə fɔːs/	(die) Luftwaffe
p. 86, 8	**dress** /dres/	(das) Kleid, (die) Kleidung
	latest /ˈleɪtɪst/	neueste(r, s)
	mostly /ˈməʊstli/	meistens, größtenteils
	(to) **be a shame** *(irr)* /ˌbi_ə ˈʃeɪm/	schade sein
	grandad *(informal)* /ˈɡrænˌdæd/	(der) Opa
	still /stɪl/	nach wie vor, trotzdem
	(to) **die** /daɪ/	sterben
	cute /kjuːt/	süß, niedlich
	childhood /ˈtʃaɪldˌhʊd/	(die) Kindheit
p. 87, 8	**speech bubble** /ˈspiːtʃ ˌbʌbl/	(die) Sprechblase
	thought bubble /ˈθɔːt ˌbʌbl/	(die) Gedankenblase
	at that time /æt_ˈðæt_taɪm/	zu jener Zeit
	darling /ˈdɑːlɪŋ/	(der) Liebling, (der) Schatz
p. 87, 9	**timeline** /ˈtaɪmlaɪn/	(die) Zeitachse
p. 89, 13	**label** /ˈleɪbl/	(das) Etikett

dress

'..., wasn't he?' oder '..., didn't he?' kannst du mit 'oder? / nicht wahr? / gell?' übersetzen.

thought bubble

Unit 4 | Part B Giving a helping hand

p. 90, 2	**argument** /ˈɑːɡjʊmənt/	(der) Streit; (das) Argument
	herself /həˈself/	sich; (sie) selbst
p. 91, 2	**annoying** /əˈnɔɪɪŋ/	ärgerlich
	(to) **join** /dʒɔɪn/	sich zu jemandem gesellen
	(to) **save** /seɪv/	aufheben; sichern
	silly /ˈsɪli/	albern, dumm
	upset /ʌpˈset/	aufgebracht; aufgeregt
	(to) be up for something *(informal, irr)* /ˌbi_ˌʌp fɔː ˈsʌmθɪŋ/	Lust zu etwas haben
	(to) hang out *(informal, irr)* /ˌhæŋ_ˈaʊt/	rumhängen, Zeit mit jemandem verbringen
	I'm in! *(informal)* /ˌaɪm_ˈɪn/	Ich bin dabei!
	tuition /tjuːˈɪʃn/	*hier:* (die) Nachhilfe
	(to) skip /skɪp/	*hier:* ausfallen lassen
	D /diː/	*etwa:* Note 4, ausreichend
	What if ...? /ˌwɒt_ˈɪf/	Was wäre, wenn ...?
	lame /leɪm/	lahm
p. 93, 5	**right now** /ˌraɪt ˈnaʊ/	jetzt, im Moment
	right /raɪt/	(das) Recht
	(to) **delete** /dɪˈliːt/	löschen
	guy /ɡaɪ/	(der) Kerl, (der) Typ
	chemistry club /ˈkemɪstri klʌb/	(die) Chemie-AG

How about ...? /ˈhaʊ_əˌbaʊt/ Wie wäre es mit ...?, Was ist mit ...?
What's up? *(informal)* /ˌwɒts_ˈʌp/ Was ist los?
What's wrong? *(informal)* /ˌwɒts_ˈrɒŋ/ Was ist los?

to **skip** = to not do something that you normally do

How r u? /ˌhaʊ_ˈɑː jʊ/ Wie geht es dir / euch?
gr8 (= great) /ɡreɪt/ großartig
sec (= second) /sek, ˈsekənd/ (die) Sekunde

	I'd (= I would) /aɪd, 'aɪ wʊd/	ich würde	
p. 94, 6	(to) **seek advice** *(irr)* /ˌsiːk‿əd'vaɪs/	Rat suchen	
	advice /əd'vaɪs/	(der) Rat, (der) Ratschlag	
	(to) **stop** /stɒp/	stoppen	**stop** ≠ start
	(to) **agree** /ə'griː/	zustimmen	
	parent /'peərənt/	(das) Elternteil	
	All the best! /ˌɔːl ðə 'best/	Alles Gute!	
	Good luck! /ˌgʊd 'lʌk/	Viel Glück!	
	(to) **chat** /tʃæt/	plaudern; chatten	
	unless /ən'les/	außer wenn	
	headline /'hedˌlaɪn/	(die) Schlagzeile; *hier:* (die) Überschrift	
	teen /tiːn/	Teenager	
	anonymous(ly) /ə'nɒnɪməs, ə'nɒnɪməsli/	anonym	
	(to) be left out *(irr)* /ˌbiː ˌleft‿'aʊt/	ausgeschlossen werden	
p. 95, 6	(to) **communicate** /kə'mjuːnɪkeɪt/	kommunizieren, sprechen	
	matter /'mætə/	(die) Angelegenheit	
	(to) **prove** *(irr)* /pruːv/	beweisen	
	official, officially /ə'fɪʃl, ə'fɪʃli/	offiziell	
	(to) **wish** /wɪʃ/	wünschen	
	shy /ʃaɪ/	schüchtern	
	(to) **apologize (= apologise)** /ə'pɒlədʒaɪz/	sich entschuldigen	
	(to) **tease** /tiːz/	hänseln, ärgern	
	helpful /'helpfl/	hilfreich, nützlich	
	(to) keep a diary *(irr)* /ˌkiːp‿ə 'daɪəri/	Tagebuch führen	
	screen time /'skriːn taɪm/	(die) Bildschirmzeit	
p. 96, 8	school counsellor /ˌskuːl 'kaʊnslə/	(der/die) Vertrauenslehrer/in	
p. 96, 9	**call** /kɔːl/	(der) Anruf, (das) Gespräch	
	helpline /'helpˌlaɪn/	*(der) telefonische Beratungsdienst*	
p. 97, 10	(to) **deal with** *(irr)* /'diːl wɪð/	sich befassen mit, umgehen mit	
	word search /'wɜːd sɜːtʃ/	(die) Wortsuche	
p. 97, 11	**company** /'kʌmpni/	(die) Firma, (das) Unternehmen	
	office manager /'ɒfɪs ˌmænɪdʒə/	(der/die) Sekretär/in	An **office manager** is a person who works in an office.
p. 98, 12	(to) **be wrong** *(irr)* /ˌbiː 'rɒŋ/	im Unrecht sein	
	hers /hɜːz/	ihre(r, s)	
	ours /'aʊəz/	unsere(r, s)	
	neighbour /'neɪbə/	(der/die) Nachbar/in	
	theirs /ðeəz/	ihre(r, s)	
p. 98, 13	(to) **allow** /ə'laʊ/	erlauben	
	(to) **stay up (late)** /ˌsteɪ‿ˌʌp 'leɪt/	lange aufbleiben	
	linking part /'lɪŋkɪŋ pɑːt/	(das) Verbindungsteil	
	linking word /'lɪŋkɪŋ wɜːd/	(das) Verbindungswort	
	rude /ruːd/	unhöflich; primitiv	

Using your mobile is a good way to **communicate**.

Früher war die britische Schreibweise von Wörtern mit '-ise', 'isation' oder '-iser' eindeutig die mit 's', nur im amerikanischen Englisch wurden alle diese Wörter mit 'z' geschrieben. Mittlerweile werden kaum noch Unterschiede gemacht. Viele Briten schreiben 'organize, organizer, realize, ...'.
In vielen Wörterbüchern wird sogar die Schreibweise mit 'z' als die häufiger vorkommende gelistet.

mine /maɪn/ meine(r, s)
yours /jɔːz/ deine(r, s); eure(r, s); Ihre(r, s)
his /hɪz/ seine(r, s)
hers /hɜːz/ ihre(r, s)
ours /'aʊəz/ unsere(r, s)
theirs /ðeəz/ ihre(r, s)

p. 99, 15	(to) **give advice** *(irr)* /ˌɡɪv_ədˈvaɪs/	Rat geben	
	back /bæk/	(der) Rücken	
	pupil /ˈpjuːpl/	(der/die) Schüler/in	**pupil** = student
	complete /kəmˈpliːt/	vollständig, komplett	
	fault /fɔːlt/	(die) Schuld, (der) Fehler	**fault** = mistake
	(to) **ask for advice** /ˌɑːsk fər_ədˈvaɪs/	um Rat bitten	
	(to) panic /ˈpænɪk/	in Panik geraten	

Unit 5 | Part A Inventions

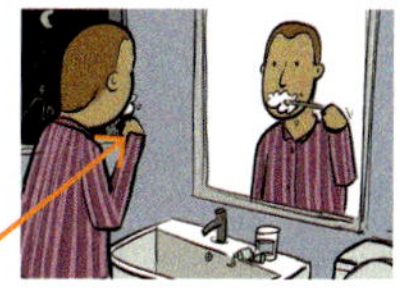

p. 103	**communication** /kəˌmjuːnɪˈkeɪʃn/	(die) Verständigung, (die) Kommunikation	
p. 104, 1	**toothbrush** /ˈtuːθbrʌʃ/	(die) Zahnbürste	**toothbrush**
	muscle /ˈmʌsl/	(der) Muskel	
	power /ˈpaʊə/	(die) Kraft	
	author /ˈɔːθə/	(der/die) Autor/in	
	electric /ɪˈlektrɪk/	elektrisch, Elektro-	
	cool /kuːl/	kühl; kalt	**cool** ≠ warm
p. 104, 2	steam locomotive /ˈstiːm ˌləʊkəˌməʊtɪv/	(die) Dampflokomotive, (die) Dampflok	
p. 105, 2	**basic** /ˈbeɪsɪk/	grundlegend, wesentlich	
	steam engine /ˈstiːm_ˌendʒɪn/	(die) Dampfmaschine	
	(to) **pull** /pʊl/	ziehen	to **pull** ≠ to push
	passenger /ˈpæsɪndʒə/	(der/die) Passagier/in	
	most /məʊst/	die meisten; am meisten	
	engine /ˈendʒɪn/	(die) Maschine, (der) Motor	An **engine** is a machine.
	American /əˈmerɪkən/	(der/die) Amerikaner/in; amerikanisch	
	television /ˈtelɪˌvɪʒn/	(der) Fernseher, (das) Fernsehen	
	working /ˈwɜːkɪŋ/	funktionierend	
	inventor /ɪnˈventə/	(der/die) Erfinder/in	
	named /neɪmd/	namens	
	horsehair /ˈhɔːsˌheə/	(das) Rosshaar	
	bone /bəʊn/	(der) Knochen	
	high-pressure /ˌhaɪ ˈpreʃə/	Hochdruck-	
	locomotive /ˌləʊkəˈməʊtɪv/	(die) Lokomotive	
	(to) patent /ˈpeɪtnt/	sich patentieren lassen	
	phone call /ˈfəʊn kɔːl/	(der) Telefonanruf	
	long-distance /ˌlɒŋ ˈdɪstəns/	Fern-	
	transatlantic /ˌtrænzətˈlæntɪk/	transatlantisch	
p. 106, 3	railway company /ˈreɪlweɪ ˌkʌmpni/	(die) Eisenbahngesellschaft	
p. 106, 4	passive /ˈpæsɪv/	(das) Passiv	
	telescope /ˈtelɪˌskəʊp/	(das) Teleskop	
p. 107, 5	**section** /ˈsekʃn/	(das) Teil, (das) Stück, (der) Abschnitt; (die) Abteilung	
	display /dɪˈspleɪ/	(die) Auslage, (die) Ausstellung	

was / were invented /ˌwɒz/ˌwɜːr_ɪnˈventɪd/
wurde/n erfunden
was made /ˌwɒz ˈmeɪd/
wurde gemacht
are used /ˌɑː ˈjuːsd/
werden benutzt
was used /ˌwɒz ˈjuːzd/
wurde verwendet
are pulled /ˌɑː ˈpʊld/
werden gezogen
was patented /ˌwɒz ˈpeɪtntɪd/
wurde patentiert
was presented /ˌwɒz priˈzentɪd/
wurde vorgestellt
was built /ˌwɒz ˈbɪlt/
wurde gebaut
was born /ˌwɒz ˈbɔːn/
wurde geboren

	scientist /ˈsaɪəntɪst/	(der/die) Wissenschaftler/in	
	space /speɪs/	(das) Weltall	**opening times** = the time of day when a shop or museum is open
p. 108, 6	**opening times** *(pl)* /ˈəʊpənɪŋ taɪmz/	(die) Öffnungszeiten	
	(to) **be located** *(irr)* /ˌbiː ləʊˈkeɪtɪd/	gelegen sein	
	in advance /ˌɪn‿ədˈvɑːns/	im Voraus	
	picnic /ˈpɪknɪk/	(das) Picknick	
	the Tube /ðə ˈtjuːb/	(die) (Londoner) U-Bahn	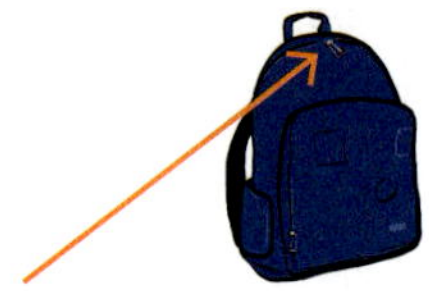
	(to) renovate /ˈrenəveɪt/	renovieren	
p. 108, 7	(to) **save** /seɪv/	sparen; retten	
	zip /zɪp/	(der) Reißverschluss	**zip**
	(to) **count** /kaʊnt/	zählen	
	(to) **appear** /əˈpɪə/	erscheinen, auftauchen	
	industry /ˈɪndəstri/	(die) Industrie	
	construction /kənˈstrʌkʃn/	(der) Bau	
	(to) button /ˈbʌtən/	knöpfen	
	onwards /ˈɒnwədz/	von ... an	**simple** = easy to understand
p. 109, 7	**simple** /ˈsɪmpl/	einfach, simpel	
	(to) **prevent** /prɪˈvent/	verhindern, vorbeugen	
	comfortable /ˈkʌmftəbl/	bequem	
	tin /tɪn/	(die) Büchse, (die) Dose	
	tool /tuːl/	(das) Werkzeug	
	accidentally /ˌæksɪˈdentli/	versehentlich, zufällig	
	(to) **grow** *(irr)* /grəʊ/	wachsen	to **grow** = to become taller
	discovery /dɪˈskʌvri/	(die) Entdeckung	
	seat belt /ˈsiːt belt/	(der) Sicherheitsgurt	
	strap /stræp/	(der) Riemen	
	leather /ˈleðə/	(das) Leder	
	(to) fasten /ˈfɑːsn/	schließen, zumachen	to **fasten** = to close
	belt /belt/	(der) Gürtel	
	seat /siːt/	(der) Sitz	
	tin opener /ˈtɪn‿ˌəʊpnə/	(der) Dosenöffner	
	inside /ˈɪnˌsaɪd/	in ... hinein	
	(to) store /stɔː/	lagern	
	(to) become infected *(irr)* /bɪˌkʌm‿ɪnˈfektɪd/	sich infizieren	
	bacteria *(pl)* /bækˈtɪəriə/	(die) Bakterien	
	antibiotic /ˌæntibaɪˈɒtɪk/	(das) Antibiotikum	
	(Petri) dish /ˈpiːtri ˌdɪʃ/	(die) Petrischale	
	lab /læb/	(das) Labor	at the **lab**
	mould /məʊld/	(der) Schimmel	
	(to) be estimated *(irr)* /ˌbi‿ˈestɪmeɪtəd/	geschätzt werden	
p. 110, 8	(to) **rate** /reɪt/	einschätzen, bewerten	
	rating /ˈreɪtɪŋ/	(die) Einschätzung, (die) Einstufung	

p. 110, 9	**electricity** /ɪˌlek'trɪsəti/	(die) Elektrizität, (der) Strom
p. 111, 10	**brochure** /'brəʊʃə/	(die) Broschüre
p. 111, 11	**practical** /'præktɪkl/	praktisch
	baker /'beɪkə/	*hier: (die) Backmaschine*
	cleaning skates *(pl)* /'kliːnɪŋ ˌskeɪts/	*(die) Reinigungsskates*
	X-ray glasses *(pl)* /'eksreɪ ˌglaːsɪz/	*(die) Röntgenbrille*
	toilet roll /baker /'beɪkə//	(die) Toilettenpapier-Rolle
p. 112, 12	**owner** /'əʊnə/	(der/die) Besitzer/in
	rich /rɪtʃ/	reich
	flour /'flaʊə/	(das) Mehl
p. 113, 15	(to) **agree on** /ə'gri‿ɒn/	sich einigen auf

She is the proud **owner** of a new blue bike.

Unit 5 | Part B Communication

p. 114, 2	**development** /dɪ'veləpmənt/	(die) Entwicklung
	writing /'raɪtɪŋ/	(die) Schrift, (das) Schreiben
	result /rɪ'zʌlt/	(das) Ergebnis
	finding /'faɪndɪŋ/	(die) Entdeckung, (das) Ergebnis
	general /'dʒenrəl/	allgemein
	(to) **give a presentation** *(irr)* /ˌgɪv‿ə ˌprezn'teɪʃn/	eine Präsentation halten
	low-tech /ˌləʊ 'tek/	technisch einfach
	on demand /ˌɒn dɪ'maːnd/	auf Anfrage
p. 115, 3	(to) **be interested in** *(irr)* /ˌbi‿'ɪntrəstɪd‿ɪn/	interessiert sein an
p. 116, 5	planner /'plænə/	(der) Kalender, (der) Planer
p. 117, 6	**network** /'netˌwɜːk/	(das) Netzwerk
	method /'meθəd/	(die) Methode
	(to) **research** /rɪ'sɜːtʃ/	recherchieren
	search engine /'sɜːtʃ‿ˌendʒɪn/	(die) Suchmaschine
	source /sɔːs/	(die) Quelle
	(to) **copy** /'kɒpi/	kopieren
	document /'dɒkjʊmənt/	(das) Dokument
	(to) be done with *(informal, irr)* /ˌbiː 'dʌn wɪð/	fertig sein mit
p. 118, 7	**rock** /rɒk/	(der) Stein, (der) Fels
	stone /stəʊn/	(der) Stein
	theory /'θɪəri/	(die) Theorie
	function /'fʌŋkʃn/	(die) Aufgabe, (die) Funktion
	BC (= before Christ) /ˌbiː 'siː, bɪˌfɔː 'kraɪst/	v. Chr. (= vor Christus)
	around /ə'raʊnd/	ungefähr
	AD (= Anno Domini) /ˌeɪ 'diː, ˌænəʊ 'dɒmɪnaɪ/	n. Chr. (= nach Christus)
	wide /waɪd/	weit

A letter is a piece of **writing**.

The boy **is interested in** buying a T-shirt.

A **method** is a way of doing something.

Wendungen wie 'isn't it?' oder 'aren't you?' nennt man Bestätigungsfragen (= *question tags*). Du kannst sie mit 'oder? / nicht wahr? / gell?' übersetzen und bildest sie, indem du die Verbform aus einem bejahten Aussagesatz verneinst.
You're connected to the Internet, **aren't** you?
She can speak Chinese, **can't** she?
Harry used a search engine, **didn't** he?
The friends like each other, **don't** they?

	tablet /ˈtæblət/	(der) Block, (die) Platte	
	clay /kleɪ/	(der) Lehm, (der) Ton	
	printing press /ˈprɪntɪŋ pres/	(die) Druckerpresse	
p. 119, 7	**rise** /raɪz/	(der) Aufstieg	
	(to) **keep in touch** *(irr)* /ˌkiːp‿ɪn ˈtʌtʃ/	Kontakt halten, in Verbindung bleiben	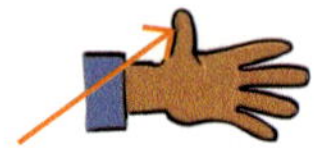
	thumb /θʌm/	(der) Daumen	**thumb**
	once more /ˌwʌns ˈmɔː/	noch einmal	
	(to) message /ˈmesɪdʒ/	eine Nachricht schicken	
	uncomplicated /ʌnˈkɒmplɪˌkeɪtɪd/	unkompliziert	
p. 119, 8	**habit** /ˈhæbɪt/	(die) Gewohnheit, (die) Angewohnheit	
p. 120, 9	challenge /ˈtʃæləndʒ/	*hier:* (die) Wette	
p. 120, 10	console /kənˈsəʊl/	(die) Konsole	
p. 121, 12	**dos and don'ts** /ˌduːz‿ən ˈdəʊnts/	was man tun und was man nicht tun sollte	
	magazine /ˌmægəˈziːn/	(die) Zeitschrift	
	password /ˈpɑːsˌwɜːd/	(das) Passwort	
	(to) **download** /ˌdaʊnˈləʊd/	herunterladen	
	(to) **click on** /ˈklɪk‿ɒn/	anklicken	
	(to) **trust** /trʌst/	vertrauen	
	anybody /ˈenibɒdi/	irgendjemand; jede(r, s)	
	(to) **treat** /triːt/	behandeln	A vet **treats** animals.
	(to) befriend /bɪˈfrend/	sich anfreunden mit	
	(to) bully /ˈbʊli/	mobben	
	respectful /rɪˈspektfl/	respektvoll	
p. 121, 13	**summary** /ˈsʌməri/	(die) Zusammenfassung	
p. 122, 14	**happy** /ˈhæpi/	zufrieden	
p. 122, 15	(to) be prepared *(irr)* /ˌbiː prɪˈpeəd/	vorbereitet sein	
p. 123, 16	**talk** /tɔːk/	(das) Gespräch, (der) Vortrag	**talk** = conversation

Hier findest du alphabetisch sortiert alle Wörter aus dem vorliegenden Buch mit der Angabe der Seite *(p.)*, auf der das Wort das erste Mal vorkommt oder auf der es zum Lernwort gemacht wird. Die Zahl hinter dem Komma bezeichnet die Aufgabe auf der Seite.
Lernwörter aus den vorigen Bänden sind mit „NHG 5" oder „NHG 6" markiert.
Die **fett** gedruckten Lernwörter solltest du dir merken.
(informal) bedeutet: Dieses Wort oder dieser Ausdruck ist umgangssprachlich.
Folgende Abkürzungen werden verwendet: *(pl)* = (unregelmäßige) Mehrzahlform, *(no pl)* = keine Mehrzahlform, *(irr)* = unregelmäßiges Verb, *(AE)* = amerikanisches Englisch, L&L = Land und Leute

A

a, an /ə/eɪ, ən/ ein(e) NHG 5
a /ə/ pro NHG 6
A /eɪ/ *etwa:* Note 1, sehr gut p. 101
abbey /ˈæbi/ Abtei(kirche) p. 78
(to) **be able to do something** *(irr)* /ˌbi‿ˌeɪbl tə ˈduː ˌsʌmθɪŋ/ etwas tun können NHG 6
about /əˈbaʊt/ über; an NHG 5; ungefähr NHG 6
(to) **be about** *(irr)* /ˌbi‿əˈbaʊt/ gehen um; handeln von NHG 5
above /əˈbʌv/ über NHG 5; oben, oberhalb p. 60, 8
(to) **go abroad** *(irr)* /ˌɡəʊ‿əˈbrɔːd/ ins Ausland gehen / fahren NHG 6
absolutely /ˈæbsəluːtli/ absolut p. 8, 2
accent /ˈæksnt/ Akzent p. 80, 2
accident /ˈæksɪdnt/ Unfall p. 45, 4
by accident /ˌbaɪ‿ˈæksɪdnt/ zufällig; aus Versehen p. 15, 12
accidentally /ˌæksɪˈdentli/ versehentlich; zufällig p. 109, 7
across the country /əˌkrɒs ðə ˈkʌntri/ im ganzen Land p. 73, 9
(to) **act** /ækt/ handeln; spielen NHG 6
(to) **act out** /ˌækt‿ˈaʊt/ nachspielen; vorspielen NHG 5
action /ˈækʃn/ Handlung NHG 5
(to) activate /ˈæktɪveɪt/ aktivieren p. 8, 2
active /ˈæktɪv/ aktiv p. 33, 2
activity /ækˈtɪvəti/ Aktivität NHG 5
actor/actress /ˈæktə, ˈæktrəs/ Schauspieler/in NHG 6
actually /ˈæktʃuəli/ eigentlich; tatsächlich NHG 6
AD (= Anno Domini) /ˌeɪ ˈdiː, ˌænəʊ ˈdɒmɪnaɪ/ n. Chr. (= nach Christus) p. 118, 7
(to) **add** /æd/ hinzufügen NHG 5
additional /əˈdɪʃnəl/ zusätzlich p. 132
address /əˈdres/ Adresse NHG 5
adjective /ˈædʒɪktɪv/ Adjektiv NHG 6
adult /ˈædʌlt/ Erwachsene/r NHG 6
in advance /ˌɪn‿ədˈvɑːns/ im Voraus p. 108, 6
adventure /ədˈventʃə/ Abenteuer NHG 6
advert (= ad) /ˈædvɜːt, æd/ Werbung; Anzeige p. 39, 9
(to) advertise /ˈædvətaɪz/ für etwas Werbung machen p. 63, 12
advice /ədˈvaɪs/ Rat(schlag) p. 94, 6
(to) **give advice** *(irr)* /ˌɡɪv‿ədˈvaɪs/ Rat geben p. 99, 15
(to) **seek advice** *(irr)* /ˌsiːk‿ədˈvaɪs/ Rat suchen p. 94, 6
(to) **be afraid of** *(irr)* /ˌbi‿əˈfreɪd‿əv/ Angst haben vor NHG 6
African /ˈæfrɪkən/ Afrikaner/in; afrikanisch p. 83, 5
after /ˈɑːftə/ nach NHG 5
after that /ˌɑːftə ˈðæt/ danach p. 66, 2
afternoon /ˌɑːftəˈnuːn/ Nachmittag NHG 5
afterwards /ˈɑːftəwədz/ anschließend; später NHG 6
again /əˈɡen/ wieder; noch einmal NHG 5
against /əˈɡenst/ gegen NHG 6
for ages *(informal)* /fər‿ˈeɪdʒɪz/ seit einer Ewigkeit p. 57, 3
... ago /əˈɡəʊ/ vor ... NHG 6
(to) **agree** /əˈɡriː/ zustimmen p. 94, 6
(to) **agree on** /əˈɡri‿ɒn/ sich einigen auf p. 113, 15
air force /ˈeə fɔːs/ Luftwaffe p. 85, 7
airport /ˈeəpɔːt/ Flughafen NHG 6
all /ɔːl/ alle; alles; ganz; völlig NHG 5
all around /ˌɔːl‿əˈraʊnd/ überall (in) p. 39, 10
all kinds of /ˌɔːl ˈkaɪndz‿əv/ alle möglichen NHG 6
all over /ˌɔːl‿ˈəʊvə/ überall NHG 6
all over the world /ˌɔːl‿ˌəʊvə ðə ˈwɜːld/ auf der ganzen Welt NHG 6
All the best! /ˌɔːl ðə ˈbest/ Alles Gute! p. 94, 6
all the time /ˌɔːl ðə ˈtaɪm/ die ganze Zeit NHG 6
(to) **be allergic to** *(irr)* /ˌbi‿əˈlɜːdʒɪk tʊ/ allergisch sein auf p. 21, 5
(to) **allow** /əˈlaʊ/ erlauben p. 98, 13
(to) **be allowed (to)** *(irr)* /ˌbi‿əˈlaʊd‿tə/ erlaubt sein, dürfen NHG 6
almost /ˈɔːlməʊst/ fast; beinahe NHG 6
alone /əˈləʊn/ allein NHG 5
along /əˈlɒŋ/ entlang NHG 6
already /ɔːlˈredi/ schon; bereits NHG 5
alright /ɔːlˈraɪt/ in Ordnung p. 45, 4
also /ˈɔːlsəʊ/ auch NHG 5
although /ɔːlˈðəʊ/ obwohl NHG 6
always /ˈɔːlweɪz/ immer NHG 5
am (= ante meridiem) /ˌeɪˈem, ˌænti məˈrɪdiəm/ morgens, vormittags *(hinter Uhrzeit zwischen Mitternacht und 12 Uhr mittags)* NHG 5
amazing *(informal)* /əˈmeɪzɪŋ/ toll NHG 6
ambulance /ˈæmbjʊləns/ Krankenwagen p. 163
(to) **call an ambulance** /ˌkɔːl‿ən‿ˈæmbjʊləns/ einen Krankenwagen rufen p. 45, 4
American /əˈmerɪkən/ Amerikaner/in; amerikanisch p. 105, 2

ancient /ˈeɪnʃnt/ alt; antik NHG 6
and /ænd/ und NHG 5
and so on /ænd ˈsəʊ‿ɒn/ und so weiter NHG 6
angry /ˈæŋgri/ zornig, wütend NHG 6
animal /ˈænɪml/ Tier NHG 5
ankle /ˈæŋkl/ (Fuß)knöchel p. 46, 5
(to) announce /əˈnaʊns/ bekannt geben p. 53
announcement /əˈnaʊnsmənt/ Mitteilung; Durchsage NHG 6
annoyed /əˈnɔɪd/ genervt NHG 6
annoying /əˈnɔɪɪŋ/ ärgerlich p. 91, 2
anonymous(ly) /əˈnɒnɪməs, əˈnɒnɪməsli/ anonym p. 94, 6
another /əˈnʌðə/ noch ein/e; ein anderer/ein anderes/eine andere NHG 5
answer /ˈɑːnsə/ Antwort NHG 5
(to) **answer** /ˈɑːnsə/ (be)antworten NHG 5
antibiotic /ˌæntibaɪˈɒtɪk/ Antibiotikum p. 109, 7
any /ˈeni/ (irgend)ein(e) NHG 5
any more /ˌeni ˈmɔː/ noch mehr p. 24, 8
anybody /ˈenibɒdi/ irgendjemand; jede(r, s) p. 121, 12
anyone /ˈeniˌwʌn/ jede(r, s); (irgend)jemand p. 67, 2
anything /ˈeniˌθɪŋ/ irgendetwas NHG 5
anyway /ˈeniweɪ/ jedenfalls NHG 6
anywhere /ˈeniˌweə/ überall; irgendwo p. 56, 2
apart /əˈpɑːt/ auseinander NHG 6
(to) **apologize (= apologise)** /əˈpɒlədʒaɪz/ sich entschuldigen p. 95, 6
(to) **appear** /əˈpɪə/ erscheinen, auftauchen p. 108, 7
apple /ˈæpl/ Apfel NHG 5
(to) apply /əˈplaɪ/ anwenden p. 8, 2
appointment /əˈpɔɪntmənt/ Termin p. 42, 1
April /ˈeɪprəl/ April NHG 5
area /ˈeəriə/ Gebiet; Region NHG 5
arena /əˈriːnə/ Arena; Stadion p. 77
argument /ˈɑːgjʊmənt/ Streit; Argument p. 90, 2
armour /ˈɑːmə/ Rüstung p. 66, 2
around /əˈraʊnd/ um; herum; umher NHG 6; ungefähr p. 118, 7
from (all) around the world /frəm‿ˌɔːl‿əˌraʊnd ðə ˈwɜːld/ aus der (ganzen) Welt p. 11, 6
(to) **arrive** /əˈraɪv/ ankommen NHG 5
art /ɑːt/ Kunst NHG 5
article /ˈɑːtɪkl/ Artikel NHG 5
arts and crafts /ˌɑːrts‿ən ˈkrɑːfts/ Basteln; Bastelarbeit p. 56, 2
as /əz/ als; wie; während NHG 5
as ... as /æz æz/ so ... wie NHG 6
as soon as /əz‿ˈsuːn‿əz/ so bald wie p. 53
as well /ˌəz‿ˈwel/ auch NHG 6
Asia /ˈeɪʒə/ Asien p. 30
(to) **ask** /ɑːsk/ fragen; bitten NHG 5
(to) **ask for advice** /ˌɑːsk fər‿ədˈvaɪs/ um Rat bitten p. 99, 15
(to) **ask questions** /ˌɑːsk‿ˈkwestʃnz/ Fragen stellen NHG 5
aspect /ˈæspekt/ Aspekt; Gesichtspunkt p. 69, 5
assembly /əˈsembli/ (Schüler)versammlung NHG 5
at /æt/ an; in; bei; um NHG 5
at first /ˌæt ˈfɜːst/ zuerst NHG 6
at home /ˌæt ˈhəʊm/ zu Hause NHG 5
at least /ˌæt ˈliːst/ mindestens; wenigstens NHG 6
at that time /æt‿ˈðæt‿taɪm/ zu jener Zeit p. 87, 8
at the doctor's /ˌæt‿ðə ˈdɒktəz/ beim Arzt/bei der Ärztin p. 31
at the same time /ˌæt‿ðə ˌseɪm ˈtaɪm/ gleichzeitig; zur gleichen Zeit p. 56, 2
at/in the back /ˌæt/ˌɪn ðə ˈbæk/ hinten NHG 5
at/in the front /ˌæt/ˌɪn ðə ˈfrʌnt/ vorne NHG 5
athlete /ˈæθliːt/ Athlet/in p. 53
(to) **do athletics** *(irr)* /ˌduː‿æθˈletɪks/ Leichtathletik machen NHG 5
atmosphere /ˈætməsˌfɪə/ Atmosphäre p. 19, 2
(to) **attend** /əˈtend/ besuchen p. 73, 9
(to) **draw attention to** *(irr)* /ˌdrɔ‿əˈtenʃn tə/ Aufmerksamkeit lenken auf p. 70, 6
(to) **pay attention (to)** *(irr)* /ˌpeɪ‿əˈtenʃn tʊ/ aufpassen; achten auf NHG 6
attraction /əˈtrækʃn/ Attraktion NHG 6
August /ˈɔːgəst/ August NHG 5
aunt /ɑːnt/ Tante NHG 5
authentic /ɔːˈθentɪk/ authentisch p. 76
author /ˈɔːθə/ Autor/in p. 104, 1
autumn /ˈɔːtəm/ Herbst NHG 6
(to) **avoid** /əˈvɔɪd/ meiden; vermeiden p. 56, 2
award ceremony /əˈwɔːd ˌserəməni/ Preisverleihung p. 53
away /əˈweɪ/ weg NHG 5
(to) **go away** *(irr)* /ˌgəʊ‿əˈweɪ/ weggehen; verschwinden NHG 6

B

back /bæk/ zurück NHG 5; Rücken p. 99, 15
at/in the back /ˌæt/ˌɪn ðə ˈbæk/ hinten NHG 5
background /ˈbækˌgraʊnd/ Hintergrund NHG 6
bacon /ˈbeɪkən/ Schinkenspeck p. 128
bacteria *(pl)* /bækˈtɪəriə/ Bakterien p. 109, 7
bad /bæd/ schlecht; schlimm NHG 5
bad /bæd/ *hier:* stark p. 42, 1
bag /bæg/ Tasche; Tüte NHG 5
bagpipes *(pl)* /ˈbægˌpaɪps/ Dudelsack p. 71, 6
(to) **bake** /beɪk/ backen NHG 5
baker /ˈbeɪkə/ Bäcker/in NHG 6
baker /ˈbeɪkə/ *hier:* Backmaschine p. 111, 11
balloon /bəˈluːn/ Luftballon NHG 5
banana /bəˈnɑːnə/ Banane NHG 5
bandage /ˈbændɪdʒ/ Verband p. 46, 5
(to) bang one's head /ˌbæŋ wʌnz ˈhed/ sich den Kopf anschlagen p. 45, 4
bangers and mash /ˌbæŋəz‿ən ˈmæʃ/ *Würstchen mit Kartoffelbrei* L&L 1
Bangladesh /ˌbæŋgləˈdeʃ/ Bangladesch p. 30
barely /ˈbeəli/ kaum p. 77
bargain /ˈbɑːgɪn/ Schnäppchen p. 60, 8

basic /ˈbeɪsɪk/ grundlegend; wesentlich p. 105, 2
basil /ˈbæzl/ Basilikum p. 131
bat /bæt/ Schläger p. 39, 10; Fledermaus p. 127
bathroom /ˈbɑːθˌruːm/ Badezimmer NHG 5
battle /ˈbætl/ Kampf p. 67, 2
battlefield /ˈbætlˌfiːld/ Schlachtfeld p. 29
BC (= before Christ) /ˌbiː ˈsiː, bɪˌfɔː ˈkraɪst/ v. Chr. (= vor Christus) p. 118, 7
(to) **be** *(irr)* /biː/ sein NHG 5
(to) **be a shame** *(irr)* /ˌbi‿ə ˈʃeɪm/ schade sein p. 86, 8
(to) **be able to do something** *(irr)* /ˌbi‿ˌeɪbl tə ˈduː ˌsʌmθɪŋ/ etwas tun können NHG 6
(to) **be about** *(irr)* /ˌbi‿əˈbaʊt/ gehen um; handeln von NHG 5
(to) be about to do something *(irr)* /ˌbi‿əˌbaʊt‿tə ˈduː ˌsʌmθɪŋ/ im Begriff sein, etwas zu tun p. 52
(to) **be afraid of** *(irr)* /ˌbi‿əˈfreɪd‿əv/ Angst haben vor NHG 6
(to) be alive *(irr)* /ˌbi‿əˈlaɪv/ leben p. 102
(to) **be allergic to** *(irr)* /ˌbi‿əˈlɜːdʒɪk tʊ/ allergisch sein auf p. 21, 5
(to) **be allowed (to)** *(irr)* /ˌbi‿əˈlaʊd‿tə/ erlaubt sein, dürfen NHG 6
(to) **be born** *(irr)* /ˌbiː ˈbɔːn/ geboren werden p. 40, 12
(to) be connected with *(irr)* /ˌbiː kəˈnektɪd wɪð/ in Verbindung gebracht werden p. 78
(to) be done with *(informal, irr)* /ˌbiː ˈdʌn wɪð/ fertig sein mit p. 117, 6
(to) be estimated *(irr)* /ˌbi‿ˈestɪmeɪtəd/ geschätzt werden p. 109, 7
(to) **be good at doing something** *(irr)* /ˌbiː ɡʊd‿ət ˈduːɪŋ ˌsʌmθɪŋ/ gut darin sein, etwas zu tun NHG 5
(to) **be good at something** *(irr)* /ˌbiː ˈɡʊd‿æt ˌsʌmθɪŋ/ gut in etwas sein NHG 6
(to) **be (good/great) fun** *(irr)* /ˌbiː ˌɡʊd/ˌɡreɪt ˈfʌn/ (viel/großen) Spaß machen NHG 5
(to) **be homesick** *(irr)* /ˌbiː ˈhəʊmˌsɪk/ Heimweh haben p. 85, 7
(to) **be interested in** *(irr)* /ˌbi‿ˈɪntrəstɪd‿ɪn/ interessiert sein an p. 115, 3
(to) be left out *(irr)* /ˌbiː ˌleft‿ˈaʊt/ ausgeschlossen werden p. 94, 6
(to) **be located** *(irr)* /ˌbiː ləʊˈkeɪtɪd/ gelegen sein p. 108, 6
(to) be lost *(irr)* /ˌbiː ˈlɒst/ sich verirrt haben p. 126
(to) be made up of *(irr)* /ˌbiː ˌmeɪd‿ˈʌp‿əv/ zusammengesetzt sein aus p. 54
(to) be missing *(irr)* /ˌbiː ˈmɪsɪŋ/ fehlen p. 124
(to) be off *(informal, irr)* /ˌbi‿ˈɒf/ *hier:* weg sein p. 52
(to) **be one's turn** *(irr)* /ˌbiː wʌnz ˈtɜːn/ an der Reihe sein NHG 5
(to) be prepared *(irr)* /ˌbiː prɪˈpeəd/ vorbereitet sein p. 122, 15
(to) **be right** *(irr)* /ˌbiː ˈraɪt/ recht haben NHG 5
(to) be up for something *(informal, irr)* /ˌbi‿ˌʌp fɔː ˈsʌmθɪŋ/ Lust zu etwas haben p. 91, 2
(to) be up to something *(irr)* /ˌbi‿ˌʌp tə ˈsʌmθɪŋ/ etwas vorhaben p. 57, 3
(to) **be worth** *(irr)* /ˌbiː ˈwɜːθ/ (sich) lohnen; wert sein p. 71, 6
(to) **be wrong** *(irr)* /ˌbiː ˈrɒŋ/ im Unrecht sein p. 98, 12
(to) **be wrong (with)** *(irr)* /ˌbiː ˈrɒŋ wɪθ/ nicht in Ordnung sein (mit) p. 48, 8
beach /biːtʃ/ Strand NHG 5
beak /biːk/ Schnabel p. 127
beak-like /ˈbiːkˌlaɪk/ *schnabelähnlich* p. 127
beard /bɪəd/ Bart p. 67, 2
beautiful /ˈbjuːtəfl/ schön NHG 5
because /bɪˈkɒz/ weil; da NHG 5
because of /bɪˈkɒz‿əv/ wegen p. 80, 2
(to) **become** *(irr)* /bɪˈkʌm/ werden NHG 6
(to) become infected *(irr)* /bɪˌkʌm‿ɪnˈfektɪd/ sich infizieren p. 109, 7
bed /bed/ Bett NHG 5
bedroom /ˈbedruːm/ Schlafzimmer NHG 5
bee /biː/ Biene NHG 6
beef /biːf/ Rindfleisch p. 23, 7
before /bɪˈfɔː/ bevor; zuvor, vorher; vor NHG 5
(to) befriend /bɪˈfrend/ sich anfreunden mit p. 121, 12
(to) **begin** *(irr)* /bɪˈɡɪn/ anfangen; beginnen NHG 5
beginning /bɪˈɡɪnɪŋ/ Anfang; Beginn NHG 6
(to) behave /bɪˈheɪv/ sich verhalten, sich benehmen p. 28
behind /bɪˈhaɪnd/ hinter NHG 5
(to) **believe (in)** /bɪˈliːv‿ɪn/ glauben (an) NHG 6
bell /bel/ Glocke NHG 6
(to) **belong (to)** /bɪˈlɒŋ/ gehören (zu) p. 40, 11
below /bɪˈləʊ/ unten, unter NHG 6
belt /belt/ Gürtel p. 109, 7
best /best/ beste(r, s) NHG 5
All the best! /ˌɔːl ðə ˈbest/ Alles Gute! p. 94, 6
the best /ðə ˈbest/ der/die/das beste NHG 5; am besten NHG 6
(to) **like best** /ˌlaɪk ˈbest/ am liebsten mögen NHG 5
better /ˈbetə/ besser NHG 6
(to) **get better** *(irr)* /ˌɡet ˈbetə/ besser / gesund werden p. 37, 7
between /bɪˈtwiːn/ zwischen NHG 5
BFF (= best friends forever) *(informal)* /ˌbi‿ef‿ˈef, ˌbest ˌfrendz fərˈevə/ *allerbeste Freunde/Freundinnen* p. 8, 2
bhaji /ˈbɑːdʒi/ *indisches Gericht* p. 23, 7
bicycle bell /ˈbaɪsɪkl bel/ Fahrradklingel p. 59, 7
(to) biff *(informal)* /bɪf/ hauen, schlagen p. 39, 10
big /bɪɡ/ groß NHG 5
bike /baɪk/ Fahrrad NHG 6
(to) **ride a bike** *(irr)* /ˌraɪd‿ə ˈbaɪk/ Fahrrad fahren NHG 5
bill /bɪl/ Rechnung p. 24, 8
billion /ˈbɪljən/ Milliarde p. 147
bin /bɪn/ Abfalleimer NHG 5
bird /bɜːd/ Vogel NHG 6
bird of prey /ˌbɜːd‿əv ˈpreɪ/ Raubvogel p. 67, 2

birthday /ˈbɜːθdeɪ/ Geburtstag NHG 5
Happy birthday (to you)! /ˌhæpi ˈbɜːθdeɪ tʊ juː/ Herzlichen Glückwunsch zum Geburtstag! NHG 5
birthplace /ˈbɜːθˌpleɪs/ Geburtsort p. 149
biscuit /ˈbɪskɪt/ Keks NHG 5
bit /bɪt/ Teil; Stück p. 125
a bit /ə ˈbɪt/ ein bisschen NHG 5
black /blæk/ schwarz NHG 5
(to) **bleed** *(irr)* /bliːd/ bluten p. 43, 1
blood /blʌd/ Blut NHG 6
blue /bluː/ blau NHG 5
board /bɔːd/ Tafel; Brett NHG 5
board game /ˈbɔːd geɪm/ Brettspiel NHG 6
boat /bəʊt/ Boot NHG 5
body /ˈbɒdi/ Körper NHG 5
(to) boil /bɔɪl/ kochen *(Flüssigkeit)* p. 160
(to) bring to the boil *(irr)* /ˌbrɪŋ tə ðə ˈbɔɪl/ zum Kochen bringen p. 12, 7
bone /bəʊn/ Knochen p. 105, 2
book /bʊk/ Buch NHG 5
(to) **book** /bʊk/ buchen, reservieren NHG 6
bookshelf /ˈbʊkˌʃelf/ Bücherregal NHG 5
boot /buːt/ Kofferraum p. 76
(to) boot /buːt/ einen Tritt geben p. 39, 10
bored /bɔːd/ gelangweilt NHG 6
boring /ˈbɔːrɪŋ/ langweilig NHG 5
(to) **borrow** /ˈbɒrəʊ/ (aus)leihen NHG 5
both /bəʊθ/ beide p. 25, 11
(to) bother /ˈbɒðə/ sich Mühe geben p. 101
bottle /ˈbɒtl/ Flasche NHG 5
(to) bounce /baʊns/ (auf)springen p. 39, 10
bowl /bəʊl/ Schüssel; Schale NHG 6
box /bɒks/ Kasten; Kiste NHG 5
boy /bɔɪ/ Junge NHG 5
bracket /ˈbrækɪt/ Klammer p. 13, 7
branch /brɑːntʃ/ Zweig; Ast p. 16, 16
bravely /breɪvli/ mutig p. 78
bread /bred/ Brot p. 15, 11
break /breɪk/ Pause NHG 5
(to) **break** *(irr)* /breɪk/ brechen, zerbrechen; kaputt machen NHG 6
breakfast /ˈbrekfəst/ Frühstück NHG 5
breathtaking /ˈbreθˌteɪkɪŋ/ atemberaubend p. 67, 2
bridge /brɪdʒ/ Brücke NHG 6
bright, brightly /braɪt,ˈbraɪtli/ hell; strahlend NHG 6
brilliant /ˈbrɪljənt/ genial, klasse NHG 5
(to) **bring** *(irr)* /brɪŋ/ mitbringen NHG 5
(to) **bring over** *(irr)* /ˌbrɪŋ‿ˈəʊvə/ herbeibringen p. 24, 8
(to) bring to the boil *(irr)* /ˌbrɪŋ tə ðə ˈbɔɪl/ zum Kochen bringen p. 12, 7
Britain /ˈbrɪtn/ Großbritannien NHG 6
British /ˈbrɪtɪʃ/ britisch NHG 6
brochure /ˈbrəʊʃə/ Broschüre p. 111, 10
broken /ˈbrəʊkən/ gebrochen p. 42, 1; zerbrochen; kaputt p. 64, 13
brother /ˈbrʌðə/ Bruder NHG 5
brown /braʊn/ braun NHG 5
(to) **brush one's teeth** /ˌbrʌʃ wʌnz ˈtiːθ/ sich die Zähne putzen NHG 5
bubble and squeak /ˌbʌbl‿ən ˈskwiːk/ *Resteessen aus gebratenem Kartoffelbrei und zerstampftem Gemüse* L&L 1
buddy *(informal)* /ˈbʌdi/ Kumpel p. 38, 8
(to) **build** *(irr)* /bɪld/ bauen NHG 5
building /ˈbɪldɪŋ/ Gebäude NHG 6
(to) bully /ˈbʊli/ mobben p. 121, 12
burdock /ˈbɜːdɒk/ Große Klette p. 127
burnt /bɜːnt/ verbrannt, angebrannt p. 18, 2
(to) bury /ˈberi/ begraben; vergraben p. 78
business /ˈbɪznəs/ Geschäft; Handel p. 89, 13
busy /ˈbɪzi/ beschäftigt NHG 5; bewegt, ereignisreich; belebt; verkehrsreich NHG 6
but /bʌt/ aber NHG 5; außer NHG 6
(to) button /ˈbʌtən/ knöpfen p. 108, 7
(to) **buy** *(irr)* /baɪ/ kaufen NHG 5
(to) buzz /bʌz/ summen, brummen p. 78
by /baɪ/ von; mit NHG 5; bei, an; *hier:* (spätestens) bis NHG 6
by *(+ Verbform mit -ing)* /baɪ/ indem NHG 6
by accident /ˌbaɪ‿ˈæksɪdnt/ zufällig; aus Versehen p. 15, 12
by heart /ˌbaɪ ˈhɑːt/ auswendig p. 14, 10
by ourselves /ˌbaɪ aʊəˈselvz/ (wir) selbst p. 125
bye /baɪ/ tschüs(s) NHG 5

C

C /siː/ *etwa:* Note 3, befriedigend p. 101
cabbage /ˈkæbɪdʒ/ Kohl p. 12, 7
tossing the caber /ˌtɒsɪŋ ðə ˈkeɪbə/ Baumstammwerfen p. 71, 6
cage /keɪdʒ/ Käfig NHG 5
cake /keɪk/ Kuchen NHG 5
calculator /ˈkælkjʊˌleɪtə/ Taschenrechner NHG 5
calendar /ˈkælɪndə/ Kalender NHG 5
call /kɔːl/ Anruf; Gespräch p. 96, 9
(to) **call** /kɔːl/ anrufen NHG 6
(to) **call an ambulance** /ˌkɔːl‿ən‿ˈæmbjʊləns/ einen Krankenwagen rufen p. 45, 4
(to) be called /ˌbiː ˈkɔːld/ heißen, genannt werden NHG 5
(to) **calm down** /ˌkɑːm ˈdaʊn/ (sich) beruhigen p. 46, 5
camera /ˈkæmrə/ Kamera; Fotoapparat NHG 6
camp /kæmp/ (Zelt)lager NHG 6
camping gear /ˈkæmpɪŋ ˌgɪə/ Campingausrüstung p. 76
camping site /ˈkæmpɪŋ ˌsaɪt/ Campingplatz p. 70, 6
can /kæn/ können NHG 5; Dose; Büchse p. 12, 7
can't (= cannot) /kɑːnt, ˈkænɒt/ nicht können NHG 5
candle /ˈkændl/ Kerze NHG 5
cap /kæp/ Mütze NHG 6
capital /ˈkæpɪtl/ Hauptstadt p. 147
caption /ˈkæpʃn/ Bildunterschrift p. 26, 12
car /kɑː/ Auto NHG 5

car boot sale /ˌkɑː ˈbuːt seɪl/ *Kofferraum-Flohmarkt* p. 55
carbohydrate /ˌkɑːbəʊˈhaɪdreɪt/ Kohlenhydrat p. 53
card /kɑːd/ Karte NHG 5
cardamom /ˈkɑːdəməm/ Kardamom p. 30
(to) **take care (of)** *(irr)* /ˌteɪk‿ˈkeər‿əv/ sich kümmern um NHG 6
(to) care about /ˈkeər‿əˌbaʊt/ sich etwas machen aus p. 32, 1
careful /ˈkeəfl/ vorsichtig NHG 6
carefully /ˈkeəfli/ vorsichtig NHG 6
Caribbean /ˌkærɪˈbiən/ karibisch p. 70, 6
carnival /ˈkɑːnɪvl/ Volksfest, Karneval p. 72, 8
carrot /ˈkærət/ Möhre; Karotte NHG 5
(to) carry /ˈkæri/ tragen p. 130
case /keɪs/ Fall NHG 6
cash /kæʃ/ Geld; Bargeld p. 24, 8
cast /kɑːst/ Gips p. 42, 1
castle /ˈkɑːsl/ Burg; Schloss NHG 6
cat /kæt/ Katze NHG 5
(to) **catch** *(irr)* /kætʃ/ fangen NHG 5
(to) **catch a cold** *(irr)* /ˌkætʃ‿ə ˈkəʊld/ sich erkälten p. 42, 1
(to) catch a plane *(irr)* /ˌkætʃ‿ə ˈpleɪn/ ein Flugzeug nehmen p. 102
category /ˈkætəgri/ Kategorie NHG 6
cathedral /kəˈθiːdrəl/ Kathedrale p. 124
(to) cause /kɔːz/ verursachen p. 127
charity /ˈtʃærəti/ Wohltätigkeits-organisation p. 57, 3
cayenne pepper /ˌkeɪen ˈpepə/ Cayennepfeffer p. 17, 17
(to) **celebrate** /ˈseləˌbreɪt/ feiern NHG 6
celebration /ˌseləˈbreɪʃn/ Feier NHG 6
centre /ˈsentə/ Zentrum NHG 6
shopping centre /ˈʃɒpɪŋ ˌsentə/ Einkaufszentrum NHG 5
century /ˈsentʃəri/ Jahrhundert NHG 6
certainly /ˈsɜːtnli/ sicher; gerne p. 22, 6
chain /tʃeɪn/ Kette NHG 6
chair /tʃeə/ Stuhl NHG 5
challenge /ˈtʃæləndʒ/ Heraus-forderung NHG 5
challenge /ˈtʃæləndʒ/ *hier:* Wette p. 120, 9
chance /tʃɑːns/ Möglichkeit; Gelegenheit p. 36, 7
change /tʃeɪndʒ/ Wechselgeld NHG 5
(to) **change** /tʃeɪndʒ/ (sich) ändern; verändern NHG 6
(to) **change lines** /ˌtʃeɪndʒ ˈlaɪnz/ umsteigen NHG 6
(to) **change one's mind** /ˌtʃeɪndʒ wʌnz ˈmaɪnd/ seine Meinung ändern NHG 6
character /ˈkærəktə/ Figur; Charakter NHG 6
charity /ˈtʃærəti/ Wohltätigkeits-organisation p. 56, 2
charity run /ˈtʃærəti rʌn/ Wohltätig-keitslauf p. 56, 2
charity shop /ˈtʃærəti ʃɒp/ *Laden, in dem gebrauchte Dinge zu Wohl-tätigkeitszwecken verkauft werden* p. 61, 8
(to) **chat** /tʃæt/ plaudern; chatten p. 94, 6
cheap /tʃiːp/ billig p. 18, 2
check /tʃek/ Überprüfung; Kontrolle p. 38, 8
(to) **check** /tʃek/ überprüfen; kontrollieren NHG 5
(to) **check out** *(informal)* /ˌtʃek‿ˈaʊt/ sich ansehen; ausprobieren p. 66, 2
(to) check out /ˌtʃek‿ˈaʊt/ aus-checken p. 27, 14
check-up /ˈtʃek‿ʌp/ Untersuchung p. 46, 5
(to) cheer /tʃɪə/ jubeln p. 53
(to) cheer somebody on /ˌtʃɪə ˌsʌmbədi‿ˈɒn/ jemanden anfeuern p. 52
(to) cheer up /ˌtʃɪər‿ˈʌp/ aufmuntern, aufheitern p. 48, 7
cheerful /ˈtʃɪəfl/ fröhlich, vergnügt p. 70, 6
cheese /tʃiːz/ Käse NHG 5
chemistry club /ˈkemɪstri klʌb/ Chemie-AG p. 93, 5
chess /tʃes/ Schach p. 35, 6
chicken /ˈtʃɪkɪn/ Huhn NHG 6
(chicken) tikka masala, (chicken) tikka /ˌtʃɪkɪn ˌtiːkə məˈsɑːlə, ˌtʃɪkɪn ˈtiːkə/ *britisch-indisches (Hühnchen-)Gericht* p. 11, 6
chickpea /ˈtʃɪkˌpiː/ Kichererbse p. 12, 7
child (*pl* **children**) /tʃaɪld, ˈtʃɪldrən/ Kind NHG 5
childhood /ˈtʃaɪldˌhʊd/ Kindheit p. 86, 8
chilli (*pl* chillies) /ˈtʃɪli, ˈtʃɪliz/ Chili; Peperoni p. 23, 7
Chinese /ˌtʃaɪˈniːz/ Chinese/Chinesin; chinesisch NHG 6
chips *(pl)* /tʃɪps/ Pommes frites NHG 5
chocolate /ˈtʃɒklət/ Schokolade NHG 5
(to) **choose** *(irr)* /tʃuːz/ wählen; sich entscheiden NHG 5
(to) **chop** /tʃɒp/ hacken p. 13, 8
chore /tʃɔː/ lästige Aufgabe; Hausarbeit NHG 5
Christian /ˈkrɪstʃən/ Christ/in; christlich NHG 6
Christmas /ˈkrɪsməs/ Weihnachten NHG 6
church /tʃɜːtʃ/ Kirche NHG 6
chutney /ˈtʃʌtni/ *würzige indische Soße* p. 63, 11
cinema /ˈsɪnəmə/ Kino NHG 5
cinnamon /ˈsɪnəmən/ Zimt p. 17, 17
city /ˈsɪti/ Stadt; Innenstadt NHG 5
city centre /ˌsɪti ˈsentə/ Innenstadt p. 28
class /klɑːs/ Klasse; Unterrichts-stunde NHG 5
classmate /ˈklɑːsˌmeɪt/ Klassen-kamerad/in; Mitschüler/in NHG 5
classroom /ˈklɑːsˌruːm/ Klassen-zimmer NHG 5
clay /kleɪ/ Lehm; Ton p. 118, 7
clean /kliːn/ sauber NHG 5
(to) **clean (up)** /kliːn, ˌkliːn‿ˈʌp/ sauber machen NHG 5
cleaning skates *(pl)* /ˈkliːnɪŋ ˌskeɪts/ *Reinigungsskates* p. 111, 11
clear /klɪə/ klar; deutlich NHG 6
(to) clear up /ˌklɪər‿ˈʌp/ aufräumen p. 73, 9
clearly /ˈklɪəli/ klar; deutlich NHG 6
clever /ˈklevə/ klug; schlau p. 126

(to) **click on** /ˈklɪk‿ɒn/ anklicken p. 121, 12
(to) **climb** /klaɪm/ auf etwas (hinauf)steigen; klettern NHG 5
climbing /ˈklaɪmɪŋ/ Klettern p. 32, 1
clock /klɒk/ Uhr NHG 5
(to) **close** /kləʊz/ zumachen; schließen NHG 5
closed /kləʊzd/ geschlossen NHG 6
clothes *(pl)* /kləʊðz/ Kleider; Kleidung NHG 5
clothing /ˈkləʊðɪŋ/ Kleidung p. 76
club /klʌb/ AG; Klub NHG 5
coach /kəʊtʃ/ Trainer/in p. 45, 4
coconut cream /ˈkəʊkəˌnʌt kriːm/ Kokosmilch p. 23, 7
coffee /ˈkɒfi/ Kaffee NHG 5
coffee grinder /ˈkɒfi ˌgraɪndə/ Kaffeemühle p. 60, 8
cold /kəʊld/ kalt NHG 5; Erkältung p. 42, 1
(to) **catch a cold** *(irr)* /ˌkætʃ‿ə ˈkəʊld/ sich erkälten p. 42, 1
(to) **collect** /kəˈlekt/ sammeln NHG 5
collection /kəˈlekʃn/ Sammlung NHG 6
colony /ˈkɒləni/ Kolonie p. 30
colour /ˈkʌlə/ Farbe NHG 5
colourful /ˈkʌləfl/ farbenfroh; bunt p. 70, 6
combat arena /ˈkɒmbæt‿əˌriːnə/ Wettkampfarena p. 66, 2
combination /ˌkɒmbɪˈneɪʃn/ Kombination; Mischung NHG 6
(to) **come** *(irr)* /kʌm/ kommen NHG 5
(to) **come back** *(irr)* /ˌkʌm ˈbæk/ zurückkommen NHG 5
(to) come by *(irr)* /ˌkʌm ˈbaɪ/ vorbeikommen p. 77
(to) **come in** *(irr)* /ˌkʌm‿ˈɪn/ hereinkommen p. 42, 1
Come on! /ˌkʌm‿ˈɒn/ Komm(t) schon! p. 39, 10
(to) come together *(irr)* /ˌkʌm təˈgeðə/ zusammenkommen p. 54
comfort food /ˈkʌmfət fuːd/ Wohlfühlessen p. 9, 2
comfortable /ˈkʌmftəbl/ bequem p. 109, 7
coming soon /ˌkʌmɪŋ ˈsuːn/ in Kürze erscheinend p. 67, 2
command /kəˈmɑːnd/ Befehl NHG 5
(to) **comment on** /ˈkɒment‿ɒn/ kommentieren NHG 6
commercial /kəˈmɜːʃl/ kommerziell, profitorientiert NHG 6
(to) **have in common** *(irr)* /ˌhæv‿ɪn ˈkɒmən/ gemeinsam haben NHG 6
(to) **communicate** /kəˈmjuːnɪkeɪt/ kommunizieren, sprechen p. 95, 6
communication /kəˌmjuːnɪˈkeɪʃn/ Verständigung; Kommunikation p. 103
community /kəˈmjuːnəti/ Gemeinschaft, Gemeinde p. 81, 2
company /ˈkʌmpni/ Firma; Unternehmen p. 97, 11
(to) **compare** /kəmˈpeə/ vergleichen NHG 6
comparison /kəmˈpærɪsn/ Vergleich NHG 6
(to) **compete** /kəmˈpiːt/ an einem Wettkampf teilnehmen; kämpfen p. 36, 7
(to) compete in /kəmˈpiːt‿ɪn/ teilnehmen an p. 53
competition /ˌkɒmpəˈtɪʃn/ Wettbewerb NHG 5
competitive /kəmˈpetətɪv/ *von Konkurrenzdenken geprägt* p. 35, 6
complete /kəmˈpliːt/ vollständig, komplett p. 99, 15
(to) **complete** /kəmˈpliːt/ vervollständigen NHG 5
completely /kəmˈpliːtli/ völlig, absolut NHG 6
compromise /ˈkɒmprəmaɪz/ Kompromiss NHG 6
con /kɒn/ Nachteil; Kontra NHG 6
(to) **concentrate** /ˈkɒnsnˌtreɪt/ sich konzentrieren p. 35, 6
concept /ˈkɒnsept/ Entwurf; Konzept NHG 6
concert /ˈkɒnsət/ Konzert NHG 6
conditional (clause) /kənˈdɪʃnəl klɔːz/ Konditional(satz) p. 44
conflict /ˈkɒnflɪkt/ Konflikt NHG 6
(to) **connect** /kəˈnekt/ verbinden p. 84, 6
connection /kəˈnekʃn/ Verbindung p. 146
(to) conquer /ˈkɒŋkə/ erobern p. 66, 2
(to) consist of /kənˈsɪst‿əv/ bestehen aus p. 54
console /kənˈsəʊl/ Konsole p. 76
construction /kənˈstrʌkʃn/ Bau p. 108, 7
(to) **contact** /ˈkɒntækt/ sich in Verbindung setzen mit NHG 6
(to) **contain** /kənˈteɪn/ enthalten p. 63, 11
container /kənˈteɪnə/ Behälter p. 136
content /ˈkɒntent/ Inhalt p. 67, 2
(to) continue to do /kənˌtɪnjuː tə ˈduː/ weiter(hin) tun, nach wie vor tun p. 125
(to) control /kənˈtrəʊl/ kontrollieren; steuern p. 30
conversation /ˌkɒnvəˈseɪʃn/ Gespräch; Unterhaltung p. 26, 13
(to) **cook** /kʊk/ kochen NHG 5; braten, backen NHG 6
cook-along video /ˈkʊk‿əˌlɒŋ ˌvɪdiəʊ/ *Mitmach-Koch-Video* p. 12, 7
cookbook /ˈkʊkˌbʊk/ Kochbuch p. 16, 14
cooked /kʊkt/ gekocht p. 23, 7
cooker /ˈkʊkə/ Herd p. 17, 17
cooking /ˈkʊkɪŋ/ Kochen; Koch- NHG 5
(to) **do the cooking** *(irr)* /ˌduː ðə ˈkʊkɪŋ/ kochen NHG 5
cool /kuːl/ kühl; kalt p. 104, 1
(to) **copy** /ˈkɒpi/ abschreiben NHG 5; kopieren p. 117, 6
coriander /ˌkɒriˈændə/ Koriander p. 17, 17
corner /ˈkɔːnə/ Ecke NHG 6
correct /kəˈrekt/ richtig, korrekt; korrigieren NHG 5
(to) **cost** *(irr)* /kɒst/ kosten NHG 5
costume /ˈkɒstjuːm/ Kostüm NHG 6
cosy /ˈkəʊzi/ gemütlich p. 19, 2
cotton /ˈkɒtn/ Baumwolle; Baumwoll- p. 125
cough /kɒf/ Husten p. 42, 1
could /kʊd/ könnte(st, n, t) NHG 5; *Vergangenheitsform von can* NHG 6

counsellor /ˈkaʊnslə/ Berater/in p. 78
(to) **count** /kaʊnt/ zählen p. 108, 7
country /ˈkʌntri/ Land NHG 6
across the country /əˌkrɒs ðə ˈkʌntri/ im ganzen Land p. 73, 9
countryside /ˈkʌntriˌsaɪd/ Land; Landschaft NHG 6
a couple of /ə ˈkʌpl‿əv/ einige, ein paar NHG 6
course /kɔːs/ Kurs NHG 6
course /kɔːs/ Gang p. 28
court /kɔːt/ Platz NHG 5
cousin /ˈkʌzn/ Cousin/e NHG 5
(to) **cover** /ˈkʌvə/ bedecken NHG 6
cow /kaʊ/ Kuh NHG 6
cracker /ˈkrækə/ Kräcker p. 23, 7
arts and crafts /ˌɑːrts‿ən ˈkrɑːfts/ Basteln; Bastelarbeit p. 56, 2
(to) crash into /ˈkræʃ‿ˌɪntʊ/ zusammenstoßen mit p. 125
cream /kriːm/ Sahne p. 16, 14
coconut cream /ˈkəʊkəˌnʌt kriːm/ Kokosmilch p. 23, 7
(to) **create** /kriˈeɪt/ erschaffen; erzeugen NHG 5
creative /kriˈeɪtɪv/ kreativ NHG 5
cricket /ˈkrɪkɪt/ Kricket p. 162
(to) **cross** /krɒs/ überqueren NHG 6
crowd /kraʊd/ Menschenmenge p. 56, 2
crowded /ˈkraʊdɪd/ überfüllt p. 57, 3
crumb /krʌm/ Krümel p. 12, 7
(to) **cry** /kraɪ/ weinen; schreien NHG 6
cucumber /ˈkjuːˌkʌmbə/ Salatgurke p. 8, 2
cue card /ˈkjuː kɑːd/ *Stichwortkarte* NHG 6
culture /ˈkʌltʃə/ Kultur NHG 6
cumin /ˈkjuːmɪn/ Kreuzkümmel p. 17, 17
cup /kʌp/ Tasse NHG 5
cupboard /ˈkʌbəd/ Schrank p. 12, 7
curious /ˈkjʊəriəs/ neugierig p. 30
curry /ˈkʌri/ Curry(gericht) p. 8, 1
curtain /ˈkɜːtn/ Vorhang p. 60, 8
customer /ˈkʌstəmə/ Kunde/ Kundin NHG 6
(to) **cut** *(irr)* /kʌt/ schneiden NHG 6
(to) cut off *(irr)* /ˌkʌt‿ˈɒf/ abschneiden p. 77
cute /kjuːt/ süß; niedlich p. 86, 8
(to) **cycle** /ˈsaɪkl/ Rad fahren, radeln NHG 6
(to) **go cycling** *(irr)* /ˌgəʊ ˈsaɪklɪŋ/ Rad fahren gehen NHG 6

D

D /diː/ *etwa:* Note 4, ausreichend p. 91, 2
dad /dæd/ Papa; Vati NHG 5
daily /ˈdeɪli/ täglich NHG 5
dance /dɑːns/ Tanz p. 36, 7
(to) **dance** /dɑːns/ tanzen NHG 5
dancer /ˈdɑːnsə/ Tänzer/in NHG 6
dancing /ˈdɑːnsɪŋ/ Tanzen NHG 5
danger /ˈdeɪndʒə/ Gefahr NHG 6
dangerous /ˈdeɪndʒərəs/ gefährlich NHG 6
dark /dɑːk/ dunkel; Dunkelheit NHG 6
darkness /ˈdɑːknəs/ Dunkelheit NHG 6
darling /ˈdɑːlɪŋ/ Liebling; Schatz p. 52
date /deɪt/ Datum NHG 5
(to) set a date /ˌset‿ə ˈdeɪt/ sich verabreden p. 101
daughter /ˈdɔːtə/ Tochter NHG 5
day /deɪ/ Tag NHG 5
some day /ˈsʌmˌdeɪ/ eines Tages p. 36, 7
day out /ˌdeɪ‿ˈaʊt/ *Ausflugstag* NHG 6
(to) **deal with** *(irr)* /ˈdiːl wɪð/ sich befassen mit, umgehen mit p. 97, 10
dear /dɪə/ liebe/r *(Anrede)* NHG 5
dear /dɪə/ Liebes *(Anrede)* p. 29
December /dɪˈsembə/ Dezember NHG 5
(to) **decide** /dɪˈsaɪd/ entscheiden; sich entscheiden NHG 5
(to) **decorate** /ˈdekəreɪt/ schmücken; dekorieren NHG 5
decoration /ˌdekəˈreɪʃn/ Dekoration; Schmuck NHG 6
decorative /ˈdekrətɪv/ dekorativ p. 63, 12
definitely /ˈdefnətli/ eindeutig, definitiv NHG 6
(to) **delete** /dɪˈliːt/ löschen p. 93, 5
delicious /dɪˈlɪʃəs/ köstlich, lecker NHG 6
on demand /ˌɒn dɪˈmɑːnd/ auf Anfrage p. 114, 2
dentist /ˈdentɪst/ Zahnarzt/ Zahnärztin p. 42, 1
to the dentist's /ˌtʊ ðə ˈdentɪsts/ in die Zahnarztpraxis p. 163
(to) **depend on** /dɪˈpend‿ɒn/ abhängen von NHG 6
(to) **describe** /dɪˈskraɪb/ beschreiben NHG 5
description /dɪˈskrɪpʃn/ Beschreibung NHG 6
design /dɪˈzaɪn/ Entwurf; Design NHG 6
(to) **design** /dɪˈzaɪn/ entwerfen NHG 5
desk /desk/ Schreibtisch NHG 5
dessert /dɪˈzɜːt/ Nachtisch p. 17, 17
(to) **destroy** /dɪˈstrɔɪ/ zerstören NHG 6
detail /ˈdiːteɪl/ Detail; Einzelheit NHG 5
(to) develop /dɪˈveləp/ erarbeiten; (sich) entwickeln p. 8, 2
development /dɪˈveləpmənt/ Entwicklung p. 114, 2
dialogue /ˈdaɪəˌlɒg/ Gespräch; Dialog NHG 5
diary /ˈdaɪəri/ Tagebuch NHG 6
diary entry /ˈdaɪəri‿ˌentri/ Tagebucheintrag NHG 6
(to) keep a diary *(irr)* /ˌkiːp‿ə ˈdaɪəri/ Tagebuch führen p. 95, 6
dictionary /ˈdɪkʃənri/ Lexikon; Wörterbuch NHG 6
(to) **die** /daɪ/ sterben p. 86, 8
different /ˈdɪfrənt/ anders; andere(r, s); verschiedene(r, s) NHG 5
difficult /ˈdɪfɪklt/ schwierig; schwer NHG 6
dining room /ˈdaɪnɪŋ ruːm/ *hier:* Speisesaal p. 66, 2
dinner /ˈdɪnə/ Abendessen NHG 5
(to) direct /daɪˈrekt/ leiten, führen p. 54
directions *(pl)* /daɪˈrekʃnz/ *hier:* Wegbeschreibungen NHG 6
(to) **give directions** *(irr)* /ˌgɪv daɪˈrekʃnz/ den Weg beschreiben NHG 6

dirty /ˈdɜːti/ dreckig; schmutzig NHG 5
disability /ˌdɪsəˈbɪləti/ Behinderung; Einschränkung p. 54
(to) **disappear** /ˌdɪsəˈpɪə/ verschwinden NHG 6
disappointed /ˌdɪsəˈpɔɪntɪd/ enttäuscht NHG 6
disappointing /ˌdɪsəˈpɔɪntɪŋ/ enttäuschend p. 18, 2
disaster /dɪˈzɑːstə/ Katastrophe p. 28
discipline /ˈdɪsəplɪn/ Disziplin p. 52
(to) **discover** /dɪˈskʌvə/ entdecken NHG 6
discovery /dɪˈskʌvri/ Entdeckung p. 109, 7
discus /ˈdɪskəs/ Diskus(werfen) p. 53
(to) **discuss** /dɪˈskʌs/ besprechen; diskutieren NHG 6
discussion /dɪˈskʌʃn/ Diskussion NHG 6
disgusting /dɪsˈgʌstɪŋ/ widerlich p. 9, 2
dish (*pl* **dishes**) /dɪʃ, ˈdɪʃɪz/ Gericht; Speise p. 7
(Petri) dish /ˈpiːtri ˌdɪʃ/ Petrischale p. 109, 7
dishwasher /ˈdɪʃˌwɒʃə/ Spülmaschine NHG 5
display /dɪˈspleɪ/ Auslage; Ausstellung p. 107, 5
(to) **display** /dɪˈspleɪ/ aushängen; zeigen NHG 5
(to) **put on display** ***(irr)*** /ˌpʊt‿ɒn dɪˈspleɪ/ ausstellen NHG 6
firework display /ˈfaɪəˌwɜːk dɪˌspleɪ/ Feuerwerk p. 67, 2
distance /ˈdɪstəns/ Ferne; Entfernung p. 136
(to) **dive** /daɪv/ tauchen p. 70, 6
diving /ˈdaɪvɪŋ/ Tauchen p. 32, 1
Diwali /dɪˈwɑːli/ *hinduistisches Fest* p. 146
dizzy /ˈdɪzi/ schwindlig p. 45, 4
(to) **do** ***(irr)*** /duː/ tun; machen NHG 5
(to) **do athletics** ***(irr)*** /ˌduː‿æθˈletɪks/ Leichtathletik machen NHG 5
(to) **do gymnastics** ***(irr)*** /ˌduː dʒɪmˈnæstɪks/ turnen NHG 5
(to) **do research** ***(irr)*** /ˌduː rɪˈsɜːtʃ/ recherchieren NHG 5
(to) **do sports** ***(irr)*** /ˌduː ˈspɔːts/ Sport treiben NHG 6
(to) **do the cooking** ***(irr)*** /ˌduː ðə ˈkʊkɪŋ/ kochen NHG 5
(to) **do the shopping** ***(irr)*** /ˌduː ðə ˈʃɒpɪŋ/ einkaufen NHG 5
doctor /ˈdɒktə/ Arzt/Ärztin p. 31
doctor's practice /ˈdɒktəz ˌpræktɪs/ Arztpraxis p. 46, 5
at the doctor's /ˌæt‿ðə ˈdɒktəz/ beim Arzt/bei der Ärztin p. 31
(to) **see a doctor** ***(irr)*** /ˌsiː‿ə ˈdɒktə/ einen Arzt/eine Ärztin aufsuchen p. 43, 1
document /ˈdɒkjʊmənt/ Dokument p. 117, 6
dog /dɒg/ Hund NHG 5
door /dɔː/ Tür NHG 6
dos and don'ts /ˌduːz‿ˌən ˈdəʊnts/ was man tun und was man nicht tun sollte p. 121, 12
double /ˈdʌbl/ doppelt, Doppel- NHG 5
down /daʊn/ hinunter; (nach) unten NHG 6
(to) **download** /ˌdaʊnˈləʊd/ herunterladen p. 121, 12
Dr (= Doctor) /ˈdɒktə/ Dr. (= Doktor) NHG 6
draft /drɑːft/ Entwurf NHG 6
dragon /ˈdrægən/ Drache NHG 6
drama /ˈdrɑːmə/ Theater-; Schauspiel- NHG 6
dramatic /drəˈmætɪk/ dramatisch p. 43, 1
(to) **draw** ***(irr)*** /drɔː/ zeichnen NHG 5
(to) **draw attention to** ***(irr)*** /ˌdrɔ‿əˈtenʃn tə/ Aufmerksamkeit lenken auf p. 70, 6
drawer /ˈdrɔːə/ Schublade p. 12, 7
drawing /ˈdrɔːɪŋ/ Zeichnung NHG 6
dream /driːm/ Traum NHG 5
dress /dres/ Kleid; Kleidung p. 86, 8
(to) **dress** /dres/ sich anziehen; sich kleiden p. 72, 8
drink /drɪŋk/ Trinken; Getränk NHG 5
(to) **drink** ***(irr)*** /drɪŋk/ trinken NHG 5
(to) **drive** ***(irr)*** /draɪv/ fahren NHG 6
drone /drəʊn/ Drohne p. 124
(to) drop /drɒp/ fallen lassen p. 39, 10
dry /draɪ/ trocken NHG 6
dry suit /ˈdraɪsuːt/ Taucheranzug p. 38, 8
during /ˈdjʊərɪŋ/ während NHG 6

E

each /iːtʃ/ jede(r, s) NHG 5
each and every /ˈiːtʃ‿ən‿ˌevri/ jede(r, s) einzelne p. 39, 10
each other /ˌiːtʃ‿ˈʌðə/ einander NHG 5
ear /ɪə/ Ohr NHG 5
earlier /ˈɜːliə/ vorhin, früher NHG 6
early /ˈɜːli/ früh NHG 6
(to) **earn** /ɜːn/ verdienen NHG 6
earth /ɜːθ/ Erde NHG 6
Easter /ˈiːstə/ Ostern NHG 6
easy /ˈiːzi/ leicht; einfach NHG 5
(to) **eat** ***(irr)*** /iːt/ essen NHG 5
(to) **eat out** ***(irr)*** /ˌiːt‿ˈaʊt/ auswärts essen; im Restaurant essen p. 25, 10
eating habit /ˈiːtɪŋ ˌhæbɪt/ Essgewohnheit p. 30
(to) echo /ˈekəʊ/ (wider)hallen p. 127
(to) **edit** /ˈedɪt/ bearbeiten NHG 5
egg /eg/ Ei NHG 5
Egypt /ˈiːdʒɪpt/ Ägypten p. 6
not ... either /ˌnɒt‿ˈaɪðə/ auch nicht p. 24, 8
either ... or ... /ˌaɪðə ˈɔː/ entweder ... oder ... NHG 6
elbow pad /ˈelbəʊ ˌpæd/ Ellenbogenschützer p. 39, 10
electric /ɪˈlektrɪk/ elektrisch; Elektro- p. 104, 1
electrical /ɪˈlektrɪkl/ elektrisch p. 142
electricity /ɪˌlekˈtrɪsəti/ Elektrizität; Strom p. 110, 9
elephant /ˈelɪfənt/ Elefant p. 62, 10
else /els/ anders; sonst NHG 5
emergency /ɪˈmɜːdʒnsi/ Notfall p. 45, 4
emergency call /ɪˈmɜːdʒnsi kɔːl/ Notruf p. 50, 13
emergency services ***(pl)*** /ɪˈmɜːdʒnsi ˌsɜːvɪsɪz/ Notdienst, Rettungsdienst p. 45, 4
(to) **emigrate** /ˈemɪgreɪt/ auswandern p. 85, 7
(to) **empty** /ˈempti/ ausleeren; ausräumen NHG 5

end /end/ Ende; Schluss NHG 5
(to) **end** /end/ enden; beenden NHG 6
in the end /ˌɪn ðiˈend/ am Ende, schließlich NHG 6
ending /ˈendɪŋ/ Ende; Schluss NHG 6
energy /ˈenədʒi/ Energie; Kraft p. 133
engine /ˈendʒɪn/ Maschine; Motor p. 105, 2
engineer /ˌendʒɪˈnɪə/ Ingenieur/in NHG 6
English /ˈɪŋglɪʃ/ Englisch; englisch NHG 5
English-speaking /ˈɪŋglɪʃ‿ˌspiːkɪŋ/ englischsprachig p. 26, 13
(to) **enjoy** /ɪnˈdʒɔɪ/ genießen NHG 5
Enjoy! /ɪnˈdʒɔɪ/ Guten Appetit! p. 17, 17
enough /ɪˈnʌf/ genug NHG 5
(to) **enter** /ˈentə/ eingeben; betreten NHG 6
entertainment /ˌentəˈteɪnmənt/ Unterhaltung NHG 6
entrance /ˈentrəns/ Eingang; Eintritt NHG 6
entry /ˈentri/ Eintritt NHG 6
entry /ˈentri/ Zutritt p. 125
diary entry /ˈdaɪəri‿ˌentri/ Tagebucheintrag NHG 6
environment /ɪnˈvaɪrənmənt/ Umwelt; Umgebung NHG 6
equipment /ɪˈkwɪpmənt/ Ausrüstung; Ausstattung NHG 5
eraser /ɪˈreɪzə/ Radiergummi NHG 5
(to) **escape** /ɪˈskeɪp/ fliehen; entkommen NHG 5
especially /ɪˈspeʃli/ besonders; vor allem NHG 6
(to) be estimated *(irr)* /ˌbi‿ˈestɪmeɪtəd/ geschätzt werden p. 109, 7
Europe /ˈjʊərəp/ Europa NHG 6
(to) evaporate /ɪˈvæpəreɪt/ verdampfen, verdunsten p. 139
even /ˈiːvn/ selbst; sogar NHG 5
evening /ˈiːvnɪŋ/ Abend NHG 5
event /ɪˈvent/ Ereignis; Veranstaltung NHG 5
ever /ˈevə/ jemals NHG 6
ever since /ˌevə ˈsɪns/ seitdem p. 101

every /ˈevri/ jede(r, s) NHG 5
each and every /ˈiːtʃ‿ən‿ˌevri/ jede(r, s) einzelne p. 39, 10
everybody /ˈevriˌbɒdi/ alle; jeder NHG 5
everyday /ˈevriˌdeɪ/ alltäglich, Alltags- NHG 6
everyone /ˈevriwʌn/ alle; jeder NHG 5
everything /ˈevriθɪŋ/ alles NHG 5
everywhere /ˈevriweə/ überall NHG 5
exactly /ɪgˈzækli/ genau NHG 6
exam /ɪgˈzæm/ Prüfung p. 100
(to) **examine** /ɪgˈzæmɪn/ untersuchen p. 46, 5
example /ɪgˈzɑːmpl/ Beispiel NHG 5
for example /fər‿ɪgˈzɑːmpl/ zum Beispiel NHG 5
excellent /ˈeksələnt/ ausgezeichnet NHG 5
except /ɪkˈsept/ außer NHG 6
exchange student /ɪksˈtʃeɪndʒ ˌstjuːdnt/ Austauschschüler/in p. 49, 10
excited /ɪkˈsaɪtɪd/ aufgeregt NHG 6
exciting /ɪkˈsaɪtɪŋ/ aufregend NHG 5
Excuse me! /ɪkˈskjuːz ˌmi/ Entschuldigung! NHG 5
exercise /ˈeksəsaɪz/ Übung NHG 6
exercise /ˈeksəsaɪz/ Bewegung p. 124
(to) exercise /ˈeksəsaɪz/ trainieren p. 36, 7
exercise book /ˈeksəsaɪz ˌbʊk/ Heft NHG 5
exhausted /ɪgˈzɔːstɪd/ erschöpft p. 36, 7
exhausting /ɪgˈzɔːstɪŋ/ anstrengend p. 34, 4
exhibition /ˌeksɪˈbɪʃn/ Ausstellung NHG 6
(to) **exist** /ɪgˈzɪst/ existieren NHG 6
(to) **expect** /ɪkˈspekt/ erwarten NHG 6
expensive /ɪkˈspensɪv/ teuer NHG 6
experience /ɪkˈspɪəriəns/ Erfahrung NHG 5
experiment /ɪkˈsperɪmənt/ Experiment; Versuch NHG 5
expert /ˈekspɜːt/ Experte/Expertin NHG 6

(to) **explain** /ɪkˈspleɪn/ erklären NHG 5
(to) **explore** /ɪkˈsplɔː/ erforschen; untersuchen NHG 6
(to) **express** /ɪkˈspres/ ausdrücken NHG 6
extra /ˈekstrə/ zusätzlich NHG 5
extremely /ɪkˈstriːmli/ äußerst, höchst; außerordentlich p. 22, 6
eye /aɪ/ Auge NHG 5
eyeball /ˈaɪˌbɔːl/ Augapfel p. 125

F

face /feɪs/ Gesicht NHG 5
fact /fækt/ Tatsache; Fakt NHG 5
fact file /ˈfækt faɪl/ Steckbrief NHG 5
(to) **fall** *(irr)* /fɔːl/ fallen p. 43, 1
(to) **fall off** *(irr)* /ˌfɔːl‿ˈɒf/ (herunter) fallen p. 51, 16
false /fɔːls/ falsch NHG 5
family /ˈfæmli/ Familie NHG 5
famous /ˈfeɪməs/ berühmt NHG 5
fancy /ˈfænsi/ nobel p. 28
fantastic /fænˈtæstɪk/ fantastisch; super NHG 5
far /fɑː/ weit NHG 5
far /fɑː/ *hier:* weit weg p. 102
farm /fɑːm/ Bauernhof NHG 6
fashion /ˈfæʃn/ Mode NHG 6
fast /fɑːst/ schnell NHG 5
(to) fasten /ˈfɑːsn/ schließen; zumachen p. 109, 7
father /ˈfɑːðə/ Vater NHG 5
fault /fɔːlt/ Schuld; Fehler p. 99, 15
favourite /ˈfeɪvrət/ Liebling; Lieblings- NHG 5
February /ˈfebruəri/ Februar NHG 5
fee /fiː/ Gebühr; Geld p. 56, 2
registration fee /ˌredʒɪˈstreɪʃn fiː/ Anmeldegebühr p. 56, 2
(to) **feed** *(irr)* /fiːd/ füttern NHG 6
feedback /ˈfiːdbæk/ Feedback; Rückmeldung NHG 5
(to) **feel** *(irr)* /fiːl/ (sich) fühlen NHG 6
feeling /ˈfiːlɪŋ/ Gefühl NHG 6
felt-tip /ˈfelt‿tɪp/ Filzstift NHG 5
festival /ˈfestɪvl/ Fest; Festival NHG 6
fever /ˈfiːvə/ Fieber p. 42, 1
a few /ə ˈfjuː/ einige; wenige NHG 6
field /fiːld/ Feld NHG 5

playing field /ˈpleɪɪŋ ˌfiːld/ Sportplatz p. 45, 4
field trip /ˈfiːld‿trɪp/ Exkursion p. 124
fight /faɪt/ Kampf; Streit p. 66, 2
(to) **fight** *(irr)* /faɪt/ bekämpfen; ankämpfen gegen NHG 6
(to) **fill** /fɪl/ füllen NHG 6
(to) **fill in** /ˌfɪl‿ˈɪn/ eintragen, ausfüllen NHG 5
filled /fɪld/ gefüllt p. 9, 2
(to) **film** /fɪlm/ drehen, filmen NHG 6
final /ˈfaɪnl/ letzte(r, s); endgültig NHG 5
finally /ˈfaɪnli/ schließlich; endlich p. 57, 3
(to) **find** *(irr)* /faɪnd/ finden NHG 5
(to) **find out** *(irr)* /ˌfaɪnd‿ˈaʊt/ herausfinden NHG 5
finding /ˈfaɪndɪŋ/ Entdeckung; Ergebnis p. 114, 2
fine /faɪn/ in Ordnung, gut NHG 5
(to) **finish** /ˈfɪnɪʃ/ beenden; enden; fertigstellen NHG 6; aufessen p. 8, 2
finished /ˈfɪnɪʃt/ fertig p. 53
finishing line /ˈfɪnɪʃɪŋ ˌlaɪn/ Ziellinie p. 52
fire /ˈfaɪə/ Feuer NHG 6
firefighter /ˈfaɪəˌfaɪtə/ Feuerwehrmann/-frau NHG 6
firework display /ˈfaɪəˌwɜːk dɪˌspleɪ/ Feuerwerk p. 67, 2
fireworks *(pl)* /ˈfaɪəˌwɜːks/ Feuerwerk NHG 6
first /fɜːst/ erste(r, s); zuerst NHG 5
at first /ˌæt ˈfɜːst/ zuerst NHG 6
fish (*pl* **fish** *or* **fishes**) /fɪʃ, fɪʃ, fɪʃɪz/ Fisch NHG 5
fish and chips /ˌfɪʃ‿ən ˈtʃɪps/ *Fisch mit Pommes* L&L 1
(to) **fit** /fɪt/ passen NHG 5
(to) **keep fit** *(irr)* /ˌkiːp ˈfɪt/ fit bleiben, (sich) fit halten p. 31
flag /flæg/ Fahne; Flagge p. 52
flat /flæt/ Wohnung NHG 6
flatbread /ˈflætbred/ Fladen p. 9, 2
flea market /ˈfliː ˌmɑːkɪt/ Flohmarkt p. 57, 3
flexible /ˈfleksəbl/ biegsam, gelenkig p. 36, 7
floor /flɔː/ Fußboden NHG 5
flour /ˈflaʊə/ Mehl p. 112, 12
flower /ˈflaʊə/ Blume NHG 6
flowerpot /ˈflaʊəˌpɒt/ Blumentopf p. 60, 8
(to) **fly** *(irr)* /flaɪ/ fliegen NHG 6
(to) **focus on** /ˈfəʊkəs‿ɒn/ sich konzentrieren auf NHG 5
folder /ˈfəʊldə/ Mappe; Ordner NHG 5
(to) **follow** /ˈfɒləʊ/ folgen; verfolgen NHG 6
following /ˈfɒləʊɪŋ/ folgende(r, s) NHG 6
food /fuːd/ Essen NHG 5
foot (*pl* **feet**) /fʊt, fiːt/ Fuß NHG 5
football /ˈfʊtˌbɔːl/ Fußball NHG 5
football 5-a-side /ˌfʊtbɔːl ˌfaɪv‿ə ˈsaɪd/ 5er-Fußball p. 54
for /fɔː/ für NHG 5
for *(+ Zeitraum)* /fɔː/ ... lang NHG 6
for ages *(informal)* /fər‿ˈeɪdʒɪz/ seit einer Ewigkeit p. 57, 3
for example /fər‿ɪgˈzɑːmpl/ zum Beispiel NHG 5
for free /fə ˈfriː/ gratis NHG 6
for some time /fə ˌsʌm ˈtaɪm/ eine Zeitlang p. 37, 7
for the first time /fə ðə ˈfɜːst‿taɪm/ zum ersten Mal NHG 6
(to) force /fɔːs/ (er)zwingen p. 76
foreign /ˈfɒrɪn/ ausländisch; fremd p. 85, 7
forest /ˈfɒrɪst/ Wald NHG 6
forever /fərˈevə/ ewig, für immer p. 56, 2
(to) **forget** *(irr)* /fəˈget/ vergessen NHG 5
fork /fɔːk/ Gabel NHG 5
form /fɔːm/ Klasse NHG 5
foxhunting *(no pl)* /ˈfɒks ˌhʌntɪŋ/ Fuchsjagd p. 14, 10
France /frɑːns/ Frankreich NHG 5
free /friː/ frei; kostenlos NHG 6
for free /fə ˈfriː/ gratis NHG 6
free time /friː ˈtaɪm/ Freizeit NHG 5
French /frentʃ/ Französisch NHG 5
fresh /freʃ/ frisch; neu NHG 6
Friday /ˈfraɪdeɪ/ Freitag NHG 5
(on) Fridays /ˈfraɪdeɪz/ freitags NHG 5
fridge /frɪdʒ/ Kühlschrank p. 12, 7
fried /fraɪd/ gebraten p. 11, 6
fried egg /ˌfraɪd‿ˈeg/ Spiegelei p. 52
friend /frend/ Freund/in NHG 5
friendly /ˈfrendli/ freundlich NHG 6
(to) **make friends (with)** *(irr)* /ˌmeɪk ˈfrendz/ sich anfreunden (mit) NHG 6
friendship /ˈfrenʃɪp/ Freundschaft NHG 6
from /frɒm/ von; aus NHG 5
from (all) around the world /frəm‿ˌɔːl‿əˌraʊnd ðə ˈwɜːld/ aus der (ganzen) Welt p. 11, 6
from all over the world /frəm‿ˌɔːl‿ˌəʊvə ðə ˈwɜːld/ aus der ganzen Welt NHG 5
at/in the front /ˌæt/ˌɪn ðə ˈfrʌnt/ vorne NHG 5
in front of /ˌɪn ˈfrʌnt‿əv/ vor NHG 5
fruit /fruːt/ Frucht; Obst NHG 5
frustrated /frʌˈstreɪtɪd/ frustriert NHG 6
full /fʊl/ voll, vollständig NHG 6; satt p. 8, 2
full of /ˈfʊl‿əv/ voller p. 76
fun /fʌn/ Spaß NHG 5; lustig; witzig NHG 6
(to) **be (good/great) fun** *(irr)* /ˌbiː ˌgʊd/ˌgreɪt ˈfʌn/ (viel/großen) Spaß machen NHG 5
(to) **have (a lot of) fun** *(irr)* /ˌhæv‿ə ˌlɒt‿əv‿ˈfʌn/ (viel) Spaß haben NHG 6
function /ˈfʌŋkʃn/ Aufgabe; Funktion p. 118, 7
funny /ˈfʌni/ lustig; komisch NHG 5
furniture /ˈfɜːnɪtʃə/ Möbel(stück) NHG 5
future /ˈfjuːtʃə/ Zukunft NHG 6

G

gallery walk /ˈgæləri wɔːk/ *Gruppendiskussion in Stationsarbeit* p. 41, 13
(to) gallop /ˈgæləp/ galoppieren p. 77
game /geɪm/ Spiel NHG 5
board game /ˈbɔːd geɪm/ Brettspiel NHG 6
gap /gæp/ Lücke NHG 5
garden /ˈgɑːdn/ Garten NHG 5
garlic /ˈgɑːlɪk/ Knoblauch p. 9, 2
gate /geɪt/ Tor NHG 6

general /ˈdʒenrəl/ allgemein p. 114, 2
geography /dʒiːˈɒgrəfi/ Erdkunde NHG 5
German /ˈdʒɜːmən/ Deutsch; deutsch NHG 5
Germany /ˈdʒɜːməni/ Deutschland NHG 5
gerund /ˈdʒerənd/ Gerundium p. 34
(to) **get** *(irr)* /get/ bekommen; holen; kaufen NHG 5; kommen; gelangen; werden NHG 6; bringen p. 24, 8
(to) get *(irr)* /get/ *hier:* gehen p. 77; verstehen p. 126
(to) **get along** *(irr)* /ˌget‿əˈlɒŋ/ sich verstehen NHG 6
(to) get away *(irr)* /ˌget‿əˈweɪ/ wegkommen, flüchten p. 102
(to) **get better** *(irr)* /ˌget ˈbetə/ besser werden, gesund werden p. 37, 7
(to) get dressed *(irr)* /ˌget‿ˈdrest/ sich anziehen p. 76
(to) get killed *(irr)* /ˌget ˈkɪld/ umgebracht werden p. 76
(to) get lost *(irr)* /ˌget ˈlɒst/ verloren gehen, sich verirren p. 124
(to) **get married** *(irr)* /ˌget ˈmærid/ heiraten p. 81, 2
(to) **get rid of** *(irr)* /ˌget ˈrɪd‿əv/ loswerden p. 61, 8
(to) get stuck *(irr)* /ˌget ˈstʌk/ festsitzen p. 102
(to) **get together** *(irr)* /ˌget‿təˈgeðə/ zusammenkommen NHG 5
(to) **get up** *(irr)* /ˌget‿ˈʌp/ aufstehen NHG 6
(to) **get well** *(irr)* /ˌget ˈwel/ gesund werden p. 44, 2
Get well soon! /ˌget ˌwel ˈsuːn/ Gute Besserung! p. 48, 7
ghost /gəʊst/ Geist; Gespenst NHG 6
ginger /ˈdʒɪndʒə/ Ingwer p. 23, 7
girl /gɜːl/ Mädchen NHG 5
(to) **give** *(irr)* /gɪv/ geben NHG 5; angeben, mitteilen NHG 6
(to) give a helping hand *(irr)* /ˌgɪv‿ə ˌhelpɪŋ ˈhænd/ helfen p. 79
(to) **give a presentation** *(irr)* /ˌgɪv‿ə ˌpreznˈteɪʃn/ eine Präsentation halten p. 114, 2
(to) give a try *(irr)* /ˌgɪv‿ə ˈtraɪ/ ausprobieren p. 100
(to) **give advice** *(irr)* /ˌgɪv‿ədˈvaɪs/ Rat geben p. 99, 15
(to) **give directions** *(irr)* /ˌgɪv daɪˈrekʃnz/ den Weg beschreiben NHG 6
(to) give off *(irr)* /ˌgɪv‿ˈɒf/ abgeben p. 127
glad /glæd/ glücklich, froh p. 52
glass /glɑːs/ Glas NHG 6
VR glasses *(pl)* /ˌviː‿ˈɑː ˌglɑːsɪz/ VR-Brille p. 125
X-ray glasses *(pl)* /ˈeksreɪ ˌglɑːsɪz/ *Röntgenbrille* p. 111, 11
glue /gluː/ Klebstoff NHG 5
(to) **go** *(irr)* /gəʊ/ gehen; fahren NHG 5
(to) **go abroad** *(irr)* /ˌgəʊ‿əˈbrɔːd/ ins Ausland gehen / fahren NHG 6
(to) **go away** *(irr)* /ˌgəʊ‿əˈweɪ/ weggehen; verschwinden NHG 6
(to) **go cycling** *(irr)* /ˌgəʊ ˈsaɪklɪŋ/ Rad fahren gehen NHG 6
(to) go for the top *(irr)* /ˌgəʊ fə ðə ˈtɒp/ sich um Höchstleistungen bemühen p. 52
(to) **go hiking** *(irr)* /ˌgəʊ ˈhaɪkɪŋ/ wandern gehen NHG 6
(to) go off *(irr)* /ˌgəʊ‿ˈɒf/ weggehen p. 77
(to) **go on** *(irr)* /ˌgəʊ‿ˈɒn/ passieren; weitergehen, weiterreden p. 26, 12
(to) **go out** *(irr)* /ˌgəʊ‿ˈaʊt/ (hinaus) gehen; ausgehen NHG 6
(to) **go riding** *(irr)* /ˌgəʊ ˈraɪdɪŋ/ reiten gehen NHG 6
(to) **go shopping** *(irr)* /ˌgəʊ ˈʃɒpɪŋ/ einkaufen gehen NHG 6
(to) **go swimming** *(irr)* /ˌgəʊ ˈswɪmɪŋ/ schwimmen gehen NHG 6
(to) **go with** *(irr)* /ˌgəʊ ˈwɪθ/ gehören zu; passen zu NHG 6
in one go /ˌɪn wʌn ˈgəʊ/ auf einmal p. 136
goal /gəʊl/ Tor NHG 5
goalkeeper /ˈgəʊlˌkiːpə/ Tormann/ Torfrau p. 54
(to) be going to *(irr)* /ˌbiː ˈgəʊɪŋ tʊ/ werden NHG 6
gone /gɒn/ weg NHG 6
good /gʊd/ gut NHG 5
(to) **be good at something** *(irr)* /ˌbiː ˈgʊd‿æt ˌsʌmθɪŋ/ gut in etwas sein NHG 6
I'm good, thanks. /aɪm ˈgʊd ˌθæŋks/ Es geht mir gut, danke. NHG 5
Good luck! /ˌgʊd ˈlʌk/ Viel Glück! p. 94, 6
Good morning! /ˌgʊd ˈmɔːnɪŋ/ Guten Morgen! NHG 5
goodbye /ˌgʊdˈbaɪ/ auf Wiedersehen NHG 5
goods *(pl)* /gʊdz/ Waren p. 30
gotta (= have got to) *(informal)* /ˈgɒtə/ müssen p. 102
government /ˈgʌvənmənt/ Regierung p. 73, 9
(to) grab /græb/ sich schnappen; greifen p. 39, 10
grammar /ˈgræmə/ Grammatik p. 10
grandad *(informal)* /ˈgrænˌdæd/ Opa p. 86, 8
grandchild (*pl* grandchildren) /ˈgrænˌtʃaɪld, ˈgrænˌtʃɪldrən/ Enkelkind p. 89, 13
grandfather /ˈgrænˌfɑːðə/ Großvater NHG 5
grandma *(informal)* /ˈgrænˌmɑː/ Oma p. 6
grandmother /ˈgrænˌmʌðə/ Großmutter NHG 5
grandpa *(informal)* /ˈgrænˌpɑː/ Opa p. 84, 6
grandparents *(pl)* /ˈgrænˌpeərənts/ Großeltern NHG 6
grape /greɪp/ (Wein)traube NHG 6
grass /grɑːs/ Gras NHG 6
gravy /ˈgreɪvi/ (Braten)soße p. 8, 2
great /greɪt/ groß; großartig NHG 5
Great Britain /ˌgreɪt ˈbrɪtn/ Großbritannien p. 85, 7
great-grandchild (*pl* great-grandchildren) /ˌgreɪt ˈgrænˌtʃaɪld, ˌgreɪt ˈgrænˌtʃɪldrən/ Urenkelkind p. 89, 13
great-grandfather /ˌgreɪt ˈgrænˌfɑːðə/ Urgroßvater p. 85, 7
great-grandmother /ˌgreɪt ˈgrænˌmʌðə/ Urgroßmutter p. 82, 4
Greece /griːs/ Griechenland p. 8, 2

Greek /griːk/ Grieche/Griechin; griechisch p. 18, 1
green /griːn/ grün NHG 5; umweltfreundlich, ökologisch p. 73, 9
greetings *(pl)* /ˈgriːtɪŋz/ Grüße p. 8, 2
grey /greɪ/ grau NHG 5
(to) grieve /griːv/ traurig sein, trauern p. 102
grilled /grɪld/ gegrillt p. 8, 2
ground /graʊnd/ Boden NHG 6
group /gruːp/ Gruppe NHG 5
(to) **grow** *(irr)* /grəʊ/ anbauen NHG 6; wachsen p. 109, 7
(to) **grow up** *(irr)* /ˌgrəʊ‿ˈʌp/ erwachsen sein / werden NHG 6; aufwachsen p. 81, 2
gruel /ˈgruːəl/ Haferschleim; Grütze p. 76
(to) **guess** /ges/ (er)raten NHG 5
guest /gest/ Gast NHG 5
guide /gaɪd/ Führer/in p. 54; Führer *(Buch)* p. 56, 2
guided /ˈgaɪdɪd/ geführt p. 124
guitar /gɪˈtɑː/ Gitarre NHG 5
guy /gaɪ/ Kerl; Typ p. 76
(you) guys *(pl, informal)* /gaɪz/ Leute *(umgangssprachl.)* NHG 6
gym (= gymnasium) /dʒɪm, dʒɪmˈneɪziəm/ Turnhalle NHG 5
(to) **do gymnastics** *(irr)* /ˌduː dʒɪmˈnæstɪks/ turnen NHG 5

H

habit /ˈhæbɪt/ Gewohnheit, Angewohnheit p. 119, 8
hair /heə/ Haar; Haare NHG 5
hairdresser /ˈheəˌdresə/ Friseur/in NHG 6
half /hɑːf/ halb NHG 5
half (*pl* **halves**) /hɑːf, hɑːvz/ Hälfte NHG 6
hall /hɔːl/ Halle p. 125
ham /hæm/ Schinken p. 131
(to) hand /hænd/ übergeben p. 53
on the one hand, ... /ˌɒn ðə ˈwʌn hænd/ einerseits ... p. 69, 5
on the other hand, ... /ˌɒn ðiˌˈʌðə hænd/ andererseits ... p. 69, 5
(to) give a helping hand *(irr)* /ˌgɪv‿ə ˌhelpɪŋ ˈhænd/ helfen p. 79
(to) **hand in** /ˌhænd‿ˈɪn/ einreichen; abgeben NHG 6
(to) hang on *(irr)* /ˌhæŋ‿ˈɒn/ sich festhalten p. 77
(to) hang out *(informal, irr)* /ˌhæŋ‿ˈaʊt/ rumhängen; Zeit mit jemandem verbringen p. 91, 2
(to) **hang (up)** *(irr)* /ˌhæŋ‿ˈʌp/ hängen, aufhängen NHG 6
(to) **happen** /ˈhæpən/ geschehen; passieren NHG 5
happy /ˈhæpi/ glücklich NHG 5; zufrieden p. 122, 14
Happy birthday (to you)! /ˌhæpi ˈbɜːθdeɪ tʊ juː/ Herzlichen Glückwunsch zum Geburtstag! NHG 5
hard /hɑːd/ hart, schwierig NHG 6; fest; kräftig p. 45, 4
hardly /ˈhɑːdli/ kaum p. 127
(to) **hate** /heɪt/ hassen; nicht ausstehen können NHG 5
(to) **have** *(irr)* /hæv/ haben; essen; trinken NHG 5
(to) **have a look at** *(irr)* /ˌhæv‿ə ˈlʊk‿ət/ sich ansehen NHG 6
(to) **have (a lot of) fun** *(irr)* /ˌhæv‿ə ˌlɒt‿əv‿ˈfʌn/ (viel) Spaß haben NHG 6
(to) **have got** *(irr)* /ˌhæv ˈgɒt/ haben NHG 5
(to) **have in common** *(irr)* /ˌhæv‿ɪn ˈkɒmən/ gemeinsam haben NHG 6
(to) **have to** *(irr)* /ˈhæv tə/ müssen NHG 5
he /hiː/ er NHG 5
head /hed/ Kopf NHG 6
(to) bang one's head /ˌbæŋ wʌnz ˈhed/ sich den Kopf anschlagen p. 45, 4
(to) head /hed/ köpfen p. 39, 10
headache /ˈhedeɪk/ Kopfschmerzen p. 42, 1
heading /ˈhedɪŋ/ Überschrift; Titel NHG 6
headline /ˈhedˌlaɪn/ Schlagzeile; *hier:* Überschrift p. 94, 6
headteacher /ˌhedˈtiːtʃə/ Schulleiter/in; Rektor/in p. 53
health /helθ/ Gesundheit p. 43, 1
healthy /ˈhelθi/ gesund NHG 6
(to) **hear** *(irr)* /hɪə/ hören NHG 5
heart /hɑːt/ Herz NHG 6
by heart /ˌbaɪ ˈhɑːt/ auswendig p. 14, 10
(to) **heat** /hiːt/ erhitzen p. 13, 8
heavy /ˈhevi/ schwer NHG 5
hedgehog /ˈhedʒˌhɒg/ Igel NHG 6
height /haɪt/ Höhe NHG 6
hello /həˈləʊ/ hallo NHG 5
helmet /ˈhelmɪt/ Helm p. 39, 10
help /help/ Hilfe NHG 5
(to) **help** /help/ helfen NHG 5
(to) **help out** /ˌhelp‿ˈaʊt/ aushelfen p. 49, 10
helpful /ˈhelpfl/ hilfreich; nützlich p. 95, 6
(to) give a helping hand *(irr)* /ˌgɪv‿ə ˌhelpɪŋ ˈhænd/ helfen p. 79
helpline /ˈhelpˌlaɪn/ *telefonischer Beratungsdienst* p. 130
her /hɜː/ ihr/ihre; sie NHG 5
herb /hɜːb/ (Gewürz)kraut p. 12, 7
here /hɪə/ hier; hierher NHG 5
Here you are! /ˌhɪə ju‿ˈɑː/ Hier, bitte! NHG 5
hers /hɜːz/ ihre(r, s) p. 98, 12
herself /həˈself/ sich; (sie) selbst p. 90, 2
(to) **hide** *(irr)* /haɪd/ verstecken, sich verstecken NHG 6
high /haɪ/ hoch NHG 5
high jump /ˈhaɪ dʒʌmp/ Hochsprung p. 53
high-pressure /ˌhaɪ ˈpreʃə/ Hochdruck- p. 105, 2
high-speed train /ˌhaɪspiːd ˈtreɪn/ Hochgeschwindigkeitszug p. 127
highlight /ˈhaɪˌlaɪt/ Höhepunkt p. 67, 2
(to) take a hike *(AE, informal, irr)* /ˌteɪk‿ə ˈhaɪk/ abhauen p. 102
(to) **go hiking** *(irr)* /ˌgəʊ ˈhaɪkɪŋ/ wandern gehen NHG 6
hill /hɪl/ Hügel NHG 6
him /hɪm/ ihm, ihn NHG 5
himself /hɪmˈself/ selbst; sich (selbst) NHG 6
Hinduism /ˈhɪnduˌɪzm/ Hinduismus NHG 6
(to) **hire** /ˈhaɪə/ mieten NHG 6
his /hɪz/ sein; seine(r, s) NHG 5
historical /hɪˈstɒrɪkl/ geschichtlich; historisch p. 146

history /ˈhɪstri/ Geschichte NHG 5
(to) **hit** *(irr)* /hɪt/ schlagen NHG 5
(to) hit *(irr)* /hɪt/ treffen; stoßen gegen p. 127
hockey stick /ˈhɒki stɪk/ Hockeyschläger p. 59, 7
(to) **hold** *(irr)* /həʊld/ (fest)halten NHG 5
hole /həʊl/ Loch NHG 5
Holi /ˈhɒli/ *hinduistisches Fest der Farben* p. 146
holiday /ˈhɒlɪdeɪ/ Feiertag NHG 6
holiday(s) /ˈhɒlɪdeɪ(z)/ Ferien; Urlaub NHG 5
home /həʊm/ nach Hause; zu Hause; daheim NHG 5; Zuhause; Haus NHG 6
at home /ˌæt ˈhəʊm/ zu Hause NHG 5
home town /ˈhəʊm ˌtaʊn/ Heimatstadt NHG 5
home-made /ˌhəʊmˈmeɪd/ hausgemacht, selbst gemacht p. 22, 6
(to) **be homesick** *(irr)* /ˌbiː ˈhəʊmˌsɪk/ Heimweh haben p. 85, 7
homework /ˈhəʊmwɜːk/ Hausaufgaben NHG 5
honest /ˈɒnɪst/ ehrlich NHG 6
honey /ˈhʌni/ Honig p. 137
hook /hʊk/ Haken p. 127
hook-and-loop fastener /ˌhʊk‿ən ˈluːp ˌfɑːsnə/ *Klettverschluss* p. 127
(to) **hope** /həʊp/ hoffen NHG 5
horrible /ˈhɒrəbl/ schrecklich; gemein NHG 6
horse /hɔːs/ Pferd NHG 6
(to) **ride a horse** *(irr)* /ˌraɪd‿ə ˈhɔːs/ reiten NHG 5
horse riding /ˈhɔːs ˌraɪdɪŋ/ Reiten p. 76
horsehair /ˈhɔːsˌheə/ Rosshaar p. 105, 2
hospital /ˈhɒspɪtl/ Krankenhaus NHG 6
hot /hɒt/ heiß NHG 6; scharf p. 19, 2
hour /ˈaʊə/ Stunde NHG 5
house /haʊs/ Haus NHG 5
how /haʊ/ wie NHG 5
How about ...? /ˈhaʊ‿əˌbaʊt/ Wie wäre es mit ...?, Was ist mit ...? p. 90, 1
How are you? /ˌhaʊ‿ˈɑː jʊ/ Wie geht es dir / euch / Ihnen? NHG 5
How much is it? /ˌhaʊ mʌtʃ‿ˈɪz‿ɪt/ Wie viel kostet es? NHG 5
however /haʊˈevə/ aber; wie auch immer p. 78
huge /hjuːdʒ/ riesig NHG 6
hundred /ˈhʌndrəd/ Hundert NHG 6
hungry /ˈhʌŋgri/ hungrig NHG 5
hurdle /ˈhɜːdl/ Hürdenlauf; Hürde p. 52
(to) **hurry (up)** /ˌhʌri‿ˈʌp/ sich beeilen NHG 5
(to) **hurt** *(irr)* /hɜːt/ wehtun, schmerzen; verletzen p. 42, 1
husband /ˈhʌzbənd/ Ehemann NHG 5
hysterical /hɪˈsterɪkl/ hysterisch p. 125

I

I /aɪ/ ich NHG 5
I don't know. /ˌaɪ ˌdəʊnt ˈnəʊ/ Ich weiß es nicht. NHG 5
I don't like ... /ˌaɪ ˈdəʊnt laɪk/ Ich mag ... nicht. NHG 5
I'd (= I would) /aɪd, ˈaɪ wʊd/ ich würde p. 93, 5
I'd love to ... /aɪd ˈlʌv tə/ Ich würde sehr gern ... NHG 5
I'm (= I am) /aɪm, ˈaɪ‿æm/ ich bin, ich heiße NHG 5
I'm good, thanks. /aɪm ˈgʊd ˌθæŋks/ Es geht mir gut, danke. NHG 5
ice /aɪs/ Eis NHG 6
ice cream /ˈaɪs ˌkriːm/ Eis NHG 5
ice hockey /ˈaɪs ˌhɒki/ Eishockey p. 129
(to) **ice-skate** /ˈaɪsˌskeɪt/ Schlittschuh laufen NHG 5
ICT (= Information and Communication Technology) /ˌaɪˌsiːˈtiː, ɪnfəˈmeɪʃn‿ən kəˌmjuːnɪˈkeɪʃn tekˌnɒlədʒi/ Informatik *(Schulfach)* NHG 5
idea /aɪˈdɪə/ Idee; Vorstellung NHG 5
if /ɪf/ wenn; falls; ob NHG 5
ill /ɪl/ krank NHG 6
illness /ˈɪlnəs/ Krankheit p. 49, 11
image /ˈɪmɪdʒ/ Bild p. 101
(to) **imagine** /ɪˈmædʒɪn/ sich etwas vorstellen NHG 5
immediately /ɪˈmiːdiətli/ sofort p. 53
immigrant /ˈɪmɪgrənt/ Einwanderer/in; Immigrant/in p. 70, 6
important /ɪmˈpɔːtnt/ wichtig NHG 5
impossible /ɪmˈpɒsəbl/ unmöglich NHG 6
impression /ɪmˈpreʃn/ Eindruck p. 100
impressive /ɪmˈpresɪv/ beeindruckend p. 70, 6
(to) **improve** /ɪmˈpruːv/ verbessern; besser werden NHG 6
in /ɪn/ in; auf NHG 5
in advance /ˌɪn‿ədˈvɑːns/ im Voraus p. 108, 6
in front of /ˌɪn ˈfrʌnt‿əv/ vor NHG 5
in general /ɪn ˈdʒenrəl/ im Allgemeinen p. 30
in my opinion /ɪn ˈmaɪ‿əˌpɪnjən/ meiner Meinung nach NHG 6
in one go /ˌɪn wʌn ˈgəʊ/ auf einmal p. 130
in order to /ˌɪn‿ˈɔːdə tʊ/ um zu p. 33, 2
in the end /ˌɪn ðiˈ‿end/ am Ende, schließlich NHG 6
I'm in! *(informal)* /ˌaɪm‿ˈɪn/ Ich bin dabei! p. 91, 2
(to) **include** /ɪnˈkluːd/ beinhalten; einbeziehen NHG 6
including /ɪnˈkluːdɪŋ/ einschließlich p. 54
independent /ˌɪndɪˈpendənt/ unabhängig p. 30
India /ˈɪndiə/ Indien p. 11, 6
Indian /ˈɪndiən/ Inder/in; indisch p. 21, 5
indoor /ˌɪnˈdɔː/ Hallen- p. 36, 7
indoors /ˌɪnˈdɔːz/ drinnen, im Haus p. 32, 1
industry /ˈɪndəstri/ Industrie p. 108, 7
(to) become infected *(irr)* /bɪˌkʌm‿ɪnˈfektɪd/ sich infizieren p. 109, 7
infection /ɪnˈfekʃn/ Infektion p. 43, 1
influence /ˈɪnfluəns/ Einfluss p. 66, 2
(to) **inform** /ɪnˈfɔːm/ informieren NHG 6
information *(no pl)* /ˌɪnfəˈmeɪʃn/ Informationen NHG 5
ingredient /ɪnˈgriːdiənt/ Zutat p. 17, 17

injury /ˈɪndʒəri/ Verletzung p. 46, 5
inline skating /ˌɪnlaɪn ˈskeɪtɪŋ/ Inlinerfahren p. 138
inside /ˈɪnˌsaɪd/ innerhalb NHG 5; innen; drinnen; hinein NHG 6
inside /ˈɪnˌsaɪd/ in ... hinein p. 109, 7
(to) inspire /ɪnˈspaɪə/ inspirieren p. 127
inspired /ɪnˈspaɪəd/ inspiriert p. 127
instruction /ɪnˈstrʌkʃn/ Anweisung; Instruktion NHG 6
interested /ˈɪntrəstɪd/ interessiert NHG 6
(to) **be interested in** *(irr)* /ˌbi‿ˈɪntrəstɪd‿ɪn/ interessiert sein an p. 115, 3
interesting /ˈɪntrəstɪŋ/ interessant NHG 5
(to) interrupt /ˌɪntəˈrʌpt/ unterbrechen p. 101
(to) **interview** /ˈɪntəˌvjuː/ interviewen, befragen NHG 5
into /ˈɪntuː/ in NHG 5
(to) **introduce** /ˌɪntrəˈdjuːs/ einführen; vorstellen NHG 5
introduction /ˌɪntrəˈdʌkʃn/ Einleitung NHG 5
(to) **invent** /ɪnˈvent/ erfinden NHG 6
invented /ɪnˈventɪd/ erfunden p. 15, 12
invention /ɪnˈvenʃn/ Erfindung NHG 6
inventor /ɪnˈventə/ Erfinder/in p. 105, 2
invitation /ˌɪnvɪˈteɪʃn/ Einladung NHG 5
(to) **invite** /ɪnˈvaɪt/ einladen NHG 5
Ireland /ˈaɪələnd/ Irland NHG 6
island /ˈaɪlənd/ Insel p. 78
it /ɪt/ es NHG 5
Italian /ɪˈtæljən/ Italiener/in; italienisch p. 18, 1
Italy /ˈɪtəli/ Italien NHG 5
item /ˈaɪtəm/ Gegenstand p. 56, 2
its /ɪts/ sein(e), ihr(e) *(sächlich)* NHG 5
itself /ɪtˈself/ (sich) selbst p. 70, 6

J

jacket /ˈdʒækɪt/ Jacke NHG 6
January /ˈdʒænjuəri/ Januar NHG 5
Japanese /ˌdʒæpəˈniːz/ Japaner/in; japanisch p. 127
jar /dʒɑː/ (Glas)gefäß p. 12, 7
javelin /ˈdʒævlɪn/ Speerwerfen p. 52
jewellery *(no pl)* /ˈdʒuːəlri/ Schmuck NHG 6
Jewish /ˈdʒuːɪʃ/ jüdisch NHG 6
job /dʒɒb/ Aufgabe; Beruf NHG 6
(to) **join** /dʒɔɪn/ mitmachen (bei) NHG 5; sich zu jemandem gesellen p. 91, 2
(to) **join in** /ˌdʒɔɪn‿ˈɪn/ sich beteiligen an; mitmachen bei NHG 6
journey /ˈdʒɜːni/ Reise; Fahrt NHG 6
juice /dʒuːs/ Saft NHG 5
juicy /ˈdʒuːsi/ saftig p. 19, 2
July /dʒʊˈlaɪ/ Juli NHG 5
jump /dʒʌmp/ Sprung p. 52
(to) **jump** /dʒʌmp/ springen NHG 5
June /dʒuːn/ Juni NHG 5
just /dʒʌst/ nur; bloß NHG 5; einfach; wirklich; gerade NHG 6

K

(to) **keep** *(irr)* /kiːp/ halten; behalten; aufbewahren NHG 5
(to) keep a diary *(irr)* /ˌkiːp‿ə ˈdaɪəri/ Tagebuch führen p. 95, 6
(to) **keep doing something** *(irr)* /ˌkiːp ˈduːɪŋ sʌmθɪŋ/ etwas weiter tun p. 57, 3
(to) **keep fit** *(irr)* /ˌkiːp ˈfɪt/ fit bleiben, (sich) fit halten p. 31
(to) **keep in touch** *(irr)* /ˌkiːp‿ɪn ˈtʌtʃ/ Kontakt halten; in Verbindung bleiben p. 119, 7
(to) keep up *(irr)* /ˌkiːp‿ˈʌp/ *hier:* hochlegen p. 46, 5
kg (= kilogram) /ˈkɪləˌgræm/ Kilogramm NHG 6
(to) **kick** /kɪk/ treten NHG 5
kid /kɪd/ Kind NHG 5
(to) **kill** /kɪl/ töten p. 14, 10
kind /kaɪnd/ Art; Sorte NHG 5
kindly /ˈkaɪndli/ freundlich p. 78
all kinds of /ˌɔːl ˈkaɪndz‿əv/ alle möglichen NHG 6
king /kɪŋ/ König NHG 6
kingdom /ˈkɪŋdəm/ Königreich p. 78
kingfisher /ˈkɪŋˌfɪʃə/ Eisvogel p. 127
kitchen /ˈkɪtʃən/ Küche NHG 5
km (= kilometre) /ˈkɪləˌmiːtə/ Kilometer p. 56, 2
km/h (= kilometres per hour) /ˌkeɪ‿em‿ˈeɪtʃ/ Kilometer pro Stunde p. 127
knee /niː/ Knie NHG 6
knee pad /ˈniː ˌpæd/ Knieschützer p. 39, 10
knife *(pl* **knives***)* /naɪf, naɪvz/ Messer NHG 5
knight /naɪt/ Ritter p. 15, 11
(to) **knock** /nɒk/ klopfen NHG 6
(to) knock over /ˌnɒk‿ˈəʊvə/ umstoßen p. 52
(to) **know** *(irr)* /nəʊ/ wissen; kennen NHG 5
I don't know. /ˌaɪ ˌdəʊnt ˈnəʊ/ Ich weiß es nicht. NHG 5
Korean /kəˈriːən/ Koreaner/in; koreanisch p. 80, 2
korma /ˈkɔːmə/ *indisches Gericht* p. 19, 2

L

lab /læb/ Labor p. 109, 7
label /ˈleɪbl/ Etikett p. 89, 13
(to) **label** /ˈleɪbl/ beschriften NHG 5
lad *(informal, Scottish)* /læd/ Junge p. 71, 6
lady /ˈleɪdi/ Frau; Dame p. 25, 11
Lahmacun /ˌlɑməˈdʒuːn/ *traditionelles türkisches Gericht* p. 9, 2
lake /leɪk/ See NHG 5
lamb /læm/ Lamm p. 22, 6
lame /leɪm/ lahm p. 91, 2
lamp /læmp/ Lampe p. 60, 8
(to) **land** /lænd/ landen p. 71, 6
language /ˈlæŋgwɪdʒ/ Sprache NHG 5
lantern /ˈlæntən/ Laterne NHG 6
large /lɑːdʒ/ groß NHG 6
lass *(informal, Scottish)* /læs/ Mädchen p. 71, 6
lassi /ˈlæsi/ *Joghurtgetränk* p. 23, 7
last /lɑːst/ letzte(r, s) NHG 5; (an)dauern NHG 6
last /lɑːst/ als Letzte(r, s) p. 53
late /leɪt/ (zu) spät NHG 5
(to) **stay up (late)** /ˌsteɪ‿ʌp ˈleɪt/ lange aufbleiben p. 98, 13
later /ˈleɪtə/ später NHG 5

latest /ˈleɪtɪst/ neueste(r, s) p. 86, 8
(to) **laugh** /lɑːf/ lachen NHG 6
lazy /ˈleɪzi/ faul NHG 6
lead /liːd/ Leine NHG 6
leader /ˈliːdə/ Leiter/in NHG 6
leaf (*pl* **leaves**) /liːf, liːvz/ Blatt NHG 6
leaflet /ˈliːflət/ Prospekt; Broschüre p. 41, 13
(to) **learn** *(irr)* /lɜːn/ lernen NHG 6
least /liːst/ am wenigsten p. 67, 2
leather /ˈleðə/ Leder p. 109, 7
(to) **leave** *(irr)* /liːv/ weggehen NHG 5; verlassen, abfahren; (übrig) lassen; zurücklassen; hinterlassen NHG 6
(to) leave behind *(irr)* /ˌliːv bɪˈhaɪnd/ zurücklassen p. 102
Lebanon /ˈlebənən/ der Libanon p. 9, 2
left /left/ links, nach links NHG 6; übrig p. 12, 7
on the left /ˌɒn ðə ˈleft/ links, auf der linken Seite NHG 5
(to) be left out *(irr)* /ˌbiː ˌleft‿ˈaʊt/ ausgeschlossen werden p. 94, 6
(to) have something left *(irr)* /ˌhæv sʌmθɪŋ ˈleft/ etwas übrig haben p. 57, 3
leg /leg/ Bein NHG 6
legend /ˈledʒnd/ Legende p. 78
lemon /ˈlemən/ Zitrone NHG 5
lemonade /ˌleməˈneɪd/ Limonade p. 23, 7
less /les/ weniger NHG 6
lesson /ˈlesn/ Stunde; Unterricht NHG 5
(to) **let** *(irr)* /let/ lassen NHG 5
(to) let in *(irr)* /ˌlet‿ˈɪn/ hereinlassen p. 28
let's ... /lets/ lass(t) uns ... NHG 5
letter /ˈletə/ Buchstabe NHG 5; Brief NHG 6
level /ˈlevl/ Stufe; Level NHG 5
library /ˈlaɪbrəri/ Bücherei NHG 5
(to) lick /lɪk/ (ab)lecken p. 29
life (*pl* **lives**) /laɪf, laɪvz/ Leben NHG 5
lifestyle /ˈlaɪfˌstaɪl/ Lebensstil p. 31
(to) **lift** /lɪft/ (hoch)heben p. 71, 6
light /laɪt/ Licht NHG 5
(to) **light** *(irr)* /laɪt/ anzünden NHG 6
like /laɪk/ wie; mögen NHG 5
I would like ... (= I'd like ...) /aɪ ˌwʊd ˈlaɪk, aɪd ˈlaɪk/ Ich würde gern ... / Ich hätte gern ... NHG 5
(to) **like best** /ˌlaɪk ˈbest/ am liebsten mögen NHG 5
(to) **like doing something** /laɪk ˈduːɪŋ ˌsʌmθɪŋ/ etwas gern tun NHG 6
like that /ˌlaɪk ˈðæt/ so p. 39, 10
line /laɪn/ Linie; Zeile NHG 5
linking part /ˈlɪŋkɪŋ pɑːt/ Verbindungsteil p. 98, 13
linking word /ˈlɪŋkɪŋ wɜːd/ Verbindungswort p. 98, 13
The Lion King /ðə ˈlaɪən ˌkɪŋ/ *Der König der Löwen (Musical)* p. 56, 2
list /lɪst/ Liste NHG 5
(to) **list** /lɪst/ auflisten NHG 5
(to) **listen (to)** /ˈlɪsn/ zuhören, anhören NHG 5
listening /ˈlɪsnɪŋ/ Hören p. 11, 6
literature /ˈlɪtrətʃə/ Literatur p. 100
little /ˈlɪtl/ klein NHG 5
a little /ə ˈlɪtl/ ein bisschen NHG 6
(to) **live** /lɪv/ leben; wohnen NHG 5
lively /ˈlaɪvli/ lebendig p. 81, 2
living /ˈlɪvɪŋ/ Lebensstil p. 31
living /ˈlɪvɪŋ/ lebend p. 76
living room /ˈlɪvɪŋ ˌruːm/ Wohnzimmer NHG 5
'll (= will) /l, wɪl/ werden NHG 6
(to) **load** /ləʊd/ laden NHG 5
loads of /ˈləʊdz‿əv/ jede Menge p. 76
locomotive /ˌləʊkəˈməʊtɪv/ Lokomotive p. 105, 2
log /lɒg/ Baumstamm p. 71, 6
logical thinking /ˌlɒdʒɪkl ˈθɪŋkɪŋ/ logische Denken p. 33, 2
lonely /ˈləʊnli/ einsam NHG 6
long /lɒŋ/ lang NHG 5
long jump /ˈlɒŋ dʒʌmp/ Weitsprung p. 52
long-distance /ˌlɒŋ ˈdɪstəns/ Fern- p. 105, 2
look /lʊk/ Aussehen; Look p. 72, 8
(to) **look** /lʊk/ aussehen NHG 5
(to) **have a look at** *(irr)* /ˌhæv‿ə ˈlʊk‿ət/ sich ansehen NHG 6
(to) **look after** /ˌlʊk‿ˈɑːftə/ sich kümmern um; aufpassen auf NHG 5
(to) **look (at)** /ˈlʊk‿ət/ (an)sehen, (an)schauen NHG 5
(to) **look for** /ˈlʊk fə/ suchen nach NHG 5
(to) **look forward to** /ˌlʊk ˈfɔːwəd‿tʊ/ sich freuen auf NHG 6
(to) look out for /ˌlʊk‿ˈaʊt fə/ *hier:* sich kümmern um p. 40, 12
(to) **look up** /ˌlʊk‿ˈʌp/ hochschauen; nachschlagen p. 35, 6
-looking /ˈlʊkɪŋ/ aussehend p. 28
(to) **lose** *(irr)* /luːz/ verlieren p. 32, 1
loser /ˈluːzə/ Verlierer/in p. 32, 1
a lot /ə ˈlɒt/ viel, sehr NHG 5
a lot (of) /ə ˈlɒt/ viel(e), jede Menge NHG 5
thanks a lot /ˌθæŋks‿ə ˈlɒt/ vielen Dank NHG 5
lots of /ˈlɒts‿əv/ viel(e) NHG 5
loud /laʊd/ laut NHG 5
love /lʌv/ viele Grüße; alles Liebe *(in Briefen)* NHG 6
(to) **love** /lʌv/ lieben, sehr mögen NHG 5
(to) **love doing something** /lʌv ˈduːɪŋ ˌsʌmθɪŋ/ etwas sehr gern tun NHG 5
lovely /ˈlʌvli/ schön p. 29
lover /ˈlʌvə/ Liebhaber/in p. 70, 6
low-tech /ˌləʊ ˈtek/ technisch einfach p. 114, 2
lower /ˈləʊə/ niedriger p. 54
loyal /ˈlɔɪəl/ treu; loyal p. 78
Good luck! /ˌgʊd ˈlʌk/ Viel Glück! p. 94, 6
(good) luck /lʌk/ Glück NHG 6
luckily /ˈlʌkɪli/ zum Glück; glücklicherweise p. 53
lunch /lʌntʃ/ Mittagessen NHG 5
lunch break /ˈlʌntʃ breɪk/ Mittagspause p. 53
lychee /ˈlaɪtʃi/ Litschi p. 140

M

machine /məˈʃiːn/ Maschine; Apparat NHG 6
made /meɪd/ hergestellt, gemacht p. 73, 9
magazine /ˌmægəˈziːn/ Zeitschrift p. 117, 6
main /meɪn/ Haupt- NHG 5

main (course) /ˈmeɪn kɔːs/ Hauptgericht p. 17, 17
main entrance /ˌmeɪn‿ˈentrəns/ Haupteingang p. 125
(to) **make** *(irr)* /meɪk/ machen NHG 5
(to) **make friends (with)** *(irr)* /ˌmeɪk ˈfrendz/ sich anfreunden (mit) NHG 6
(to) make money *(irr)* /ˌmeɪk ˈmʌni/ Geld verdienen p. 165
(to) **make notes** *(irr)* /ˌmeɪk ˈnəʊts/ sich Notizen machen NHG 5
(to) **make somebody do something** *(irr)* /ˌmeɪk ˌsʌmbədi ˈduː ˌsʌmθɪŋ/ jemanden dazu bringen, etwas zu tun p. 37, 7
(to) **make sure** *(irr)* /ˌmeɪk ˈʃɔː/ darauf achten, dass ... NHG 6
(to) make sure *(irr)* /ˌmeɪk ˈʃɔː/ sich versichern; achten auf p. 124
(to) **make up** *(irr)* /ˌmeɪk‿ˈʌp/ erfinden, sich ausdenken NHG 6
man (*pl* **men**) /mæn, men/ Mann NHG 5
(to) manage /ˈmænɪdʒ/ zurechtkommen, es schaffen p. 29
many /ˈmeni/ viele NHG 5
map /mæp/ Karte NHG 5
March /mɑːtʃ/ März NHG 5
mark /mɑːk/ Note; Zensur NHG 6
(to) **mark** /mɑːk/ markieren, kennzeichnen p. 50, 14
market /ˈmɑːkɪt/ Markt NHG 5
(to) **be married** *(irr)* /ˌbiː ˈmærid/ verheiratet sein NHG 6
(to) **get married** *(irr)* /ˌget ˈmærid/ heiraten p. 81, 2
(to) **marry** /ˈmæri/ heiraten p. 85, 7
masala /məˈsɑːlə/ *Gewürzmischung* L&L 1
mashed potatoes *(pl)* /ˌmæʃt pəˈteɪtəʊz/ Kartoffelbrei p. 8, 1
match /mætʃ/ Spiel NHG 5
(to) **match** /mætʃ/ passen zu NHG 6
(to) **match (with/to)** /mætʃ/ zuordnen NHG 5
maths *(informal)* /mæθ/ Mathe *(Schulfach)* NHG 5
matter /ˈmætə/ Angelegenheit p. 95, 6
What's the matter? /ˌwɒts‿ðə ˈmætə/ Was ist los? p. 42, 1
May /meɪ/ Mai NHG 5
may /meɪ/ können; dürfen NHG 6
maybe /ˈmeɪbi/ vielleicht NHG 5
me, to me /miː/ mir; mich; ich NHG 5
meal /miːl/ Mahlzeit; Essen NHG 5
(to) **mean** *(irr)* /miːn/ meinen; bedeuten NHG 6
meaning /ˈmiːnɪŋ/ Bedeutung p. 46, 5
meanwhile /ˈmiːnˌwaɪl/ inzwischen; unterdessen p. 77
meat /miːt/ Fleisch p. 12, 7
mechanic /mɪˈkænɪk/ Mechaniker / Mechanikerin NHG 6
the media /ðə ˈmiːdiə/ die Medien p. 14, 9
mediation /ˌmiːdiˈeɪʃn/ Sprachmittlung; Mediation p. 15, 12
medical /ˈmedɪkl/ medizinisch p. 51, 16
medicine /ˈmedsn/ Medizin; Medikamente p. 43, 1
medieval /ˌmediˈiːvl/ mittelalterlich p. 76
(to) **meet** *(irr)* /miːt/ treffen; sich treffen NHG 5; kennenlernen NHG 6
Nice to meet you. /ˌnaɪs tə ˈmiːt jə/ Schön, dich / euch / Sie zu treffen. NHG 5
meeting /ˈmiːtɪŋ/ Versammlung; Treffen NHG 6
meeting point /ˈmiːtɪŋ pɔɪnt/ Treffpunkt p. 125
member /ˈmembə/ Mitglied NHG 5
memory /ˈmemri/ Erinnerung p. 80, 2
(to) **mention** /ˈmenʃn/ erwähnen p. 67, 2
menu /ˈmenjuː/ Speisekarte; Menü NHG 5
mess /mes/ Unordnung p. 29
message /ˈmesɪdʒ/ Nachricht; Botschaft NHG 5
(to) message /ˈmesɪdʒ/ eine Nachricht schicken p. 119, 7
method /ˈmeθəd/ Methode p. 117, 6
metre /ˈmiːtə/ Meter NHG 6
middle /ˈmɪdl/ Mitte NHG 5
the Middle Ages *(pl)* /ðə ˌmɪdl‿ˈeɪdʒɪz/ Mittelalter p. 77
might /maɪt/ könnte(st, n, t) NHG 6
mile /maɪl/ Meile NHG 6
milk /mɪlk/ Milch NHG 5
milkshake /ˈmɪlkˌʃeɪk/ Milchshake p. 52
(to) mime /maɪm/ mimen, pantomimisch darstellen p. 49, 11
minced meat /ˌmɪnst ˈmiːt/ Hackfleisch p. 9, 2
mind /maɪnd/ Geist; Verstand p. 102
(to) **change one's mind** /ˌtʃeɪndʒ wʌnz ˈmaɪnd/ seine Meinung ändern NHG 6
mine /maɪn/ meine(r, s) p. 18, 2
mineral water /ˈmɪnrəl ˌwɔːtə/ Mineralwasser p. 23, 7
mischief /ˈmɪstʃɪf/ Unfug p. 76
(to) **miss** /mɪs/ vermissen; verpassen NHG 5
missing /ˈmɪsɪŋ/ fehlend NHG 5
(to) be missing *(irr)* /ˌbiː ˈmɪsɪŋ/ fehlen p. 124
mistake /mɪˈsteɪk/ Fehler p. 147
mix /mɪks/ Mischung p. 30
(to) **mix** /mɪks/ sich (ver)mischen NHG 6
mixed /mɪkst/ gemischt p. 23, 7
mixture /ˈmɪkstʃə/ Mischung p. 81, 2
mobile (phone) /ˈməʊbaɪl/ Handy NHG 6
modal verb /ˈməʊdl vɜːb/ Modalverb p. 47, 6
model /ˈmɒdl/ Modell NHG 6
Monday /ˈmʌndeɪ/ Montag NHG 5
(on) Mondays /ˈmʌndeɪz/ montags NHG 5
money /ˈmʌni/ Geld NHG 5
(to) make money *(irr)* /ˌmeɪk ˈmʌni/ Geld verdienen p. 165
pocket money /ˈpɒkɪt ˌmʌni/ Taschengeld p. 57, 3
month /mʌnθ/ Monat NHG 5
mood /muːd/ Laune; Stimmung NHG 6
moon /muːn/ Mond NHG 5
more /mɔː/ mehr; weitere NHG 5
morning /ˈmɔːnɪŋ/ Morgen NHG 5
Morocco /məˈrɒkəʊ/ Marokko p. 12, 7
mosque /mɒsk/ Moschee NHG 6

most /məʊst/ die meisten; am meisten p. 105, 2
most of the time /ˈməʊst‿əv ðə ˌtaɪm/ meistens p. 37, 7
mostly /ˈməʊstli/ meistens, größtenteils p. 86, 8
mother /ˈmʌðə/ Mutter NHG 5
mould /məʊld/ Schimmel p. 109, 7
mountain /ˈmaʊntɪn/ Berg NHG 5
mountain biking /ˈmaʊntɪn ˌbaɪkɪŋ/ Mountainbikefahren p. 80, 2
move /muːv/ Bewegung NHG 5
on the move /ˌɒn ðə ˈmuːv/ unterwegs p. 102
(to) **move** /muːv/ umziehen NHG 6; (sich) bewegen p. 36, 7
(to) move out /ˌmuːv‿ˈaʊt/ ausziehen p. 139
(to) **move something** /ˈmuːv ˌsʌmθɪŋ/ etwas wegräumen, etwas woanders hinstellen NHG 6
moving /ˈmuːvɪŋ/ beweglich NHG 6
Mr /ˈmɪstə/ Herr *(Anrede)* NHG 5
Mrs /ˈmɪsɪz/ Frau *(Anrede)* NHG 5
Ms /mɪz/ Fr. (= Frau) *(Anrede)* p. 53
much /mʌtʃ/ viel NHG 5; sehr p. 60, 8
mud /mʌd/ Schlamm p. 72, 8
muddy /ˈmʌdi/ matschig; schlammig p. 70, 6
multicultural /ˌmʌltiˈkʌltʃərəl/ multikulturell p. 71, 6
mum /mʌm/ Mama; Mutti NHG 5
muscle /ˈmʌsl/ Muskel p. 104, 1
mushroom /ˈmʌʃruːm/ Pilz p. 128
music /ˈmjuːzɪk/ Musik NHG 5
musician /mjʊˈzɪʃn/ Musiker/in NHG 6
Muslim /ˈmʊzləm/ Muslim/in; muslimisch NHG 6
must /mʌst/ müssen NHG 6
mustn't (= must not) /ˈmʌsnt, mʌst ˈnɒt/ nicht dürfen NHG 6
my /maɪ/ mein(e) NHG 5
myself /maɪˈself/ mir/mich/ich (selbst) p. 36, 7
mythical /ˈmɪθɪkl/ sagenumwoben p. 78

N

naan bread /ˈnɑːn bred/ *indisches Fladenbrot* p. 19, 2
(to) **name** /neɪm/ (be)nennen NHG 5
named /neɪmd/ namens p. 105, 2
national park /ˌnæʃnl ˈpɑːk/ Nationalpark NHG 6
nature /ˈneɪtʃə/ Natur NHG 5
near /nɪə/ nahe, in der Nähe von NHG 5
nearly /ˈnɪəli/ fast; beinahe p. 77
necessary /ˈnesəsri/ notwendig, erforderlich NHG 5
(to) **need** /niːd/ brauchen NHG 5
(to) **need to** /ˈniːd‿tʊ/ müssen NHG 5
negative /ˈnegətɪv/ negativ NHG 6
neighbour /ˈneɪbə/ Nachbar/in p. 98, 12
neighbourhood /ˈneɪbəˌhʊd/ Viertel; Nachbarschaft NHG 5
neither /ˈnaɪðə, ˈniːðə/ auch nicht p. 57, 3
nervous /ˈnɜːvəs/ nervös NHG 5
net /net/ Netz NHG 5
network /ˈnetˌwɜːk/ Netzwerk p. 117, 6
never /ˈnevə/ nie, niemals NHG 5
new /njuː/ neu NHG 5
New Year /ˌnjuː ˈjɪə/ Neujahr NHG 6
news *(no pl)* /njuːz/ Neuigkeit; Nachrichten p. 46, 5
newspaper /ˈnjuːzˌpeɪpə/ Zeitung NHG 6
next /nekst/ nächste(r, s) NHG 5; dann, als Nächstes NHG 6
next to /ˈnekst‿tə/ neben NHG 5
nice /naɪs/ schön; nett NHG 5
Nice to meet you. /ˌnaɪs tə ˈmiːt jə/ Schön, dich / euch / Sie zu treffen. NHG 5
night /naɪt/ Nacht; Abend NHG 6
no /nəʊ/ kein(e); nein NHG 5
no longer /ˌnəʊ ˈlɒŋgə/ nicht mehr p. 73, 9
no one /ˈnəʊ wʌn/ keiner NHG 6
nobody /ˈnəʊbədi/ niemand; keiner p. 57, 3
noise /nɔɪz/ Geräusch; Lärm NHG 6
noodle /ˈnuːdl/ Nudel p. 11, 6
north /nɔːθ/ Norden; Nord- p. 19, 2
North Africa /ˌnɔːθ‿ˈæfrɪkə/ Nordafrika p. 9, 2
northern /ˈnɔːðən/ nördlich, Nord- NHG 6
nose /nəʊz/ Nase NHG 5
not /nɒt/ nicht NHG 5
not … either /ˌnɒt‿ˈaɪðə/ auch nicht p. 24, 8
not any /ˌnɒt‿ˈeni/ kein(e) NHG 5
not anymore /ˌnɒt‿ˌeni ˈmɔː/ nicht mehr NHG 6
not anyone /ˌnɒt‿ˈeniwʌn/ niemand p. 70, 6
not anything /ˌnɒt‿ˈeniˌθɪŋ/ nichts NHG 6
not anywhere /ˌnɒt‿ˈeniˌweə/ nirgendwo NHG 6
not at all /ˌnɒt‿ət‿ˈɔːl/ überhaupt nicht p. 124
not yet /nɒt ˈjet/ noch nicht NHG 6
note /nəʊt/ Nachricht; Notiz NHG 5
(to) **note** /nəʊt/ beachten, zur Kenntnis nehmen NHG 6
notepad /ˈnəʊtˌpæd/ Notizblock NHG 5
(to) **make notes *(irr)*** /ˌmeɪk ˈnəʊts/ sich Notizen machen NHG 5
nothing /ˈnʌθɪŋ/ nichts NHG 6
(to) **notice** /ˈnəʊtɪs/ bemerken; wahrnehmen NHG 6
noticeboard /ˈnəʊtɪsˌbɔːd/ Schwarzes Brett NHG 5
noun /naʊn/ Hauptwort; Substantiv; Nomen NHG 5
November /nəʊˈvembə/ November NHG 5
now /naʊ/ jetzt NHG 5
nowhere /ˈnəʊweə/ nirgends; nirgendwo p. 53
number /ˈnʌmbə/ Zahl; Nummer; Anzahl NHG 5
phone number /ˈfəʊn ˌnʌmbə/ Telefonnummer NHG 5
nurse /nɜːs/ Krankenschwester; Krankenpfleger NHG 6

O

o'clock /əˈklɒk/ Uhr *(bei Nennung einer Uhrzeit)* NHG 5
object /ˈɒbdʒekt/ Gegenstand NHG 6
occasion /əˈkeɪʒn/ Gelegenheit; Anlass p. 21, 5
October /ɒkˈtəʊbə/ Oktober NHG 5
octopus /ˈɒktəpəs/ Tintenfisch p. 8, 2

odd /ɒd/ merkwürdig, seltsam p. 63, 12
odd one out /ˌɒd wʌn‿ˈaʊt/ *Wort, das nicht zu den anderen passt* p. 16, 15
of /əv/ von; aus NHG 5
Of course! /əv ˈkɔːs/ Natürlich! NHG 5
off /ɒf/ von; hinunter, herunter NHG 6
offer /ˈɒfə/ Angebot p. 128
(to) **offer** /ˈɒfə/ anbieten NHG 6
office /ˈɒfɪs/ Büro NHG 5
office manager /ˈɒfɪs ˌmænɪdʒə/ Sekretär/in p. 97, 11
official, officially /əˈfɪʃl, əˈfɪʃli/ offiziell p. 95, 6
often /ˈɒfn/ oft; häufig NHG 5
oh dear *(informal)* /əʊ ˈdɪə/ oje p. 43, 1
oil /ɔɪl/ Öl p. 17, 17
old /əʊld/ alt NHG 5
the Olympics *(pl)* /ðiˌəˈlɪmpɪks/ Olympische Spiele p. 54
OMG! (= Oh my God!) /ˌəʊ‿em ˈdʒiː/ Oh mein Gott! p. 26, 12
on /ɒn/ auf; an; in NHG 5
on /ɒn/ *hier:* über p. 124
on demand /ˌɒn dɪˈmɑːnd/ auf Anfrage p. 114, 2
on one's own /ˌɒn ˌwʌnz‿ˈəʊn/ allein NHG 5
on the left /ˌɒn ðə ˈleft/ links, auf der linken Seite NHG 5
on the move /ˌɒn ðə ˈmuːv/ unterwegs p. 102
on the one hand, ... /ˌɒn ðə ˈwʌn hænd/ einerseits ... p. 69, 5
on the other hand, ... /ˌɒn ðiˌˈʌðə hænd/ andererseits ... p. 69, 5
on the right /ˌɒn ðə ˈraɪt/ rechts, auf der rechten Seite NHG 5
on time /ˌɒn ˈtaɪm/ pünktlich NHG 5
once /wʌns/ früher p. 146
once again /ˌwʌns‿əˈgen/ abermals p. 53
once more /ˌwʌns ˈmɔː/ noch einmal p. 119, 7
once upon a time /ˌwʌns‿əˌpɒn‿ə ˈtaɪm/ es war einmal p. 78
one /wʌn/ ein(e); eins NHG 5; eine(r, s) p. 64, 13
this one /ˈðɪs wʌn/ diese(r, s) hier p. 63, 11
these ones /ˈðiːz wʌnz/ diese p. 60, 8
onion /ˈʌnjən/ Zwiebel p. 9, 2
only /ˈəʊnli/ nur, bloß; erst; einzige(r, s) NHG 5
onto /ˈɒntə/ auf, in NHG 6
onwards /ˈɒnwədz/ von ... an p. 108, 7
open /ˈəʊpən/ offen; geöffnet NHG 5
(to) **open** /ˈəʊpən/ öffnen; aufmachen NHG 5; sich öffnen, aufgehen; eröffnen NHG 6
open-air /ˌəʊpən‿ˈeə/ im Freien p. 70, 6
tin opener /ˈtɪn‿ˌəʊpnə/ Dosenöffner p. 109, 7
opening times *(pl)* /ˈəʊpənɪŋ taɪmz/ Öffnungszeiten NHG 6
operator /ˈɒpəˌreɪtə/ Telefonist/in p. 45, 4
opinion /əˈpɪnjən/ Meinung; Ansicht NHG 6
in my opinion /ɪn ˈmaɪ‿əˌpɪnjən/ meiner Meinung nach NHG 6
opposite /ˈɒpəzɪt/ Gegenteil NHG 5
or /ɔː/ oder NHG 5
orange /ˈɒrɪndʒ/ Orange; Apfelsine; orange NHG 5
order /ˈɔːdə/ Reihenfolge; Ordnung NHG 6
order /ˈɔːdə/ Befehl p. 125
in order to /ˌɪn‿ˈɔːdə tʊ/ um zu p. 33, 2
(to) **take an order** *(irr)* /ˌteɪk‿ən‿ˈɔːdə/ eine Bestellung aufnehmen p. 22, 6
(to) **order (in)** /ˈɔːdə, ˌɔːdər‿ˈɪn/ bestellen p. 8, 2
(to) **organize (= organise)** /ˈɔːgənaɪz/ organisieren NHG 6
organizer /ˈɔːgəˌnaɪzə/ Organisator/ Organisatorin p. 70, 6
original /əˈrɪdʒnəl/ ursprünglich, p. 17, 17
originally /əˈrɪdʒnəli/ ursprünglich p. 6
other /ˈʌðə/ andere(r, s) NHG 5
otherwise /ˈʌðəˌwaɪz/ sonst, im Übrigen p. 101
our /aʊə/ unser(e) NHG 5
ours /ˈaʊəz/ unsere(r, s) p. 98, 12
ourselves /aʊəˈselvz/ uns; wir selbst p. 36, 7
out /aʊt/ heraus, hinaus; aus NHG 5; draußen NHG 6
out and about /ˌaʊt‿ən‿əˈbaʊt/ unterwegs p. 63, 12
out of /ˈaʊt‿əv/ aus NHG 6
out of breath /ˌaʊt‿əv ˈbreθ/ außer Atem p. 77
outdoor /ˌaʊtˈdɔː/ Outdoor-, im Freien p. 33, 2
outdoors /ˌaʊtˈdɔːz/ draußen; im Freien p. 32, 1
outside /ˌaʊtˈsaɪd/ außen; (nach) draußen NHG 5
over /ˈəʊvə/ über, hinüber; vorbei NHG 5
all over the world /ˌɔːl‿ˌəʊvə ðə ˈwɜːld/ auf der ganzen Welt NHG 6
over there /ˌəʊvə ˈðeə/ dort (drüben) NHG 5
overcooked /ˌəʊvəˈkʊkt/ verkocht p. 19, 2
ow (= ouch) *(informal)* /aʊ, aʊtʃ/ aua, autsch p. 42, 1
own /əʊn/ eigene(r, s) NHG 5
on one's own /ˌɒn ˌwʌnz‿ˈəʊn/ allein NHG 5
owner /ˈəʊnə/ Besitzer/in p. 112, 12

P

p (= penny, *pl* **pence)** /piː, ˈpeni, pens/ Penny *(brit. Währung)* NHG 5
p. (= page) /peɪdʒ/ Seite p. 9, 2
(to) **pack** /pæk/ packen NHG 5
packaging /ˈpækɪdʒɪŋ/ Verpackung p. 73, 9
packed /pækt/ voll p. 132
packet /ˈpækɪt/ Packung NHG 5
page /peɪdʒ/ Seite NHG 5
pain /peɪn/ Schmerz p. 102
painful /ˈpeɪnfl/ schmerzhaft p. 43, 1
(to) **paint** /peɪnt/ (an)malen NHG 5
painting /ˈpeɪntɪŋ/ Bild; Gemälde NHG 5
pair /peə/ Paar NHG 6
(a pair of) trousers /ə ˌpeər‿əv ˈtraʊzəz/ Hose NHG 5
palace /ˈpæləs/ Palast NHG 6
palak paneer /ˌpɑːlək pəˈnɪə/ *indisches Gericht* p. 23, 7
pancake /ˈpænˌkeɪk/ Pfannkuchen p. 29
(to) panic /ˈpænɪk/ in Panik geraten p. 77

paper /ˈpeɪpə/ Papier NHG 6
paper /ˈpeɪpə/ *hier:* Klausur p. 101
paprika /ˈpæprɪkə/ Paprikapulver p. 17, 17
paragraph /ˈpærəˌɡrɑːf/ Absatz; Abschnitt NHG 6
Paralympic /ˌpærəˈlɪmpɪk/ paralympisch p. 54
the Paralympic Games *(pl)* /ðə ˌpærəlɪmpɪk‿ˈɡeɪmz/ Paralympische Spiele p. 54
the Paralympics *(pl)* /ðə ˌpærəˈlɪmpɪks/ *Olympische Spiele für Menschen mit Behinderungen* p. 54
parent /ˈpeərənt/ Elternteil p. 94, 6
parents ***(pl)*** /ˈpeərənts/ Eltern NHG 5
(to) park /pɑːk/ parken p. 76
parliament /ˈpɑːləmənt/ Parlament NHG 6
part /pɑːt/ Teil NHG 5; Rolle p. 65, 15
(to) **pass** /pɑːs/ geben, herüberreichen NHG 5
passenger /ˈpæsɪndʒə/ Passagier/in p. 105, 2
passive /ˈpæsɪv/ Passiv p. 106
password /ˈpɑːsˌwɜːd/ Passwort p. 121, 12
past /pɑːst/ nach; Vergangenheit NHG 5; vorbei; vorüber NHG 6
past progressive /ˌpɑːst prəʊˈɡresɪv/ Verlaufsform der Vergangenheit p. 68
pasta /ˈpæstə/ Nudeln p. 8, 1
pastry /ˈpeɪstri/ Brandteig; Blätterteig p. 23, 7
(to) pat /pæt/ einen Klaps geben p. 39, 10
(to) patent /ˈpeɪtnt/ sich patentieren lassen p. 105, 2
path /pɑːθ/ Weg; Pfad NHG 6
(to) **pay** ***(irr)*** /peɪ/ (be)zahlen NHG 5
(to) **pay attention (to)** ***(irr)*** /ˌpeɪ‿əˈtenʃn tʊ/ aufpassen; achten auf NHG 6
payment /ˈpeɪmənt/ Bezahlung NHG 6
PE (= Physical Education) /ˌpiː‿ˈiː, ˌfɪzɪkl‿edjʊˈkeɪʃn/ Sport *(Schulfach)* NHG 5
(to) peel /piːl/ schälen p. 29

pen /pen/ Stift NHG 5
pencil /ˈpensl/ Bleistift NHG 5
pencil case /ˈpensl ˌkeɪs/ Federmäppchen NHG 5
pencil sharpener /ˈpensl ˌʃɑːpnə/ Bleistiftspitzer NHG 5
people /ˈpiːpl/ Leute; Menschen NHG 5
pepper /ˈpepə/ Paprika; Pfeffer p. 12, 7
per /pɜː/ pro NHG 5
perfect /ˈpɜːfɪkt/ perfekt NHG 5
(to) **perform** /pəˈfɔːm/ aufführen; durchführen NHG 6
performance /pəˈfɔːməns/ Aufführung; Leistung NHG 6
permission /pəˈmɪʃn/ Erlaubnis; Genehmigung NHG 6
personal /ˈpɜːsnəl/ persönlich NHG 5
pet /pet/ Haustier NHG 5
(Petri) dish /ˈpiːtri ˌdɪʃ/ Petrischale p. 109, 7
phew *(informal)* /fjuː/ puh p. 46, 5
phone /fəʊn/ Telefon NHG 5
phone call /ˈfəʊn kɔːl/ Telefonanruf p. 105, 2
phone number /ˈfəʊn ˌnʌmbə/ Telefonnummer NHG 5
photo /ˈfəʊtəʊ/ Foto NHG 5
(to) **take a photo** ***(irr)*** /ˌteɪk‿ə ˈfəʊtəʊ/ ein Foto machen NHG 5
photograph /ˈfəʊtəˌɡrɑːf/ Fotografie; Foto NHG 6
photographer /fəˈtɒɡrəfə/ Fotograf/in NHG 6
phrase /freɪz/ Satz; Ausdruck NHG 5
physical /ˈfɪzɪkl/ körperlich p. 35, 6
piano /piˈænəʊ/ Klavier NHG 5
(to) **pick up** /ˌpɪk‿ˈʌp/ aufheben; abholen NHG 5
pickpocket /ˈpɪkˌpɒkɪt/ Taschendieb/in p. 69, 5
picnic /ˈpɪknɪk/ Picknick p. 108, 6
picture /ˈpɪktʃə/ Bild NHG 5
(to) **take a picture** ***(irr)*** /ˌteɪk‿ə ˈpɪktʃə/ ein Foto machen NHG 5
piece /piːs/ Stück; Teil NHG 6
piece of art /ˌpiːs‿əv‿ˈɑːt/ Kunstwerk p. 126
pile /paɪl/ Stapel; Haufen p. 101

place /pleɪs/ Ort; Platz; Haus, Zuhause NHG 5
(to) **place** /pleɪs/ platzieren; stellen NHG 5
(to) **take place** ***(irr)*** /ˌteɪk ˈpleɪs/ stattfinden NHG 6
(to) **plan** /plæn/ planen NHG 5
plane /pleɪn/ Flugzeug NHG 6
(to) catch a plane *(irr)* /ˌkætʃ‿ə ˈpleɪn/ ein Flugzeug nehmen p. 102
planner /ˈplænə/ Kalender; Planer p. 116, 5
plant /plɑːnt/ Pflanze NHG 6
plaster /ˈplɑːstə/ Gips; Pflaster p. 43, 1
plastic /ˈplæstɪk/ Plastik NHG 6
plate /pleɪt/ Teller NHG 5
platform /ˈplætˌfɔːm/ Bahnsteig; Plattform NHG 6
play /pleɪ/ Spiel; (Theater)stück NHG 6
(to) **play** /pleɪ/ spielen NHG 5
player /ˈpleɪə/ Spieler/in NHG 5
playground /ˈpleɪˌɡraʊnd/ Spielplatz NHG 5
playing /ˈpleɪɪŋ/ Spielen NHG 5
playing field /ˈpleɪɪŋ ˌfiːld/ Sportplatz p. 45, 4
please /pliːz/ bitte NHG 5
pleased /pliːzd/ erfreut; zufrieden p. 53
pm (= post meridiem) /ˌpiːˈem, ˌpəʊst məˈrɪdiəm/ nachmittags; abends *(hinter Uhrzeit zwischen 12 Uhr mittags und Mitternacht)* NHG 5
pocket /ˈpɒkɪt/ (Hosen)tasche p. 69, 5
pocket money /ˈpɒkɪt ˌmʌni/ Taschengeld p. 57, 3
poem /ˈpəʊɪm/ Gedicht NHG 5
poet /ˈpəʊɪt/ Dichter/in p. 39, 10
point /pɔɪnt/ Punkt NHG 5
(to) **point (at/to)** /pɔɪnt/ deuten (auf); zeigen (auf) NHG 5
Poland /ˈpəʊlənd/ Polen NHG 5
police /pəˈliːs/ Polizei p. 125
police officer /pəˈliːs‿ɒfɪsə/ Polizeibeamter/Polizeibeamtin NHG 6
Polish /ˈpəʊlɪʃ/ Polnisch; polnisch p. 83, 5

polite /pəˈlaɪt/ höflich NHG 6
poor /pɔː/ arm NHG 6
poppadom /ˈpɒpədəm/ *dünnes indisches Brot* p. 23, 7
popular /ˈpɒpjʊlə/ beliebt NHG 6
population /ˌpɒpjʊˈleɪʃn/ Bevölkerung p. 83, 5
pork /pɔːk/ Schweinefleisch p. 140
porridge /ˈpɒrɪdʒ/ Haferbrei p. 52
positive /ˈpɒzətɪv/ positiv NHG 6
possibility /ˌpɒsəˈbɪləti/ Möglichkeit NHG 6
possible /ˈpɒsəbl/ möglich p. 46, 5
(to) **post** /pəʊst/ posten; bekannt geben NHG 6
postcard /ˈpəʊstˌkɑːd/ Postkarte; Ansichtskarte NHG 5
pot /pɒt/ Topf p. 12, 7
potato (*pl* **potatoes**) /pəˈteɪtəʊ, pəˈteɪtəʊz/ Kartoffel p. 8, 2
pound (= £) /paʊnd/ Pfund *(britische Währung)* NHG 5
powder /ˈpaʊdə/ Pulver p. 30
power /ˈpaʊə/ Kraft p. 104, 1
practical /ˈpræktɪkl/ praktisch p. 111, 11
practice /ˈpræktɪs/ Übung; Training NHG 6; Praxis p. 42, 1
doctor's practice /ˈdɒktəz ˌpræktɪs/ Arztpraxis p. 46, 5
(to) **practise** /ˈpræktɪs/ üben; trainieren NHG 5
prayer /preə/ Gebet NHG 6
(to) **prefer** /prɪˈfɜː/ vorziehen; bevorzugen p. 32, 1
(to) **prepare** /prɪˈpeə/ vorbereiten NHG 5; zubereiten p. 17, 17
(to) **prepare for** /prɪˈpeə fɔː/ sich vorbereiten auf p. 68, 3
(to) be prepared *(irr)* /ˌbiː prɪˈpeəd/ vorbereitet sein p. 122, 15
present /ˈpreznt/ Geschenk NHG 5; Gegenwart NHG 6
present perfect /ˌpreznt ˈpɜːfɪkt/ Perfekt p. 10
present progressive /ˌpreznt prəʊˈgresɪv/ Verlaufsform der Gegenwart p. 22, 6
(to) **present (to)** /priˈzent/ präsentieren, vorstellen NHG 5
presentation /ˌpreznˈteɪʃn/ Präsentation; Vortrag NHG 5
(to) **give a presentation *(irr)*** /ˌgɪv‿ə ˌpreznˈteɪʃn/ eine Präsentation halten p. 114, 2
pretty /ˈprɪti/ ziemlich NHG 5
(to) **prevent** /prɪˈvent/ verhindern, vorbeugen p. 109, 7
price /praɪs/ Preis *(Kosten)* p. 60, 8
price tag /ˈpraɪs tæg/ Preisschild p. 60, 8
printing press /ˈprɪntɪŋ pres/ Druckerpresse p. 118, 7
prize /praɪz/ Preis; Gewinn p. 35, 6
pro /prəʊ/ Vorteil; Pro NHG 6
probably /ˈprɒbəbli/ wahrscheinlich NHG 6
No problem. /ˌnəʊ ˈprɒbləm/ *hier:* Keine Ursache. p. 46, 5
(to) **produce** /prəˈdjuːs/ herstellen NHG 6; produzieren p. 73, 9
product /ˈprɒdʌkt/ Produkt p. 147
profile /ˈprəʊfaɪl/ Profil; Porträt p. 33, 2
programme /ˈprəʊgræm/ Programm NHG 6
project /ˈprɒdʒekt/ Projekt NHG 6
(to) **promise** /ˈprɒmɪs/ versprechen p. 46, 5
(to) **pronounce** /prəˈnaʊns/ aussprechen NHG 6
prop /prɒp/ Requisite p. 27, 14
prop word /ˈprɒp wɜːd/ Stützwort p. 64, 13
properly /ˈprɒpəli/ richtig p. 47, 6
(to) **protect** /prəˈtekt/ beschützen NHG 6
proud(ly) /ˈpraʊd(li)/ stolz NHG 6
(to) **prove *(irr)*** /pruːv/ beweisen p. 95, 6
pub /pʌb/ Kneipe p. 19, 2
public /ˈpʌblɪk/ öffentlich NHG 6
the public /ðə ˈpʌblɪk/ die Öffentlichkeit NHG 6
(to) **publish** /ˈpʌblɪʃ/ veröffentlichen; herausgeben NHG 6
pudding /ˈpʊdɪŋ/ Nachspeise L&L 1
(to) **pull** /pʊl/ ziehen p. 105, 2
pumpkin /ˈpʌmpkɪn/ Kürbis NHG 6
pupil /ˈpjuːpl/ Schüler/in p. 99, 15
purple /ˈpɜːpl/ violett; lila NHG 5
(to) **push** /pʊʃ/ schieben; stoßen NHG 6
(to) **put *(irr)*** /pʊt/ setzen; stellen; legen NHG 5
(to) **put in *(irr)*** /ˌpʊt‿ˈɪn/ hineintun, hinzufügen p. 13, 8
(to) **put on *(irr)*** /ˌpʊt‿ˈɒn/ anlegen; auftragen p. 46, 5; anziehen *(Kleidung)* p. 68, 3
(to) **put on display *(irr)*** /ˌpʊt‿ɒn dɪˈspleɪ/ ausstellen NHG 6
(to) **put together *(irr)*** /ˌpʊt‿təˈgeðə/ zusammenstellen; zusammensetzen NHG 6
(to) **put up *(irr)*** /ˌpʊt‿ˈʌp/ aufhängen; aufstellen NHG 6
puzzle /ˈpʌzl/ Rätsel p. 33, 2

Q

quality /ˈkwɒləti/ Qualität p. 18, 2
quantifier /ˈkwɒntɪˌfaɪə/ *hier:* Mengenangabe p. 16, 13
quarter /ˈkwɔːtə/ Viertel NHG 5
queen /kwiːn/ Königin NHG 6
question /ˈkwestʃn/ Frage NHG 5
queue /kjuː/ Schlange; Reihe p. 100
quick /kwɪk/ schnell, kurz p. 12, 7
quickly /ˈkwɪkli/ schnell NHG 6
quiet /ˈkwaɪət/ leise; ruhig NHG 5
quite /kwaɪt/ ziemlich NHG 6
quotation /kwəʊˈteɪʃn/ Zitat p. 148

R

rabbit /ˈræbɪt/ Kaninchen NHG 5
race /reɪs/ Rennen p. 52
railway company /ˈreɪlweɪ ˌkʌmpni/ Eisenbahngesellschaft p. 106, 3
rain /reɪn/ Regen NHG 6
(to) **rain** /reɪn/ regnen NHG 5
rainy /ˈreɪni/ regnerisch NHG 5
(to) raise /reɪz/ aufziehen, großziehen p. 78
(to) **rate** /reɪt/ einschätzen; bewerten p. 110, 8
rather /ˈrɑːðə/ eher, lieber NHG 6
rather than /ˈrɑːðə ðæn/ anstatt NHG 6
rating /ˈreɪtɪŋ/ Einschätzung; Einstufung p. 110, 8

raw /rɔː/ roh p. 21, 5
RE (= Religious Education) /ˌɑːr‿ˈiː, reˌlɪdʒəs‿edjʊˈkeɪʃn/ Religion *(Schulfach)* NHG 5
(to) **reach** /riːtʃ/ erreichen p. 33, 2
(to) **react (to)** /riˈækt/ reagieren (auf) NHG 6
reaction /riˈækʃn/ Reaktion NHG 6
(to) **read** ***(irr)*** /riːd/ lesen NHG 5
(to) **read along** ***(irr)*** /ˌriːd‿əˈlɒŋ/ mitlesen NHG 5
(to) read out *(irr)* /ˌriːd‿ˈaʊt/ (laut) vorlesen p. 47, 5
reading /ˈriːdɪŋ/ Lesen NHG 5; Lesung p. 43, 1
ready /ˈredi/ fertig, bereit NHG 5
real /rɪəl/ wirklich; echt NHG 6
(to) **realize (= realise)** /ˈrɪəlaɪz/ sich bewusst sein, erkennen NHG 6
really /ˈrɪəli/ wirklich NHG 5
reason /ˈriːzn/ Grund NHG 6
for no reason /fə ˌnəʊ ˈriːzn/ ohne Grund, grundlos p. 14, 10
(to) receive /rɪˈsiːv/ erhalten; empfangen p. 127
receptionist /rɪˈsepʃnɪst/ Empfangsdame/Empfangschef p. 42, 1
recipe /ˈresəpi/ Rezept p. 12, 7
(to) recognize (= recognise) /ˈrekəgnaɪz/ erkennen p. 78
(to) **recommend** /ˌrekəˈmend/ empfehlen NHG 6
record /ˈrekɔːd/ Rekord p. 53
(to) **record** /riˈkɔːd/ aufnehmen NHG 5
recording /riˈkɔːdɪŋ/ Aufnahme NHG 5
red /red/ rot NHG 5
(to) **reduce** /rɪˈdjuːs/ reduzieren p. 73, 9
(to) register /ˈredʒɪstə/ registrieren, anmelden p. 76
registration /ˌredʒɪˈstreɪʃn/ *Überprüfung der Anwesenheit* NHG 5
registration fee /ˌredʒɪˈstreɪʃn fiː/ Anmeldegebühr p. 56, 2
regular /ˈregjʊlə/ üblich, normal NHG 6
regularly /ˈregjʊləli/ regelmäßig p. 36, 7
relative /ˈrelətɪv/ Verwandte/r NHG 6
relative clause /ˌrelətɪv ˈklɔːz/ Relativsatz p. 58
(to) **relax** /rɪˈlæks/ entspannen NHG 5
relaxed /rɪˈlækst/ entspannt NHG 6
relaxing /rɪˈlæksɪŋ/ entspannend p. 35, 6
relay /ˈriːleɪ/ Staffellauf p. 53
religious /rəˈlɪdʒəs/ religiöse(r, s) NHG 6
(to) **remember** /rɪˈmembə/ sich erinnern an NHG 5
(to) **remove** /rɪˈmuːv/ entfernen NHG 6
(to) renovate /ˈrenəveɪt/ renovieren p. 108, 6
(to) **repair** /rɪˈpeə/ reparieren NHG 6
(to) **repeat** /riˈpiːt/ wiederholen NHG 5
(to) **reply** /rɪˈplaɪ/ antworten; erwidern NHG 6
(to) **report** /rɪˈpɔːt/ sich melden NHG 6
(to) report /rɪˈpɔːt/ berichten; melden p. 30
reported speech /ˌrɪ pɔːtɪd ˈspiːtʃ/ indirekte Rede p. 92
(to) **research** /rɪˈsɜːtʃ/ recherchieren p. 117, 6
(to) **do research** ***(irr)*** /ˌduː rɪˈsɜːtʃ/ recherchieren NHG 5
reservation /ˌrezəˈveɪʃn/ Reservierung p. 22, 6
respect /rɪˈspekt/ Respekt; respektieren NHG 6
respectful /rɪˈspektfl/ respektvoll p. 121, 12
(to) **rest** /rest/ ausruhen p. 46, 5
result /rɪˈzʌlt/ Ergebnis p. 114, 2
(to) **return** /rɪˈtɜːn/ zurückgeben NHG 6
review /rɪˈvjuː/ Kritik; Rezension p. 18, 2
(to) rewrite *(irr)* /ˌriːˈraɪt/ überarbeiten, umschreiben p. 22, 6
rhyming word /ˈraɪmɪŋ wɜːd/ Reimwort p. 39, 10
rice /raɪs/ Reis NHG 5
rich /rɪtʃ/ reich p. 112, 12
(to) **get rid of** ***(irr)*** /ˌget ˈrɪd‿əv/ loswerden p. 61, 8
(to) **ride** ***(irr)*** /raɪd/ fahren; reiten NHG 5
(to) **ride a bike** ***(irr)*** /ˌraɪd‿ə ˈbaɪk/ Fahrrad fahren NHG 5
(to) **ride a horse** ***(irr)*** /ˌraɪd‿ə ˈhɔːs/ reiten NHG 5
riding /ˈraɪdɪŋ/ Reiten p. 34
(to) **go riding** ***(irr)*** /ˌgəʊ ˈraɪdɪŋ/ reiten gehen NHG 6
right /raɪt/ richtig NHG 5; rechts, nach rechts; genau; direkt NHG 6; Recht p. 93, 5
(to) **be right** ***(irr)*** /ˌbiː ˈraɪt/ recht haben NHG 5
on the right /ˌɒn ðə ˈraɪt/ rechts, auf der rechten Seite NHG 5
right now /ˌraɪt ˈnaʊ/ jetzt; im Moment p. 93, 5
rightful /ˈraɪtfl/ rechtmäßig p. 78
ripple /ˈrɪpl/ leichte Welle p. 127
rise /raɪz/ Aufstieg p. 119, 7
river /ˈrɪvə/ Fluss NHG 6
riverside /ˈrɪvəˌsaɪd/ Flussufer p. 80, 2
road /rəʊd/ Straße NHG 5
roast /rəʊst/ Braten; gebraten, geröstet p. 8, 2
robot /ˈrəʊbɒt/ Roboter p. 125
rock /rɒk/ Stein; Fels p. 118, 7
role /rəʊl/ Rolle NHG 6
role play /ˈrəʊl pleɪ/ Rollenspiel NHG 6
(to) **roll** /rəʊl/ rollen p. 39, 10
rolled /rəʊld/ gerollt p. 9, 2
Roman /ˈrəʊmən/ Römer/in; römisch NHG 6
room /ruːm/ Platz; Raum; Zimmer NHG 5
waiting room /ˈweɪtɪŋ ˌruːm/ Wartezimmer p. 46, 5
root /ruːt/ Wurzel p. 79
round /raʊnd/ rund NHG 5; (um ...) herum NHG 6
rowing /ˈrəʊɪŋ/ Rudern p. 32, 1
royal /ˈrɔɪəl/ königlich NHG 6
The Royal Air Force /ðə ˌrɔɪəl‿ˈeə fɔːs/ Königliche Luftwaffe p. 85, 7
rubbish /ˈrʌbɪʃ/ Müll NHG 5
rude /ruːd/ unhöflich; primitiv p. 98, 13
ruin /ˈruːɪn/ Ruine p. 78

rule /ruːl/ Regel NHG 5
(to) **rule** /ruːl/ herrschen, regieren NHG 6
ruler /ˈruːlə/ Lineal NHG 5
run /rʌn/ Lauf p. 56, 2
(to) **run** ***(irr)*** /rʌn/ laufen; rennen NHG 6; leiten, betreiben p. 69, 5
runner /ˈrʌnə/ Läufer/in NHG 6
running race /ˈrʌnɪŋ reɪs/ Wettrennen p. 54
rural /ˈrʊərəl/ ländlich p. 145
(to) rush /rʌʃ/ eilen p. 78

S

sad /sæd/ traurig NHG 6
safe /seɪf/ sicher; ungefährlich NHG 6
safety /ˈseɪfti/ Sicherheit NHG 6
salad /ˈsæləd/ Salat p. 8, 2
salmon /ˈsæmən/ Lachs p. 22, 6
salt /sɔːlt/ Salz NHG 5
the same /ðə ˈseɪm/ der/die/das Gleiche; derselbe/dieselbe/dasselbe NHG 5
at the same time /æt‿ðə ˌseɪm ˈtaɪm/ gleichzeitig; zur gleichen Zeit p. 56, 2
samosa /səˈməʊsə/ *indische gefüllte Teigtasche* p. 23, 7
Saturday /ˈsætədeɪ/ Samstag NHG 5
(on) Saturdays /ˈsætədeɪz/ samstags NHG 5
sauce /sɔːs/ Soße p. 8, 1
sausage /ˈsɒsɪdʒ/ Wurst; Würstchen p. 8, 1
(to) **save** /seɪv/ aufheben; sichern p. 91, 2; sparen; retten p. 108, 7
savoury /ˈseɪvəri/ pikant; salzig p. 8, 2
(to) **say** ***(irr)*** /seɪ/ sagen NHG 5
(to) **scan** /skæn/ absuchen, überfliegen p. 33, 2
scared /skeəd/ verängstigt, ängstlich NHG 6
(to) be scared (of) /ˌbiː ˈskeəd‿əv/ Angst haben (vor) NHG 5
scary /ˈskeəri/ Furcht erregend NHG 6
scene /siːn/ Szene NHG 5
school /skuːl/ Schule NHG 5
school counsellor /ˌskuːl ˈkaʊnslə/ Vertrauenslehrer/in p. 96, 8
school grounds ***(pl)*** /ˈskuːl ˌgraʊndz/ Schulgelände NHG 6
schoolbag /ˈskuːlˌbæg/ Schultasche NHG 5
science /ˈsaɪəns/ Naturwissenschaft NHG 5
the Science Museum /ðə ˈsaɪəns mjuːˌziːəm/ Naturwissenschafts-museum p. 81, 2
scientist /ˈsaɪəntɪst/ Wissen-schaftler/in p. 107, 5
(a pair of) scissors /ˈsɪzəz/ Schere NHG 5
score /skɔː/ Punktestand p. 76
Scotland /ˈskɒtlənd/ Schottland NHG 5
screen /skriːn/ Bildschirm NHG 6
screen time /ˈskriːn taɪm/ Bild-schirmzeit p. 95, 6
script /skrɪpt/ Drehbuch; Skript NHG 6
search /sɜːtʃ/ Suche NHG 5
(to) **search** /sɜːtʃ/ suchen NHG 5
search engine /ˈsɜːtʃ‿ˌendʒɪn/ Suchmaschine p. 117, 6
(to) **search the Internet** /ˌsɜːtʃ ði‿ˈɪntənet/ im Internet suchen NHG 5
seaside /ˈsiːˌsaɪd/ (Meeres)küste; Meer NHG 6
season /ˈsiːzn/ Saison p. 14, 10
seat /siːt/ Sitz p. 109, 7
(to) **take a seat** ***(irr)*** /ˌteɪk‿ə ˈsiːt/ sich setzen p. 22, 6
seat belt /ˈsiːt belt/ Sicherheitsgurt p. 109, 7
second /ˈsekənd/ Sekunde; zweite(r, s) NHG 5
second-hand /ˌsekənd ˈhænd/ gebraucht p. 56, 2
secret /ˈsiːkrət/ geheim p. 126
section /ˈsekʃn/ Teil, Stück, Abschnitt; Abteilung p. 107, 5
(to) **see** ***(irr)*** /siː/ sehen NHG 5; ***hier:*** empfangen, drannehmen p. 42, 1
(to) **see a doctor** ***(irr)*** /ˌsiː‿ə ˈdɒktə/ einen Arzt/eine Ärztin aufsuchen p. 43, 1
See you (soon)! /ˌsiː juː ˈsuːn/ Bis bald! NHG 6
seed /siːd/ Samen p. 127
(to) **seek advice** ***(irr)*** /ˌsiːk‿ədˈvaɪs/ Rat suchen p. 94, 6
(to) seem /siːm/ scheinen p. 100
selection /sɪˈlekʃn/ Auswahl p. 23, 7
(to) **sell** ***(irr)*** /sel/ verkaufen p. 57, 3
seller /ˈselə/ Verkäufer/in p. 60, 8
(to) **send** ***(irr)*** /send/ schicken NHG 5
sentence /ˈsentəns/ Satz NHG 5
September /sepˈtembə/ September NHG 5
series /ˈsɪəriːz/ Folge; Serie p. 35, 6
serious /ˈsɪəriəs/ ernst p. 70, 6
(to) **serve** /sɜːv/ servieren; reichen für p. 9, 2
session /ˈseʃn/ Stunde; Session NHG 5
set /set/ ***hier:*** Einstellung p. 113, 15
(to) set a date /ˌset‿ə ˈdeɪt/ sich verabreden p. 101
(to) **set the table** /ˌset ðə ˈteɪbl/ den Tisch decken NHG 5
(to) **set up** ***(irr)*** /ˌset‿ˈʌp/ aufbauen p. 74, 12
several /ˈsevrəl/ einige; verschie-dene p. 62, 10
Shakshuka /ʃəkˈʃuːkə/ ***traditionelles israelisches und nordafrikani-sches Gericht*** p. 9, 2
shall /ʃæl/ sollen; werden p. 57, 3
(to) **be a shame** ***(irr)*** /ˌbi‿ə ˈʃeɪm/ schade sein p. 86, 8
(to) **share** /ʃeə/ teilen NHG 5
she /ʃiː/ sie NHG 5
sheet /ʃiːt/ Blatt; Bogen NHG 6
shelf (*pl* **shelves**) /ʃelf, ʃelvz/ Regal NHG 5
(to) shine ***(irr)*** /ʃaɪn/ scheinen p. 52
ship /ʃɪp/ Schiff p. 102
shirt /ʃɜːt/ Hemd NHG 5
shoe /ʃuː/ Schuh NHG 6
(to) **shoot** ***(irr)*** /ʃuːt/ schießen p. 39, 10
shop /ʃɒp/ Geschäft; Laden NHG 5
shop assistant /ˈʃɒp‿əˌsɪstnt/ Verkäufer/in NHG 6
shopping /ˈʃɒpɪŋ/ Einkaufen; Einkaufs- NHG 5
(to) **do the shopping** ***(irr)*** /ˌduː ðə ˈʃɒpɪŋ/ einkaufen NHG 5

(to) **go shopping** ***(irr)*** /ˌɡəʊ ˈʃɒpɪŋ/ einkaufen gehen NHG 6
shopping centre /ˈʃɒpɪŋ ˌsentə/ Einkaufszentrum NHG 5
short /ʃɔːt/ kurz NHG 5
should /ʃʊd/ sollte(st, n, t) NHG 6
shoulder /ˈʃəʊldə/ Schulter p. 51, 16
(to) shout /ʃaʊt/ rufen; schreien p. 77
(to) **shout at somebody** /ˈʃaʊt‿ət ˌsʌmbədi/ jemanden anschreien NHG 6
(to) **show** ***(irr)*** /ʃəʊ/ zeigen NHG 5
(to) show somebody around *(irr)* /ˌʃəʊ ˌsʌmbədi‿əˈraʊnd/ jemanden herumführen p. 124
(to) show to the table *(irr)* /ˌʃəʊ tə ðə ˈteɪbl/ zum Tisch führen p. 22, 6
shy /ʃaɪ/ schüchtern p. 95, 6
sick /sɪk/ krank NHG 6
side /saɪd/ Seite NHG 6
side (dish) /ˈsaɪd‿dɪʃ/ Beilage p. 19, 2
on the side /ˌɒn ðə ˈsaɪd/ als Beilage p. 22, 6
sight /saɪt/ Sehenswürdigkeit NHG 5
sighted /ˈsaɪtɪd/ sehend p. 54
sign /saɪn/ Zeichen; Schild NHG 6
(to) **sign** /saɪn/ unterschreiben p. 46, 5
(to) sign up (for) /ˌsaɪn‿ˈʌp/ sich anmelden p. 52
silly /ˈsɪli/ albern; dumm p. 91, 2
similar /ˈsɪmɪlə/ ähnlich NHG 6
simple /ˈsɪmpl/ einfach; simpel p. 109, 7
simple past /ˌsɪmpl ˈpɑːst/ einfache Vergangenheit p. 82
simply /ˈsɪmpli/ einfach NHG 6
since /sɪns/ seit NHG 6
since /sɪns/ da; weil p. 52
(to) **sing** ***(irr)*** /sɪŋ/ singen NHG 5
(to) **sing along** ***(irr)*** /ˌsɪŋ‿əˈlɒŋ/ mitsingen NHG 5
singer /ˈsɪŋə/ Sänger/in NHG 6
singing /ˈsɪŋɪŋ/ singend p. 59, 7
single /ˈsɪŋgl/ einzelne(r, s) NHG 6
sir/Sir /sɜː/ Sir; Herr *(Anrede vor Vornamen)* p. 22, 6
sister /ˈsɪstə/ Schwester NHG 5
(to) **sit** ***(irr)*** /sɪt/ sitzen p. 33, 2
(to) **sit down** ***(irr)*** /ˌsɪt‿ˈdaʊn/ sich hinsetzen NHG 5
site /saɪt/ Stelle; Platz p. 73, 9
size /saɪz/ Größe NHG 5
skateboarding /ˈskeɪtbɔːdɪŋ/ Skateboardfahren NHG 5
cleaning skates *(pl)* /ˈkliːnɪŋ ˌskeɪts/ *Reinigungsskates* p. 111, 11
skating /ˈskeɪtɪŋ/ *hier:* Skateboardfahren p. 40, 12
skill /skɪl/ Fähigkeit; Geschick p. 33, 2
skill /skɪl/ Fertigkeit; Kompetenz p. 9, 2
(to) **skim** /skɪm/ überfliegen p. 18, 2
(to) skip /skɪp/ *hier:* ausfallen lassen p. 91, 2
skirt /skɜːt/ Rock NHG 5
sleep /sliːp/ Schlaf p. 36, 7
(to) **sleep** ***(irr)*** /sliːp/ schlafen NHG 5
(to) sleep in *(irr)* /ˌsliːp‿ˈɪn/ ausschlafen p. 129
(to) **slice** /slaɪs/ in Scheiben schneiden p. 13, 8
slide /slaɪd/ Folie p. 41, 13
slide show /ˈslaɪd ʃəʊ/ Bildschirmpräsentation p. 41, 13
slow, slowly /sləʊ, ˈsləʊli/ langsam NHG 6
small /smɔːl/ klein NHG 5
smart /smɑːt/ schlau, clever NHG 6
(to) **smile** /smaɪl/ lächeln NHG 6
so /səʊ/ also; deshalb; daher NHG 5
so far /ˈsəʊ fɑː/ bisher NHG 6
so that /ˈsəʊ ðæt/ damit NHG 6
soccer *(AE)* /ˈsɒkə/ Fußball p. 39, 10
sock /sɒk/ Socke p. 64, 13
soft /sɒft/ weich p. 17, 17
solution /səˈluːʃn/ Lösung NHG 6
(to) **solve** /sɒlv/ lösen NHG 6
some /sʌm/ einige, ein paar; etwas NHG 5
some day /ˈsʌmˌdeɪ/ eines Tages p. 36, 7
somebody /ˈsʌmbədi/ jemand; irgendwer NHG 6
someone /ˈsʌmwʌn/ jemand; irgendwer NHG 5
something /ˈsʌmθɪŋ/ etwas NHG 5
sometimes /ˈsʌmtaɪmz/ manchmal NHG 5
somewhere /ˈsʌmweə/ irgendwo NHG 6
son /sʌn/ Sohn NHG 5
song /sɒŋ/ Lied NHG 5
soon /suːn/ bald p. 43, 1
See you (soon)! /ˌsiː juː ˈsuːn/ Bis bald! NHG 6
coming soon /ˌkʌmɪŋ ˈsuːn/ in Kürze erscheinend p. 67, 2
sore throat /ˌsɔː ˈθrəʊt/ Halsschmerzen p. 42, 1
sorry /ˈsɒri/ es tut mir leid, Entschuldigung NHG 5
sort /sɔːt/ Sorte; Art NHG 6
(to) **sort** /sɔːt/ sortieren NHG 5
sound /saʊnd/ Geräusch; Klang NHG 6
(to) **sound** /saʊnd/ klingen, sich anhören NHG 5
sound wave /ˈsaʊnd weɪv/ Schallwelle p. 127
soup /suːp/ Suppe p. 20, 3
sour /ˈsaʊə/ sauer p. 140
source /sɔːs/ Quelle p. 117, 6
south /saʊθ/ Süden; Süd- p. 83, 5
South Asian /ˌsaʊθ‿ˈeɪʒn/ südasiatisch p. 83, 5
South India /ˌsaʊθ‿ˈɪndiə/ Südindien p. 30
south-west /ˌsaʊθˈwest/ Südwest- p. 70, 6
soy /sɔɪ/ Soja p. 143
space /speɪs/ Raum; Platz NHG 6; Weltall p. 107, 5
Spain /speɪn/ Spanien p. 80, 2
(to) **speak** ***(irr)*** /spiːk/ sprechen; reden NHG 5
This is ... speaking. /ðɪs‿ɪz ... ˈspiːkɪŋ/ Hier spricht ... p. 42, 1
special /ˈspeʃl/ besondere(r, s); besonders NHG 5
speciality /ˌspeʃiˈæləti/ Spezialität p. 9, 2
species (*pl* **species**) /ˈspiːʃiːz, ˈspiːʃiːz/ Art; Spezies NHG 6
spectacle /ˈspektəkl/ Spektakel p. 71, 6
spectacular /spekˈtækjʊlə/ atemberaubend; spektakulär p. 67, 2

speech bubble /ˈspiːtʃ ˌbʌbl/ Sprechblase p. 87, 8
(to) **spell** ***(irr)*** /spel/ buchstabieren NHG 5
spelling /ˈspelɪŋ/ Buchstabieren; Rechtschreibung NHG 6
(to) **spend** ***(irr)*** /spend/ verbringen *(Zeit)*; ausgeben *(Geld)* NHG 6
spice /spaɪs/ Gewürz p. 12, 7
spicy /ˈspaɪsi/ würzig; scharf p. 9, 2
spider /ˈspaɪdə/ Spinne p. 26, 12
(to) spin *(irr)* /spɪn/ drehen, einen Drall geben p. 39, 10; spinnen p. 77
spinach /ˈspɪnɪdʒ/ Spinat p. 23, 7
Spinning Jenny /ˌspɪnɪŋ ˈdʒeni/ *Feinspinnmaschine* p. 125
spinning wheel /ˈspɪnɪŋ ˌwiːl/ Spinnrad p. 76
spirit /ˈspɪrɪt/ Geist; Stimmung p. 53
spoken /ˈspəʊkən/ gesprochen p. 30
spoon /spuːn/ Löffel NHG 5
sport /spɔːt/ Sport; Sportart NHG 5
sports day /ˈspɔːts deɪ/ *Sportfest* p. 52
sporty /ˈspɔːti/ sportlich p. 37, 7
sprained /spreɪnd/ verstaucht p. 46, 5
spring /sprɪŋ/ Frühling NHG 6
spring roll /ˈsprɪŋ rəʊl/ Frühlingsrolle p. 137
stage /steɪdʒ/ Bühne NHG 6
stair /steə/ Stufe NHG 6
stairs ***(pl)*** /steəz/ Treppe NHG 6
stall /stɔːl/ Stand p. 56, 2
(to) **stand** ***(irr)*** /stænd/ stehen NHG 6
(to) **stand for** ***(irr)*** /ˈstænd fɔː/ stehen für NHG 6
star /stɑː/ Stern NHG 5
(to) stare at /ˈsteər‿æt/ anstarren p. 28
start /stɑːt/ Anfang; Beginn NHG 5
(to) **start** /stɑːt/ anfangen; beginnen NHG 5
starter /ˈstɑːtə/ Vorspeise p. 17, 17
(to) starve /stɑːv/ verhungern p. 12, 7
statement /ˈsteɪtmənt/ Äußerung, Aussage NHG 5
station /ˈsteɪʃn/ U-Bahn-Station; Bahnhof NHG 5
station /ˈsteɪʃn/ *hier:* Station p. 125

(to) **stay** /steɪ/ bleiben; wohnen NHG 5
(to) **stay away from** /ˌsteɪ‿əˈweɪ frɒm/ meiden; sich fernhalten von p. 18, 2
(to) **stay up (late)** /ˌsteɪ‿ˌʌp ˈleɪt/ lange aufbleiben p. 98, 13
(to) **steal** ***(irr)*** /stiːl/ stehlen p. 69, 5
steam engine /ˈstiːm‿ˌendʒɪn/ Dampfmaschine p. 105, 2
steam locomotive /ˈstiːm ˌləʊkəˌməʊtɪv/ Dampflokomotive; Dampflok p. 105, 2
steam machine /ˈstiːm‿məˈʃiːn/ Dampfmaschine p. 126
steel drum /ˌstiːl ˈdrʌm/ *Steeldrum* p. 71, 6
step /step/ Stufe; Schritt NHG 5
(to) **step** /step/ treten; steigen NHG 6
stick /stɪk/ Stock p. 127
(to) stick *(irr)* /stɪk/ festhängen p. 76
(to) stick to *(irr)* /ˈstɪk tʊ/ kleben; *hier:* sich halten an p. 127
still /stɪl/ (immer) noch NHG 5; nach wie vor, trotzdem p. 86, 8
still /stɪl/ still; bewegungslos p. 33, 2
(to) **stir in** /ˌstɜːr‿ˈɪn/ einrühren; unterrühren p. 13, 8
vegetable stock /ˈvedʒtəbl stɒk/ Gemüsebrühe p. 17, 17
stomach /ˈstʌmək/ Magen; Bauch p. 43, 1
stomach ache ***(no pl)*** /ˈstʌmək‿ˌeɪk/ Bauchschmerzen p. 42, 1
stone /stəʊn/ Stein p. 118, 7
(to) **stop** /stɒp/ stehen bleiben; anhalten NHG 5; aufhören NHG 6; stoppen p. 94, 6
(to) store /stɔː/ lagern p. 109, 7
story /ˈstɔːri/ Geschichte, Erzählung NHG 5
storytelling /ˈstɔːriˌtelɪŋ/ Geschichtenerzählen p. 84, 6
straight on /ˌstreɪt‿ˈɒn/ geradeaus NHG 6
strange /streɪndʒ/ sonderbar; merkwürdig NHG 6
strap /stræp/ Riemen p. 109, 7
strategy /ˈstrætədʒi/ Strategie p. 35, 6
straw /strɔː/ Strohhalm p. 73, 9

strawberry /ˈstrɔːbri/ Erdbeere p. 25, 10
streamer /ˈstriːmə/ Wimpel; Fähnchen p. 52
street /striːt/ Straße NHG 5
strength /streŋθ/ Kraft; Stärke p. 33, 2
stress /stres/ Betonung NHG 6
(to) **stress** /stres/ stressen p. 36, 7
stressed /strest/ gestresst p. 36, 7
strict /strɪkt/ streng NHG 6
string /strɪŋ/ Schnur; Kordel NHG 6
strong /strɒŋ/ stark p. 81, 2
student /ˈstjuːdnt/ Schüler/in NHG 5; Student/in p. 66, 2
(to) **study** /ˈstʌdi/ studieren; lernen p. 82, 4
stuff ***(informal)*** /stʌf/ Zeug NHG 6
stupid /ˈstjuːpɪd/ dumm, blöd NHG 6
(to) stutter /ˈstʌtə/ stottern p. 78
style /staɪl/ Stil NHG 6
(to) style /staɪl/ frisieren p. 68, 3
subject /ˈsʌbdʒɪkt/ Schulfach NHG 5; Thema; Betreff *(in Emails)* NHG 6
(to) succeed /səkˈsiːd/ Erfolg haben p. 78
success /səkˈses/ Erfolg p. 53
successful /səkˈsesfl/ erfolgreich p. 61, 8
such /sʌtʃ/ so; solch p. 71, 6
such as /ˈsʌtʃ‿æz/ wie p. 30
suddenly /ˈsʌdnli/ plötzlich NHG 6
sugar /ˈʃʊgə/ Zucker NHG 6
(to) **suggest** /səˈdʒest/ vorschlagen NHG 6
suggestion /səˈdʒestʃn/ Vorschlag NHG 6
summary /ˈsʌməri/ Zusammenfassung p. 121, 13
summer /ˈsʌmə/ Sommer NHG 5
sun /sʌn/ Sonne NHG 5
Sunday /ˈsʌndeɪ/ Sonntag NHG 5
(on) Sundays /ˈsʌndeɪz/ sonntags NHG 5
sunny /ˈsʌni/ sonnig NHG 5
sunshine /ˈsʌnˌʃaɪn/ Sonnenschein NHG 5
sure /ʃɔː/ sicher NHG 5
(to) **make sure** ***(irr)*** /ˌmeɪk ˈʃɔː/ darauf achten, dass ... NHG 6

surprise /sə'praɪz/ Überraschung p. 29
surprised /sə'praɪzd/ überrascht; erstaunt NHG 6
surprising /sə'praɪzɪŋ/ überraschend NHG 6
(to) sweat /swet/ schwitzen p. 52
Sweden /'swi:dn/ Schweden p. 81, 2
Swedish /'swi:dɪʃ/ schwedisch p. 81, 2
sweet /swi:t/ süß NHG 5; Süßigkeit NHG 6
(to) **swim** *(irr)* /swɪm/ schwimmen NHG 5
swimming /'swɪmɪŋ/ Schwimmen NHG 5
(to) **go swimming** *(irr)* /ˌgəʊ 'swɪmɪŋ/ schwimmen gehen NHG 6
swimming pool /'swɪmɪŋ pu:l/ Schwimmbad NHG 5
(to) **switch off** /ˌswɪtʃ‿'ɒf/ ausschalten p. 41, 13
(to) **switch on** /ˌswɪtʃ‿'ɒn/ einschalten NHG 5
swollen /'swəʊlən/ geschwollen p. 42, 1
sword /sɔ:d/ Schwert p. 76
syllable /'sɪləbl/ Silbe p. 20, 4

T

table /'teɪbl/ Tisch NHG 5; Tabelle NHG 6
(to) **set the table** /ˌset ðə 'teɪbl/ den Tisch decken NHG 5
table tennis /'teɪbl ˌtenɪs/ Tischtennis NHG 5
tablet /'tæblət/ Block; Platte p. 118, 7
(to) **take** *(irr)* /teɪk/ nehmen; bringen; benötigen; brauchen NHG 5; dauern NHG 6
(to) take a hike *(AE, informal, irr)* /ˌteɪk‿ə 'haɪk/ abhauen p. 102
(to) **take a photo** *(irr)* /ˌteɪk‿ə 'fəʊtəʊ/ ein Foto machen NHG 5
(to) **take a picture** *(irr)* /ˌteɪk‿ə 'pɪktʃə/ ein Foto machen NHG 5
(to) **take a seat** *(irr)* /ˌteɪk‿ə 'si:t/ sich setzen p. 22, 6
(to) **take an order** *(irr)* /ˌteɪk‿ən‿'ɔ:də/ eine Bestellung aufnehmen p. 22, 6
(to) **take an X-ray** *(irr)* /ˌteɪk‿ən 'eksreɪ/ eine Röntgenaufnahme machen p. 42, 1
(to) **take away** *(irr)* /ˌteɪk‿ə'weɪ/ wegnehmen; mitnehmen NHG 6
(to) **take care (of)** *(irr)* /ˌteɪk‿'keər‿əv/ sich kümmern um NHG 6
(to) take in *(irr)* /ˌteɪk‿'ɪn/ aufnehmen p. 78
(to) **take notes (on)** *(irr)* /ˌteɪk 'nəʊts/ sich Notizen machen (zu) NHG 5
(to) **take out** *(irr)* /ˌteɪk‿'aʊt/ hinausbringen NHG 5
(to) take out *(irr)* /ˌteɪk‿'aʊt/ herausnehmen p. 29
(to) **take part in** *(irr)* /ˌteɪk 'pɑ:t‿ɪn/ teilnehmen an NHG 6
(to) **take place** *(irr)* /ˌteɪk 'pleɪs/ stattfinden NHG 6
(to) **take turns** *(irr)* /ˌteɪk 'tɜ:nz/ sich abwechseln NHG 6
(to) take up time *(irr)* /ˌteɪk‿ʌp 'taɪm/ Zeit beanspruchen p. 136
takeaway /'teɪkəˌweɪ/ Essen zum Mitnehmen; Imbissbude p. 18, 1
talented /'tæləntɪd/ talentiert p. 125
talk /tɔ:k/ Gespräch; Vortrag p. 123, 16
(to) **talk about** /'tɔ:k‿əˌbaʊt/ sprechen über NHG 5
(to) **talk (to)** /tɔ:k/ sprechen (mit); reden (mit) NHG 5
tall /tɔ:l/ groß NHG 6
target task /'tɑ:gɪt ˌtɑ:sk/ Zielaufgabe p. 17, 17
task /tɑ:sk/ Aufgabe NHG 5
taste /teɪst/ Geschmack p. 60, 8
(to) **taste** /teɪst/ schmecken NHG 6
tasty /'teɪsti/ lecker p. 20, 3
tea /ti:/ Tee NHG 5
(to) **teach** *(irr)* /ti:tʃ/ unterrichten NHG 5
teacher /'ti:tʃə/ Lehrer/in NHG 5
(to) **tease** /ti:z/ hänseln, ärgern p. 95, 6
teaspoon /'ti:ˌspu:n/ Teelöffel p. 17, 17
technique /tek'ni:k/ Technik p. 52
technology /tek'nɒlədʒi/ Technologie; Technik NHG 6
teddy bear /'tedi beə/ Teddybär p. 69, 5
teen /ti:n/ Teenager p. 94, 6
(to) **brush one's teeth** /ˌbrʌʃ wʌnz 'ti:θ/ sich die Zähne putzen NHG 5
telephone /'telɪˌfəʊn/ Telefon NHG 6
telescope /'telɪˌskəʊp/ Teleskop p. 106, 4
television /'telɪˌvɪʒn/ Fernseher; Fernsehen p. 105, 2
(to) **tell** *(irr)* /tel/ erzählen NHG 5
temp (= temperature) /'temprɪtʃə/ Temperatur p. 113, 15
tender /'tendə/ zart p. 143
tent /tent/ Zelt p. 70, 6
term /tɜ:m/ Trimester; Begriff NHG 5
terrible /'terəbl/ schrecklich NHG 5
(to) **text** /tekst/ eine Textnachricht schreiben NHG 5
text (message) /'tekst ˌmesɪdʒ/ Textnachricht NHG 5
Textiles Gallery /'tekstaɪlz ˌgæləri/ *Bereich im Museum, in dem es um Stoffe geht* p. 125
Thai /taɪ/ Thailänder/in; thailändisch p. 18, 1
than /ðæn/ als *(bei Vergleich)* NHG 6
thank you /'θæŋk ju/ danke NHG 5
thanks /θæŋks/ danke NHG 5
thanks a lot /ˌθæŋks‿ə 'lɒt/ vielen Dank NHG 5
I'm good, thanks. /aɪm 'gʊd ˌθæŋks/ Es geht mir gut, danke. NHG 5
that /ðæt/ das; der/die/das (dort); dass NHG 5; so NHG 6
that's (= that is) /ðæts, 'ðæt‿ɪz/ *hier:* das kostet NHG 5
the /ðə/ der/die/das NHG 5
theatre /'θɪətə/ Theater NHG 6
their /ðeə/ ihr(e) NHG 5
theirs /ðeəz/ ihre(r, s) p. 98, 12
them /ðem/ sie; ihnen NHG 5
theme /θi:m/ Thema NHG 6
themselves /ðəm'selvz/ sich; selbst p. 126
then /ðen/ dann NHG 5
theory /'θɪəri/ Theorie p. 118, 7
there /ðeə/ dort; dahin NHG 5

there are /ðeər‿'ɑ:/ dort sind; es gibt NHG 5
there's (= there is) /ðeəz, ðeər‿'ɪz/ dort ist; es gibt NHG 5
these (*pl of* **this**) /ði:z/ diese; das NHG 5
they /ðeɪ/ sie NHG 5
thin /θɪn/ dünn p. 9, 2
thing /θɪŋ/ Ding; Gegenstand NHG 5
(to) **think** *(irr)* /θɪŋk/ denken; glauben NHG 5
(to) **think about** *(irr)* /'θɪŋk‿əˌbaʊt/ denken an, nachdenken über NHG 5
(to) **think of** *(irr)* /'θɪŋk‿əv/ denken an, sich ausdenken NHG 5
logical thinking /ˌlɒdʒɪkl 'θɪŋkɪŋ/ logisches Denken p. 33, 2
third /θɜ:d/ dritte(r, s) NHG 5
this /ðɪs/ diese(r, s) NHG 5
This is ... speaking. /ðɪs‿ɪz ... 'spi:kɪŋ/ Hier spricht ... p. 42, 1
this way /'ðɪs weɪ/ hier entlang p. 22, 6
those (*pl of* **that**) /ðəʊz/ diese, jene NHG 5
thought /θɔ:t/ Gedanke p. 80, 1
thought bubble /'θɔ:t ˌbʌbl/ Gedankenblase p. 87, 8
thousand /'θaʊznd/ tausend NHG 6
sore throat /ˌsɔ: 'θrəʊt/ Halsschmerzen p. 42, 1
throne /θrəʊn/ Thron p. 78
through /θru:/ durch NHG 6
throughout /θru:'aʊt/ während p. 67, 2
throw /θrəʊ/ Wurf p. 53
(to) **throw** *(irr)* /θrəʊ/ werfen NHG 5
(to) **throw away** *(irr)* /ˌθrəʊ‿ə'weɪ/ wegwerfen NHG 6
throwing /'θrəʊɪŋ/ Weitwurf p. 53
thumb /θʌm/ Daumen p. 119, 7
Thursday /'θɜ:zdeɪ/ Donnerstag NHG 5
(on) Thursdays /'θɜ:zdeɪz/ donnerstags NHG 5
tidy /'taɪdi/ ordentlich; aufgeräumt NHG 5
(to) **tidy (up)** /'taɪdi, ˌtaɪdi‿'ʌp/ aufräumen NHG 5

tie /taɪ/ Krawatte NHG 5
till /tɪl/ bis NHG 5
time /taɪm/ Zeit; Mal NHG 5
all the time /ˌɔ:l ðə 'taɪm/ die ganze Zeit NHG 6
at that time /æt‿'ðæt‿taɪm/ zu jener Zeit p. 87, 8
at the same time /ˌæt ‿ðə ˌseɪm 'taɪm/ gleichzeitig; zur gleichen Zeit p. 56, 2
for some time /fə ˌsʌm 'taɪm/ eine Zeitlang p. 37, 7
for the first time /fə ðə 'fɜ:st‿taɪm/ zum ersten Mal NHG 6
most of the time /'məʊst‿əv ðə ˌtaɪm/ meistens p. 37, 7
on time /ˌɒn 'taɪm/ pünktlich NHG 5
What time is it? / What's the time, please? /wɒt‿'taɪm‿ɪz‿ɪt, ˌwɒts ðə 'taɪm pli:z/ Wie spät ist es (bitte)? NHG 5
(to) take up time *(irr)* /ˌteɪk‿ʌp 'taɪm/ Zeit beanspruchen p. 136
time travelling /'taɪm ˌtrævlɪŋ/ Zeitreisen p. 126
timeline /'taɪmlaɪn/ Zeitachse p. 87, 9
timetable /'taɪmteɪbl/ Stundenplan NHG 5; Fahrplan NHG 6
tin /tɪn/ Büchse; Dose p. 109, 7
tin opener /'tɪn‿ˌəʊpnə/ Dosenöffner p. 109, 7
tip /tɪp/ Tipp NHG 6
tired /'taɪəd/ müde NHG 6
title /'taɪtl/ Titel; Überschrift NHG 6
to /tʊ/ (um) zu; in; nach; zu; an; bis; vor NHG 5
toad in the hole /ˌtəʊd‿ɪn ðə 'həʊl/ *Bratwürste in einem Yorkshire Pudding* L&L 1
today /tə'deɪ/ heute NHG 5; heutzutage NHG 6
toe /təʊ/ Zeh NHG 5
together /tə'geðə/ zusammen NHG 5
toilet /'tɔɪlət/ Toilette NHG 5
toilet roll /'tɔɪlət rəʊl/ Toilettenpapier-Rolle p. 111, 11
Tokyo /'təʊkiəʊ/ Tokio p. 54
tomato (*pl* **tomatoes**) /tə'mɑ:təʊ, tə'mɑ:təʊz/ Tomate NHG 5
tomorrow /tə'mɒrəʊ/ morgen NHG 5

ton /tʌn/ Tonne p. 73, 9
tonight /tə'naɪt/ heute Abend p. 28
too /tu:/ auch; zu NHG 5
tool /tu:l/ Werkzeug p. 109, 7
tooth (*pl* **teeth**) /tu:θ, ti:θ/ Zahn p. 42, 1
toothache *(no pl)* /'tu:θeɪk/ Zahnschmerzen p. 42, 1
toothbrush /'tu:θbrʌʃ/ Zahnbürste p. 104, 2
top /tɒp/ beste(r, s) NHG 5; oberes Ende; Spitze NHG 6
(to) go for the top *(irr)* /ˌgəʊ fə ðə 'tɒp/ sich um Höchstleistungen bemühen p. 52
topic /'tɒpɪk/ Thema NHG 5
tor /tɔ:/ Felsturm p. 78
torch /tɔ:tʃ/ Taschenlampe NHG 6
(to) toss /tɒs/ werfen p. 71, 6
tossing the caber /ˌtɒsɪŋ ðə 'keɪbə/ Baumstammwerfen p. 71, 6
(to) **touch** /tʌtʃ/ berühren NHG 5
(to) **keep in touch** *(irr)* /ˌki:p‿ɪn 'tʌtʃ/ Kontakt halten; in Verbindung bleiben p. 119, 7
tournament /'tʊənəmənt/ Turnier p. 35, 6
towards /tə'wɔ:dz/ in Richtung, zu; gegenüber NHG 6
tower /'taʊə/ Turm NHG 6
town /taʊn/ Stadt NHG 5
toy /tɔɪ/ Spielzeug NHG 5
track /træk/ *hier:* Bahn p. 53
trade /treɪd/ Handel p. 30
(to) trade /treɪd/ Geschäfte machen; handeln p. 30
traditional /trə'dɪʃnəl/ traditionell NHG 6
train /treɪn/ Zug NHG 5
(to) **train** /treɪn/ trainieren p. 33, 2
transatlantic /ˌtrænzət'læntɪk/ transatlantisch p. 105, 2
(to) translate /træns'leɪt/ übersetzen p. 15, 11
transport /'trænspɔ:t/ Transport; Verkehrsmittel NHG 6
(to) transport /træns'pɔ:t/ transportieren p. 130
travel /'trævl/ Reise NHG 6
(to) **travel** /'trævl/ reisen; fahren NHG 5

travel guide /ˈtrævl gaɪd/ Reiseführer *(Buch)* p. 62, 10
travelling /ˈtrævlɪŋ/ Reisen NHG 6
(to) **treat** /triːt/ behandeln p. 121, 12
tree /triː/ Baum NHG 5
trick /trɪk/ Trick; Kunststück NHG 5
trip /trɪp/ Ausflug; Fahrt NHG 6
triple jump /ˈtrɪpl dʒʌmp/ Dreisprung p. 53
trophy /ˈtrəʊfi/ Trophäe p. 53
trouble /ˈtrʌbl/ Ärger; Schwierigkeiten NHG 6
(a pair of) trousers /ə ˌpeər‿əv ˈtraʊzəz/ Hose NHG 5
truck /trʌk/ Lastwagen p. 102
true /truː/ wahr NHG 5
(to) **trust** /trʌst/ vertrauen p. 121, 12
(to) **try** /traɪ/ (aus)probieren; versuchen NHG 5
(to) give a try *(irr)* /ˌgɪv‿ə ˈtraɪ/ ausprobieren p. 100
(to) **try on** /ˌtraɪ‿ˈɒn/ anprobieren p. 60, 8
(to) **try out** /ˌtraɪ‿ˈaʊt/ ausprobieren p. 17, 17
the Tube /ðə ˈtjuːb/ (Londoner) U-Bahn p. 108, 6
Tuesday /ˈtjuːzdeɪ/ Dienstag NHG 5
(on) Tuesdays /ˈtjuːzdeɪz/ dienstags NHG 5
tuition /tjuːˈɪʃn/ *hier:* Nachhilfe p. 91, 2
tunic /ˈtjuːnɪk/ Tunika p. 76
Turkey /ˈtɜːki/ die Türkei p. 9, 2
Turkish /ˈtɜːkɪʃ/ türkisch p. 18, 1
turmeric /ˈtɜːmərɪk/ Kurkuma p. 30
(to) **turn** /tɜːn/ abbiegen NHG 6
(to) turn around /ˌtɜːn‿əˈraʊnd/ sich umdrehen p. 77
(to) **turn off** /ˌtɜːn‿ˈɒf/ ausschalten p. 39, 10
(to) **turn over** /ˌtɜːn‿ˈəʊvə/ (sich) umdrehen p. 71, 6
(to) turn to /ˈtɜːn tʊ/ (sich) wenden an p. 127
(to) **be one's turn** *(irr)* /ˌbiː wʌnz ˈtɜːn/ an der Reihe sein NHG 5
(to) **take turns** *(irr)* /ˌteɪk ˈtɜːnz/ sich abwechseln NHG 6
TV (= television) /ˌtiː ˈviː, ˈtelɪˌvɪʒn/ Fernsehen; Fernseher NHG 6
(to) **watch TV** /ˌwɒtʃ tiː ˈviː/ Fernsehen gucken NHG 5
twice /twaɪs/ zweimal p. 36, 7
twin /twɪn/ Zwilling; Zwillings- NHG 5
type /taɪp/ Art NHG 6
typical /ˈtɪpɪkl/ typisch NHG 5

U

ugly /ˈʌgli/ hässlich NHG 6
the UK (= United Kingdom) /ðə ˌjuː ˈkeɪ, juːˌnaɪtɪd ˈkɪŋdəm/ Vereinigtes Königreich NHG 6
umbrella /ʌmˈbrelə/ Regenschirm p. 126
uncle /ˈʌŋkl/ Onkel NHG 5
uncomplicated /ʌnˈkɒmplɪˌkeɪtɪd/ unkompliziert p. 119, 7
under /ˈʌndə/ unter NHG 5
underground /ˈʌndəˌgraʊnd/ U-Bahn NHG 6
(to) **understand** *(irr)* /ˌʌndəˈstænd/ verstehen NHG 5
unfortunately /ʌnˈfɔːtʃnətli/ unglücklicherweise NHG 6
unit /ˈjuːnɪt/ Kapitel p. 41, 13
university /ˌjuːnɪˈvɜːsəti/ Universität p. 81, 2
unless /ənˈles/ außer wenn p. 94, 6
(to) unscramble /ʌnˈskræmbl/ ordnen, in die richtige Reihenfolge bringen p. 9, 2
until /ənˈtɪl/ bis NHG 6
unusual /ʌnˈjuːʒuəl/ ungewöhnlich NHG 5
up /ʌp/ nach oben; hinauf; oben NHG 5
What's up? *(informal)* /ˌwɒts‿ˈʌp/ Was ist los? p. 90, 2
(to) be up for something *(informal, irr)* /ˌbi‿ˌʌp fɔː ˈsʌmθɪŋ/ Lust zu etwas haben p. 91, 2
(to) be up to something *(irr)* /ˌbi‿ˌʌp tə ˈsʌmθɪŋ/ etwas vorhaben p. 57, 3
(to) upcycle /ˈʌpsaɪkl/ upcyceln p. 63, 12
upset /ʌpˈset/ aufgebracht; aufgeregt p. 91, 2
upstairs /ˌʌpˈsteəz/ (nach) oben p. 100
us /ʌs/ uns NHG 5
the USA (= United States of America) /ðə ˌjuˌesˈeɪ, juːˌnaɪtɪd ˌsteɪts‿əv‿əˈmerɪkə/ USA; Vereinigte Staaten von Amerika NHG 6
use /juːs/ Verwendung; Einsatz p. 73, 9
(to) **use** /juːz/ benutzen NHG 5
used to + ***infinitive*** /ˈjuːst‿tuː/ früher + *Vergangenheitsform* NHG 6
useful /ˈjuːsfl/ nützlich NHG 5
user /ˈjuːzə/ Benutzer/in p. 127
usual /ˈjuːʒuəl/ gewöhnlich, üblich p. 29
usually /ˈjuːʒuəli/ gewöhnlich; normalerweise NHG 5

V

(to) **vacuum** /ˈvækjuəm/ staubsaugen NHG 5
vegan /ˈviːgən/ Veganer/in; vegan p. 14, 10
vegetable /ˈvedʒtəbl/ Gemüse p. 17, 17
vegetable stock /ˈvedʒtəbl stɒk/ Gemüsebrühe p. 17, 17
vegetarian /ˌvedʒəˈteəriən/ Vegetarier/in; vegetarisch p. 8, 2
veggie *(informal)* /ˈvedʒi, ˈvedʒtəbl/ Gemüse p. 12, 7
Velcro® /ˈvelkrəʊ/ *Klettverschluss* p. 127
verse /vɜːs/ Strophe; Vers NHG 6
version /ˈvɜːʃn/ Version, Fassung NHG 5
very /ˈveri/ sehr NHG 5
the very first /ðə ˌveri ˈfɜːst/ der/die/das allererste p. 101
very much /ˌveri ˈmʌtʃ/ sehr NHG 6
vet /vet/ Tierarzt/-ärztin NHG 6
victory /ˈvɪktri/ Sieg NHG 6
Vietnamese /vɪˌetnəˈmiːz/ Vietnamese/Vietnamesin; vietnamesisch p. 18, 1
view /vjuː/ (Aus)sicht NHG 6
Viking /ˈvaɪkɪŋ/ Wikinger/in; Wikinger- p. 66, 1
village /ˈvɪlɪdʒ/ Dorf p. 81, 2
vindaloo /ˌvɪndəˈluː/ *indisches Gericht* p. 19, 2
visit /ˈvɪzɪt/ Besuch NHG 5

(to) **visit** /ˈvɪzɪt/ besuchen NHG 6
visitor /ˈvɪzɪtə/ Besucher/in NHG 6
voice /vɔɪs/ Stimme NHG 6
VR glasses *(pl)* /ˌviːˈɑː ˌɡlɑːsɪz/ VR-Brille p. 125

W

(to) **wait** /weɪt/ warten, erwarten NHG 5
waiter/waitress /ˈweɪtə, ˈweɪtrəs/ Kellner/in p. 22, 6
waiting room /ˈweɪtɪŋ ˌruːm/ Wartezimmer p. 46, 5
(to) **wake up** *(irr)* /ˌweɪkˈʌp/ aufwachen NHG 6
(to) wake up *(irr)* /ˌweɪkˈʌp/ aufwecken p. 76
walk /wɔːk/ Spaziergang
(to) **walk** /wɔːk/ gehen NHG 5
walking stick /ˈwɔːkɪŋ stɪk/ Spazierstock; Krückstock p. 127
wall /wɔːl/ Wand NHG 6
(to) wander around /ˌwɒndərəˈraʊnd/ umherstreifen p. 125
(to) **want (to)** /wɒnt/ wollen NHG 5
war /wɔː/ Krieg p. 85, 7
World War II /ˌwɜːld ˌwɔː ˈtuː/ Zweiter Weltkrieg p. 85, 7
(to) **warn** /wɔːn/ warnen p. 22, 6
warrior /ˈwɒriə/ Krieger/in p. 66, 2
(to) **wash** /wɒʃ/ waschen; sich waschen NHG 5
waste /weɪst/ Abfall p. 73, 9
watch /wɒtʃ/ (Armband)uhr NHG 6
(to) **watch** /wɒtʃ/ beobachten; ansehen NHG 5
(to) **watch TV** /ˌwɒtʃ tiː ˈviː/ Fernsehen gucken NHG 5
water /ˈwɔːtə/ Wasser NHG 5
way /weɪ/ Weg; Art NHG 5
this way /ˈðɪs weɪ/ hier entlang p. 22, 6
we /wiː/ wir NHG 5
(to) **wear** *(irr)* /weə/ tragen *(Kleidung)* NHG 5
weather /ˈweðə/ Wetter NHG 5
web page /ˈwebˌpeɪdʒ/ Webseite; Internetseite p. 11, 6
Wednesday /ˈwenzdeɪ/ Mittwoch NHG 5
(on) Wednesdays /ˈwenzdeɪz/ mittwochs NHG 5
week /wiːk/ Woche NHG 5
weekend /ˌwiːkˈend/ Wochenende NHG 5
weight /weɪt/ Gewicht p. 133
weight training /ˈweɪtˌtreɪnɪŋ/ Krafttraining p. 32, 1
welcome (to) /ˈwelkəm tʊ/ willkommen (in) NHG 5
You're welcome. /ˌjɔː ˈwelkəm/ Gern geschehen.; Keine Ursache. p. 65, 15
well /wel/ nun NHG 5; gut NHG 6
(to) **get well** *(irr)* /ˌɡet ˈwel/ gesund werden p. 44, 2
well done /ˌwel ˈdʌn/ gut gemacht NHG 6
well-known /ˌwelˈnəʊn/ bekannt; berühmt p. 78
West African /ˌwestˈæfrɪkən/ Westafrikaner/in; westafrikanisch p. 81, 2
Western /ˈwestən/ West-, westlich p. 30
wet /wet/ nass NHG 6
what /wɒt/ was; welche(r, s) NHG 5
What about ...? /ˌwɒtəˌbaʊt ˈ.../ Was ist mit ...? / Wie wäre es mit ...? NHG 5
What if ...? /ˌwɒtˈɪf/ Was wäre, wenn ...? p. 91, 2
What time is it? /wɒtˈtaɪmɪzɪt/ Wie spät ist es? NHG 5
What ... would you like? /ˌwɒt ... wəd jə ˈlaɪk/ Was für ein / eine ... hättest du / hättet ihr / hätten Sie gern? NHG 5
What's on? *(informal)* /ˌwɒtsˈɒn/ Was ist los? NHG 6
What's the matter? /ˌwɒtsðə ˈmætə/ Was ist los? p. 42, 1
What's the time, please? /ˌwɒts ðə ˈtaɪm pliːz/ Wie spät ist es, bitte? NHG 5
What's up? *(informal)* /ˌwɒtsˈʌp/ Was ist los? p. 90, 2
What's wrong? *(informal)* /ˌwɒtsˈrɒŋ/ Was ist los? p. 90, 2
whatever /wɒtˈevə/ was (auch immer) NHG 6
wheel /wiːl/ Rad NHG 6
wheelchair /ˈwiːltʃeə/ Rollstuhl p. 36, 7
when /wen/ wann; wenn; als NHG 5
whenever /wenˈevə/ wann auch immer p. 63, 12
where /weə/ wo; wohin NHG 5
which /wɪtʃ/ welche(r, s); was NHG 5
while /waɪl/ während NHG 6; Weile p. 85, 7
(to) whip cream /ˌwɪp ˈkriːm/ Sahne schlagen p. 29
white /waɪt/ weiß NHG 5
who /huː/ wer; der/die/das NHG 5
whole /həʊl/ ganz, gesamt NHG 6
whose /huːz/ wessen NHG 5
why /waɪ/ warum NHG 5
wide /waɪd/ weit p. 118, 7
wife (*pl* **wives**) /waɪf, waɪvz/ Ehefrau NHG 5
WiFi /ˈwaɪ faɪ/ WLAN p. 113, 15
wildlife /ˈwaɪldˌlaɪf/ Tier- und Pflanzenwelt; Flora und Fauna NHG 6
will /wɪl/ werden NHG 6
(to) **win** *(irr)* /wɪn/ gewinnen p. 32, 1
window /ˈwɪndəʊ/ Fenster NHG 5
winner /ˈwɪnə/ Gewinner/in p. 53
(to) **wish** /wɪʃ/ wünschen p. 95, 6
with /wɪð/ mit; bei NHG 5
without /wɪðˈaʊt/ ohne NHG 5
wizard /ˈwɪzəd/ Zauberer p. 78
woman (*pl* **women**) /ˈwʊmən, ˈwɪmɪn/ Frau NHG 5
won't /wəʊnt/ nicht werden NHG 6
(to) **wonder** /ˈwʌndə/ sich fragen NHG 6
wonderful /ˈwʌndəfl/ wunderbar, wundervoll NHG 6
wood /wʊd/ Holz NHG 6
wooden /ˈwʊdn/ Holz-, hölzern p. 76
word /wɜːd/ Wort NHG 5
word search /ˈwɜːd sɜːtʃ/ Wortsuche p. 97, 10
word web /ˈwɜːd web/ Wortnetz NHG 5
wordbank /ˈwɜːdbæŋk/ *Wortsammlung* NHG 5

work /wɜːk/ Arbeit; Werk NHG 5
(to) **work** /wɜːk/ arbeiten NHG 5; funktionieren NHG 6
(to) work out /ˌwɜːk‿ˈaʊt/ ausarbeiten p. 100; *hier:* aufgehen p. 101
workbook /ˈwɜːkbʊk/ Arbeitsheft p. 8, 1
working /ˈwɜːkɪŋ/ funktionierend p. 105, 2
workout /ˈwɜːkaʊt/ Training p. 36, 7
worksheet /ˈwɜːkʃiːt/ Arbeitsblatt p. 14, 9
world /wɜːld/ Welt NHG 5
all over the world /ˌɔːl‿ˌəʊvə ðə ˈwɜːld/ auf der ganzen Welt NHG 6
from all over the world /frəm‿ˌɔːl‿ˌəʊvə ðə ˈwɜːld/ aus der ganzen Welt NHG 5
from (all) around the world /frəm‿ˌɔːl‿əˌraʊnd ðə ˈwɜːld/ aus der (ganzen) Welt p. 11, 6
World War II /ˌwɜːld ˌwɔː ˈtuː/ Zweiter Weltkrieg p. 85, 7
world-famous /ˌwɜːld ˈfeɪməs/ weltberühmt p. 70, 6
worried /ˈwʌrid/ beunruhigt; besorgt NHG 6
(to) **worry** /ˈwʌri/ sich Sorgen machen NHG 5
worse /wɜːs/ schlechter, schlimmer NHG 6
the worst /ðə ˈwɜːst/ der/die/das schlechteste/schlimmste; am schlechtesten/schlimmsten NHG 6
would /wʊd/ würde(st, n, t) NHG 5
I would like ... (= I'd like ...) /aɪ ˌwʊd ˈlaɪk, aɪd ˈlaɪk/ Ich würde gern ... / Ich hätte gern ... NHG 5
Would you like ...? /ˌwʊd juː ˈlaɪk/ Hättest du / Hättet ihr / Hätten Sie gern ...? NHG 5
wound /wuːnd/ Wunde p. 42, 1
wrist /rɪst/ Handgelenk p. 42, 1
(to) **write** *(irr)* /raɪt/ schreiben NHG 5
(to) **write down** *(irr)* /ˌraɪt‿ˈdaʊn/ aufschreiben NHG 5
writing /ˈraɪtɪŋ/ Schrift; Schreiben p. 114, 2
written /ˈrɪtn/ schriftlich NHG 6
wrong /rɒŋ/ falsch NHG 6
(to) **be wrong** *(irr)* /ˌbiː ˈrɒŋ/ im Unrecht sein p. 98, 12
(to) **be wrong (with)** *(irr)* /ˌbiː ˈrɒŋ wɪθ/ nicht in Ordnung sein (mit) p. 48, 8
What's wrong? *(informal)* /ˌwɒts‿ˈrɒŋ/ Was ist los? p. 90, 2

X

X-ray /ˈeksreɪ/ Röntgenbild p. 46, 5
(to) **take an X-ray** *(irr)* /ˌteɪk‿ən ˈeksreɪ/ eine Röntgenaufnahme machen p. 42, 1
X-ray glasses *(pl)* /ˈeksreɪ ˌɡlɑːsɪz/ *Röntgenbrille* p. 111, 11

Y

year /jɪə/ Jahr NHG 5; Schuljahr; Klasse NHG 6
yellow /ˈjeləʊ/ gelb NHG 5
yes /jes/ ja NHG 5
yesterday /ˈjestədeɪ/ gestern NHG 6
yet /jet/ schon; noch p. 46, 5
Yorkshire pudding /ˌjɔːkʃə ˈpʊdɪŋ/ *britische gebackene Beilage* p. 8, 2
you /juː/ du; dich; dir; man; ihr; euch; Sie; Ihnen NHG 5
young /jʌŋ/ jung NHG 6
your /jɔː/ dein(e); euer/eure; Ihr(e) NHG 5
yours /jɔːz/ deine(r, s); eure(r, s); Ihre(r, s) NHG 6
yours sincerely /ˌjɔːz sɪnˈsɪəli/ mit freundlichen Grüßen *(am Ende eines formellen Briefes)* NHG 6
yourself /jɔːˈself/ dir, dich; sich NHG 5
youth club /ˈjuːθ ˌklʌb/ Jugendklub NHG 6
yummy *(informal)* /ˈjʌmi/ lecker p. 8, 1

Z

zero waste /ˌzɪərəʊ ˈweɪst/ verpackungsfrei p. 73, 9
zip /zɪp/ Reißverschluss p. 108, 7

Names

First names

Agata *(f.)* /əˈgɑːtə/
Alex *(m., f.)* /ˈælɪks/
Alexander *(m.)* /ˌælɪgˈzɑːndə/
Amira *(f.)* /əˈmiːrə/
Andy *(m., f.)* /ˈændi/
Anna *(f.)* /ˈænə/
Arthur *(m.)* /ˈɑːθə/
Ava *(f.)* /ˈeɪvə/
Ayaz *(m.)* /ˈaɪəz/
Becky *(f.)* /ˈbeki/
Ben *(m.)* /ben/
Benjamin *(m.)* /ˈbendʒəmɪn/
Billie *(m., f.)* /ˈbɪli/
Bob *(m., f.)* /bɒb/
Cathy *(f.)* /ˈkæθi/
Chloe *(f.)* /ˈkləʊi/
Chris *(m., f.)* /krɪs/
Claire *(f.)* /kleə/
Dan *(m.)* /dæn/
Daniel *(m.)* /ˈdænjəl/
Delia *(f.)* /ˈdiːliə/
Demir *(m.)* /deˈmɪə/
Ector *(m.)* /ˈektə/
Edward *(m.)* /ˈedwəd/
Edyta *(f.)* /əˈdiːtə/
Ellie *(f.)* /ˈeli/
Emily *(f.)* /ˈeməli/
Emma *(f.)* /ˈemə/
Eric *(m.)* /ˈerɪk/
Erika *(f.)* /ˈerɪkə/
Faisal *(m.)* /ˈfaɪsl/
Filip *(m.)* /ˈfɪlɪp/
Fiona *(f.)* /fiˈəʊnə/
Gemma *(f.)* /ˈdʒemə/
George *(m.)* /dʒɔːdʒ/
Harry *(m., f.)* /ˈhæri/
Harvey *(m.)* /ˈhɑːvi/
Jack *(m.)* /dʒæk/
Jacob *(m.)* /ˈdʒeɪkəb/
Jada *(f.)* /ˈdʒeɪdə/
James *(m.)* /dʒeɪmz/
Jamie *(m.)* /ˈdʒeɪmi/
Jan *(m., f.)* /dʒæn, jæn, jɑːn/
Jason *(m.)* /ˈdʒeɪsn/
Jemima *(f.)* /dʒɪˈmaɪmə/
Jenna *(f.)* /ˈdʒenə/
Jill *(f.)* /dʒɪl/
Joe *(m., f.)* /dʒəʊ/
John *(m.)* /dʒɒn/
Joshua *(m.)* /ˈdʒɒʃjuə/
Juan *(m.)* /wɑːn/
Karim *(m.)* /kəˈriːm/
Katie *(f.)* /ˈkeɪti/
Kay *(m., f.)* /keɪ/
Kristin *(f.)* /krɪˈstiːn/
Laura *(f.)* /ˈlɔːrə/
Leon *(m.)* /ˈliːən/
Leona *(f.)* /liˈəʊnə/
Levi *(m.)* /ˈliːvaɪ/
Lily *(f.)* /ˈlɪli/
Linda *(f.)* /ˈlɪndə/
Logie *(m.)* /ˈləʊgi/
Louise *(f.)* /luˈiːz/
Lucy *(f.)* /ˈluːsi/
Makena *(f.)* /məˈkiːnə/
Margo *(f.)* /ˈmɑːgəʊ/
Marianne *(f.)* /ˌmæriˈæn/
Martin *(m.)* /ˈmɑːtɪn/
Matilda *(f.)* /məˈtɪldə/
Matt *(m.)* /mæt/
Matthew *(m.)* /ˈmæθjuː/
Merlin *(m.)* /ˈmɜːlɪn/
Mia *(f.)* /ˈmiːə/
Michael *(m.)* /ˈmaɪkl/
Michelle *(f.)* /miːˈʃel/
Mira *(f.)* /ˈmaɪrə/
Nils *(m.)* /nɪlz/
Noah *(m.)* /ˈnəʊə/
Oliver *(m.)* /ˈɒlɪvə/
Olivia *(f.)* /əˈlɪviə/
Ollie *(m.)* /ˈɒli/
Paolo *(m.)* /pəˈəʊləʊ/
Paul *(m.)* /pɔːl/
Pavel *(m.)* /ˈpɑːvl/
Peter *(m.)* /ˈpiːtə/
Phil *(m.)* /fɪl/
Radek *(m.)* /ˈrɑːdek/
Raymond *(m.)* /ˈreɪmənd/
Richard *(m.)* /ˈrɪtʃəd/
Robert *(m.)* /ˈrɒbət/
Ryan *(m.)* /ˈraɪən/
Sally *(f.)* /ˈsæli/
Sam *(m., f.)* /sæm/
Sami *(m.)* /ˈsæmi/
Sarah *(f.)* /ˈseərə/
Sebastian *(m.)* /səˈbæstiən/
Sheree *(f.)* /ʃəˈriː/
Sophie *(f.)* /ˈsəʊfi/
Stephen *(m.)* /ˈstiːvn/
Steven *(m.)* /ˈstiːvn/
Suzy *(f.)* /ˈsuːzi/
Tarek *(m.)* /ˈtærɪk/
Thomas *(m.)* /ˈtɒməs/
Tim *(m.)* /tɪm/
Toby *(m.)* /ˈtəʊbi/
Tom *(m.)* /tɒm/
Tony *(m., f.)* /ˈtəʊni/
Uther *(m.)* /ˈjuːθə/
William *(m.)* /ˈwɪljəm/
Zara *(f.)* / ˈzɑːrə/

Families

Addis /ˈædɪs/
Adil /əˈdiːl/
Baird /beəd/
Barlow /ˈbɑːləʊ/
Bell /bel/
Bohlin /ˈbɔːlɪn/
Carter /ˈkɑːtə/
Cooper /ˈkuːpə/
Dill /dɪl/
Dunkerley /ˈdʌŋkərli/
Durand /ˈdʌrənd/
Eilish /ˈaɪlɪʃ/
Fisher /ˈfɪʃə/
Fleming /ˈflemɪŋ/
Graham /ˈgreɪəm/
Hamilton /ˈhæmltən/
Hawk /hɔːk/
Hawking /ˈhɔːkɪŋ/
Hill /hɪl/
Kellog /ˈkelɒg/
Kershaw /ˈkɜːʃɔː/
Kogan /ˈkəʊgən/
Miller /ˈmɪlə/
Norris /ˈnɒrɪs/
Patel /pəˈtel/
Peters /ˈpiːtəz/
Rogers /ˈrɒdʒəz/
Rosen /ˈrəʊzn/
Spratt /spræt/
Stephenson /ˈstiːvnsən/
Strauss /straʊs/
Thomas /ˈtɒməs/
Tomlinson /ˈtɒmlɪnsən/
Trevithick /ˈtrevɪθɪk/
Watson /ˈwɒtsn/
Watt /wɒt/
Weston /ˈwestən/
Zephaniah /ˌzefəˈnaɪə/

Other names

Adventuring Andy /ədˌventʃərɪŋ‿ˈændi/
American football /əˌmerɪkən ˈfʊtˌbɔːl/
Arundel Castle /ˈærəndl kɑːsl/
Ayaz London /ˌaɪəzˈlʌndən/
bangers and mash /ˌbæŋəz‿ən ˈmæʃ/
Barbican /ˈbɑːbɪkən/
Barley Hall /ˌbɑːli ˈhɔːl/
bhaji /ˈbɑːdʒi/
The Black Horse /ðə ˌblæk ˈhɔːs/
bubble and squeak /ˌbʌbl‿ən ˈskwiːk/
burdock /ˈbɜːdɒk/
(chicken) tikka (masala), (chicken) tikka /ˌtʃɪkɪn ˌtiːkə məˈsɑːlə, ˌtʃɪkɪn ˈtiːkə/
Dim Sum /ˌdɪm ˈsʌm/
Diwali /dɪˈwɑːli/
Double /ˈdʌbl/
East India Company /ˌiːst‿ˌɪndiə ˈkʌmpni/
Farmhouse /ˈfɑːmˌhaʊs/
Feastival /ˈfiːstɪvl/
Foodlover /ˈfuːdˌlʌvə/
Glastonbury Abbey /ˌglæstənbəri‿ˈæbi/
Glastonbury Tor /ˌglæstənbəri ˈtɔː/
The Highland Games /ðə ˈhaɪlənd geɪmz/
Hindi /ˈhɪndi/

hippo roller /ˈhɪpəʊ ˌrəʊlə/
Holi /ˈhɒli/
Holland Park /ˌhɒlənd ˈpɑːk/
Hyde Park /ˌhaɪd ˈpɑːk/
Isabel3589 /ˌɪzəbel ˌθriː faɪv‿eɪt ˈnaɪn/
Jorvik /ˈjɔː vɪk/
kari /ˈkɑːri/
kebab /kɪˈbæb/
The King's Head /ðə ˌkɪŋz ˈhed/
kingfisher /ˈkɪŋˌfɪʃə/
korma /ˈkɔːmə/
Lahmacun /ˌlɑməˈdʒuːn/
lassi /ˈlæsi/
The London Eye /ðə ˌlʌndən‿ˈaɪ/
Lonelygirl /ˌləʊnliˈɡɜːl/
Lyceum Theatre /laɪˌsiːəm ˈθɪətə/
Manchester Cathedral /ˌmæntʃɪstə kəˈθiːdrəl/
Margherita /ˌmɑːɡəˈriːtə/
masala /məˈsɑːlə/
The Museum of London /ðə mjuːˌziːəm‿əv ˈlʌndən/
naan /nɑːn/
Nazi /ˈnɑːtsi/
Notting Hill /ˌnɒtɪŋ ˈhɪl/
Notting Hill Carnival /ˌnɒtɪŋ hɪl ˈkɑːnɪvl/
The Olympics *(pl)* /ðiˌəˈlɪmpɪks/
one-pot pasta /ˌwʌnˌpɒt ˈpæstə/
The Palace of India /ðə ˌpæləs‿əv‿ˈɪndiə/
palak paneer /ˌpɑːlək pəˈnɪə/
The Paralympic Games *(pl)* /ðə ˌpærəlɪmpɪk‿ˈɡeɪmz/
The Paralympics *(pl)* /ðə ˌpærəˈlɪmpɪks/
Pizza Extra /ˌpiːtsə‿ˈekstrə/
poppadom /ˈpɒpədəm/
Portobello Market /ˌpɔːtəˌbeləʊ ˈmɑːkɪt/
Portobello Road /ˌpɔːtəˌbeləʊ ˈrəʊd/
Preppy Rappy /ˌprepi ˈræpi/
reggae /ˈreɡeɪ/
The Royal Air Force /ðə ˌrɔɪəl‿ˈeə fɔːs/
samosa /səˈməʊsə/
The Science and Industry Museum / ðə ˌsaɪəns‿ən‿ˈɪndəstri mjuːˌziːəm/
The Science Museum /ðə ˈsaɪəns mjuːˌziːəm/
Shakshuka /ʃəkˈʃuːkə/
sitting volleyball /ˌsɪtɪŋ ˈvɒlibɔːl/
Skatepark Project /ˈskeɪtpɑːk ˌprɒdʒekt/
spaghetti bolognese /spəˌɡeti ˈbɒləˌneɪz/
Spinning Jenny /ˌspɪnɪŋ ˈdʒeni/
St James /sənt ˈdʒeɪmz/
Sunnyday /ˌsʌniˈdeɪ/
Sushi Blue /ˌsuːʃi ˈbluː/
The Taj Mahal /ðə ˌtɑːdʒ məˈhɑːl/
Tamil /ˈtæməl/
Textiles Gallery /ˈtekstaɪlz ˌɡæləri/
Tiramisu /ˌtɪrəmiˈsuː/
toad in the hole /ˌtəʊd‿ɪn ðə ˈhəʊl/
Tokyo /ˈtəʊkiəʊ/
Trouble /ˈtrʌbl/
Uther Pendragon /ˌjuːθə penˈdræɡən/
Velcro® /ˈvelkrəʊ/
Viking Lodge /ˈvaɪkɪŋ lɒdʒ/
vindaloo /ˌvɪndəˈluː/
Wonton /ˌwɒnˈtɒn/
Yorkshire pudding /ˌjɔːkʃə ˈpʊdɪŋ/

Geographical Names

Asia /ˈeɪʒə/
Avalon /ˈævəlɒn/
Bangladesh /ˌbæŋɡləˈdeʃ/
Battersea /ˈbætəsi/
Bayswater /ˈbeɪzˌwɔːtə/
Berlin /bɜːˈlɪn/
Braemar /ˌbreɪˈmɑː/
Brighton /ˈbraɪtn/
Bristol /ˈbrɪstl/
Britain /ˈbrɪtn/
Brixton /ˈbrɪkstən/
China /ˈtʃaɪnə/
Chinatown /ˈtʃaɪnəˌtaʊn/
the Cotswolds /ðə ˈkɒtswəʊldz/
Edinburgh /ˈedɪnbərə/
Egypt /ˈiːdʒɪpt/
Elephant & Castle /ˌelɪfənt‿ən ˈkɑːsl/
England /ˈɪŋɡlənd/
Exeter /ˈeksɪtə/
Exhibition Road /ˌeksɪˈbɪʃn rəʊd/
Finsbury Park /ˈfɪnzbəri pɑːk/
Germany /ˈdʒɜːməni/
Ghana /ˈɡɑːnə/
Glastonbury /ˈɡlæstənbəri/
Golders Green /ˌɡəʊldəz ˈɡriːn/
Great Britain /ˌɡreɪt ˈbrɪtn/
Greece /ɡriːs/
Hammersmith /ˈhæməsmɪθ/
Highland /ˈhaɪlənd/
India /ˈɪndiə/
Isle of Wight /ˌaɪl‿əv ˈwaɪt/
Israel /ˈɪzreɪl/
Italy /ˈɪtəli/
Japan /dʒəˈpæn/
Korea /kəˈrɪə/
Lebanon /ˈlebənən/
Leeds /liːdz/
Liverpool /ˈlɪvəpuːl/
London /ˈlʌndən/
Los Angeles /lɒs‿ˈændʒəliːz/
Manchester /ˈmæntʃɪstə/
Mars /mɑːz/
Merton /ˈmɜːtn/
Morocco /məˈrɒkəʊ/
New Delhi /ˌnjuː ˈdeli/
North Africa /ˌnɔːθ‿ˈæfrɪkə/
Pakistan /ˌpɑːkɪˈstɑːn/
Poland /ˈpəʊlənd/
Scotland /ˈskɒtlənd/
South India /ˌsaʊθ‿ˈɪndiə/
South Kensington /ˌsaʊθ ˈkenzɪŋtən/
Southall /ˈsaʊθɔːl/
Spain /speɪn/
Stoke-on-Trent /ˌstəʊk‿ɒn ˈtrent/
Sweden /ˈswiːdn/
Trinidad /ˈtrɪnɪdæd/
Turkey /ˈtɜːki/
the UK (= United Kingdom) /ðə ˌjuː ˈkeɪ, juːˌnaɪtɪd ˈkɪŋdəm/
the USA (= United States of America) /ðə ˌju‿es‿ˈeɪ, juːˌnaɪtɪd ˌsteɪts‿əv‿əˈmerɪkə/
Wales /weɪlz/
York /jɔːk/

Numbers

0 oh, zero, nil /əʊ, ˈzɪərəʊ, nɪl/
1 one /wʌn/
2 two /tuː/
3 three /θriː/
4 four /fɔː/
5 five /faɪv/
6 six /sɪks/
7 seven /sevn/
8 eight /eɪt/
9 nine /naɪn/
10 ten /ten/
11 eleven /ɪˈlevn/
12 twelve /twelv/
13 **thir**teen /ˌθɜːˈtiːn/
14 fourteen /ˌfɔːˈtiːn
15 **fif**teen /ˌfɪfˈtiːn/
16 sixteen /ˌsɪksˈtiːn/
17 seventeen /ˌsevnˈtiːn/
18 **eigh**teen /ˌeɪˈtiːn/
19 nineteen /ˌnaɪnˈtiːn/
20 **twen**ty /ˈtwenti/

21 twenty-one /ˌtwentiˈwʌn/
30 **thir**ty /ˈθɜːti/
33 thirty-three /ˌθɜːtiˈθriː/
40 **for**ty /ˈfɔːti/
45 forty-five /ˌfɔːtiˈfaɪv/
50 **fif**ty /ˈfɪfti/
56 fifty-six /ˌfɪftiˈsɪks/
60 sixty /ˈsɪksti/
67 sixty-seven /ˌsɪkstiˈsevn/
70 seventy /ˈsevnti/
78 seventy-eight /ˌsevntiˈeɪt/
80 **eigh**ty /ˈeɪti/
89 eighty-nine /ˌeɪtiˈnaɪn/
90 ninety /ˈnaɪnti/

100 a/one hundred /ə/wʌn ˈhʌndrəd/
101 one hundred and one /wʌn ˌhʌndrəd‿ən ˈwʌn/
200 two hundred /tuː ˈhʌndrəd/

1,000 one thousand /ə/wʌn ˈθauznd/
2,000 two thousand /tuː ˈθauznd/

> **!** Bei Zahlen mit vier oder mehr Ziffern werden, falls erforderlich, im Englischen Kommata verwendet, keine Punkte!

1st **first** /fɜːst/
2nd **second** /ˈsekənd/
3rd **third** /θɜːd/
4th fourth /fɔːθ/
5th **fif**th /fɪfθ/
6th sixth /sɪksθ/
7th seventh /sevnθ/
8th **eigh**th /eɪtθ/
9th **nin**th /naɪnθ/
10th tenth /tenθ/
11th eleventh /ɪˈlevnθ/
12th **twelf**th /twelfθ/
13th thirteenth /ˌθɜːˈtiːnθ/
19th nineteenth /ˌnaɪnˈtiːnθ/
20th twent**ie**th /ˈtwentiəθ/

21st twenty-first /ˌtwentiˈfɜːst/
22nd twenty-second /ˌtwentiˈsekənd/
23rd twenty-third /ˌtwentiˈθɜːd/

30th thirt**ie**th /ˈθɜːtiəθ/
40th fort**ie**th /ˈfɔːtiəθ/
50th fift**ie**th /ˈfɪftiəθ/
60th sixt**ie**th /ˈsɪkstiəθ/
70th sevent**ie**th /ˈsevntiəθ/
80th eight**ie**th /ˈeɪtiəθ/
90th ninet**ie**th /ˈnaɪntiəθ/
100th hundredth /ˈhʌndrədθ/

> **!** Daten schreibst du im britischen Englisch so:
> 1 August, 2 January, 5 November
> oder so: 1st / 1st August,
> 2nd / 2nd January, 5th / 5th November

> **!** Jahreszahlen sprichst du so aus:
> 1939 nineteen thirty-nine
> 1951 nineteen fifty-one
> 2010 two thousand and ten

$\frac{1}{2}$ a / one half /ə/wʌn ˈhɑːf/
$\frac{1}{3}$ a / one third /ə/wʌn ˈθɜːd/
$\frac{1}{4}$ a / one quarter /ə/wʌn ˈkwɔːtə/
$\frac{1}{8}$ a / one eighth /ə/wʌn‿ˈeɪtθ/
$\frac{3}{4}$ three quarters /θriː ˈkwɔːtəz/

Irregular verbs

infinitive	simple past	past participle	German
(to) be /biː/	was/were /wɒz/wɜː/	been /biːn/	sein
(to) become /bɪˈkʌm/	became /bɪˈkeɪm/	become /bɪˈkʌm/	werden
(to) begin /bɪˈgɪn/	began /bɪˈgæn/	begun /bɪˈgʌn/	anfangen; beginnen
(to) bleed /bliːd/	bled /bled/	bled /bled/	bluten
(to) break /breɪk/	broke /brəʊk/	broken /ˈbrəʊkən/	(zer)brechen; kaputt machen
(to) bring /brɪŋ/	brought /brɔːt/	brought /brɔːt/	mitbringen
(to) build /bɪld/	built /bɪlt/	built /bɪlt/	bauen
(to) buy /baɪ/	bought /bɔːt/	bought /bɔːt/	kaufen
(to) catch /kætʃ/	caught /kɔːt/	caught /kɔːt/	fangen
(to) choose /tʃuːz/	chose /tʃəʊz/	chosen /ˈtʃəʊzn/	wählen; sich entscheiden
(to) come /kʌm/	came /keɪm/	come /kʌm/	kommen
(to) cost /kɒst/	cost /kɒst/	cost /kɒst/	kosten
(to) cut /kʌt/	cut /kʌt/	cut /kʌt/	schneiden
(to) deal with /ˈdiːl wɪð/	dealt with /ˈdelt wɪð/	dealt with /ˈdelt wɪð/	sich befassen mit, umgehen mit
(to) do /duː/	did /dɪd/	done /dʌn/	machen; tun
(to) draw /drɔː/	drew /druː/	drawn /drɔːn/	zeichnen
(to) drink /drɪŋk/	drank /dræŋk/	drunk /drʌŋk/	trinken
(to) drive /draɪv/	drove /drəʊv/	driven /ˈdrɪvn/	fahren
(to) eat /iːt/	ate /et/eɪt/	eaten /ˈiːtn/	essen
(to) fall /fɔːl/	fell /fel/	fallen /ˈfɔːlən/	fallen
(to) feed /fiːd/	fed /fed/	fed /fed/	füttern
(to) feel /fiːl/	felt /felt/	felt /felt/	(sich) fühlen
(to) fight /faɪt/	fought /fɔːt/	fought /fɔːt/	bekämpfen; ankämpfen gegen
(to) find /faɪnd/	found /faʊnd/	found /faʊnd/	finden
(to) fly /flaɪ/	flew /fluː/	flown /fləʊn/	fliegen
(to) forget /fəˈget/	forgot /fəˈgɒt/	forgotten /fəˈgɒtən/	vergessen
(to) get /get/	got /gɒt/	got /gɒt/	bekommen; holen; kaufen; kommen, gelangen; werden; bringen
(to) give /gɪv/	gave /geɪv/	given /ˈgɪvn/	geben; angeben, mitteilen
(to) go /gəʊ/	went /went/	gone /gɒn/	gehen; fahren
(to) grow /grəʊ/	grew /gruː/	grown /grəʊn/	wachsen; anbauen
(to) hang (up) /ˌhæŋ‿ˈʌp/	hung (up) /ˌhʌŋ‿ˈʌp/	hung (up) /ˌhʌŋ‿ˈʌp/	hängen, aufhängen
(to) have /hæv/	had /hæd/	had /hæd/	haben; essen; trinken
(to) hear /hɪə/	heard /hɜːd/	heard /hɜːd/	hören
(to) hide /haɪd/	hid /hɪd/	hidden /ˈhɪdn/	(sich) verstecken
(to) hit /hɪt/	hit /hɪt/	hit /hɪt/	schlagen; stoßen gegen
(to) hold /həʊld/	held /held/	held /held/	(fest)halten
(to) hurt /hɜːt/	hurt /hɜːt/	hurt /hɜːt/	wehtun, schmerzen; verletzen

Irregular verbs

infinitive	simple past	past participle	German
to) keep /ki:p/	kept /kept/	kept /kept/	aufbewahren; (be)halten
(to) know /nəʊ/	knew /nju:/	known /nəʊn/	wissen; kennen
(to) learn /lɜ:n/	learnt/learned /lɜ:nt/lɜ:nd/	learnt/learned /lɜ:nt/lɜ:nd/	lernen
(to) leave /li:v/	left /left/	left /left/	weggehen; verlassen, abfahren; (übrig) lassen; zurücklassen; hinterlassen
(to) let /let/	let /let/	let /let/	lassen
(to) light /laɪt/	lit /lɪt/	lit /lɪt/	anzünden
(to) lose /lu:z/	lost /lɒst/	lost /lɒst/	verlieren
(to) make /meɪk/	made /meɪd/	made /meɪd/	machen
(to) mean /mi:n/	meant /ment/	meant /ment/	meinen; bedeuten
(to) meet /mi:t/	met /met/	met /met/	(sich) treffen; kennenlernen
(to) pay /peɪ/	paid /peɪd/	paid /peɪd/	(be)zahlen
(to) prove /pru:v/	proved /pru:vd/	proved/proven /pru:vd/'pru:vn/	beweisen
(to) put /pʊt/	put /pʊt/	put /pʊt/	setzen; stellen; legen
(to) read /ri:d/	read /red/	read /red/	lesen
(to) rewrite /ˌri:ˈraɪt/	rewrote /ˌri:ˈrəʊt/	rewritten /ˌri:ˈrɪtn/	überarbeiten, umschreiben
(to) ride /raɪd/	rode /rəʊd/	ridden /ˈrɪdn/	fahren; reiten
(to) run /rʌn/	ran /ræn/	run /rʌn/	laufen; rennen; leiten, betreiben
(to) say /seɪ/	said /sed/	said /sed/	sagen
(to) see /si:/	saw /sɔ:/	seen /si:n/	sehen; empfangen, drannehmen
(to) sell /sel/	sold /səʊld/	sold /səʊld/	verkaufen
(to) send /send/	sent /sent/	sent /sent/	schicken
(to) shine /ʃaɪn/	shone /ʃɒn/	shone /ʃɒn/	scheinen
(to) shoot /ʃu:t/	shot /ʃɒt/	shot /ʃɒt/	schießen
(to) show /ʃəʊ/	showed /ʃəʊd/	shown /ʃəʊn/	zeigen
(to) sing /sɪŋ/	sang /sæŋ/	sung /sʌŋ/	singen
(to) sit /sɪt/	sat /sæt/	sat /sæt/	sitzen
(to) sit down /ˌsɪt‿ˈdaʊn/	sat down /ˌsæt‿ˈdaʊn/	sat down /ˌsæt‿ˈdaʊn/	sich hinsetzen
(to) sleep /sli:p/	slept /slept/	slept /slept/	schlafen
(to) speak /spi:k/	spoke /spəʊk/	spoken /ˈspəʊkən/	reden; sprechen
(to) spell /spel/	spelt/spelled /spelt/speld/	spelt/spelled /spelt/speld/	buchstabieren
(to) spend /spend/	spent /spent/	spent /spent/	ausgeben *(Geld)*; verbringen *(Zeit)*
(to) spin /spɪn/	spun/span /spʌn/spæn/	spun /spʌn/	spinnen; drehen
(to) stand /stænd/	stood /stʊd/	stood /stʊd/	stehen
(to) steal /sti:l/	stole /stəʊl/	stolen /ˈstəʊlən/	stehlen
(to) stick /stɪk/	stuck /stʌk/	stuck /stʌk/	festhängen
(to) swim /swɪm/	swam /swæm/	swum /swʌm/	schwimmen

Irregular verbs

infinitive	simple past	past participle	German
(to) take /teɪk/	took /tʊk/	taken /ˈteɪkən/	nehmen; bringen; benötigen; brauchen; dauern
(to) teach /tiːtʃ/	taught /tɔːt/	taught /tɔːt/	unterrichten
(to) tell /tel/	told /təʊld/	told /təʊld/	erzählen
(to) think /θɪŋk/	thought /θɔːt/	thought /θɔːt/	denken; glauben
(to) throw /θrəʊ/	threw /θruː/	thrown /θrəʊn/	werfen
(to) understand /ˌʌndəˈstænd/	understood /ˌʌndəˈstʊd/	understood /ˌʌndəˈstʊd/	verstehen
(to) wake up /ˌweɪk‿ˈʌp/	woke up /ˌwəʊk‿ˈʌp/	woken up /ˌwəʊkən‿ˈʌp/	aufwachen; aufwecken
(to) wear /weə/	wore /wɔː/	worn /wɔːn/	tragen *(Kleidung)*
(to) win /wɪn/	won /wʌn/	won /wʌn/	gewinnen
(to) write /raɪt/	wrote /rəʊt/	written /ˈrɪtn/	schreiben

Tipp:

Einige Verben bilden das **simple past** und das **past participle** nach einem ähnlichen Muster. Wenn du sie dir in Gruppen sortierst, kannst du dir die Formen vielleicht besser merken.
Findest du weitere Beispiele für diese Gruppen oder andere Gruppen?

bring	brought	brought	mitbringen
buy	bought	bought	kaufen
catch	c**au**ght	c**au**ght	fangen
fight	fought	fought	bekämpfen
think	thought	thought	denken; glauben

sing	sang	sung	singen
swim	swam	swum	schwimmen

draw	drew	dr**a**wn	zeichnen
fly	flew	flown	fliegen
grow	grew	grown	wachsen
know	knew	known	kennen; wissen
throw	threw	thrown	werfen

cost	cost	cost	kosten
cut	cut	cut	schneiden
hit	hit	hit	schlagen
let	let	let	lassen
put	put	put	legen, setzen, stellen

Seite Lern-phasen	Inhalte	Kompetenzen	Sprachliche Mittel
7	**Unit 1 – Food (Kompetenzschwerpunkt: Schreiben)**		
	PART A – Delicious dishes		
8 Activate	Über verschiedene (Lieblings-) Gerichte lesen und sprechen	**Reading:** *text messages* und *blog posts* lesen **Speaking:** über Lieblingsgerichte sprechen, Fragen stellen	**Wortschatz** *food, likes and dislikes*
10 Practise	Strukturen bewusst machen und festigen	**Writing:** über etwas schreiben, das noch andauert bzw. Auswirkungen auf die Gegenwart hat	**Strukturen** *present perfect* **Wortschatz** *food*
11 Develop	Essen in der Schulkantine Eine Mahlzeit zubereiten	**Listening:** einem Gespräch folgen **Reading:** einen Dialog lesen, einen Limerick verstehen **Viewing:** einen Videoclip verstehen **Mediation:** einen Podcast sprachmitteln	**Wortschatz** *food, ingredients, recipe*
16 Practise	Strukturen festigen, Vorbereitung auf die Target task	**Writing:** ein *word web* zum Thema *cooking* erstellen	**Strukturen** *quantifiers*
17 Apply	**Target task** Our international cookbook	**Writing:** ein Rezept aufschreiben	**Wortschatz** *food, quantities*
	PART B – At a restaurant		
18 Activate	Restaurants in der eigenen Umgebung Verschiedene Restaurants in Großbritannien	**Speaking:** über Restaurants in der eigenen Umgebung sprechen, Bewertungskriterien für Restaurants finden **Reading:** Restaurantkritiken lesen	**Wortschatz** *food, eating out*
20 Practise	Strukturen bewusst machen und festigen	**Writing:** Vergleiche anstellen	**Strukturen** *comparison of adjectives*
21 Develop	Einen Restaurantbesuch planen Im Restaurant ein Gericht aussuchen und bestellen	**Listening:** einen Dialog verstehen **Speaking:** über ein Bild sprechen, eine Szene beschreiben **Reading:** einer Speisekarte Informationen entnehmen **Writing:** eine Textnachricht schreiben, eine Restaurantkritik verfassen **Viewing:** einen Videoclip verstehen	**Wortschatz** *at a restaurant*
26 Practise	Strukturen festigen, Vorbereitung auf die Target task	**Writing:** verschiedene Restaurant-szenen beschreiben und weiterführen	**Wortschatz** *at a restaurant* **Strukturen** *present progressive*
27 Apply	**Target task** Our restaurant role play **Check out** Selbsteinschätzung	**Speaking:** ein Rollenspiel vorbereiten und präsentieren	**Wortschatz** *at the restaurant*
28 Story	Jamie and Lucy: Delicious disaster	**Reading:** ein Kapitel der Fortsetzungsgeschichte lesen	
30 Challenge	Curious about curry?	**Reading:** einen Artikel über Herkunft, Geschichte und Bedeutung des Curry lesen	

Seite Lern-phasen	Inhalte	Kompetenzen	Sprachliche Mittel
55	**Unit 3 – What's on? (Kompetenzschwerpunkt: Lesen)**		
	PART A – At the car boot sale		
56 Activate	Über verschiedene Freizeitangebote lesen	**Speaking:** darüber sprechen, was man am Wochenende gern macht **Reading:** einen Flyer verstehen	**Wortschatz** *What's on?*
58 Practise	Strukturen bewusst machen und festigen	**Writing:** Personen und Gegenstände näher beschreiben	**Strukturen** *relative clauses*
59 Develop	Etwas über *car boot sales* erfahren Kaufen und Verkaufen	**Listening:** einen Dialog verstehen, Bilder zuordnen **Reading:** einem Dialog folgen **Viewing:** einen Videoclip verstehen **Speaking:** nach Preisen fragen und Auskunft erteilen **Writing:** die Geschichte eines Gegenstandes schreiben **Mediation:** bei einem Verkaufsgespräch vermitteln	**Wortschatz** *buying and selling*
64 Practise	Strukturen festigen, Vorbereitung auf die Target task	**Writing:** Verkaufsdialoge	**Strukturen** *prop words "one" and "ones"* **Wortschatz** *buying and selling*
65 Apply	Target task Secondhand-Shopping	**Speaking:** eine Flohmarkt-Szene entwickeln und als Rollenspiel präsentieren	**Wortschatz** *buying and selling*
	PART B – Festivals		
66 Activate	Das *Jorvik Viking Festival* kennenlernen	**Reading:** einem Poster Informationen entnehmen, einen Blogeintrag lesen **Speaking:** über ein Festival sprechen	**Wortschatz** *What's on?, events*
68 Practise	Strukturen bewusst machen und festigen	**Writing:** über Vergangenes schreiben **Speaking:** Fragen über Vergangenes stellen und beantworten	**Strukturen** *past progressive* **Wortschatz** *What's on?*
69 Develop	Mehr über das *Jorvik Viking Festival* erfahren Weitere Großveranstaltungen im Vereinigten Königreich kennenlernen	**Listening:** Statements zum *Jorvik Viking Festival* verstehen **Reading:** Blogeinträge verstehen und Notizen machen **Speaking:** Fragen über verschiedene Veranstaltungen stellen und beantworten **Viewing:** einer Slideshow folgen **Mediation:** einen Zeitungsartikel sprachmitteln	**Wortschatz** *What's on?, festivals*
74 Practise	Strukturen festigen, Vorbereitung auf die Target task	**Writing:** Situationen beschreiben	**Strukturen** *past progressive*
75 Apply	Target task A blog post Check out Selbsteinschätzung	**Writing:** einen Blogeintrag über ein Festival oder eine Veranstaltung schreiben	**Wortschatz** *What's on?, events*
76 Story	Jamie and Lucy: Medieval mischief	**Reading:** ein Kapitel der Fortsetzungsgeschichte lesen	
78 Challenge	The legend of King Arthur	**Reading:** einen Sachtext über Glastonbury und den sagenhaften *King Arthur* lesen	

Bildquellen

|Alamy Stock Photo, Abingdon/Oxfordshire: agefotostock 71.2; Allsorts Stock Photo 108.1; Alternative Occasions 67.5; Ammentorp Photography 80.1; Art Directors & TRIP 92.3; Baker, Darren 80.2; Baldesare, Paul 79.2; Ballard, Laura Clay 62.5; Barton, William 83.2; BasPhoto 103.1; Cavan Images 67.3; Chilvers, Clive 70.2; Classic Picture Library 109.1; Dack, Simon 155.1; Daemmrich, Bob 54.1, 54.2, 54.3; Dale, Veryan 79.4; David R. Frazier Photolibrary, Inc. 59.1; Doering, Olaf 119.6; Doyle, Paul 71.1; E.J.Westmacott 55.2; Farrell, Wayne 70.1; Fernandez, Antonio Guillem 79.1; Gilbert, Jeff 55.3; Gustafsson, Jeppe 63.1; Hoare, Jeremy 83.4; Hrda, Lucia 72.5; Huang, I-Wei 59.5; Image Source 92.2; Imagebroker 65.1; imageBROKER 65.2; Janine Wiedel Photolibrary 79.3; John Freeman 111.1; Karki, Hari 19.3; Liasi, Theodore 38.1; Lloyd 78.1; Lordprice Collection 108.2; Lyons, David 72.3; MBI 31.2; Muller, Cora 59.2; Noir, Nathaniel 19.1; PA Images 66.1, 67.2, 67.6; Pearson, David 73.1; Pound, Philip 72.1; PURPLE MARBLES YORK 1 66.2; Reinholds, Aigars 62.1; Richardson, Jason 72.4; Rivera M, Carlos J 18.1; robertharding 30.4; Roger Cracknell 01/classic 72.2; Saxena, Ashok 83.1; Spitzbart, Wolfgang 75.2; Tack, Jochen 75.1; Torontonian 15.2; True Images 119.1; Vorobiev, Mikhail 62.4; Walmsley, Alan 67.1, 67.4; WENN Rights Ltd 83.3; Whitefoot, Tracey 78.2; Yarvin World Journeys 62.2; YAY Media AS 59.7. |Alamy Stock Photo (RMB), Abingdon/Oxfordshire: anther Media GmbH 62.3; Art Directors & TRIP 7.3; Camandona, Fabio 31.1; Finizio, Roberto 149.1; MacDonald, Dennis 35.1; Picture Partners 127.5; Studioshots 169.2; World History Archive 106.1; © Mike Booth 104.10. |Amortegui, Miguel, Brighton: 15.1, 25.1, 38.2, 48.6, 62.6, 96.1, 110.2. |Arrandale, Denise, Neumünster: 49.2. |Courtesy of Kopernik, kopernik.info: 130.1, 133.1, 136.1. |Fast, Lisa, Hannover: 13.1, 59.3, 120.1, 166.1. |fotolia.com, New York: davidevison 146.1; denis_vermenko 7.5; ExQuisine 20.1; fergregory 78.3; Gennadiy Poznyakov 148.2; Gorilla 34.2; RRF 104.8; Shaiith 20.2; Steiner, C. 20.4; Stocksnapper 127.2. |Getty Images, München: AFP 66.3; Stringer 40.1; Wheeler, Nik 55.1. |Getty Images (RF), München: fstop123 92.1; Mcbride, Joe 39.1. |Hardy, Helen, Braunschweig: 120.3. |Interfoto, München: Delimont, Danita/Merrill, John & Lisa 36.1. |iStockphoto.com, Calgary: aggiebilly Titel; Arnese, Claudio 59.4; Circle Creative Studio 81.1; coffeekai 31.3; Daisy-Daisy 31.4; dejankrsmanovic 65.3; Elizaquibel, Jorge 81.2; HAYKIRDI 33.1; Iaroshenko, Maryna 9.2; kissesfromholland 104.7; mgstudyo 92.4; Okea 112.1; perrygerenday 63.3; Philary 18.2; Ridofranz 31.5; serikbaib 59.9; SolStock 7.1; undefined undefined 103.3; visual7 147.1; Wirestock 168.2; Yobro10 36.2; © travellinglight 14.1, 30.3. |mauritius images GmbH, Mittenwald: Westend61 /Fischinger, Mareen 7.4. |Nordzieke, Paula: 89.1, 89.2, 89.3, 89.4, 89.5, 89.6. |OKAPIA KG - Michael Grzimek & Co., Frankfurt/M.: BIOS/Labat, Jean-Michel 118.1; Groß 127.4; imagebroker/Robiller, Franz Christoph 127.3; Vock, Karl Gottfried 127.1. |PantherMedia GmbH (panthermedia.net), München: Popov, Andriy 49.1, 49.3; Schmid, Christophe 154.1. |Picture-Alliance GmbH, Frankfurt a.M.: Bildagentur-online 8.2; Schönherr, Maximilian 104.9; ZB/Thieme, Wolfgang 110.1. |Science Museum Group © The Board of Trustees of the Science Museum: Boer War rations, gravy soup. 1965-239/6/2/5Science Museum Group Collection Online. Accessed September 20, 2023. https , Lizenz Creative Commons Zero 109.2. |Shutterstock.com, New York: Agarianna76 139.1, 142.1, 145.1; AJR_photo 33.3; auremar 169.1; chrisdorney 84.1; DenPhotos 103.4; Es sarawuth 103.2; Esin, Deniz 9.1; Gingell, Ben 36.3; gkrphoto 19.2; Kumar Barui, Tutun 59.8; Marius GODOI 63.2; Monkey Business Images 7.2; muzsy 34.1; Rehorst, Bernd 59.6; yackers1 8.3. |stock.adobe.com, Dublin: Alvaro 8.1; Aphotostudio 148.3; asife 37.1; cougarsan 48.5; denisgorelkin 119.2, 119.3, 119.4, 119.5; guteksk7 120.2; Iakov Kalinin 82.1; mdurson 33.2; nikolaydonetsk 8.4; peregrinus 48.3; Richardt, Dagmar 118.2; Schwier, Christian 168.1; sergojpg 148.1; sinhyu 109.3; somegirl 30.1; Sughra 48.1, 48.2; UJac 20.3; valvectors 48.4; victoria p. 30.2. |Todd, Gary, Henan: Anyang-Museum 118.3. |Visuelle Lebensfreude - Bodem + Sötebier GbR, Hannover: 11.1, 11.2, 11.3, 11.4, 11.5, 104.1, 104.2, 104.3, 104.4, 104.5, 104.6.

Textquellen

14 „Vegan Steven“ Benjamin Zephaniah, „The little book of vegan poems – Explicit vegan lyrics“, AK Press, Edinburgh, 2002.

39 „Choose your sports“, Martin Dejnicki, Toronto, Canada. 25.7.2022: https://wordswan.com/author/martin-dejnicki/sports-poems

39 „Skateboarding“, Margo L. Dill, St. Louis, Missouri, USA. 26.7.2022: https://www.scrapbook.com/poems/cat/38.html

39 „What Can You Do With a Football?“, James Carter, „Journey to The Centre Of My Brain“, London, Macmillan Children's Books, 2012.

114 „On the Move Again“, „On the Move: Poems About Migration“ by Michael Rosen with drawings by Quentin Blake, Walker Books Ltd., London, 2020.

Shetland Islands
Orkney Islands
Lewis
Outer Hebrides
Skye
Aberdeen
Ben Nevis 1344 m
Balmoral
Scotland
Glasgow
Edinburgh
Tweed
Atlantic Ocean
North Sea